The Rights of Older Persons

Also in this series

AN AMERICAN CIVIL LIBERTIES UNION HANDBOOK

THE RIGHTS OF OLDER PERSONS

SECOND EDITION
Completely Revised and Up-to-Date

Robert N. Brown
with
Legal Counsel for the Elderly

General Editor of the Handbook Series:
Norman Dorsen, President, ACLU

SOUTHERN ILLINOIS UNIVERSITY PRESS
CARBONDALE AND EDWARDSVILLE

92 91 90 89   4 3 2 1

Library of Congress Cataloging-in-Publication Data

Brown, Robert N., 1944–
    The rights of older persons.

    (An American Civil Liberties Union handbook)
    1. Aged—Legal status, laws, etc.—United
States. 2. Old age assistance—Law and
legislation—United States. 3. Aged—
Medical care—Law and legislation—United
States. I. Legal Counsel for the Elderly
(Washington, D.C.) II. Title. III. Series.
KF390.A4B76 1988   346.7301'3   88-2030
ISBN 0-8093-1432-0   347.30613

The paper used in this publication meets the minimum requirements of
American National Standard for Information Sciences—Permanence of
Paper for Printed Library Materials, ANSI Z39.48-1984.   ∞™

Contents

Preface

This guide sets forth your rights under present law and offers suggestions on how you can protect your rights. It is one of a continuing series of handbooks published in cooperation with the American Civil Liberties Union.

The hope surrounding these publications is that Americans informed of their rights will be encouraged to exercise them. Through their exercise, rights are given life. If they are rarely used, they may be forgotten and violations may become routine.

This guide offers no assurances that your rights will be respected. The laws may change and, in some of the subjects covered in these pages, they change quite rapidly. An effort has been made to note those parts of the law where movement is taking place but it is not always possible to predict accurately when the law *will* change.

Even if the laws remain the same, interpretations of them by courts and administrative officials often vary. In a federal system such as ours, there is a built-in problem of the differences between state and federal law, not to speak of the confusion of the differences from state to state. In addition, there are wide variations in the ways in which particular courts and administrative officials will interpret the same law at any given moment.

If you encounter what you consider to be a specific abuse of your rights you should seek legal assistance. There are a number of agencies that may help you, among them ACLU affiliate offices, but bear in mind that the ACLU is a limited-purpose organization. In many communities, there are federally funded legal service offices which provide assistance to poor persons who cannot afford the costs of legal representation. In general, the rights that the ACLU defends are freedom of inquiry and expression, due process of law, equal protection of the laws, and privacy. The authors in this series have discussed other rights in these books (even though they sometimes fall outside the ACLU's usual concern) in order to provide as much guidance as possible.

These books have been planned as guides for the people directly affected: therefore the question and answer format. In some of these areas there are more detailed works available for "experts." These guides seek to raise the largest issues and inform the nonspecialist of the basic law on the subject. The authors of the books are themselves specialists who understand the need for information at "street level."

No attorney can be an expert in every part of the law. If you encounter a specific legal problem in an area discussed in one of these handbooks, show the book to your attorney. Of course, he will not be able to rely *exclusively* on the handbook to provide you with adequate representation. But if he hasn't had a great deal of experience in the specific area, the handbook can provide helpful suggestions on how to proceed.

Norman Dorsen, President
American Civil Liberties Union

The principal purpose of this handbook, and others in this series, is to inform individuals of their legal rights. The authors from time to time suggest what the law should be, but the author's personal views are not necessarily those of the ACLU. For the ACLU's position on the issues discussed in this handbook, the reader should write to Librarian, ACLU, 132 West 43 Street, New York, NY 10036.

Acknowledgments

This book is the product of a great deal of work, not only my own but that of many others. My coauthors—all of whom legally represent older persons on a regular basis—contributed the skills, insights, and wisdom of their vast experience. Wayne Moore, Director of Legal Counsel for the Elderly, with whom most of my coauthors are associated, made available to me the counsel's staff and resources. Similarly, the Pension Rights Center, the Walter P. Reuther Senior Centers of Metropolitan Detroit, and the Society for the Right to Die allowed members of their staffs to take time from their other duties to contribute to this book. The contribution of Kenneth Morse was written by him in his private capacity. No official support or endorsement by the United States Equal Opportunity Commission or any other agency of the United States Government is intended or should be inferred.

My coauthors of the first edition—Clifford D. Allo, Alan D. Freeman, and Gordon W. Netzorg—were unable to participate in this new edition, but I acknowledge their contribution to it. A number of attorneys improved the book by reading and commenting upon chapter drafts. Assisting in this way were: Frank S. Bloch, Howard C. Eglit, Burton D. Fretz, Kathleen A. Gmeiner, Patricia Nemore, John S. Regan, Roger Schwartz, Eileen P. Sweeney, and Jay W. Tower. My thanks also go to a large group of law students who did research, checked cites, and performed other essential tasks during the two years this revision has been underway.

In the final stages of preparing the book for publication, I was assisted by several individuals. Anthony S. Kogut, an attorney specializing in representing older persons, prepared a revision of the civil service retirement section of the book. A chapter revised by Shirley A. Cushing was omitted due to space limitations. Her efforts are appreciated. Suzanne Sattler edited the appendixes, and Suzanne Dreifus edited or proofread several chapters. Lionel Postic, Robert Postic, and Margaret Kurtzweil also were indispensable in a number of capacities. The assistance of former student Dawn White also is acknowledged.

I also am indebted to Dean Bernard Dobranski of the University of Detroit School of Law for allocating funds to support my research, to the staff of the University of Detroit School of Law Library for their assistance, and to the school's support and secretarial staff, particularly Kathy Abdelnour, Katy Graham, and Jenny McAlonan, for their help.

My greatest debt is to my family. My daughter Alexa Jane Brown and my wife, Claire Pilliod Brown, encouraged and sustained me during the long period of the book's preparation. This book is dedicated to the memory of my father, A. Edward Brown, who died shortly before the manuscript was completed.

Robert N. Brown

Introduction

The late Henry Friendly, a distinguished federal judge, described the Social Security Act as "almost unintelligible to the uninitiated." The same could be said of the Employee Retirement Income Security Act (ERISA) and other laws important to older persons. The purpose of this book is to explain these laws to older persons, their families, nonlawyer professionals such as social workers and nurses who have regular contact with the elderly, and lawyers who represent older persons. The book's title thus refers primarily to the right of older persons to receive benefits promised by law—Social Security, Supplemental Security Income, Medicare, etc.—and to be protected against behavior proscribed by law such as employment discrimination based on age. Also covered are subjects critically important to older persons and their families—e.g., the rights of adults with impairments allegedly preventing them from making decisions about their personal, financial, and medical wellbeing.

The primary focus of the book is on present laws. Readers should be aware, however, that many of the rights of older persons are the product of legislative action. For several decades older persons have enjoyed a favored status with state and federal lawmakers. The social legislation of the New Deal was expanded by the Great Society programs of the 1960s. The 1970s also saw an extension of laws benefiting older persons. More recently, however, this climate is beginning to change. While solicitude for older persons continues among lawmakers, pressures to cut back on these benefits are increasing. Indeed, benefit reductions and budget cutbacks already threaten many of these programs. Existing programs will continue and needed expansions, such as adequate public funding for long-term care, will occur only if older persons and those concerned about their wellbeing continue to be forceful advocates for these programs.

My coauthors and I have discussed most major laws affecting older persons as well as court decisions and rules issued by the government agencies responsible for administering these laws. Because these agencies, such as the Social Security Administration and state health and welfare bureaucracies, play so large a role in the lives of older persons, we have spent considerable time discussing these agencies and have provided hints on how to avoid pitfalls that can deprive you of your rights. Please remember that the laws we discuss are subject to change. This book is current as of August 1988 and therefore does not reflect changes occurring since then.

Robert N. Brown

PART ONE
The Right to an Adequate Income

One of the most basic needs of older persons is an adequate income to ensure that the last years of life are lived in comfort and dignity. For many older persons, the key to an adequate income is the opportunity to continue to work as long as desired. Others wish to work because of the esteem or personal satisfaction gained from employment. Until very recently, our society denied this opportunity to older workers by requiring that they cease work upon reaching a certain age, usually 65 or 70. Mandatory retirement, long accepted as part of our industrial economy, is being replaced by a system in which workers can continue in their jobs as long as they wish or until they no longer are able to work. Even with the abandonment of mandatory retirement, older workers fare badly in the workplace — they often are the last hired and the first fired. This topic, age discrimination in employment, is discussed in chapter 6.

Most older persons prefer to retire. For these individuals, pension payments from their employers are critical to their economic wellbeing. Sadly, large numbers of older persons retire only to learn that the pension on which they relied will not be paid or will be substantially less than anticipated. Others are threatened with the loss of their pensions when their former employers' businesses fail. To redress these problems Congress enacted the Pension Reform Act of 1974 (ERISA) which provides important protections for workers' pensions. More recently Congress enacted other laws to protect workers and their dependents. Pensions are discussed in chapters 4 and 5.

The most important sources of income for older persons, however, are government benefit programs. The best known of these is the Old Age, Survivors, and Disability Insurance Program, popularly called Social Security, which provides income to retired and disabled workers and their families. Another government benefit program providing essential financial assistance to needy older persons is the Supplemental Security Income program (SSI). SSI also is important because eligibility for SSI often brings with it eligibility for Medicaid and thus assistance in paying for needed medical services. These programs are discussed in chapters 1 and 2. Chapter 3 discusses the increasingly important and complex subject of the benefits available under Social Security and SSI to disabled workers and their families. Chapter 4 briefly describes the benefits available to railroad retirees and retired federal civil servants.

The programs described in this part form the economic foundation for older persons. Together these programs have improved substantially the economic status of older persons. Despite these gains, however, significant numbers of older persons continue to be impoverished. This is particularly so for older women and members of minority groups, many of whom had irregular contact with the workforce. In addition, program complexities diminish their effectiveness, and gaps in coverage leave many older persons unprotected. Continued advocacy is needed to assure that existing programs fulfill their objectives and that needed enhancements are enacted.

1

Social Security

What is Social Security?

Social Security is the popular name for the Old Age, Survivors, and Disability Insurance program (OASDI) created by the Social Security Act of 1935 and administered by the Social Security Administration (SSA).[1] Under this program, benefits are paid to workers and their dependents (husbands or wives and children) and to the survivors of workers. Social Security was created in response to the devastating effects of the Great Depression and is designed to provide economic security to workers and their families by providing a source of income to these persons after the worker has retired, died, or is unable to work because of a disability.

What benefits are available under Social Security?

There are three types of Social Security benefits: old age or disability benefits, which are payable to the worker;[2] benefits for dependents of retired or disabled workers;[3] and benefits for the surviving family of a worker who has died,[4] including a lump-sum death benefit ($255) payable to the deceased worker's survivors.[5] In 1987 more than thirty-eight million individuals received in excess of $200 billion under Social Security.[6]

How is Social Security financed?

Social Security is financed by taxes on workers and employers. During 1988 the taxes that finance Social Security are taken only from the first $45,000 a worker earns.[7] In 1988 the tax paid by wage earners is 7.51 percent (the wage earner's employer also contributes 7.51 percent) and by the self-employed, 13.02 percent. This payroll tax will increase gradually in the next few years until 1990 when it will be 7.65 percent for wage earners and their employers, and 15.3 percent for the self-employed.[8] However, after 1989 only one half of the self-employment tax will be considered part of net earnings, and self-employed persons will get an income tax deduction equal to one-half of the self-employment tax.

Since the contributions made each year (by presently employed workers) finance the benefits paid that year (to retired and disabled workers and workers' families and survivors), the Social Security system remains solvent only as long as there are enough workers contributing each year to cover the costs of the benefits paid that year. From 1975 to 1977 the system operated at a deficit, as more benefits were paid than contributions made. To restore the financial integrity of the system, Congress amended the Social Security Act in late 1977 and in 1983. Among the changes were increases in the tax rate and in the amount of wages taxed and the mandatory coverage of employees of nonprofit organizations and all newly hired civilian employees of the federal government. These changes assure that the system will remain solvent, but they are costly to workers whose Social Security contributions will increase substantially.

Do benefit levels depend on the amount of contributions?

In general, the amount of benefits a worker receives depends upon how much he has contributed and the amount of quarters he has earned (see the next section). However, a worker's benefit also is affected by whether he has dependents and by how long he and his dependents survive. Thus, two individuals who worked the same length of time at the same wage will receive different amounts under Social Security if one of the workers has dependents and the other does not. Also a person may receive more benefits than she and her employer contributed if she lives a long time after retirement, while another person may receive less in benefits than her contributions if she dies soon after retiring.

ELIGIBILITY

Who is eligible for Social Security?

Unlike some public benefit programs that base eligibility on need, Social Security benefits are payable based upon a work record. It is possible for an entire family to receive benefits based on the earnings record of one individual. Although the details of Social Security eligibility are too complex to explain completely, in general, there are two parts to Social Security eligibility. First, a family member must have worked in employment which is "covered" by the Social Security system.[9]

Second, the person must have worked long enough to have acquired "insured" status.[10]

What is "covered employment"?

Nearly all work (including self-employment and part-time work) counts toward eligibility for Social Security benefits. In fact, nine out of ten workers in this country are covered by Social Security.[11]

The Social Security Amendments of 1983 made these changes with respect to coverage:

- All federal and legislative branch employees (except reemployed civil service annuitants) hired on or after 1 January 1984 (there are exceptions for federal and legislative branch employees who were participating in a federal retirement system prior to 1 January 1984), all members of Congress, the president, federal judges, and most executive-level political appointees of the federal government, effective 1 January 1984, are covered under Social Security.
- Current and future employees of private tax-exempt nonprofit organizations are covered, effective 1 January 1984, on a mandatory basis.
- States are prohibited from terminating coverage of state and local government employees if the termination has not gone into effect by 20 April 1983, and those that have terminated coverage may elect to be covered again.[12]

A particularly acute problem concerns those workers employed in jobs which are covered but whose employers do not comply with reporting requirements and do not pay Social Security taxes for them.[13] Farmworkers and domestic workers frequently find themselves ineligible for Social Security payments at retirement because their work has not been credited to them by their employers. In addition, spouses working together (e.g., in small proprietorships such as grocery stores and other family businesses such as farms) often do not report the income of each spouse separately. Consequently, many spouses will find that they do not have coverage when they apply for benefits.

When are domestic workers covered?

Domestic workers such as housekeepers, cooks, and gardeners have been covered by Social Security since 1951.[14] A domestic worker's wages are covered by Social Security if one employer pays him or her $50 or more in cash in a 3-month calendar quarter.[15] The domestic worker receives one quarter of coverage for each $470 (1988) of his or her covered wages, up to a maximum of four quarters for the year. Work in a domestic job is not covered employment if less than $50 is earned during a quarter or if less than $50 is earned from any single employer during a quarter. Responsibility for withholding Social Security tax and paying the tax lies with the employer. The employer is subject to criminal penalties (e.g., a fine of up to $10,000 and imprisonment for not more than five years) if he or she willfully fails to collect or truthfully account for and pay over the appropriate tax.[16]

When are farmworkers covered?

A farmworker's wages are covered if he or she receives $150 or more in cash pay during a year from any one employer or if he or she works for one employer for twenty or more days during a year and is paid in cash for work which is computed on the basis of time rather than piecework.[17]

Effective 31 December 1987, the twenty-day test is eliminated. Instead, a farmworker's wages are covered if the employer pays $2,500 or more to all employees during the taxable year. However, farmwork by foreign workers lawfully admitted to this country on a temporary basis is not covered by Social Security.[18] When the farmworker is hired and paid by a crewleader, the crewleader is the farmworker's employer and is responsible for reporting the farm laborer's work and for withholding and paying Social Security taxes for him. If a farmworker is hired and paid directly by a farmer or if the crewleader is a farmer's employee (and there is a written agreement establishing this fact), it is the farmer's responsibility to report work and pay taxes.[19] Farmwork by a sharecropper also is covered by Social Security, but the sharecropper is self-employed and is responsible for paying Social Security taxes himself.[20]

How does a person acquire "insured status"?

Insured status is the second essential ingredient to Social Security eligibility; it is acquired by working in covered employment for a sufficient number of calendar quarters (January–

March, April–June, July–September, October–December). There are three basic insured statuses: fully insured, currently insured, and specially insured for disability benefits. Each kind of insured status controls eligibility for a different Social Security benefit. The number of quarters one must work to attain each status varies according to the status and to the person's age and other factors (see table 1).

TABLE 1.
Insured Status Required for Each Social Security Benefit

Monthly Social Security benefits can be paid to:	*If the worker:*
A retired worker age 62 or over	Is fully insured.
A disabled worker under age 65	Would have been fully insured had he or she attained age 62 in the month the disability began and (except in the case of a person disabled because of blindness) has 20 quarters of coverage out of the 40 calendar quarters ending with the quarter in which the disability began.
A worker disabled before age 31 who does not have sufficient quarters of coverage to meet the above requirement (A worker may be disabled after age 31 if he or she had subsequent period(s) of disability.)	Has quarters of coverage in one-half of the quarters elapsing in the period after attaining age 21 and up to and including the quarter of becoming disabled, but no fewer than 6 or, if disabled in a quarter before attaining age 24, he or she has 6 quarters of coverage in the 12 calendar-quarter period immediately before he or she became disabled.
The spouse of a person entitled to disability or retirement insurance benefits, if he or she is: (a) Age 62 or over (may be divorced spouse in certain circumstances); or (b) Caring for a child who is under age 16 or disabled and entitled to benefits	Is fully insured or insured for disability benefits, whichever is applicable, as shown above.

Monthly Social Security benefits can be paid to:	*If the worker:*
A dependent, unmarried child of a person entitled to disability or retirement insurance benefits if the child is: (a) Under age 18; or (b) Age 18 or over and qualified as a full-time student; or (c) Age 18 or over and under a disability which began before the child reached age 22	Is insured for retirement or disability benefits, whichever is applicable, as shown above.
A widow(er) (may be surviving divorced spouse in certain circumstances) age 60 or over	Is fully insured.
A widow(er) and, under certain conditions, a surviving divorced spouse, if the widow(er), or divorced spouse is caring for a child entitled to benefits if the child is under age 16 or disabled	Is either fully or currently insured.
A disabled widow(er) (may be surviving divorced spouse in certain circumstances) age 50 or over but under age 60 whose disability began within a certain period	Is fully insured.
A dependent, unmarried child of a deceased worker if the child is: (a) Under age 18; or (b) Age 18 or over and qualified as a full-time student; or (c) Age 18 or over and under a disability which began before the child reached age 22	Is either fully or currently insured.
The dependent parents age 62 or over of the deceased worker	Is fully insured.

A special monthly cash payment can be made to:	*If the person*
A person age 72 or over who is not insured for regular Social Security benefits	Attained age 72 before 1968 or, if he or she attains 72 after 1967, has at least 3 quarters of coverage for each calendar year elapsing after 1966 and before the year he or she attains age 72.

The lump-sum death payment will be paid in the following order of priority:	*If the worker is:*
(a) The widow(er) of the deceased wage earner who was living in the same household as the deceased wage earner at the time of death;	Either fully or currently insured.
(b) The widow(er) (excluding a divorced spouse) who is eligible for or entitled to benefits based on the deceased wage earner's record for the month of death;	
(c) Children who are eligible for or entitled to benefits based on the deceased wage earner's record for the month of death	

If no surviving widow(er) or child as defined above survives, no lump sum is payable.

Source: *Social Security Handbook*, ninth ed. (1986), pp. 28–29.

How are quarters of coverage accumulated?

In general, a person is credited with coverage for each calendar quarter after 1936 and before 1978 in which he earned cash wages of $50 or more.[21] A person will be credited with coverage for each calendar quarter after 1950 and before 1978 in which he earned $100 while *self-employed*.[22] In 1978 the system changed. A person was credited with a quarter of coverage for each $250 earned during that year, with a maximum of four quarters of coverage available.[23] Now, a similar rule continues to be followed; one need not work in each quarter of a year but must meet the minimum annual amounts. The amount of earnings required to gain credit for a quarter of coverage is announced each November.[24] Annual amounts for 1979, 1980, 1981, 1982, 1983, 1984, 1985, 1986, 1987, and 1988 are $260, $290, $310, $340, $370, $390, $410, $440, $460, and $470 respectively.

What is fully insured status?

A worker must be fully insured for most types of Social Security benefits (see table 1). Generally, a worker is fully insured if she has earned quarters of coverage equal to the number of elapsed years between 1950 (or the year she reached age 21, if after 1950) and the year she reached age 62, became disabled, or died.

Example: Joan reached age 62 in 1987. She needs 36 quarters of coverage to be fully insured.

$$\begin{array}{r} 1987 \\ -\ 1951 \\ \hline 36 \end{array}$$

Individuals born on 2 January 1929 or later need 40 quarters of coverage to be fully insured. All quarters of coverage credited to an individual's Social Security account are counted, including those acquired before 1951 and after retirement age.[25]

What is currently insured status?

For certain types of survivor's beneftis (see table 1), the deceased worker must have had 6 quarters of coverage during the full 13-quarter period ending with the calendar quarter in which he died, most recently became entitled to disability benefits, or became entitled to retirement benefits.

What is disability insured status?

In addition to being fully insured, a disabled worker must have a recent attachment to the work force. That is, he must meet a special test for disability benefits. This test is explained below.

• Disabled before 24: Worker needs credit for 1½ years of

work (6 quarters) in the 3 years (12 quarters) before disability starts.

- Disabled between 24 and 31: Worker needs credit for half the time between the 21st birthday and the time disability starts.
- Disabled at 31 or later: Worker must be fully insured, and 5 years of the work (20 quarters) must be in the 10-year period (40 quarters) just before disability starts. (NOTE. Blind people need only to be fully insured.)

What if I lack a few quarters of coverage for eligibility?

By working in a covered job, you could gain the quarters needed for eligibility. But when looking for additional quarters of covered employment, be certain that the work is covered by Social Security.

Several public employment programs financed by federal funds exist which encourage older persons to work in public service positions—as tutors, recreation leaders, and social-service aides in programs such as the Foster Grandparent Program, the Senior Aide Program, and VISTA. Work as a VISTA or a Peace Corps volunteer is covered employment.[26] Workers in the Retired Senior Volunteer, Greenthumb, Foster Grandparent, and Senior Aide Programs gain credit toward Social Security, depending on the identity of the employer and the application of the common-law employer-employee relationship test.[27] Generally, a common-law employee is one who may be told what to do and how, when, and where to do it by his or her employer.[28] Another source of covered employment available to a person needing additional quarters of coverage is work in the home of that person's own child. Not all work in the home of one's child is covered. But since 1968 work by a parent in the home of a child caring for grandchildren under 18 (or who are older but need personal care because of mental or physical impairment) is covered when there is need because a parent of the grandchildren is absent through death or divorce.[29]

In addition, until 31 December 1987, one spouse cannot work for another spouse and receive quarters of coverage, but one spouse can work for another spouse's corporation. Similarly, both spouses can work together and receive quarters of coverage in a business in which they both share in management decisions and general operation of the business. Effective for wages paid after 31 December 1987, the work of an individual in the employ of her spouse's trade or business will be considered covered employment.[30]

How are Social Security benefits computed?

Figuring one's benefits is difficult and requires the use of tables. Rather than describe how to compute the amounts of benefits here, we have included the necessary tables and a description of how to figure benefits in Appendix E.

Who is eligible for retirement benefits?

A worker who is 62, fully insured, and has retired is eligible for retirement benefits.[31] However, the benefits paid to an individual who retires at 62 are lower than those received after retirement at age 65.[32] Similarly, a person who defers retirement until after 65 receives higher benefits than if he had retired at 65.[33]

Is a worker's family eligible for Social Security retirement benefits?

Yes. In addition to the worker, his spouse and children may be eligible for benefits.

When are spouses eligible for retirement benefits?

A spouse who is 62 or who is younger and caring for the worker's child(ren) (either under the age of 16, or disabled before age 22) is eligible for retirement benefits based on his or her spouse's eligibility.[34] In most cases, he or she will receive half of his or her spouse's benefits, but the amount may be less. In addition to the worker's present spouse, his or her divorced spouse also will be eligible for Social Security benefits if he or she is at least 62, if he or she and the worker were married for at least ten years before their divorce became final, and if he or she is unmarried. Benefits will not be terminated when the divorced spouse either remarries the former spouse who is entitled to retirement benefits or when the divorced spouse marries an individual entitled to spouse's, widow(er)'s, mother's, father's, parent's, or childhood disability benefits (the individual must be age 18 or over).[35] In addition, if the divorced spouse has been divorced from his or her former spouse for at least two years, he or she may receive benefits on the former spouse's work record, even if the former spouse is still working. Moreover, work deductions because of the former spouse's earnings will not be made from the benefits payable to the divorced spouse. The divorced spouse must meet the other requirements for eligibility (e.g., he or she is at least age 62 and had been married to the former spouse for at least ten years before the divorce), and the former spouse must be at least age 62. This provision is effective for benefits beginning January 1985.[36]

Are the children of a retired worker eligible for benefits?

Yes. A child who is unmarried, under age 18 (or under age 19 and attending elementary or secondary school full time), or age 18 or over with a disability (which began before the child reached age 22), and is dependent on a retired worker is eligible for benefits.[37] The term "child" includes adopted children, stepchildren, and—under some circumstances—grandchildren.[38] A child's benefit is usually half of the benefit paid his or her retired parent. The child's benefit will be reduced when the total amount of benefits payable on a worker's earnings record exceeds the maximum amount of benefits that can be paid on that record.[39]

Who is eligible for disability insurance benefits?

A person is eligible for disability insurance benefits if he is disabled, is fully insured, and has worked enough to have acquired twenty quarters of coverage (five years) in the last forty quarters (ten years) before becoming disabled.[40] As is true of retirement benefits, disability insurance benefits are available to a disabled worker's family.[41]

Who is eligible for survivors' benefits?

Survivors' benefits are payable to the husband or wife of the deceased worker as well as to the worker's parents and children. To be eligible, the parent must be age 62 or older and must have been receiving at least one-half support from the worker, generally at the time of the worker's death.[42] In addition to monthly cash benefits, a lump-sum death payment is available upon the death of the worker to the worker's widow or widower who was either living with the worker at the time of his or her death or was eligible for benefits on the worker's earnings record for the month of the worker's death. If there is no qualified widow or widower, the benefits will go to any children eligible for benefits on the worker's earnings record for the month of that worker's death.[43]

When is a widow(er) entitled to benefits?

A widow(er) who is 60 or older, or is between 50 and 60 and is disabled, will receive monthly survivors' benefits if his or her deceased spouse was fully insured at the time of death.[44] A surviving divorced spouse who meets these requirements, is now unmarried (or remarried after meeting the requirements for widow(er) benefits), and was married to the deceased at least ten years also is eligible for widow(er)'s benefits.[45] To be considered a widow or widower by the SSA, you must have been married to the worker (now deceased) for at least nine months, or be the biological parent of the worker's child, or be the adoptive parent of the worker's child, or the worker must be the adoptive parent of your child.[46] A widow(er) also may be eligible for mother's or father's insurance benefits. If his or her spouse died fully or currently (six quarters of coverage in the previous thirteen quarters) insured and if he or she is unmarried and is caring for the deceased spouse's minor (under the age of 16) or disabled (before age 22) child, he or she is eligible for mother's or father's insurance benefits.[47] Widow(er)'s benefits will be between 82½ and 100 percent of the deceased spouse's basic monthly benefits, while mother's or father's insurance benefits will be about 75 percent of the deceased spouse's basic monthly benefits.[48]

Are children entitled to survivors' benefits?

Unmarried children are eligible for survivor's benefits if their parent died or became disabled while fully or currently insured.[49] The definitions of "child" and "dependent" are the same for survivors' benefits as for retirement benefits. A child is eligible for three-quarters of the deceased parent's basic monthly benefit, unless a family maximum has been reached.[50]

When are parents eligible for survivors' benefits?

The parent of a worker who died while currently insured is eligible for monthly survivor's benefits if the parent is at least 62 and was dependent on the deceased worker for half of his or her support. A parent's benefit usually will be 82½ percent of the deceased worker's benefits.[51]

What is the maximum amount of benefits that can be paid on a work record?

Congress has established a maximum amount (called the family maximum) that generally can be paid a family, regardless of the number of entitled beneficiaries on a worker's record. The family maximum is determined according to the method of computing the Primary Insurance Amount (PIA) (usually the amount received for retirement at age 65) and the kind of benefits payable to the worker. For example, if a worker first became eligible or died in 1979 or later, the family maximum is computed by adding fixed percentages of predetermined dollar amounts (called "bend points") which are part of the PIA. The formula in effect for 1988 is 150 percent of the first $407 of the PIA, plus 272 percent of the excess of PIA over $407 through $588, plus 134 percent of the excess PIA over $588 through $767, plus 175 percent of the excess PIA over $767. These "bend points" usually change each year.

The family maximum for disability benefits is 85 percent of the Average Indexed Monthly Earnings of the worker, but not less than the PIA nor more than 150 percent of the PIA.

All the benefit rates, except the retirement or disability insurance benefits and benefits payable to a divorced spouse or surviving divorced spouse, are subject to reduction to bring the total monthly benefits payable within the family maximum.[52] Note that the total benefits payable to the family group are not necessarily reduced when monthly benefits are not payable to one member of the group. For example, if the spouse continues to work, his or her benefit can be used to increase the benefits of others in the family group, usually eligible children. For a discussion of the family maximum, see the *Social Security Handbook*, ninth edition, pages 108–15.

APPLYING FOR BENEFITS

How do I apply for Social Security benefits?

To receive Social Security benefits, you are required to fill out an application and supply the Social Security Administration with proof of necessary information, such as your age and identity. Application forms for each kind of benefit available can be obtained from SSA offices throughout the country. If you are unable to go to the SSA office to apply in person, you can send the completed application to the office, or the SSA can send a representative to your home. While you may accept assistance in completing the application you are required to sign it yourself. However, if a person is mentally or physically incapable of signing an application, a legal guardian, caregiver, or other interested person may complete and sign the application.[53]

Most applications for Social Security benefits are made on official Social Security forms. However, any written indication of an intention to file for benefits which identifies the individual seeking benefits can serve as an application. If it is followed by completion of an official application within six months of a request by the SSA to complete a formal application, an informal application of this sort may be construed as a temporary application.[54] Also, an application for one benefit—retirement benefits, for example—will serve as an application for other benefits to which you are entitled, such as spouse's benefits or Medicare. Similarly, under some circumstances, an application for Railroad Retirement or Veterans Administration benefits is treated as an application for Social Security benefits.[55] However, if you intend to apply for disability benefits, you should state this clearly on an application or in a written statement.

When should I apply for Social Security benefits?

If it is possible to anticipate eligibility for benefits (retirement, a birthday), application can be made in advance. Obviously there will be other circumstances which cannot be anticipated, such as the death of a spouse. Nevertheless, be certain to file your application for benefits promptly. Retirement and survivors' (not based on disability) benefits will not be paid for any month earlier than six months before the month of application. (You can receive disability benefits as far back as twelve months before the month you apply.)[56] A person who waits until age 67 to apply for retirement benefits will receive retroactive benefits for only six months and not for the entire period since his or her 65th birthday. An application for a lump-sum death benefit must be filed within two years after the date of death unless "good cause" is shown.[57]

What proof of eligibility is required?

You have the burden of establishing your eligibility for Social Security benefits. For this reason it is best that you have available to you your birth and marriage documents when submitting the application to the SSA. However, if you cannot locate them, do not wait to apply until the documents are found. Apply immediately, since delay in applying for benefits can result in loss of benefits. The *Social Security Handbook* lists the proof you will need to establish your eligibility for Social Security benefits.[58]

What is acceptable proof of age?

The best proof of age is an original public or church record of birth or of baptism made before your fifth birthday.[59] Next best is a certified copy of such a record. If neither of these is available, other evidence of age, such as a school or census record, a Bible or other family record, a religious record of confirmation or baptism in youth or early adult life, an insurance policy, marriage record, employment or labor union record, a fraternal organization record, a military record, a voting record, a delayed birth certificate or a birth certificate of your child showing your age, or a physician's or midwife's record of birth, or a passport. For a person born in a foreign country, there should be available a record of entry into the United States and, perhaps, a naturalization record. Statements by family members or other persons who know you also can be used to establish your age. If there is a conflict in establishing age—some documents indicating one age, others another age—you should attempt to corroborate your claim with as many documents and statements as you can obtain. In general, the SSA gives more weight to old documents than to more recent documents.[60] In one case, however, in which a dispute arose as to a claimant's age, a court reversed the SSA's decision (based on her original birth certificate, a census record, and her son's birth certificate) that the claimant was not 62, even though the claimant had submitted a corrected birth certificate showing her to be 62. The court discounted the census record because of errors on its face, and held that the correction on the birth certificate must be given full faith and credit.[61] It is improper for the SSA to rely rigidly on an old document when there is more persuasive evidence based on more recent records or statements.[62] It is

TABLE 2.
The Evidence Usually Required to Be Submitted to the Social Security Administration in Claims for Monthly Benefits or the Lump-Sum Death Payment

Beneficiary	Age	Relationship			Dependency or support	School attendance	Child in care	Death of a worker
		Marriage	Divorce	Parent-child				
Insured person	X							
Spouse (62 or over)	X	X						
Spouse under 62 (child in care)		X		X			X	
Divorced spouse (62 or over)	X	X	X					
Child...........	X			X	X	X		In survivor claims
Widow(er) (60 or over, 50 or over if disabled)..........	X	X						X
Surviving divorced spouse ...	X	X	X					X
Widow(er) under 62 or surviving divorced mother or father (child in care)		X	X	X			X	X
Parent....................	X			X	X			X
Lump-sum death payment: A. Surviving spouse living in same household		X						X
B. Eligible surviving spouse, excluding divorced spouse	X	X						X
C. Eligible children	X			X	X	X		X

Source: Social Security Handbook, ninth edition (1986), p. 230. This is merely a summary of requirements. See text for details.

your task, therefore, to urge the SSA to base its decision on the documents you produce, despite other inconsistent evidence.

What is acceptable proof of marriage?

Social Security benefits are available to wives and husbands of wage earners and to their widows and widowers. To obtain these benefits, it is often necessary to establish proof of marriage.[63] This can be done by showing the SSA your original certificate of marriage or a certified copy of the public or church record of your marriage. If none of these is available, an affidavit signed by the person who performed the marriage ceremony or statements from persons who witnessed the marriage, may also serve as proof of marriage.[64]

Some states recognize common-law marriages (in which a man and woman agree to live together as husband and wife but do not go through a marriage ceremony). A common-law marriage will be accepted by the SSA as a valid marriage if the state in which the agreement was made recognizes such marriages.[65] If the SSA requires proof of a common-law marriage, this may be established in the following ways.[66] If both wife and husband are living, each should submit an affidavit confirming the agreement to live together as husband and wife, and each should obtain a statement from a blood relative confirming the agreement. If one spouse is no longer living, the surviving spouse should submit an affidavit attesting the marriage and should obtain statements from two persons with knowledge of the marriage, preferably blood relatives of the deceased spouse.

Ordinarily, the SSA will pay wife's or husband's benefits to one person only. Thus, if a man has been married three times, only his current wife will receive benefits.[67] An exception to this rule is made when a couple was married for at least 10 years before obtaining a divorce.[68] In this situation, the SSA will pay benefits both to the current spouse and to the spouse who was divorced after 10 years of marriage or more. However, if a person remarries without having obtained a valid divorce from a prior spouse, the problem arises as to which spouse will receive benefits, since benefits are usually paid to only one spouse. The present spouse may establish entitlement to benefits by submitting proof of a ceremonial marriage and a signed statement that he or she went through the marriage ceremony in good faith and believing that the marriage was valid. Both parties to this second marriage should, if they are living, submit statements testifying to their lack of knowledge of an impediment to a valid marriage.[69] But even these steps—taken carefully— will not necessarily ensure the receipt of benefits by the present spouse. If the former spouse already receives benefits from the SSA, the present spouse's application will be denied. And if the present spouse receives benefits, they may be cut off if the former spouse later applies for benefits.[70]

Sometimes it is necessary to establish that a marriage has been validly terminated.[71] This is true when a person seeks benefits as a divorced spouse or widow(er) or when he or she wishes to establish the validity of a later marriage. Establishing the termination of a marriage involves submitting a certified copy of a decree of divorce or annulment or—when the marriage ended as a result of the death of the spouse—a certified copy of the death certificate.

How can I prove the existence of a parent-child relationship?
Children of a retired, disabled, or deceased worker may be eligible for Social Security benefits. If benefits are sought for such children, it may be necessary to establish the parentage of the worker.[72] If the child is legitimate, a birth or baptismal certificate usually will suffice. If, however, the worker was not married to the mother of the child, parentage can be established by submitting one of the following documents: a written acknowledgment of paternity by the worker, a court decree declaring that the worker is the parent of the child, or a court decree ordering the worker to support the child because he is the child's father. If none of these are available, other evidence that the worker is or was the parent of the child and lived with the child or contributed to the child's support can be submitted.

A written acknowledgment of parentage by the worker can be an income tax return listing the child, a will referring to the child as his, an application for insurance naming the child as his, or a letter acknowledging parentage. If a court decree of paternity is used, the decree must identify the worker and the child and must include a specific finding of paternity. If a court order for support is used, it must identify the child and the worker as the parent and must direct the worker to contribute to the child's support. Other evidence might include hospital, church, or school records; court orders not meeting the requirements just mentioned; or statements from physicians, relatives, or others acknowledging the relationship between the child and the worker. Such statements should include the basis for the person's knowledge of the relationship. Evidence that the worker and the child's mother were living together when the child was conceived is also relevant. Yet another way for an illegitimate child to establish eligibility is to demonstrate that he or she could inherit the worker's (i.e., the parent's) personal property in the state where the parent has his or her permanent home at the time the child applies for benefits, if the parent dies without a will. If the parent is deceased, the SSA will look at the laws that were in effect at the time the parent died in the state where the parent had his or her permanent home.[73] When benefits are sought for an adopted child, adoption can be proved by submitting a copy of the court decree of adoption or a copy of the amended birth certificate issued after the adoption.[74] When benefits are sought for a stepchild, it may be necessary to establish that the child is the natural or adopted child of the husband or wife of the worker and to prove that the child's parent is validly married to the worker. To obtain child's benefits for a grandchild, it is necessary to demonstrate that the grandchild was living with and receiving support from the grandparent and that the child's parents were dead or disabled when the grandparent became eligible for Social Security benefits or—in the case of survivor's benefits—that the grandchild has been adopted by the surviving grandparent.

How can proof of receiving support be established?

Eligibility for some kinds of Social Security benefits depends upon proof that the person seeking benefits is (or was) supported by the worker. Parents seeking benefits have to establish that half of their support was derived from their deceased child just as the eligibility of some minor children depends upon establishing that they are (or were) supported by the worker.[75]

The time during which support must have been provided varies according to the type of benefits sought, but usually it is a period of time (often one year) immediately prior to application for benefits or prior to the time the worker died or became eligible for benefits.[76] However, if because of illness, unemployment, or death, it is not possible to establish that the support was given continuously for 12 months, an attempt should be made to prove that the worker provided support for at least three months and that no other person provided substantial support on a continuing and permanent basis during the crucial period. Another possibility is to show that the worker had begun making substantial contributions a short time before the support requirements had to be met and intended to continue to make contributions on a permanent and continuing basis.[77] Children's dependency can be established by proof that the child and the worker were living together in the same household and by the submission of a statement detailing the amount of the child's income and the amount and type of support supplied by the worker.

DECISIONS AND APPEALS

How long does it take the Social Security Administration to act on an application for benefits?

It depends on the kind of benefits sought and on how quickly evidence on your claim can be obtained. Claims for retirement or survivors' benefits are acted on more quickly than claims for disability benefits, which require more complicated evidence. Generally, you can expect to receive a check for retirement or survivors' benefits within sixty to ninety days after submitting the application. Since it is the applicant's responsibility to supply all information requested by the SSA, delays in receiving benefits can be avoided by obtaining requested information promptly. Disability applications take an average of three to six months. To date, Congress has not imposed any time limits on the SSA that require it to act on applications with reasonable promptness. In contrast, local welfare departments are required to act on applications for welfare within forty-five days of the date the application was submitted.[78] If the department fails to do so, the applicant can sue to expedite the department's decision. The SSA's slowness in acting on applications for benefits and in processing appeals has prompted several lawsuits which allege that these delays violate the constitutional and statutory rights of Social Security applicants.[79] However, the Supreme Court has ruled that it is inappropriate for courts to set mandatory time limits within which to process administrative appeals.[80] So in the future, courts will only be able to remedy individual cases involving delay. One helpful provision exists to aid applicants for survivors' or retirement benefits. If ninety days pass from the time you submit the last information the SSA requested and your check has not arrived, you may demand (by writing to the local SSA office) to be paid. Within fifteen days of the demand, the SSA is required to send a check to you.[81]

Are advance payments available before the SSA reaches its final decision?

Yes. The SSA is authorized to make advance payments when there is evidence that a person is entitled to benefits, even if more evidence may be needed to make a final decision. These payments may be made without waiting the 30- or 90-day periods necessary for an expedited payment.[82]

In addition, the SSA has recently implemented an "immediate payment" program in which the SSA will issue immediate payment of up to $200: (1) to an individual who is currently eligible for either Social Security or Supplemental Security Income benefits but has not received his or her check; or (2) to an individual who has been approved for either Social Security or Supplemental Security Income but has not started receiving his or her monthly checks. These payments are made when the eligible individual cannot wait the 7- to 10-day time period required for having a critical payment processed and when further delay in payment would deprive the individual of food and/ or shelter, endanger his health, or cause the SSA "extremely adverse public relations."[83]

How are applicants notified of decisions by the SSA concerning Social Security benefits?

In most cases applicants receive a notice or letter from the SSA relaying its decision. If the decision is favorable, the letter specifies the amount of the benefits. Unfortunately, when the decision is unfavorable, the notice sent by the SSA seldom adequately reveals the reason for the decision. Form letters are used which explain the reason for denying an application in vague, general terms. The letters also inform the applicant that he or she is entitled to appeal the adverse decision, and they explain how to appeal. But because these letters are usually unsatisfactory, some courts have required that the notices be changed to explain more completely how a person can appeal an adverse decision by the SSA.[84]

If you are receiving Social Security benefits and the SSA decides to reduce or terminate them, you are entitled to receive written notice of this decision and an explanation of your appeal rights. In most cases, you will receive this notice *before* your check is reduced or terminated. Unfortunately, however, if you disagree with the decision and want to appeal it, you usually are not entitled to continue to receive benefits while the appeal is pending, unless you are being terminated from disability because of medical improvement or unless your benefits are being reduced because of an overpayment.

Only written applications can ensure that you will receive all the benefits to which you are entitled. A reversal on appeal of a formal denial will result in your receiving retroactive benefits from the date of your application, whereas if your request is denied orally or informally, no appeal can follow. You will have to reapply, and you will receive benefits only as far back as the later, formal or written application, *not* back to the month of the original informal application.[85]

Do I have a right to appeal if the SSA decides against my claim?

Absolutely! The SSA often makes mistakes in deciding applications for Social Security benefits. This is especially true of applications for disability benefits, of which nearly half the denials that are appealed are reversed on appeal. Although fewer mistakes are made in applications for retirement and survivors' benefits, mistakes *are* made. You should definitely file an appeal if you believe your claim was denied wrongly. Furthermore, unless you do appeal, the decision denying your benefits becomes final.[86] If you later decide that the denial was erroneous and reapply for benefits, the SSA may point to the earlier denial and refuse to reopen your case.[87]

Can I appeal if the SSA stops sending my checks or reduces the amount of my checks?

Certainly! Just as you are entitled to appeal a decision by the SSA that you do not qualify for Social Security benefits in the first place, so also are you entitled to appeal a termination or reduction of your benefits.[88] Possible reasons for reducing or canceling benefits are discussed below. Unfortunately, however, the effectiveness of the appeals system in protecting the rights of Social Security recipients is reduced by the fact that in most cases your benefits will be reduced or cut off *before* your appeal is heard. However, there are two situations which afford the opportunity for a prior hearing: 1) termination from disability benefits because of medical improvement and 2) reduction of checks because of being overpaid. (*See* below for details of these two situations.)

The refusal of the SSA to provide a hearing *before* benefits are reduced or terminated has prompted a number of lawsuits by Social Security recipients. These suits are based on the Fifth Amendment of the U.S. Constitution, which states that "no person shall be . . . deprived of life, liberty or property, without due process of law" and on a 1970 decision of the U.S. Supreme Court, *Goldberg v. Kelly*,[89] in which the Court ruled that welfare recipients are entitled to advance notice and a hearing before their welfare benefits are reduced, suspended, or terminated. Several federal judges ruled that Social Security recipients are entitled to a hearing before their benefits are reduced or cut off by the SSA. However, on appeal the U.S. Supreme Court reversed these decisions, ruling that the Constitution does *not* require that Social Security recipients be given a hearing before their benefits are cut off.

A case decided by the Court, *Mathews v. Eldridge*,[90] involved Social Security disability benefits. The Court acknowledged that the appeals system was very slow and that many Social Security recipients rely heavily (even exclusively) on their Social Security benefits to provide the necessities of life. Nevertheless, the Court said that it would be difficult and costly for the SSA to provide hearings before benefits are cut off and said that because disability decisions are based on "objective" medical evidence, providing a hearing before benefits are cut off would not substantially improve the present system. As a result of this ruling, recipients of disability benefits clearly do not have a constitutional right to a hearing *before* their benefits are cut off. However, disability recipients whose benefits will be terminated because the SSA has determined that they have improved medically may now elect to receive benefits through the administrative law judge (ALJ) hearing stage. This new provision applies only to determinations made prior to 1 January 1989.[91]

The impact of the *Eldridge* decision on recipients of retirement and survivors' benefits, however, is less clear. To some extent, the Court's holding in *Eldridge* was based on the *type* of facts involved—medical evidence which the Court felt was "objective" in nature and which typically was reduced to writing. Other Social Security decisions are not based on such evidence, and courts may decide that an oral hearing before benefits are cut off is necessary to protect the rights of recipients. The SSA continues to refuse to provide a hearing before terminating benefits, but the Supreme Court has ruled that a hearing is required on the issue of waiver in overpayment cases before benefits can be reduced or terminated.[92] Thus, if Social Security benefits are reduced or cut off, a recipient should check with a lawyer or see whether it is possible to file a suit requiring that benefits be continued while an appeal is pending.

How do I appeal?

Begin an appeal by notifying the SSA that you disagree with its decision. This can be done by calling or visiting an SSA office to discuss the problem. In these informal discussions, the problem may be resolved. If not, you can then file a formal request for an appeal. This request should be in writing—either on a special form the SSA has for this purpose (which you can obtain from an SSA office) or in a letter you write yourself.[93] An appeal must begin within sixty days of receiving notice from the SSA of their unfavorable decision.[94]

The SSA appeals process has several stages, the first of which is called "reconsideration." During this stage the SSA's original decision (called an "initial determination") is reconsidered or reviewed. You are entitled to submit further evidence in support of your claim during reconsideration, but you are not given an opportunity to appear personally on your behalf or to call witnesses to support your claim, unless it is a disability medical improvement case.[95]

The next stage of appeal is a hearing before an administrative law judge. If you are notified by the SSA that it has reconsidered your claim and has decided to uphold its original decision, you have sixty days in which to request a hearing.[96] Again, your request should be in writing, either by letter or on an SSA form. (Make sure you do not waive your right to a hearing by checking the wrong box on the SSA form.) The judge who will hear your claim is a lawyer who works for a separate division of the SSA called the Office of Hearings and Appeals. SSA judges are not involved in the daily administration of Social Security. Many of them conduct hearings in an open and fair manner—but, unfortunately, some do not. You are entitled to have an attorney or friend represent you at the hearing,[97] to use anything as evidence for the judge to consider in reaching his decision, and to call any witnesses you want to testify. If a witness, such as a doctor, is unwilling to come to the hearing voluntarily, you can have him subpoenaed (ordered to appear, in other words). You also have the right to cross-examine witnesses called by the SSA at the hearing. A record is kept of the hearing, and the judge gives his decision in writing, usually several weeks after the hearing is held. If you have not obtained all the information you want the judge to consider by the time the hearing is held, you may request the judge to hold the record open for several weeks to allow time to obtain the additional information. Usually your request will be granted.[98]

Is the SSA represented by a lawyer at the hearing?

No. The SSA does not have a representative at these hearings, but since the administrative law judge makes sure that the position of the SSA is considered, in a sense he serves three roles—as representative of the SSA, as assistant to the claimant in fully developing the record, and as judge. He usually is able to fill the first two roles without being unfair to claimants. However, if the judge appears to be acting unfairly or does not ensure that all information that is necessary to make a fair decision has been included, this can be pointed out on appeal if he decides against the claim.

What should I do to prepare for the hearing?

Usually, several months pass after your request for a hearing before the hearing is held. About twenty days before the hearing, you will be notified by letter of the time and place of the hearing. If the time or place scheduled is inconvenient for you, you may request that it be rescheduled.[99] Your request will be granted if "good cause" is shown.

Before the hearing, gather all of the evidence favorable to your case that can be obtained. This gathering of information should begin before you receive notification of the date of the hearing, since there will then be little time to obtain medical and other records needed to win your case. Also review your file at the SSA hearing office, to be certain that it contains all of the information you wish the judge to consider. The file will be available before the hearing, allowing ample opportunity to examine it then.

If you have witnesses you want to have testify at the hearing, you should call or meet with them to discuss their testimony and to determine whether they will appear at the hearing voluntarily. If there is any question as to a witness' willingness to appear, you must notify the judge's office in order to have the witness subpoenaed and to explain the necessity of his testimony. The judge's office must be notified at least five days before the hearing.[100]

Finally, you are entitled to travel reimbursement or advance payment of travel expenses when you are required to travel seventy-five miles or more (within the U.S.) one way to a hearing. In addition, your representative and necessary witnesses (unsubpoenaed) are also entitled to reimbursement for their travel expenses. Generally, reimbursement is limited to the cost of travel by the most economical and expeditious means of transportation available and appropriate to your condition of health. Subpoenaed witnesses are paid the same fees and mileage they would receive if they had been subpoenaed by a federal district court.[101] For reimbursement and in the case of advance payment of travel expenses, you must submit to the SSA an itemized list of what you spent, with supporting receipts.[102]

Can I appeal an adverse decision by an administrative law judge?

Yes. If the judge does not rule in your favor, you may file an appeal with the SSA's Appeals Council, an appellate body located in Arlington, Virginia. The request for an appeal should be made in writing and must be filed within sixty days of your receipt of the decision by the administrative law judge.[103] Only if there is some special feature of your case will the Appeals Council actually hear the appeal. If the council does accept the appeal, it acts much like an appellate court—that is, a claimant can submit a legal brief but cannot call witnesses as at a trial.[104] The claimant is entitled to make an oral argument before the council, but this is done only rarely.[105] Occasionally, the council will review an administrative law judge's decision favorable to a claimant, and this sometimes results in reversal of the favorable decision. But of all the cases decided by the administrative law judge only about 10 percent of the cases are reversed.[106] Although the Appeals Council rarely issues decisions favorable to claimants, one must nonetheless go through this appeal stage before seeking judicial review.

Can I take the SSA to court?

Yes. However, before the case can be heard by a court, it must go through an administrative appeal within the SSA. This means that the case must first be reconsidered and then heard by an administrative law judge. If the judge's decision is unfavorable, it must then be reviewed by the Appeals Council. Only after the Appeals Council has acted on the case may it go to court.[107] You then have sixty days in which to file a suit in a federal district court requesting that the decision of the SSA be overturned.[108]

In such suits the court considers whether the decision of the SSA should be upheld. If the judge concludes that the SSA applied the law properly and that there is evidence in the record to support the decision of the SSA, the judge will uphold the SSA.[109] If, however, the judge concludes that the SSA was mistaken as to what legal rule controlled the case or that there is insufficient evidence in the record to support the decision of the SSA, the judge will rule in favor of the claimant. About 60 percent of the Social Security cases which reach court result in the SSA's decision being reversed or remanded.[110] So if you are dissatisfied with the decision of the SSA and you have exhausted all of the appeals available within the SSA, do not hesitate to file an action in court seeking to have the SSA's decision reversed.

Most suits against the SSA allege that it has made factual errors in determining a person's eligibility for Social Security benefits. These suits would be argued on the basis of facts such as a person's disability or age. Other suits against the SSA allege that the SSA made an error in procedure, that a policy or procedure of the SSA violates either the Social Security Act or the Constitution, or that a provision of the act itself is unconstitutional. An example of the first type of case is *Mathews v. Eldridge*,[111] in which a Social Security disability recipient alleged that the SSA's procedures were unconstitutional because they did not provide a hearing before terminating his disability benefits. An example of the last type of case is *Weinberger v. Salfi*,[112] in which Mrs. Salfi alleged that the act's requirement that she be married to her husband for at least nine months prior to his death in order to qualify for widow's benefits was unconstitutional.

When the purpose of a suit is to establish the illegality of the Social Security Act itself or of a regulation of the SSA, the requirement that all administrative appeals must be exhausted before going to court may not apply. When the suit challenges a provision of the act as unconstitutional, for example, if it discriminates on the basis of sex, SSA regulations provide an expedited appeals process.[113] Under this process a person whose application for benefits has been denied must request that the denial be reconsidered by the SSA. If the denial is upheld on reconsideration, the person may petition the Social Security Administration for waiver of the remainder of the Social Security appeals process. If a waiver is granted, the person can go directly to federal court to contest the constitutionality of the Social Security Act provision under which her application for benefits was denied. Expediting such cases is justified by the principle that only a court can rule on the constitutionality of the act.

Furthermore, it may be possible to go directly to federal court without exhausting all administrative appeals even if a waiver is not granted. This occurred in *Mathews v. Eldridge*,[114] which challenged the constitutionality of the SSA regulations that denied Mr. Eldridge the opportunity for a hearing before his disability benefits were terminated. In those few cases which seek to challenge an SSA procedure, full use of the administrative appeals process may not be necessary. However, one should never attempt to skip the SSA appeals process without consulting a lawyer.

Do I have the right to an attorney or other person to represent me?

Certainly. People claiming or receiving Social Security benefits are entitled to have anyone assist them in dealing with the SSA.[115] It is a good idea to have such assistance, since statistics indicate that applicants assisted by an attorney or other skilled representative are successful in obtaining benefits more often than applicants who do not have such help.[116] Your representative can be an attorney or social worker or simply a friend or relative. It should, however, be someone who is experienced in handling these types of cases. You can involve a representative in your case at any point—at the time of application for benefits or later when you decide to request a hearing. In general though it is a good idea to involve a representative early in the process— perhaps after your application has been denied—so that the representative can help to obtain necessary evidence as soon as possible. The best opportunity to win a Social Security case is at the hearing. Therefore, if you intend to obtain help, you should do so *before* the hearing and be certain that the attorney or other representative is familiar with Social Security cases. (See below for information on how to find an attorney.)

Courts sometimes overturn decisions unfavorable to claimants who were unrepresented by a lawyer at an SSA hearing and who had difficulty presenting their case without a lawyer's help. When it is clear that the claimant's case was harmed because no lawyer was present to ensure that all important evidence was introduced, courts often require the SSA to give the claimant another opportunity to present his or her claim.[117]

How should I go about finding an attorney?

The SSA does not provide free attorneys to represent claimants and often will not provide help in finding them. You may look for an attorney employed by a legal-services program funded by the government or for one in private practice. Legal-services attorneys frequently handle Social Security cases, and they usually charge no fee for their services. But unless the program is funded by the Older Americans Act, you must generally have minimal income and assets to qualify for the program's services. You might also contact the state Office on Aging or local agency on aging. They may have lists of attorneys funded through the Older Americans Act to provide free or reduced fee services to individuals age 60 or older. (See appendices B and D for addresses and telephone numbers of legal services for the elderly and state agencies on aging.)

An attorney in private practice will expect a fee for representing a Social Security claimant. The usual arrangement, however, is that the attorney will charge the claimant only if he is successful in obtaining benefits. If he is successful, he will expect to be paid from the award obtained from the SSA. The amount of the fee is to be determined by the SSA.[118] The attorney is required to submit a request for approval of a fee to the SSA after the case has been decided.[119] The SSA will then review the request and authorize payment to the attorney directly from the award according to the *smallest* of: 25 percent of the award, the fee agreed upon by the claimant and the attorney, or an amount which in the judgment of the SSA is a "reasonable fee" for the services. Occasionally, the SSA will authorize the attorney to charge a sum in addition to 25 percent of the award.[120] If it is necessary for the attorney to file suit against the SSA and suit is successful, the attorney may request the court to authorize an additional fee under either the Social Security Act or the Equal Access to Justice Act.[121] Under the Equal Access to Justice Act, a court may award fees to the attorney if the government's position was not substantially justified and if it would not be inequitable to do so. These fees do not come out of the claimant's award; they are paid by the government. In any case, you should discuss the matter of fees when you first meet with an attorney about representation in a Social Security case. You should not agree to a fee arrangement which violates the system just described nor pay an attorney any money in advance except to cover any expense in preparing the case. Furthermore, it is illegal for an attorney to request a fee which violates this system or to request a fee in advance. In addition to refusing to agree to such an arrangement, you should inform the SSA and the grievance committee of your local bar association about the illegal request.

If you do not qualify for or cannot secure the assistance of a publicly funded organization or an attorney, you should contact the local bar association, a local law school, a local Social Security district office or the local Office of Hearings and Appeals. The bar association may have a list of attorneys who are experienced in Social Security cases. Law schools often have clinical programs that provide Social Security representation by law students under the supervision of clinical instructors. Generally, their services are free. And the Office of Hearings and Appeals should have a list of organizations that provide free legal services. Finally, you may want to contact the National Organization of Social Security Claimants' Representatives (NOSSCR) (1-800-431-2804 [toll free for calls from outside New York State] or 914-735-8812 [for calls in New York State; call collect]) for names and telephone numbers of attorneys in your area.

If you retain a representative you will be asked to fill out a form notifying the SSA of your choice. If the representative is a nonattorney, he must sign this notice.[122] After this form has been filled out and filed with the SSA, the representative can speak on your behalf and is authorized to examine your Social Security file and otherwise obtain information about you from the SSA. You can pay such a representative or not, but you are under no obligation to do so. If you decide to pay a nonattorney representative, the arrangements are made between you and the representative; however the SSA must first approve the fee.[123]

RECEIVING AND LOSING BENEFITS AND THE REDUCTION OF BENEFITS

Who will receive my benefits if I am unable to care for myself?

Social Security benefits are usually paid directly to the recipient, however, if the SSA determines that you are unable to take care of yourself, your benefits will be paid to someone who will be responsible for using these benefits to take care of you. The person entrusted with the responsibility of receiving benefits for your care is called a "representative payee."[124]

If you are alleged to be incapable of caring for yourself, the SSA usually requests medical evidence be submitted showing this is true. Normally, a statement from a doctor is required, but other evidence such as statements by relatives, neighbors, and others can be used. Likewise, if you have been declared legally incompetent, the court order declaring incompetency can be submitted to the SSA. Once the SSA establishes that you are not capable of caring for yourself, it will appoint someone to receive your benefits and use these benefits for your care. Normally, it prefers to appoint your spouse or another close relative or your legal guardian as representative payee, but it may appoint a friend, a public or private agency, or an institution.

A representative payee has the legal obligation to use your benefits to meet first the cost of your present needs, such as food, clothing, and rent.[125] If you are in an institution, the benefits are paid to the institution for your care. If money is left over after present needs have been met, the representative payee can use the benefits to take care of your legal dependents and also to pay off any previous debts you may have incurred. A Social Security recipient and the representative payee sometimes disagree as to how this remaining money is to be spent. For example, SSA regulations do not specifically require that the recipient be given spending money. This is especially problematic when an institution where the recipient resides has been appointed representative payee. For then the representative payee (the institution) might use the recipient's benefits to pay the institution's bills without reserving money for personal needs, such as cigarettes, hair care products, or a private telephone. SSA regulations direct the representative payee to use the Social Security check "for those items which will aid in the beneficiary's recovery or release from the institution."[126] The SSA has interpreted this to require that an institutionalized Social Security recipient be given spending money each month.[127] Similarly, a representative payee can use Social Security benefits to hire a lawyer to obtain the release of a Social Security recipient from an institution.[128]

A representative payee is required to maintain records of his use of the Social Security recipient's benefits. Any portion of the benefits held in a bank must be kept in a separate account. Investments by the representative payee of a Social Security recipient's money must comply with state law governing investments by fiduciaries—some states prohibit fiduciaries from investing in stock, for example. Representative payees are required to report periodically to the SSA to demonstrate that they have used Social Security benefits properly. If it is determined by the administration that the payee has not utilized funds properly, the payee can be discharged and a new payee appointed. In this case, the recipient may have to sue the payee in a state court to recover the misused funds. The SSA will not reimburse for the misused funds unless benefits have continued to a payee after evidence of misuse was submitted to the SSA or when actions taken have been contrary to SSA policy or regulations. When the SSA does not reimburse the beneficiary it will seek restitution from the payee for the beneficiary and submit the case to the office of the Inspector General for consideration of civil suit or criminal prosecution.[129] Under the Social Security Disability Benefits Reform Act of 1984, however, if a representative payee is found guilty of defrauding the SSA and if the court determines that such violation includes a willful misuse of funds, the court may require full or partial restitution to the individual as well as payment of a fine and/or the imposition of a prison sentence.[130]

You can resist efforts to have a representative payee appointed for you.[131] Simply request the SSA not to appoint a payee, and until a determination has been made that a payee is needed, your benefits usually will continue to be paid to you. If the SSA decides that a payee should be appointed, you can appeal this decision unless you are legally incompetent.[132] Furthermore, you can appeal the decision as to who your representative payee will be.[133]

Can my Social Security benefits be terminated?

Social Security benefits can be reduced or terminated for a number of reasons. This was established in 1960 by the U.S. Supreme Court in *Fleming v. Nestor*.[134] Mr. Nestor had immigrated to the United States from Bulgaria in 1930 and had lived and worked in this country ever since. In 1955 he retired and became eligible for Social Security retirement benefits. However, in 1956 he was deported from this country because he had been a member of the Communist party during the 1930's. Arguing that he had done nothing illegal—membership in the Communist party was not illegal during the time he was a member—and that Social Security retirement benefits were property which could not be taken from him by the government, Mr. Nestor filed suit to overturn the SSA decision terminating his benefits. The federal judge who heard his case agreed with Mr. Nestor that Social Security benefits were property which could not be taken from him. On appeal, however, the U.S. Supreme Court disagreed, stating that a Social Security recipient has no vested right to receive benefits even though the benefits stem from taxes paid as a worker.

So the Court's decision in the *Nestor* case makes it clear that there is no absolute right to receive Social Security. Congress can establish conditions of eligibility for Social Security benefits, and Congress is free to change these conditions. However, Congress normally makes changes that either take effect years after the change is made or apply only to new applicants. Unless the conditions imposed by Congress are unconstitutional (or unless the SSA imposes conditions not authorized by Congress), a person must meet all conditions of eligibility to qualify for benefits.

Under present law there are several circumstances that can result in reduction or loss of Social Security benefits. For instance, a person such as Mr. Nestor who is deported from the United States will have his benefits terminated.[135] Similarly, a person convicted of crimes such as espionage or treason may have his benefits terminated, [136] as may an alien who is absent from the United States for more than six months although this depends on the country to which he has moved.[137] And payment of retirement benefits to convicted felons is prohibited while they are in prison, effective for months following April 1983.[138]

Other circumstances leading to loss or reduction of benefits affect a larger number of people. Disability benefits, for example, may be terminated if it is determined that a person has recovered from his or her disability[139] or if he or she fails to accept rehabilitation services.[140] Another example is the case of a woman receiving benefits because of a dependent child; she will lose these benefits if the SSA determines the child is no longer living with her.[141] And divorced spouses may lose their benefits if they remarry.[142] In most cases, however, reduction or loss of Social Security benefits occurs when individuals earn more than the allowable limit while collecting benefits.

Can I work and still receive Social Security benefits?

Social Security retirement benefits are designed to replace earnings lost as a result of retirement. As a result, a person is permitted to earn only a limited amount of money and still retain full Social Security retirement benefits.[143] If more than the allowable limit is earned, benefits are reduced by one dollar for every two dollars earned over the allowable limit.[144] This rule is referred to as the "retirement test." The rule applies to all persons under the age of 70 receiving Social Security retirement benefits. Persons 70 or older may earn any amount of money without loss of any benefits.[145] During 1988 a person aged 65 through 69 may earn up to $8,400 per year without suffering any loss of Social Security benefits, and a person between 62 and 65 may earn up to $6,120.[146] These figures are based on the level of Social Security benefits, and they change each year.

A special rule allows people to receive benefits for the remainder of the year during which they retire, regardless of their earnings before retirement. Under this rule a person can get a full benefit for any month the person's wages do not exceed the monthly exempt amount and if the person does not perform substantial services in self-employment. The monthly exempt amount in 1988 is $700 if you are 65 or older and $510 if you are under 65.[147] This monthly test also applies during the year benefits begin for children or for a mother or father who receives benefits because she or he has been caring for a young child. And it applies in the first year of entitlement to a second type of benefit, such as retirement or widow(er)'s benefits. (There must be a break in entitlement of at least one month before an individual becomes entitled to a different benefit.)[148] The special monthly test can apply for only the first year in which a person has little or no earnings for one or more months. In all other years, the amount of benefits payable depends on a person's total annual earnings (except as explained above).

The special monthly test differs depending on whether the person works as an employee or is self-employed. For an employee, it does not matter when the wages are actually paid; the controlling factor is when the money is earned. For the self-employed, the main consideration is whether the person is active in his or her business and is performing "substantial services."[149] Unlike employees, who usually know how much they earn each month, self-employed people often do not know whether they will have a profit or a loss until the end of the year. The money a self-employed person receives from his or her business in a given month may vary considerably and often may be for work during some earlier month. For these reasons, the SSA does not use monthly earnings to decide how work affects payments for self-employed people. Self-employed people can get checks if they do not perform "substantial services." The SSA decides whether services as a self-employed person are substantial by looking at the amount of time the individual devotes to the business, the kind of services performed, and how the services compare with what the individual did in the past. In general, more than forty-five hours of self-employment in a month is considered substantial. Less than forty-five hours in a month is not considered substantial services. However, forty-five hours of work or less may be considered substantial if it involves the management of a sizeable business or is in a highly skilled occupation. Fewer than fifteen hours a month is never considered substantial, regardless of the size of the business or the value of the service.[150]

The retirement test penalizes only *earned* income. A person may have any amount of *unearned* income and suffer no reduction in benefits.[151] If a person receives $9,000 per year in dividends from stock, that person will receive full Social Security benefits, but if a person earns $9,000 per year, his or her benefits will be reduced. Congress has moved to alleviate the harshness of the test by increasing the amount a person can earn without losing benefits. After 1989, the earnings test benefit withholding rate will decrease to one dollar for each three dollars of excess earnings for individuals who attain full retirement age (age 65 in 1990).[152]

How does the SSA keep track of my postretirement earnings?

To enforce the retirement test, the SSA requires that recipients of retirement benefits submit a report each year predicting their monthly and annual earnings. The SSA will require those who are most likely to underestimate their earnings in a given year to report semiannually. If the report predicts excess earnings, benefits will be reduced or suspended until the excess has been collected.[153] For example, a person who informs the SSA that he or she will earn $9,400 during 1988 by earning over $700 per month, and he or she is 65 or older will have "excess earnings" of $500 for the year. (The term "excess earnings" includes only the portion of earnings that results in a reduction of Social Security benefits, not the entire sum in excess of the yearly maximum.) Since benefits are reduced by one dollar for every two dollars earned over the allowable limit, the "excess earnings" in this example are $500, one-half of the $1,000 earned in excess of the allowable limit of $8,400. If this person's Social Security benefits are $350 per month, the SSA will collect the excess earnings of $500 by suspending benefits for January, and by reducing the February benefit.[154] Beginning in March, your full benefits would be restored and would continue for the balance of the year because the excess has been fully collected.

Excess earnings of the retired individual are charged against and cause deductions from the total monthly family benefit (i.e., the benefits of the retired individual, his or her spouse, and his or her child). Excess earnings are not charged against disability insurance benefits or the benefits of an entitled divorced spouse who had been divorced from the retired individual at least two years.[155]

Another report may be required at the end of the year if no original report was filed or if the original report was inaccurate (i.e., the person earned more or less than predicted in the original report). In addition, the SSA checks with the Internal Revenue Service (IRS) to make sure that earnings reports are accurate and to catch persons who earned money but failed to file a report with the SSA. As a result of the second report or the check with the IRS, the SSA may determine that a person has been overpaid—that a person received full benefits in a month(s) in which excess earnings occurred. When this happens, the SSA will attempt to collect the overpayment by reducing or terminating future benefits.[156]

What can I do if the SSA claims I have been overpaid?

If you are notified by the SSA of an overpayment, the first step is to contact the SSA to discuss the situation with them. If you disagree with the SSA and your discussions are to no avail, you can appeal this determination by use of the normal SSA appeals system.[157]

The SSA will probably ask you to repay overpaid benefits. Repayment can occur in several ways. The SSA can suspend your checks until the overpaid amount has been recovered, or it can reduce your monthly checks and recover the overpaid amount over a period of time.[158]

However, the administration cannot recover an overpayment if (1) you were not at fault in allowing the overpayment *and* if (2) recovery of the overpayment would be either "against equity and good conscience" or "defeat the purpose of the Social Security Act."[159] Therefore, if it is claimed that you have been overpaid, you should request waiver of recovery and attempt to persuade the SSA that the overpayments were not your fault and that to require repayment would either violate equity and good conscience or defeat the purpose of the Social Security Act.

At Fault. In determining whether a person is at fault, the administration considers all relevant circumstances, including the person's age, intelligence, education, and physical and mental condition.[160] The SSA considers a person to be at fault if:

1. the person has given the SSA an incorrect statement concerning eligibility for benefits or amount of benefits which the person knew (or should have known) to be incorrect;[161]
2. the person failed to give the SSA information he knew (or should have known) to be important;[162] or
3. the person accepted a payment which he knew (or should have known) was incorrect.[163]

Furthermore, the SSA may consider a person to be at fault even though the SSA itself was partially to blame for the overpayment.

It is important to provide the SSA with a plausible explanation as to why the error occurred. Examples of circumstances that have been held not to be the fault of the recipient include reliance upon erroneous information from an official source with the SSA with respect to an interpretation of the Social Security Act or regulations,[164] reasonable belief that only take-home pay is used to compute compliance with the retirement test,[165] mistakes in computing earnings resulting from inaccurate reporting by the employer,[166] and earnings at a higher rate than expected.[167]

In determining "without fault," the SSA must assess what *you* actually knew or should have known about the event that caused the overpayment. If, for example, you suffered from a particular medical problem that may have contributed to the overpayment and inhibited your knowledge of the overpayment, you should emphasize this fact. Or if overpayment was caused by the person on whose earnings record you are receiving benefits, you should show that you had no knowledge of the event which caused the overpayment.

Recovery against Equity and Good Conscience. Even if you establish that you were not at fault in receiving an overpayment, the SSA will seek to recover the overpayments unless you also establish that such a recovery would be "against equity and good conscience" or that the "purpose of the Social Security Act" would be defeated by a recovery. Repayment of Social Security benefits is against equity and good conscience when a person has given up a valuable right or has changed his or her financial position for the worse in reliance upon receiving the benefits that now are alleged to have been improperly paid.[168]

To establish that recovery would be against equity and good conscience, you must establish that you relied—to your financial detriment—upon the correctness of the SSA's determination of your entitlement to benefits. An example of such reliance is that you quit your job after being notified of your entitlement to retirement benefits and are now unable to find employment.[169] Another example is if a man died without leaving an estate, and his widow paid for his funeral expenses in reliance on receipt of a lump-sum death benefit. If it is determined later that the man did not have sufficient quarters of coverage to be eligible for benefits, recovery from the widow would not be in equity and good conscience since she incurred a financial obligation in reliance on receipt of the benefits.[170]

The critical ingredient in establishing that recovery would be against equity and good conscience is that you have changed your financial situation for the worse in reliance upon the correctness of payments or were unaware that someone else received incorrect payments on the same work record. Your financial worth is not a critical ingredient in this determination. Rich or poor, a person who has changed his financial position, or did not know that benefits were incorrectly paid to another person on the same earnings record, should meet the requirements.[171]

Recovery defeating the purpose of the Social Security Act. Another way to avoid repaying an overpaid amount is to establish that recovery of the overpayment would "defeat the purpose of Title II of the Social Security Act."[172] The purpose of the act is to provide necessary income to retirees, disabled workers, and their dependents and survivors. If you can establish that you have limited income and assets and need continued payment of Social Security benefits to meet the ordinary and necessary expenses of life, recovery will be inappropriate.[173] To establish your need for continued payment of benefits, you should provide the SSA with a statement of your living expenses such as food, clothing, rent, mortgage payments, utility payments, medical expenses, and other necessary expenses of living.[174] Once it has been established that payment of benefits is essential to meeting your necessary expenses, it would defeat the purpose of the act to require that you repay the overpaid amount.

If you are unable to establish that no recovery should take place, you may nevertheless be able to persuade the SSA to recover the overpayment over a period of time by deducting a small amount each month from your monthly benefits. It is possible to spread repayment over a period of time if withholding the full amount each month would defeat the purpose of Title II (that is, if you are dependent on Social Security benefits as your primary source of income), if recoupment can be made by partial withholding within a reasonable time period, and if the overpayment was not the product of willful false statements or misrepresentation.[175]

Under current SSA procedures, a request for either a reconsideration or a waiver made within thirty days of your receipt of the notice of overpayment will suspend the recovery. In addition, you have a right to a personal conference on the issue of waiver prior to any proposed recovery.[176]

What should I do if I do not receive my Social Security check?
Social Security checks should arrive on the third day of each month. If the third of the month falls on a weekend, the checks will be sent so as to arrive before the weekend. If your check is late, you should notify the SSA immediately. They usually will ask that you wait until the sixth of the month to be certain that the check is not still in the mail.

If by the sixth of the month your check still has not arrived, inform the SSA of this fact. They will search their computer to determine whether a check has been issued to you. If a check has not been issued, they will determine the reason why. Common reasons are that the SSA has determined that you are no longer entitled or that your benefits should be reduced for some reason. The law requires that the SSA notify you of such a decision before your benefits are reduced or cut off. Sometimes, however, this required notice is not sent. If the SSA determines that your benefits have been terminated or reduced, the local office should send you a notice of the reason for termination and of your right to appeal this termination or reduction of benefits.

If the SSA records reveal that you should have received a check but that none was issued, a check should be sent to you immediately and you should receive it within ten to fourteen days.

If the computer indicates that a check has been issued to you, the administration will consult the Treasury Department to learn whether the check has been negotiated—that is, whether it has been cashed and returned to the Treasury Department. If the check has been issued but not negotiated, they will stop payment on the check and send a new check to you. You should receive this check by approximately the twentieth of the month.

If the computer search reveals that your check has been cashed and returned to the Treasury Department, a photocopy of the check will be sent to you to determine if the signature on the check is yours or whether the check has been forged. This process is a lengthy one, taking as long as six months to a year. And a replacement check will not be sent until it is determined whether the check has been forged.

In order to prevent checks from being lost or stolen, you can apply for "direct deposit" of Social Security checks by signing a Form SF-1199, which can be obtained at and is sent to the SSA by a financial institution. Before signing Form SF-1199, however, you should discuss the procedure for direct deposit with a financial institution representative to learn its conditions.

Finally, if a monthly check has not been lost or stolen but has not arrived by the fifteenth day of the month after the month in which the check was due, you may demand payment, and the SSA must pay within fifteen days of the demand.[177] This demand should be in writing. The SSA denies this procedure to a person who has appealed an SSA determination denying benefits,[178] or claimed disability benefits.

Will delaying retirement increase my benefits?

Yes. If you do not receive retirement benefits in one or more months after the month in which you reach retirement age (currently 65), either because you continued to work or simply did not apply for benefits, your benefits will be increased by a certain percentage. This delayed retirement credit is one-fourth of one percent of your monthly benefit amount *times* the number of months—beginning with the month of reaching age 65 and ending with the month before reaching age 70 (72 before 1984)—for which you were fully insured but did not receive benefits. Under the Social Security Act Amendments of 1983, for persons who attain age 65 in 1990 or later, the one-fourth of one percent rate will be increased by one-twenty-fourth of one percent in each even year until the rate reaches two-thirds of one percent for persons reaching age 66 in 2009 and later. (The retirement age will gradually increase in the next century to age 67.)

If a deceased person had earned delayed retirement credits, the SSA will compute that person's surviving spouse's or surviving divorced spouse's benefit based on the person's regular primary insurance amount plus the amount of the delayed retirement credit.[179]

What should I do if I am paid less than I am entitled to receive?

If you receive a Social Security check for less than you are entitled to, you should immediately notify the SSA. If the SSA agrees that you have been underpaid, payments can be made in a single check to you or can be added to your next several checks. If the SSA insists that the correct amount has been paid, you can file an appeal through the normal SSA appeals process.

What happens if I die before I receive Social Security benefits to which I am entitled?

If you should die before the SSA has arranged to pay an amount to which you are entitled, the benefits will be paid to your spouse if he or she is alive and living with you at the time of your death or is entitled to Social Security dependents' benefits. Otherwise, those benefits will be paid to your child(ren), parent(s), or your legal representative (i.e., the administrator or executor of your estate).[180]

THE GOVERNMENT PENSION OFFSET AND THE TAXATION OF SOCIAL SECURITY BENEFITS

How will my government pension affect my Social Security benefits?

If you have a federal, state or local government pension, a 1977 change in the Social Security law called the "government pension offset" may affect you. It may reduce the amount of your Social Security check as a spouse, divorced spouse, surviving spouse, or surviving divorced spouse—dollar for dollar—by the amount of all or some of your government pension.[181]

However, the offset applies only to Social Security benefits for a spouse or surviving spouse. It does not apply to Social Security retirement or disability benefits based on your own work covered by the program, even if you also receive a government pension.

This offset is effective for individuals applying for Social Security benefits in or after December 1977, unless one of the following two exceptions is met:

Exception 1. The offset will not apply for any month if you:

1. began to receive or were eligible to receive your federal, state or local government pension before December 1982. This means you must have met the age and length-of-service requirements for your pension before December 1982, even though you did not apply for your pension before then;
2. meet all the requirements for entitlement to Social Security spouse's or surviving spouse's benefits that were in effect and being administered in January 1977. (At that time, a divorced woman's marriage must have lasted at least twenty years rather than ten years as required today. And a husband or widower must have received at least one-half support from his wife.)

Exception 2. The offset will not apply for months after November 1982 if you:

1. received or were eligible to receive your federal, state, or local government pension before 1 July 1983; and
2. were receiving at least one-half support from your spouse at the time he became entitled to benefits, began a period of disability, or died. (This provision applies to men and women.)

If you are not exempt from the offset, the amount of your government pension that will be used for figuring the offset against your Social Security spouse's or surviving spouse's benefits will depend on when you first became eligible for the pension (not when you actually apply for it). Before July 1983, all of your pension will be used. For July 1983 or later, two-thirds of your pension will be used. (Effective with benefits for December 1984 on, the two-thirds reduction rate applies regardless of when you were first eligible for a governmental pension.)

In addition to the exceptions mentioned earlier, the offset will not apply to you if (1) the government job your pension is based on is covered by Social Security on your last day of employment (generally this is the official termination date as shown on your separation papers); or (2) you are entitled to Social Security benefits based on an application filed before December 1977. Although you may not be eligible for monthly payments on your spouse's Social Security record because of the offset, you may be able to get Medicare protection at age 65.

I now receive Social Security benefits. How does the income taxation of Social Security benefits affect me?

Beginning in 1984, a portion of your Social Security (or Tier I Railroad Retirement) benefits may be taxable. The amount to be included in gross income will be the lesser of: (1) one-half of the net benefits you received (amounts withheld to recover an overpayment are subtracted from the gross benefits, but Medicare premium deductions are not) or (2) one-half of the excess of your combined income over a base amount. (The base amounts are: $25,000 for an individual; $32,000 for a couple filing jointly; and $0 for a couple filing separately.)

Your combined income is your modified adjusted gross income (defined below) plus one-half of your net Social Security or Tier I Railroad Retirement benefits. (Tier II and vested dual Railroad Retirement benefits are generally taxed in the same manner as private pensions.) Your modified adjusted gross income is your adjusted gross income plus any tax-exempt interest you received plus the deduction for a married couple when both work plus amounts earned in a foreign country, a U.S. possession, or Puerto Rico that are excluded from gross income.[182]

The following example demonstrates how Social Security benefits are taxed.

Example: John Ash, who is single, recieved $8,000 in Social Security benefits in 1987. His adjusted gross income for 1987 was $24,000. He received $2,000 in tax-exempt interest. The relevant calculations are illustrated below:

(1) Adjusted gross income. $24,000
(2) Plus: All tax exempt interest. . . . . + 2,000
(3) Modified adjusted gross income $26,000

(4) Plus One-half of Social Security benefits . . . + 4,000

(5) "Combined income" $30,000

(6) Less: Base amount for an individual . . . . . . − 25,000

(7) Excess above base amount for an
individual . . . . $ 5,000

(8) One-half of excess over the base amount . . . 2,500

(9) One-half of Social Security benefits 4,000

(10) Amount includable in gross income (lesser
of (8) or (9)) . . . . $ 2,500

For more information on the taxation of Social Security and Railroad Retirement benefits, consult the Internal Revenue Service publication, "Tax Information on Social Security Benefits (and Tier I Railroad Retirement Benefits)" (IRS Publication 915).

RIGHT TO INFORMATION
AND PROTECTION FROM CREDITORS

Can I rely upon oral statements by the Social Security Administration?

Generally, advice given to you by employees of the SSA over the telephone or during visits to the office is accurate. However, errors sometimes are made by SSA employees, and you should be cautious about relying upon oral advice that affects your rights to benefits. If you are in doubt about the correctness of advice given by an SSA employee, you should not hesitate to speak to an SSA supervisor, your lawyer, or other representative for confirmation of the advice, and you should make use of manuals and brochures issued by the SSA to confirm such advice.

The importance of not relying upon an oral denial of benefits can be seen in a case decided recently by the Supreme Court. The case involved a woman who inquired orally of an SSA worker whether she was eligible for "mother's insurance benefits." The SSA worker erroneously told her that she was not, and the woman left the SSA office without having filed a written application. She eventually filed an application after learning that in fact she was eligible. She received retroactive benefits only from the date of the written application, not from the date of the oral inquiry. The Supreme Court held that the SSA worker's conduct did not excuse the woman's failure to file a written application.[183]

How can I learn whether the SSA is giving me credit for my earnings?

You have a right to know whether the SSA has given you full credit for all of your earnings.[184] Your eligibility for Social Security benefits as well as the amount of benefits you will receive depends upon the records the SSA maintains of your earnings. Keep track of these records if you work irregularly or for employers who may not have paid Social Security taxes for you.

To obtain a free copy of the Social Security records on your earnings, go to your local Social Security office to fill out a form requesting this information. If you believe that your Social Security records are incorrect, inform your local Social Security office of the errors. You have the burden of demonstrating that an error has been made and of providing evidence to support your claim that you have not been properly credited for wages earned or income earned through self-employment. Copies of your federal income tax return, pay stubs, and other records can be used to demonstrate that your account has not been fully credited.

The burden of establishing proof of an error becomes greater if more than three years have passed since the alleged error was made. A time limit of three years, three months, and fifteen days has been set by the SSA within which claims of errors usually must be submitted.[185] So, a claim that an error was made concerning work in 1985 should be pointed out to the Social Security Administration no later than 15 April 1989.[186] Because of this time limitation for correcting errors in Social Security Administration records of your earnings, you should request a report of your earnings record at least every two years.

There are, however, many exceptions to the three year limit, so you should continue to press a claim that there are earnings missing or incorrectly set forth on the record, even if more than three years have elapsed from the time of the error. In addition, you should seek the assistance of an attorney.

Do I have a right to have information in my Social Security file kept secret?

Yes, for the most part. In general, it is illegal for an SSA employee to disclose information from an SSA file to the public. There are some exceptions to this rule, however. Information can be given to other government agencies for legitimate government purposes, and your Social Security number and some information about your Social Security coverage sometimes can be given to your past and present employers.[187]

Do I have a right to see my Social Security file?

Yes. You and your authorized representative are entitled to see all nonmedical information in your Social Security file.[188] In addition, if you or your representative authorize others to see this information, it should be shown to them.[189] Similarly, medical information from your file should be disclosed to you or your authorized representative. However, if the responsible SSA official believes that direct access to a medical record may have an "adverse effect" on you, he will send it to your designated representative.[190]

If the SSA refuses to disclose information from your file to you, you are entitled to sue the SSA to obtain the information. The Freedom of Information Act authorizes such suits where federal agencies refuse to allow an individual access to information about him or her possessed by the agencies.[191]

Can a creditor attach my Social Security benefits?

No. The Social Security Act specifically provides that Social Security benefits cannot be attached or garnished by a creditor.[192] Thus, if you owe money to a store or loan company, your Social Security benefits cannot be attached by your creditor to collect the debt. The rule against attachment of Social Security benefits applies to money in a bank account if the money resulted from your depositing Social Security checks in the bank.[193] In other words, the rule forbids attachment of any money you own so long as the money can be traced to your Social Security checks. On the other hand, if you have spent money derived from Social Security checks to buy a car or television, the car or television can be attached by your creditors.

This rule forbidding attachment of Social Security benefits applies even if your creditor is a state or local government. This was established in 1973 by the U.S. Supreme Court in *Philpott v. Essex County Welfare Board*,[194] in which the Court ruled that a county welfare department could not sue a Social Security recipient to recover welfare payments made to the recipient even though the recipient had promised the welfare department that he would repay the department if he was declared eligible for Social Security benefits. The only exceptions to this rule are that the federal government can take your Social Security benefits to collect back taxes owed the federal government, and your Social Security benefits can be attached to enforce a court order obligating you to pay child support or alimony.[195]

NOTES

1. 42 U.S.C. §§ 301 *et seq.* (1982), *as amended; See also* 20 C.F.R. §§ 404.1–.2127 (1987).

2. *See* 42 U.S.C. §§ 402(a), 423(a)(1) (1982).

3. 42 U.S.C. §§ 402(b) (wife's benefits), 402(c) (husband's benefits), 402(d) (children's benefits) (1982).

4. 42 U.S.C. §§ 402(e) (widow's benefits), 402(f) (widower's benefits), 402(d) (surviving children's benefits), 402(h) (surviving parent's benefits), 402(g) (surviving mother's benefits) (1982).

5. 42 U.S.C. § 402(i) (1982); 20 C.F.R. §§ 404.390–.392 (1987).

6. 51 *Social Security Bulletin* 5, (June 1988).

7. 52 Fed. Reg. 41672, 41673 (Oct. 29, 1987).

8. *U.S. Department of Health and Human Services, Social Security Handbook* 206, 211 (9th ed. 1986) [*Social Security Handbook*].

9. *See* 42 U.S.C.S. § 410 (Supp. 1986) for a list of employment categories not covered by Social Security.

10. 42 U.S.C. §§ 414, 423(c) (1982); 20 C.F.R. § 404.101–.120 (1987).

11. *Social Security Handbook supra* note 8, at 6; 49 *Social Security Bulletin* 7 (June 1986).

12. Pub. L. No. 98-21, §§ 101–103, amending 42 U.S.C. §§ 410, 418 (Supp. I 1983).

13. It is the doing of work covered under Social Security and not the actual payment of taxes at the time the work is done that determines eligibility. But if taxes are not paid and recorded by the administration, the SSA will presume that no wages were paid. 42 U.S.C. § 405(c)(5) (1982).

14. 42 U.S.C. § 410(a)(3) (1982); 20 C.F.R. § 404.1058 (1987). *See also* 26 C.F.R. § 31.3121(a)(7)-1 (1987). Not all domestic service has Social Security coverage; domestic employment for a son or daughter after

1968 will be covered only in some situations, 42 U.S.C. § 410(a)(3)(b) (1982); 20 C.F.R. § 404.1015 (1987).

15. 42 U.S.C. § 409(g)(2) (1982), *as amended by* Social Security Amendments of 1977, Pub. L. No. 95-216, 91 Stat. 1509, 1536, 1552; §§ 315,352; 20 C.F.R. § 404.1058 (1987).

16. 26 U.S.C. §§ 3102(a), 7202 (1982).

17. 42 U.S.C. § 410(f) (1982); 20 C.F.R. § 404.1056 (1987); Pub. L. No. 100-203, 101 Stat. 1330–287, § 9002 (Dec. 22, 1987) (to be codified in 26 U.S.C. § 3121(a)(8), 42 U.S.C. § 409(h)).

18. 42 U.S.C. § 410(a)(1) (1982); 20 C.F.R. § 404.1016 (1987).

19. 42 U.S.C. § 410(n) (1982); 20 C.F.R. § 404.1010 (1987).

20. 42 U.S.C. § 411(a)(1) (1982); 20 C.F.R. § 404.1017 (1987).

21. 42 U.S.C. § 413(a)(2) (1982). In a few limited circumstances, the SSA will use one of several other definitions of "quarter of coverage" if it is to the advantage of the claimant. *Id. See also* 42 U.S.C. § 413(c) (1982).

22. *Id.*

23. Pub. L. No. 95-216, 91 Stat. 1509, 1552, § 352 (Dec. 20, 1977).

24. *Id.*

25. *Social Security Handbook, supra* note 8, at 22. The calculation used in this example is generally reliable. However, there are exceptions for persons who turned age 62 in 1973 and 1974. Until 1975 the computation for men required that quarters acquired between age 62 and 65 be counted, while for women, only quarters acquired before 62 were counted. This method of computation discriminated against men who retired early—i.e., before age 65—and resulted in lower benefits than women who retired at the same age and with the same work record would receive. Pub. L. No. 92-603, Oct. 30, 1972, changed this inequity by amending 42 U.S.C. §§ 409(i), 414(a)(1), 415(b)(3), 416(i)(3)(A), 423(a)(2), 423(c)(1)(A), 427(a)(b), and 26 U.S.C. § 3121(a)(9) (1982) so that since 1975 men and women can now retire under the same benefit formula. *See Califano v. Webster*, 430 U.S. 313 (1977); 20 C.F.R. § 404.115 (1987).

26. 20 C.F.R. §§ 404.1018(e)–(g) (1987).

27. *Social Security Handbook, supra* note 8, at 141.

28. *Id.* at 118–23; 20 C.F.R. § 404.1007 (1987).

29. 42 U.S.C. § 410(a)(3)(B) (1982); 26 U.S.C. § 3121(b)(3)(B) (1982); 20 C.F.R. § 404.1015 (1987). The mental or physical condition of the child or parent which causes the need for an adult's care must last at least four consecutive weeks in the calendar quarter when the work is performed. 20 C.F.R. § 404.1015(a)(4)(i) (1987).

30. 26 U.S.C. § 3121(b)(3) (1982); 20 C.F.R. § 404.1015(b) (1987); Pub. L. No. 100-203, 101 Stat. 1330–287, 1330–288, § 9004 (Dec. 22, 1987), amending 26 U.S.C. § 3121(b)(3), 42 U.S.C. § 210(a)(3).

31. 42 U.S.C. § 402(a) (1982).
32. A worker who retires at age 62 will receive only 80 percent of the benefit amount that he would have received by delaying his retirement to age 65. 42 U.S.C. § 402(q)(1) (1982). For retirement at age 63, benefits are reduced approximately 13.2 percent; and at age 64 approximately 6.6 percent. *Id.* The benefits of a person who retires early are recomputed when he reaches age 65 to adjust for any months between retirement and age 65 when benefits were not paid. 42 U.S.C. §§ 402(q)(6), (7) (1982). This would occur, for example, if during the period after retirement but prior to age 65 the claimant's benefits were reduced because he earned too much money, as explained below.
33. 42 U.S.C. § 402(w), *as amended by* Pub. L. No. 98-21, 97 Stat. 65, 79, § 114.
34. 42 U.S.C. §§ 402(b)(1), (c)(1), (1982); 20 C.F.R. § 404.330 (1987). The terms "wife" and "husband" are defined in 42 U.S.C. §§ 416(b), (f) (1982).
35. 42 U.S.C. §§ 416(d)(1), (4) (1982); 20 C.F.R. § 404.332(b)(3) (1987). Benefits are not available to divorced wives younger than 62 even if they are caring for children. *Mathews v. de Castro*, 429 U.S. 181 (1976). A surviving divorced spouse who remarries will remain eligible for benefits if he or she remarries someone entitled to certain types of Social Security benefits. 42 U.S.C. §§ 402(b)(3), (c)(4) (1982).
36. 42 U.S.C.S. §§ 402 (b)(5), (c)(5) (Supp. 1986); 20 C.F.R. §§ 404. 331–.333, .415–.417 (1987).
37. 42 U.S.C. § 402(d) (1982).
38. 42 U.S.C. § 416(e) (1982); 20 C.F.R. §§ 404.350–.365 (1987). The eligibility of illegitimate children for children's benefits has been the subject of frequent litigation. *See, e.g., Jimenez v. Weinberger*, 417 U.S. 628 (1974); *Mathews v. Lucas*, 427 U.S. 495 (1976); *Norton v. Mathews*, 427 U.S. 524 (1976). They are eligible for benefits; however, along with grandchildren, stepchildren, and adopted children, they must meet certain additional requirements which establish that they were dependent upon the wage earner. 42 U.S.C. § 416(h)(2), (3) (1982); 20 C.F.R. §§ 404.354–.366 (1987). Illegitimate children will be deemed dependent if they can prove that they would be entitled to inherit from the worker under state law if he or she were to die without leaving a will. 42 U.S.C. § 416(h)(2)(A) (1982); 20 C.F.R. §§ 404.354–.355 (1987).
39. 42 U.S.C.S. §§ 403(a), 415 (Supp. 1986).
40. 42 U.S.C. §§ 423(a), (c) (1982). *See also* 42 U.S.C. § 416(i) (1982).
41. *See generally* 42 U.S.C. § 402 (1982).
42. 42 U.S.C. §§ 402(e)–(h) (1982).
43. 42 U.S.C. § 402(i) (1982); 20 C.F.R. §§ 404.390–.395 (1987).

44. 42 U.S.C. §§ 402(e)(1)(B), (f)(1)(B) (1982). For purposes of eligibility for survivors' benefits, disability has a different meaning than for eligibility for disability insurance benefits. Whereas a person need only be precluded from "substantial gainful employment" to be eligible for disability insurance benefits on his or her own work record, a widow (or widower) between 50 and 65 must be precluded from "*any* gainful employment" to be eligible for survivors' benefits based on disability. 42 U.S.C. § 423(d)(2)(B) (1982).

45. 42 U.S.C. §§ 402(e)(1)(B), (f)(1)(B) (1982). *See also* 42 U.S.C. § 416(d)(2) (1982), *as amended* by Social Security Amendments of 1977, Pub. L. No. 95-216, 91 Stat. 1509, 1548, § 337. The remarriage of a surviving divorced spouse can affect his or her eligibility for benefits, although remarriage after meeting the eligibility requirements for benefits (e.g., the disability criteria) no longer will result in termination of eligibility. 42 U.S.C. §§ 402(e)(1), (3); 402(f)(1), (4) (1982), *as amended* by the Social Security Amendments of 1983, Pub. L. No. 98-21, 97 Stat. 65, 92–93, § 131. However, under the SSA's regulations, the remarriage must also occur after the worker's death. 20 C.F.R. § 404.336(e)(4) (1987). *But see Pirus v. Bowen*, CCH UNEMPL. INS. REP. ¶ 17, 679 C.D. Cal. 1987 (court invalidated rule).

46. 42 U.S.C. §§ 416(c), (g) (1982). In certain circumstances, such as the accidental death of an employee, the nine-month marriage requirement may be waived. *See* 42 U.S.C. § 416(k) (1982). The nine-month requirement was upheld by the U.S. Supreme Court in *Weinberger v. Salfi*, 422 U.S. 750 (1975).

47. 42 U.S.C. § 402(g)(1) (1982).

48. 42 U.S.C. §§ 402(g)(2), (e)(2)(B), (f)(3)(B) (1982).

49. 42 U.S.C. § 402(d)(1) (1982).

50. 42 U.S.C. § 402(d)(2) (1982).

51. 42 U.S.C. § 402(h) (1982).

52. 42 U.S.C. § 403(a) (1982).

53. 20 C.F.R. §§ 404.611–.612 (1987).

54. 20 C.F.R. § 404.630 (1987). *Tuck v. Finch*, 430 F.2d 1075 (4th Cir. 1970). The SSA often, but not always, records informal contacts. Where the existence of such a contact can be proven, eligibility may be established even if a formal application has not been submitted.

55. 20 C.F.R. §§ 404.611, .623 (1987).

56. 42 U.S.C. § 402(j)(1) (1982). In cases where granting retroactive benefits would result in benefits being actuarially reduced, benefits will not be paid earlier than the month of application. *Id. See also* 20 C.F.R. § 404.621(a)(1)(ii) (1987).

57. 42 U.S.C. § 402(i) (1982); 20 C.F.R. § 404.621(b) (1987).

58. *Social Security Handbook supra* note 8, at 238–48.

59. *See* 20 C.F.R. § 404.716 (1987) regarding proof of age.

60. *Social Security Handbook supra* note 8, at 238–41.

61. *Bennett v. Schweiker*, 532 F. Supp 837 (D.D.C. 1982).

62. *Blanks v. Richardson*, 439 F.2d 1158 (5th Cir. 1971); *Bennett v. Schweiker, supra*, at note 61.

63. *See* 20 C.F.R. § 404.723 (1987).

64. *See* 20 C.F.R. § 404.725 (1987).

65. *See* 42 U.S.C. § 416(h)(1) (1982); 20 C.F.R. § 404.726 (1987).

66. *See* 20 C.F.R. § 404.726 (1987).

67. *See* 42 U.S.C. § 402(b)(1) (1982).

68. 42 U.S.C. §§ 402(b)(1), 416(d)(1) (1982); 20 C.F.R. § 404.331 (1987).

69. *See* 42 U.S.C. § 416(h)(1)(B) (1982); 20 C.F.R. § 404.727 (1987).

70. A great number of lawsuits have involved this issue. *See, e.g., Rosenberg V. Richardson*, 538 F.2d 487 (2d Cir. 1976); *Garcia v. Secretary of HHS*, 760 F.2d 4 (1st Cir. 1985); *Gordon v. Bowen*, 801 F.2d 1275 (11th Cir. 1986) (deemed widow was entitled to receive benefits notwithstanding fact that legal widow once received such benefits on deceased wage earner's account). The SSA has "acquiesced" in the *Rosenberg* ruling in the Second Circuit that allows both the legal widow and the "deemed" widow to receive benefits at the same time. The SSA's Acquiescence Ruling will apply only to states in the Second Circuit (Connecticut, New York, and Vermont) and will apply through all levels of the SSA administrative appeal process. *See* 51 Fed. Reg. 20354, 20355 (June 4, 1986).

71. *See* 20 C.F.R. §§ 404.720, .728 (1987).

72. *See* 42 U.S.C. §§ 416(h)(2)–(3) (1982); 20 C.F.R. §§ 404.730–750 (1987). Similar problems can arise in establishing eligibility for parents' benefits.

73. 42 U.S.C. § 416(h)(2)(A) (1982); 20 C.F.R. §§ 404.354–.355 (1987).

74. Children who are adopted after the worker has become entitled to benefits must meet a special dependency test. 42 U.S.C. §§ 416(e), (h) (1982); 20 C.F.R. § 404.362(b) (1987).

75. 42 U.S.C. §§ 402(d)(1)(C), (h)(1)(B)(i) (1982); 20 C.F.R. §§ 404.736, .750 (1987).

76. 20 C.F.R. §§ 404.362, .366, .370 (1987).

77. *Id*.

78. 45 C.F.R. § 206.10(a)(3) (1987).

79. *See, e.g., White v. Mathews*, 559 F.2d 852 (2d Cir. 1977).

80. *Heckler v. Day*, 104 S. Ct. 2249 (1984) (Classwide mandatory deadlines for appeals are improper). On remand, the Second Circuit Court of Appeals held that the district court can consider some form of classwide relief other than mandatory time limits. *Barnett and Day v. Bowen*, 794 F.2d 17(2d Cir. 1986). *See also Barnett v. Bowen*, 665 F.

Supp. 1096 (D. Vt. 1987) (The court held that the SSA must notify class members of their right to seek court relief if their request for reconsideration or hearing has been unreasonably delayed.).

81. 42 U.S.C. § 405(q)(2)(B)(ii) (1982); 20 C.F.R. § 404.1810(c)(3) (1987).

82. 42 U.S.C. § 405(q)(3) (1982); 20 C.F.R. § 404.1810(e) (1987).

83. SSA Program Operations Manual System (POMS), §§ SI E02004.100 *et. seq.* (9/85); RS E02801.030 *et. seq.* (8/85).

84. *Elliott v. Weinberger*, 564 F.2d 1219 (9th Cir. 1977), *aff'd in part, rev'd in part on other grounds, sub nom. Califano v. Yamasaki*, 442 U.S. 682 (1979).

85. 42 U.S.C. §§ 402(j), 423(a)(2), (b) (1982); 20 C.F.R. §§ 404.601, .621 (1987). *Accord, Schweiker v. Hanson*, 451 U.S. 785, 786 (1981).

86. 20 C.F.R. § 404.905 (1987).

87. 20 C.F.R. § 404.957(c) (1987). However, you can request that the earlier decision be reopened. If you request reopening of the earlier decision within twelve months of the initial determination, you have a right to have the decision reopened for any reason. If you wait longer than twelve months to request reopening, you must show "good cause" to have the case reopened, and the decision whether to reopen is within the discretion of the SSA and cannot be reviewed by a court unless there is a constitutional issue involved. 20 C.F.R. § 404.972 (1987). *See Califano v. Sanders*, 430 U.S. 99 (1977).

88. 20 C.F.R. § 404.902(h) (1987).

89. 397 U.S. 254 (1970).

90. 424 U.S. 319 (1976).

91. 42 U.S.C.S. § 423(g) (Law. Co-op. 1973 & Supp. 1988).

92. *Califano v. Yamasaki*, 442 U.S. 682 (1979).

93. Administration regulations require written requests. 20 C.F.R. §§ 404.908, .909 (1987).

94. 20 C.F.R. § 404.909(a) (1987). Under some circumstances, additional time can be obtained in which to appeal. *See* 20 C.F.R. §§ 404.909(b), .911 (1987).

95. 20 C.F.R. § 404.913 (1987); 51 Fed. Reg. 288–309 (Jan. 3, 1986) (to be codified in 20 C.F.R. §§ 404.907–.961; 416.1407–.1461).

96. 20 C.F.R. § 404.933(b) (1987). An extension of time in which to appeal can be obtained in some circumstances. *See supra* note 94; and 51 Fed. Reg. 18611, 18617 (May 21, 1986) (to be codified in 20 C.F.R. § 404.1597a (g)) (proposed rules).

97. The various rights of a claimant at the hearing are contained in 20 C.F.R. §§ 404.944–.965, .1703–.1740 (1987).

98. 20 C.F.R. § 404.944 (1987).

99. 20 C.F.R. §§ 404.936, .938, .957 (1987).

100. 20 C.F.R. § 404.950(d) (1987).

101. 20 C.F.R. § 404.950(d)(4) (1987).
102. 20 C.F.R. §§ 404.999a–.999d (1987).
103. 20 C.F.R. § 404.968 (1987). An extension of time in which to appeal can be obtained in some circumstances. *See supra* note 94.
104. 20 C.F.R. §§ 404.975–.976 (1987).
105. 20 C.F.R. § 404.976(c) (1987).
106. Dixon, *The Welfare State and Mass Justice: A Warning from the Social Security Disability Program*, 1972 *Duke L. J.* 681, 697n.76 (1972); *Office of Hearings and Appeals Operational Report*, Sept. 30, 1986, at 27 (rate of outright reversal was under 10 percent in FY 1986).
107. 42 U.S.C. § 405(g) (1982); 20 C.F.R. § 404.981 (1987).
108. *Id.* An extension of time in which to appeal can be obtained in some circumstances. *See supra* note 94; 20 C.F.R. § 404.982 (1987).
109. 42 U.S.C. § 405(g) (1982).
110. Fried, "A Disability Appeal Primer: Appeals to Federal Court in Social Security and Supplemental Security Income Disability Cases," 9 *West's Social Security Reporting Service* 245, 246 (July 1985).
111. 424 U.S. 319 (1976).
112. 422 U.S. 749 (1975).
113. 20 C.F.R. §§ 404.923–.928 (1987).
114. 424 U.S. 319, 331, (1976). A difficult issue left unresolved by the Supreme Court in *Mathews* is whether 28 U.S.C. § 1361 (mandamus jurisdiction) can be used to provide a court with jurisdiction to hear a challenge to SSA procedures. Many lower courts have held that it can be. *See, e.g., Ganem v. Heckler*, 746 F.2d 844 (D.C. Cir. (1984). The Supreme Court has ruled that 5 U.S.C. § 702 (the Administrative Procedure Act) does not provide such jurisdiction. *Califano v. Sanders*, 430 U.S. 99 (1977).
115. 20 C.F.R. § 404.1705 (1987).
116. *See* Popkin, "The Effect of Representation on Nonadversary Proceedings—A Study of Three Disability Programs," 62 *Cornell L. Rev. 989 (1977); Participant Involvement in Request for Hearing Cases For Fiscal Year 1983*, May 1984 (Office of Hearings and Appeals, Social Security Administration).
117. *See Narrol v. Heckler*, 727 F.2d 1303 (D.C. Cir. 1984).
118. 20 C.F.R. §§ 404.1720–.1735 (1987).
119. 20 C.F.R. § 404.1720(b) (1987).
120. 20 C.F.R. §§ 404.1725–.1730 (1987).
121. 42 U.S.C. § 406(b)(1) (1982); 28 U.S.C. § 2412, amended by Pub. L. No. 99-80, 99 Stat. 183 (1985).
122. 20 C.F.R. § 404.1707 (1987). Form SSA-1696 ("Appointment of Representative") is used.
123. 20 C.F.R. § 404.1720(b) (1987).

124. 42 U.S.C. § 405(j) 1982); 20 C.F.R. § 404.2001 (1987).

125. 20 C.F.R. §§ 404.2035, .2040 (1987).

126. 20 C.F.R. § 404.2040(b) (1987).

127. SSA POMS §§ GN 00602.001-00602.020 (4/83) (part 2).

128. *Social Security Ruling* 66-42 (1966).

129. National Senior Citizens Law Center (NSCLC), Washington Weekly, Feb. 14, 1987, pp. 26–27.

130. Pub. L. No. 98-460, 98 Stat. 1764, 1810, § 16(c), amending 42 U.S.C. § 408. *See also Jordan v. Heckler*, 744 F.2d 1397, 1399 (10th Cir. 1984) (The SSA can only request that the payee make restitution.)

131. 20 C.F.R. § 404.2030 (1987).

132. 20 C.F.R. § 404.902(o) (1987).

133. 20 C.F.R. § 404.902(p) (1987). Under the Social Security Disability Benefits Reform Act of 1984, the SSA must ensure that representative payee certifications are adequately reviewed. Pub. L. No. 98-460, 98 Stat. 1764, 1809, § 16 (a), amending 42 U.S.C. § 405(j).

134. 363 U.S. 603 (1960).

135. 42 U.S.C. § 402(n) (1982).

136. 42 U.S.C. § 402(u) (1982).

137. 42 U.S.C. § 402(t) (1982).

138. 42 U.S.C. § 402(x) (Supp. I 1983).

139. 42 U.S.C. § 416(i)(2)(D) (1982).

140. 42 U.S.C. §§ 422(b)(1)–(2) (1982).

141. 42 U.S.C. § 403(c) (1982).

142. *See, e.g.*, 42 U.S.C. §§ 402(e), (f) (1982) *as amended* by Social Security Amendments of 1983, Pub. L. No. 98-21, 97 Stat. 65, 92 § 131; (1985); 20 C.F.R. §§ 404.332–.336 (1987).

143. 42 U.S.C. § 402(b) (1982); 20 C.F.R. §§ 404.416, .428–.456 (1987).

144. 42 U.S.C. § 403(f)(3) (1982); 20 C.F.R. § 404.430 (1987).

145. 42 U.S.C. § 403(f)(1)(B) (1982); 20 C.F.R. § 404.430(a)(3) (1987).

146. 42 U.S.C. § 403(f)(8) (1982); 52 Fed. Reg. 41672, 41674 (Oct. 29, 1987).

147. *Id.*; 20 C.F.R. §§ 404.430–.447 (1987); U.S. Department of Health and Human Services, "How work affects your Social Security check" (Feb. 1984). The exempt amounts will be redetermined each year. 20 C.F.R. § 404.430 (1987).

148. 20 C.F.R. § 404.435(c)(4) (1987).

149. 20 C.F.R. § 404.446 (1987).

150. 20 C.F.R. § 404.447 (1987).

151. 42 U.S.C. §§ 403(b), (f) (1982).

152. Pub. L. No. 98-21, Title III, § 347, Apr. 20, 1983, 97 Stat. 138.

153. 20 C.F.R. § 404.456 (1987).

154. Slightly different rules apply during the calendar year in which a person retires. During the first year of retirement, benefits will be

reduced only for months in which an employee earns more than one-twelfth of the applicable yearly maximum. 42 U.S.C. § 403(f) (1982). For the self-employed, benefits will be reduced during the first year of retirement only during months in which the self-employed person renders substantial services in self-employment. *Id.* For example, if a person at age 65 retires on 30 June 1987 and receives benefits from July through October but returns to work during November and December, earning over $700 each month, benefits would be reduced only for November and December, since these are the only months after retirement during which more than $700 (the monthly exempt amount for those 65 or older) was earned.

155. 20 C.F.R. §§ 404.415–.416, .434–.441 (1987); *Social Security Handbook, supra* note 8, at 253–56.

156. 20 C.F.R. §§ 404.501–.502 (1987).

157. 20 C.F.R. § 404.902(j) (1987).

158. 20 C.F.R. § 404.502 (1987).

159. 42 U.S.C. § 404(b) (1982); 20 C.F.R. § 404.506 (1987).

160. 20 C.F.R. § 404.507 (1987).

161. 20 C.F.R. § 404.507(a) (1987).

162. 20 C.F.R. § 404.507(b) (1987).

163. 20 C.F.R. § 404.507(c) (1987).

164. 20 C.F.R. § 510 (b) (1987). *See Michalak v. Weinberger*, 416 F. Supp. 1213 (S.D. Tex. 1976).

165. 20 C.F.R. § 404.510(a) (1987).

166. 20 C.F.R. § 404.510(f)(3) (1987).

167. 20 C.F.R. § 404.510(f)(2) (1987).

168. 42 U.S.C. § 404(b) (1982); 20 C.F.R. § 404.509 (1987). One court has extended the meaning of "against equity and good conscience" to include situations where the insured had no knowledge that benefits were being incorrectly paid. *Groseclose v. Bowen*, 809 F.2d 502 (8th Cir. 1987) (daughter who lived away from home received incorrectly paid benefits). *Accord*, 53 Fed. Reg. 25481 (July 7, 1988) (to be codified at 20 C.F.R. § 404.509) (example 4).

169. 20 C.F.R. § 404.509 (1987) (example 1).

170. 20 C.F.R. § 404.509 (1987) (example 3).

171. 20. C.F.R. § 404.509 (1987); *see supra* note 168.

172. 42 U.S.C. § 404(b) (1982); 20 C.F.R. § 404.508 (1987).

173. *See, e.g., Sierakowski v. Sec. of HEW*, 504 F.2d 831 (6th Cir. 1974); *Hatfield v. Richardson*, 380 F. Supp. 1048 (D.D.C. 1974).

174. 20 C.F.R. § 404.508 (1987).

175. 20 C.F.R. § 404.502(c) (1987).

176. SSA POMS §§ GN 02201.060 (part 2) (3/83), GN 02270.001-GN

02270.020 (part 2) (3/83); *Califano v. Yamasaki*, 442 U.S. 682 (1979); *Yamasaki v. Schweiker*, 680 F.2d 588 (9th Cir. 1982).

177. 42 U.S.C. § 405(q)(2)(B)(i) (1982); 20 C.F.R. § 404.1810(c)(2) (1987).

178. 42 U.S.C. § 405(q)(5) (1982); 20 C.F.R. § 404.1810(b)(2) (1987).

179. Pub. L. No. 98-21, 97 Stat. 65, 79, § 114, amending 42 U.S.C. § 402(w); 50 Fed. Reg. 27615 (July 5, 1985) (proposed rules); 20 C.F.R. § 404.313(a) (1987).

180. 20 C.F.R. § 404.503 (1987).

181. Pub. L. No. 98–21, 97 Stat. 65, 131, § 337, amending 42 U.S.C. §§ 402(b)(4)(A), (c)(2)(A), (e)(7)(A), (f)(2)(A), (g)(4)(A) (1982); 20 C.F.R. § 404.408a (1987); 51 Fed. Reg. 23051, 23052 (June 25, 1986) (to be codified in 20 C.F.R. §§ 404.408a(b)(4), (d)(2)); U.S. Dep't. of Health and Human Services, "Government Pension Offset—How It May Affect You" (Apr. 1983); *Social Security Handbook, supra* note 8, at 269–70.

182. 26 U.S.C. § 86 (Supp. I 1983).

183. *Schweiker v. Hanson*, 450 U.S. 785 (1981).

184. 20 C.F.R. § 404.810 (1987).

185. 20 C.F.R. §§ 404.820–.822 (1987).

186. *Id*. The time limit for establishing an error will be extended if you have filed an application for benefits within the time limit. 20 C.F.R. § 404.822(c)(2) (1987).

187. *See generally* 42 U.S.C. § 1306 (1982); 20 C.F.R. § 401.100 *et. seq.* (1987).

188. 20 C.F.R. § 401.405 (1987); 45 C.F.R. § 5b.5 (1987).

189. 45 C.F.R. § 5b.9 (1987).

190. 45 C.F.R. § 5b.6 (1987).

191. 5 U.S.C. § 552 (1982); 20 C.F.R. §§ 422.444–.449 (1987).

192. 42 U.S.C. § 407 (Supp. I 1983), as amended by Pub. L. No. 98-21, Title III, § 335(a), Apr. 20, 1983, 97 Stat. 130.

193. *Dionee v. Bouley*, 757 F.2d 1344 (1st Cir. 1985); *Finberg v. Sullivan*, 634 F.2d 50 (3d Cir. 1980); *Harris v. Bailey*, 574 F. Supp. 966 (W.D. Va. 1983). However, the Michigan Supreme Court has ruled that after a Social Security recipient dies, creditors may be able to attach Social Security funds, which are part of his estate. *Matter of Estate of Vary*, 401 Mich. 340, 258 N.W.2d 11 (1977).

194. 409 U.S. 413 (1973). *See also Ellender v. Schweiker*, 575 F. Supp. 590 (S.D.N.Y. 1983) (The SSA is also prohibited from attaching Social Security benefits).

195. 26 U.S.C. § 6331 (1982); 42 U.S.C. § 659 (Supp. I 1983).

2

Supplemental Security Income

What is Supplemental Security Income?

Supplemental Security Income (SSI) is a federal program of cash assistance for aged, blind, and disabled individuals who have little income and few assets.[1] The program provides monthly checks from the federal government of (in 1988) up to $354 for an individual and up to $532 for a couple. Some states supplement this basic federal grant by paying an additional amount to eligible individuals and couples.[2] SSI is administered by the Social Security Administration (SSA) although in some states, the state welfare department participates in the administration of the state's supplementation program. In 1986 approximately $11.7 billion was paid to people enrolled in the SSI program—about $9.5 billion by the federal government and about $2.2 billion by the states.[3]

Despite the large number of individuals currently receiving SSI, there are many individuals who have not applied even though they qualify for benefits. Many simply do not know that they are eligible or have never heard of the program. This chapter is designed to inform individuals about the eligibility requirements for SSI and of their rights under federal law. The SSI program has been a successful program, providing low-income individuals with cash assistance for a reasonable living standard. Just as important, even a small SSI benefit in most states automatically qualifies the recipient for Medicaid benefits (see chapter 8).

Who is eligible for SSI?

To be eligible for SSI, a person must be 65 or older,[4] blind,[5] or disabled[6] and must be relatively poor—that is, his income and assets cannot exceed certain levels established by Congress. In addition, a person must be either a citizen of the United States or an alien lawfully admitted to the United States for permanent residence.[7]

What resources can I have and still be eligible for SSI?

The SSA defines resources as "cash or other liquid assets or any real or personal property that an individual owns and could convert to cash to be used for his support and maintenance."[8] To be eligible for SSI, a single person cannot have countable resources in 1988 worth more than $1,900 and a couple cannot have countable resources worth more than $2,850. These figures will be increased by $100 and $150, so that in 1989 they will be $2,000 for an individual and $3,000 for a couple.[9] The higher limit for couples applies even if only one of the spouses is eligible for SSI (for example, if the husband is 67 and the wife 60).

What assets are not counted in determining eligibility for SSI?

A number of valuable assets are not counted by the SSA in determining eligibility for SSI:

1. Homestead (family home). The value of your family home and the land surrounding it is ignored completely by the SSA in determining whether you are eligible for SSI.[10] You can have a house worth any amount of money and still be eligible for SSI so long as you are using the house as your residence and you meet the other requirements. And even if you are not currently living in your home, it will be considered an excluded resource as long as you intend to return to it.[11]

2. Household goods and personal effects. You can have household goods such as furniture and personal effects such as jewelry and clothing worth up to a total of $2,000 in equity value without having these items counted in determining your eligibility for SSI. If your goods and effects exceed $2,000 in value, only the excess is counted.[12] Furthermore, certain goods and effects are excluded altogether in determining your eligibility. Totally excluded are wedding and engagement rings and personal effects for medical reasons such as prosthetic devices and wheelchairs.[13]

3. Automobiles and other vehicles. An individual or married couple may own one car, and it will not be counted as a resource so long as its current value (retail market value) is $4,500 or less.[14] If its value exceeds $4,500, only the excess over $4,500 is counted against the 1988 resource maximums of $1,900 and $2,850. However, if

your car is used for transportation to employment or to obtain medical services for a specific medical problem or is specially equipped for a handicapped person, it is not counted as a resource at all regardless of its market value.[15]

4. Life insurance. Some life-insurance policies are excluded altogether in determining SSI eligibility, and others are excluded if their value does not exceed $1,500. Excluded altogether are burial policies and policies having no cash surrender value, such as term life-insurance policies. Policies with a cash surrender value are excluded if their face value does not exceed $1,500.[16]

5. Property essential for self-support. Property of a trade or business (such as land, building, equipment, inventory), or nonbusiness income producing property (such as land that produces rents) "essential to self-support" are excluded by up to $6,000 of your equity in the income producing property if it produces a net annual income of at least 6 percent of the excluded equity. Nonbusiness property used to produce goods or services necessary for an individual's daily activities (such as land used to produce vegetables or livestock only for personal consumption) is excluded if the individual's equity in the property does not exceed $6,000. Personal property required by the individual's employer for work (such as tools, safety equipment, or uniforms) is excluded, regardless of value, while the individual is working. Property is regarded as essential for self-support if it is a significant factor in producing income necessary for your support.[17]

6. Cash received from an insurance company to replace lost or damaged excluded property is not counted, so long as it is used to replace the lost or damaged property.[18]

7. Burial spaces and funds (up to $1,500 plus accrued interest) separately set aside for burial expenses are excluded. Interest accrued on the excluded funds are also excluded.[19]

Can I dispose of extra assets to qualify for SSI?

Yes, but they must be disposed of for fair market value. If you dispose of *nonexcluded* resources for less than fair market value prior to 1 July 1988 for the purposes of establishing SSI or Medicaid eligibility, you will be charged with the difference between the fair market value and the amount of compensation received. The difference is referred to as "uncompensated value" and is counted toward the resource limit for a period of twenty-four months from the date of transfer, or until full compensation has been received, or—if the transferred asset is returned—on the date of return.

If you make such a transfer, the SSA will presume that you did so for the purpose of establishing eligibility for either SSI or Medicaid unless you can furnish convincing evidence that you transferred the resource exclusively for another reason. Convincing evidence may be documentary or nondocumentary evidence which shows that the transfer was ordered by a court (e.g., a support order) or that at the time of transfer you "could not have anticipated becoming eligible due to the existence of other circumstances which would have precluded eligibility" (e.g., you had ample income and resources to live. In addition, effective 1 April 1988, the SSA must issue regulations providing for the suspension of this transfer provision in cases of undue hardship.[20] Transfers made on or after 1 July 1988 will no longer affect SSI eligibility. However, transfers of assets for less than fair market value made within thirty months of the application for Medicaid by institutionalized individuals may affect Medicaid eligibility.[21] (See Chapter 8.)

Is jointly owned property counted?

It may be. If you own property jointly with others and you cannot sell your share without the permission of the other owners, the value of the property will not be counted in determining your SSI eligibility.[22] However, if you can sell your share, it may be counted, but problems may arise in determining the value of your share of the jointly held property.[23] The SSA may regard your share of the property to be more valuable than you believe it is. If this occurs, you should not hesitate to appeal the SSA's determination.

How are jointly held bank accounts treated?

Prior to 1 August 1982, if you had *unrestricted* access to the funds in a joint bank account, even if all of the funds in it did not belong to you, the SSA considered all of the funds as belonging to you. Beginning 1 August 1982, you may now demonstrate that not all of the funds belong to you where you have unrestricted access. You must sign a statement containing a perjury clause, giving your allegations regarding ownership of the funds and your reasons for establishing the joint account, and recounting who made deposits to and withdrawals from the account and how withdrawals were spent.[24]

Is property owned by my relatives counted?

For the most part, no. However, the entire value of property held by your spouse is regarded by the SSA as available to you and is counted in determining the amount of resources you have.[25] This process is called "deeming." For example, if you are 65 and your wife is 62 and you have $1,000 in a bank account in your name, and she has $1,900 in a bank account in her name, the SSA will regard you as having $2,900 in resources. Because a couple may have countable resources totalling only $2,850 (1988), you will be ineligible for SSI, since you have $50 more than is allowed.

How do resources in excess of allowable maximums affect eligibility for SSI?

Generally when your resources exceed allowable maximums, you are not eligible for SSI benefits. You are expected either to spend your cash assets or sell other resources and spend the sale proceeds until your total resources are within the maximums allowed. There is no rule forbidding persons intending to apply for SSI from selling assets at fair market value in order to become eligible for SSI. As soon as your assets are within allowable limits, you are eligible for SSI.

However, when your total countable liquid resources (i.e., cash, stocks, bonds, etc.) do not exceed three times the monthly SSI federal benefit rate, $1062 (1988) for an individual or $1596 (1988) for a couple, you still can be eligible to receive SSI benefits immediately if you comply with certain conditions. Moreover, you are not required to dispose of real property for so long as it cannot be sold because it is jointly owned and its sale would cause undue hardship, due to loss of housing, for the other owner(s); its sale is barred by legal impediment; or the owner's reasonable efforts to sell it have been unsuccessful.[26]

How much income can I have and be eligible for SSI?

The SSA defines income as "anything you receive in cash or in kind that you can use to meet your needs for food, clothing, or shelter."[27] Under this definition, income includes both earned and unearned income,[28] and it includes both cash and noncash income such as food or clothing.[29] Noncash income is referred to by the SSA as income "in-kind."[30]

To be eligible for federal SSI benefits in 1988, your countable monthly income cannot exceed $354 for an individual or $532 for a couple. However, since many kinds of income are not counted in determining SSI eligibility, you may be eligible for SSI even though your actual income is considerably higher than these figures. Furthermore, if you live in a state that supplements SSI by paying additional benefits, you may be eligible for state supplemental benefits even though your income is too high to be eligible for federal SSI benefits. Determining how much income you are receiving is crucial in deciding whether you are eligible for SSI and how large your benefits will be. Therefore, you should not hesitate to appeal an SSA decision concerning your income.

What is considered earned income?

The SSA regards as earned income the gross amount of wages you receive from a job (that is, the amount before taxes and insurance are deducted) and your net earnings from self-employment (that is, the amount you receive after deducting business expenses such as wages paid an employee).[31] Earned income is usually money, but it also can be income in-kind, such as food or clothing.

What is considered unearned income?

Any income you receive other than earned income is treated by the SSA as unearned income.[32] Common examples of unearned income include Social Security, Veterans' benefits, worker's compensation benefits, unemployment insurance benefits, pensions,[33] gifts, alimony, inheritances,[34] and lottery winnings and other prizes.[35]

What is income in-kind?

Income is not limited to cash received by an individual or couple; it includes noncash such as food, clothing, or shelter. Payments in-kind can be either earned or unearned income. For example, if a person works for another and receives food rather than cash, the noncash payment is regarded as earned income.[36] Unearned income in-kind includes gifts of food, clothing, or shelter.

How is the value of income in-kind determined?

In determining the value of earned income in-kind, the SSA assesses the current market value of the income in-kind received.[37] For example, if you work as a hotel clerk, earning $100 per month and use of a room, your monthly income will be $100 plus the current market value of your room.

Because determining the current market value of income in-kind is difficult, the SSA has adopted a different way of assigning value to *unearned* income in-kind. Instead of actually determining the value of such income, the SSA presumes that the income is worth $138 (1988) per month for one person and $197.33 (1988) per month for a couple.[38] If you believe that this "presumed value" is wrong, you must prove that the value of the food, clothing, housing, etc., that you are receiving is worth less than its "presumed value." You do this by supplying the Social Security Administration with documents establishing the actual value of your unearned income.

If, for example, your daughter buys all of your food for you each month, the SSA will presume that this food is worth $138 a month and will treat you as having $138 of unearned income each month. However, if the food is worth only $60 per month and you can prove this by presenting your daughter's grocery bills, it will treat you as having received only $60 per month of unearned income.

A particularly complicated problem involving income in-kind arises when you live in the household of another person. If you receive both room and board, the SSA does not determine the actual value of this room and board; instead, the administration presumes that the value of the room and board is equal to one-third of the maximum SSI payment ($118 in 1988) available to you.[39] If you live with your daughter, then, and receive both room and board from her, your SSI payment will be reduced by one-third even if the value of the room and board is less than this amount. This rule substantially harms SSI applicants who have the need but are unable to pay their full share of living costs until they start receiving their SSI benefits. Although the reduction may apply to them in the month in which they first receive benefits, they should return to the local SSA office in the next month and show that they are now paying a fair share of the household expenses and have the one-third reduction removed. In cases where the one-third reduction prevents applicants from paying their fair share of living expenses, they can argue that the remainder of their share is being paid for them as a loan. And they should document this "loan" in writing.[40]

The one-third reduction rule does not apply to all situations in which you are living with family or friends. The rule does not apply, for example, if your are receiving *only* room or board but not both.[41] However, in this situation the SSA will presume that the value of the room or board that you are receiving is worth $138 (1988) per month ($197.33 in 1988 per month for a couple). So—where applicable—to avoid being penalized unfairly, you must establish that the value of the room or board is less than $138 per month.

The one-third reduction rule also does not apply if you are living in your own home with friends or family members, or in a commercial establishment such as a hotel, or if your are paying your pro-rata share of the household expenses (food, rent, utilities, etc.).[42] Thus, if you and your daughter are living in an apartment that you have rented or if your daughter is staying in your home that you own, the one-third reduction rule does not apply. However, the SSA will include as income any rent or help with the cost of groceries that your daughter provides and will presume that its value is $138 (in 1988) per month unless you can prove it is not worth this much or you establish that you are paying your pro-rata share of the household expenses.

It is apparent that rules governing unearned income in-kind are complicated. Therefore, do not accept SSA's decisions in this area without consulting a lawyer or other representative. Mistakes are frequently made, and SSA decisions can be appealed.

What income is excluded in determining eligibility for SSI?

Eligibility for SSI is based on how much "countable" income you have. For a variety of reasons, many kinds of income are excluded *completely* in determining your countable income. Also excluded *completely* is the first $20 of income (earned or unearned) you receive each month.[43] In addition, only *part* of your earned income is counted in determining whether you are eligible for SSI.

The following kinds of income are not countable in determining your eligibility for SSI:

1. income-tax refunds[44]
2. property-tax or food-sales-tax refunds[45]
3. Medicare Part B premium paid by an insurance company or by Medicaid[46]
4. wages received from VISTA, the Foster Grandparent Program, the Retired Senior Volunteer Program, the Senior Companion Program[47]
5. the value of home produce consumed by your family[48]
6. the value of free meals provided under Title 7 of the Older Americans Act[49]
7. certain payments for foster care of children[50]
8. medical care or services (including incidental room and board) paid by an insurance company or by Medicaid[51] and noncash social services (such as advice or training or cash given to you by the Veterans Administration to purchase aid and attendance)[52]
9. cash or other property received from the sale or exchange of a resource (but this cash or property will be treated as a resource and thus may affect your eligibility)[53]
10. insurance payments for the replacement of a resource (again, however, these payments may be treated as a resource and so may affect your eligibility)[54]
11. cash payments by a state or local government agency which are based upon need[55]
12. the value of housing assistance from the federal government[56]
13. up to $10 per month of infrequently received earned income and up to $20 per month of infrequently received unearned income[57]
14. cash provided by a nongovernment social services program under certain circumstances [58]
15. any support or maintenance assistance (e.g., food, clothing, and shelter) provided in-kind by a private nonprofit organization.[59]

There are other types of income excluded as provided by federal laws other than the Social Security Act.[60]

In addition to forms of income that are excluded altogether in determining your eligibility for SSI, other income is *partially* excluded in making this determination. The principal example of this is earned income. As mentioned above, the first $20 of income you receive each month is excluded altogether in determining your SSI eligibility. Also excluded is the first $65 ($85 if you have only earned income) you earn each month.[61] In addition, one-half of your monthly earnings in excess of $65 is excluded in determining your eligibility.[62] Because of these exclusions, a person can earn up to $792 and a couple up to $1148 per month in 1988 and still be eligible for some SSI benefits.

Does the SSA count income received by my relatives in determining SSI eligiblity?

For the most part, no. If you are single, only your own income will be counted in determining whether you are eligible for SSI.[63] However, if you are married and living with your spouse, both of your incomes will be counted.[64] If both you and your spouse are applying for SSI, the normal rules governing income exclusions apply and your "countable" incomes will be added together to determine whether you are eligible for benefits. If you are eligible, you and your spouse will receive the level of benefits (Federal Benefit Rate) paid a couple (up to $532 per month in 1988). Slightly different rules apply if only one of you is applying for SSI benefits.[65] For example: John is 65 and has no income. Jane, his wife, is 58 and not eligible for SSI. She works and regularly makes $200 per month (before taxes). To determine John's SSI payment amount in light of Jane's income—which is deemed available to him—a three-step calculation must be done. First, determine the *monthly* earned and unearned income of Jane, i.e., $200. As this is more than the difference between the monthly SSI federal benefit for a couple and the federal benefit for an individual ($178), Jane's income cannot be ignored. Second, as Jane and John have no unearned income, the calculations involve only earned income. Add Jane's *monthly* earned income to John's ($200 + 0 = $200). Disregard the first $20 ($200 − 20 = $180). And also disregard $65 of earned income ($180 − 65 = $115). Divide the remainder in half ($115 ÷ 2) to get the countable earned income ($57.50). Third, subtract this countable income from the *monthly* federal benefit rate for a couple ($532 − 57.50 = $474.50). Had this figure been below $354 (the amount John would receive if he were applying as an individual), then it would have been John's monthly SSI payment amount. Because it exceeds that amount, John will simply receive $354 for that month.[66]

If I sponsor an alien, will either I or the person I sponsor be eligible for SSI?

Under recent changes to the Social Security Act, the income and resources of a sponsor are deemed to aliens for three years beginning with the month the alien is admitted to the United States for permanent resident status. Before any income and resources are deemed, certain "allocations" are made for the sponsor, the sponsor's spouse, and their dependents.[67] The sponsor-to-alien deeming provisions supplement the other deeming rules; they do not replace them. For example, if the alien's ineligible spouse is also his sponsor, the spouse-to-spouse deeming rules (described above) apply, not the sponsor-to-alien deeming rules. In addition, if both the sponsor and the alien are married and eligible for SSI, the SSA will treat them as a couple. In sponsor-to-alien deeming, the allocation for the sponsor is equal to the SSI federal benefit rate ($354 in 1988), and the allocations for the sponsor's spouse and dependents are one-half the federal benefit rate each ($177 in 1988). The countable resources deemed to an alien are those in excess of the amount allowable under SSI for an individual ($1,900 in 1988).

How is eligibility determined and the amount of benefits computed?

SSI eligibility and the amount of benefits you will be paid is determined on a monthly basis. In addition, the SSA will generally determine the amount of your benefit based on your income and other circumstances (e.g., living arrangement) existing in the second month prior to the current month. However, both eligibility and payment amount will be determined on the current month's circumstances when you apply for the first time and when your benefits are being reinstated following a period of ineligibility.[68] See appendix F for an illustration of this new method of calculation.

How do I apply for SSI benefits?

The process for applying for SSI benefits is very similar to the process for applying for Social Security benefits. Application is made on a written form provided by the SSA.[69] However, you can initiate an application by contacting a Social Security office requesting an application form.[70] Your application will be considered effective on the date it is received at the Social Security office or if it is mailed on the date it was postmarked.[71] Benefits will be paid back to the date an application is filed, unless you are not eligible for SSI on that date. Thus, the SSI payment for the first month of eligibility will be prorated by the number of days in the month for which there is an effective application.[72]

As with Social Security benefits, the burden of establishing your eligibility for SSI rests with you. You will need to prove that you are 65 or older or are blind or disabled, and you also will have to supply the Social Security Administration with proof concerning your income, your resources, and your living situation. The Social Security Administration is required to help you obtain proof needed to establish your eligibility for SSI.[73] For the most part, the process of applying for SSI benefits is similar to applying for Social Security. The same documents used to prove your age,[74] blindness, or disability for Social Security benefits can be used when applying for SSI benefits.[75] However, inasmuch as SSI eligibility is based partly on your income and assets, detailed proof regarding these matters also is required. For this reason you should collect documents concerning your income, resources, citizenship, marital status, and living arrangements before going to the Social Security office to apply for SSI. Documents that may be useful are checking and savings account statements, rent receipts, deeds, and certificates of title for automobiles and other property. However, do not delay in submitting your application until all of these documents are assembled. If there is difficulty in obtaining any of these documents, you should apply first and obtain the documents later, so as not to lose benefits as a result of your delay in submitting an application.

Under recent legislation, the IRS is now authorized to release tax information to the SSA for the purpose of determining SSI income and assets eligibility. The IRS is also authorized to release information to other government agencies administering AFDC, Medicaid, unemployment compensation, and food stamps. However, this new law includes certain protections. The SSA (or other government agency) "may [not] terminate, deny, suspend, or reduce any benefits of an individual" until it has "taken appropriate steps to independently verify information relating to:

- the amount of the asset or income involved; whether the individual actually has (or had) access to such asset or income for his [or her] own use; and
- the period or periods when the individual actually had such asset or income."

Furthermore, a person must be afforded the opportunity to contest the agency's findings "in the same manner as applies to other information and findings relating to eligibility factors under the program."[76]

Several problems surround the application process. One is that persons applying for SSI sometimes are told informally by SSA employees that they are not eligible; consequently, they do not file an official application form. A person whose application has been informally denied cannot appeal the informal denial. However, under certain circumstances the date of an oral inquiry about SSI benefits can be used as the date of application. An application on a prescribed form must be filed within sixty days of the SSA notice to you telling you of the need to file an application.[77] If this SSA notice is not sent to you, you should argue that the 60-day limit does not apply.[78]

Another problem in the application process is the lack of any time limit in which the SSA has to decide on your eligibility. In applying for Medicaid benefits, you are entitled to a decision on your application within sixty days.[79] No such time limit exists for SSI applications, and the SSA sometimes is very slow in processing applications for SSI benefits, particularly when eligibility is based upon disability. As a consequence, months can go by before a person is declared eligible for benefits.

As part of the process of applying for SSI benefits, the SSA may require that you also apply for benefits you may be entitled to but are not receiving.[80] For example, if you are eligible for VA benefits, Social Security benefits, pensions, or worker's compensation benefits, the SSA may require you to apply for these benefits before it will grant you eligibility for SSI. This rule applies only to benefits that count as income in determining SSI eligibility and does not include Medicare and Medicaid.

Can I obtain benefits while my SSI application is pending?

You may be able to. Because of the delay in processing SSI applications, Congress and the SSA have provided several ways in which a person may obtain some help while his or her application is pending. For example, SSI applicants sometimes have difficulty establishing their age. If you establish financial eligibility for SSI and provide the SSA with a document (at least three years old) indicating that you are at least 65 years old, you can obtain advance payments even if the SSA wants further proof of age.[81]

If you apply for SSI based upon disability, you can obtain benefits while your application is processed if you are determined to be "presumptively disabled."[82] To be eligible for special benefits because of presumptive disability, you must establish your financial eligibility for SSI and you must be suffering from so severe a disability that your eligibility for benefits is extremely likely. Examples of impairments which are sufficient in this case are amputation of two limbs, or of a leg at the hip, or of a foot as a result of diabetes; allegation of total deafness; confinement to a bed or immobility without a wheelchair, walker, or crutches because of a longstanding condition; allegation of a stroke of at least four months ago or of cerebral palsy, muscular dystrophy, or AIDS as defined by the Centers for Disease Control.[83] If you establish financial eligibility as well as a serious disability of this type, you are eligible for up to three months of SSI benefits while your application for benefits is pending. If you later are determined not to be eligible for SSI because you are found not to be disabled, you do not have to repay the benefits you have received in the meantime.[84]

In addition to these specialized forms of temporary assistance, an applicant for SSI in 1988 is entitled to up to $354 (or $532 for a couple), plus any federally administered State supplementary payment, if he shows a strong likelihood that he will be eligible for benefits (i.e., that he is poor enough) and if a financial emergency exists which requires immediate assistance.[85] Examples of such financial emergencies include lack of food, clothing, shelter, or medical care.[86]

Moreover, the SSA has recently implemented an "immediate payment" program under which the SSA will issue an immediate payment of up to $200:(1) to an individual who is currently eligible for either Social Security Insurance or Supplemental Security Income benefits but has not received his or her check; or (2) to an individual who has been approved for either Social Security or Supplemental Security Income but has not started receiving his or her monthly checks. These payments are made when the eligible individual cannot wait the 7- to 10-day time period required for having a critical payment processed and when further delay in payment would deprive the individual of food and/or shelter, endanger his health, or cause the SSA extremely adverse public relations." Only one emergency payment can be issued under each program every thirty days.[87]

In addition, almost all states have a general-assistance program under which a person with very limited income and assets can obtain welfare benefits. If you need help while your SSI application is pending (or when your SSI benefits have been terminated or suspended), you can apply to the local welfare department for general-assistance payments.

To encourage states to provide benefits to persons applying for SSI whose applications have not yet been acted upon (or to persons whose SSI benefits have been terminated or suspended), Congress amended the Social Security Act to provide that if a state gives benefits to such individuals during the period his application or appeal is pending, the state will be reimbursed for these benefits out of the first SSI check (i.e., the check representing all benefits to which you are entitled from the time you applied to the time the SSA makes its decision) received after the person has been ruled eligible for SSI.[88] If this happens, the first check (which usually will be for several months of benefits) will be sent to the state welfare department, which will deduct the amount of public assistance benefits paid to the person while his application was pending and then forward the balance of the check to the person. However, before the SSA will send your first check to your state welfare agency, it must receive assurances from the state that you have signed an authorization permitting the SSA to withhold your first check, and there must be an interim assistance agreement in effect between your state and the SSA.[89]

How are SSI benefits paid?

SSI benefits are paid monthly in the form of multicolored U.S. Treasury checks that usually arrive soon after the first of the month. When both members of a couple are eligible for SSI, each receives a check for one-half of the monthly amount the couple is entitled to receive.[90] However, as with Social Security checks, if a person is determined to be unable to care for him- or herself, the checks may be sent to a "representative payee."[91] The rules governing representative payees for SSI beneficiaries are similar to those of representative payees for Social Security recipients. Certain SSI recipients, however, do not receive their SSI checks directly. The SSI checks of individuals determined by the SSA to be alcoholics or drug addicts are sent automatically to a representative payee regardless of the ability of the individual to take care of his own needs.[92]

Does where I live affect my SSI benefits?

Yes, in a number of ways. Because there is great variation among the states as to whether they supplement the federal SSI payment, where you live will have an impact on how much money you receive. In addition, while SSI payments are available to residents of all fifty states and the District of Columbia, SSI is not available to individuals living outside the United States (including residents of Puerto Rico, Guam, and the Virgin Islands).[93]

Your SSI benefits also will be affected by your living arrangements—that is, by whether you are living in your own home, in the house of a friend or relative, or in an institution such as a hospital or retirement home. Federal SSI benefits are reduced by one-third if you are living in the household of another and receiving support and maintenance. Living in an institution also may affect your benefits. Persons in public institutions, such as a prison or state mental hospital, are not eligible for SSI benefits at all.[94] If you are in a medical institution such as a hospital or nursing home, and more than 50 percent of your care is being paid for by Medicaid, you will receive only $30 per month from SSI because, theoretically, your principal needs are being met by Medicaid.[95] However, if you are in a nonmedical residential institution such as a retirement home, in many states your payment will be greater than if you were living alone because the cost of such facilities is frequently several hundred dollars per month.[96]

In addition, you will lose your eligibility for SSI for any month during all of which you are outside the United States. If you are outside of the United States for thirty consecutive days or more, you are not considered back in the United States (and thus are not eligible for benefits) until you are back for thirty consecutive days.[97]

Can I apply as an individual when I live with an unrelated person of the opposite sex who is not legally my spouse?

If you "hold" yourselves out to the community in which you live as husband and wife, the SSA will treat you as a couple. If you are living with an unrelated person of the opposite sex, the SSA will ask you the following questions to determine if you are "holding" yourselves out to the community in which you live as husband and wife:

- what names are the two of you known by?
- do you introduce yourselves as husband and wife? If not, how are you introduced?
- what names are used on mail for each of you?
- who owns or rents the place where you live?
- do any deeds, leases, time payment papers, tax papers, or any other papers show you as husband and wife?[98]

If the SSA determines that you are "holding out" as husband and wife, even if you are not legally married (for example, you both are currently married to someone else), you must apply for benefits as a couple. Consequently, if you both are eligible, your federal SSI benefits would be no more than $532 (in 1988), not $708 ($354 × 2), the maximum amount (in 1988) of federal SSI for two individuals applying separately. These amounts could be higher if your state supplements the federal SSI payment.

What should I do if my check does not arrive on time?

Lost or stolen SSI checks are handled very much like lost or stolen Social Security checks. You should promptly notify the local Social Security office if your check does not arrive on time. As with Social Security checks, if the SSA determines that no check has been issued to you and that you are entitled to a check for that month, a new check will be issued which should be received in about ten to fifteen days. However, if it appears that the check has been cashed, replacement of the check will take a long time because of the need to contact the Treasury Department to determine whether a forgery has occurred.[99] If you need temporary assistance while waiting for your SSI check to be replaced, you can apply to the local welfare department for emergency assistance.

In order to prevent your check from being stolen or lost, you may want to have it deposited directly into your bank account. You can apply for "direct deposit" of your check by signing Form SF-1199, which is sent to a Social Security office by the financial institution. You should discuss the procedure for direct deposit with your financial institution to learn its procedures and conditions.

What should I do if the check I receive is for less than the amount I believe I am entitled to?

As with Social Security benefits, if your SSI check is for less than you believe you are entitled to, contact the Social Security office to discuss the problem and appeal if necessary.

What should I do if the SSA claims I have been overpaid?

The SSA may decide you have been receiving larger benefit checks than you are entitled to, or that you should not be receiving SSI checks at all. If this happens, they must notify you in writing of their conclusion that you have been overpaid.[100] If you disagree, you can contact the SSA to try to persuade them informally that they are wrong. If your informal discussions are unsuccessful, you can appeal the decision through the usual SSI appeals process.[101] If you notify the SSA promptly (within thirty days of your receipt of the notice) that you disagree with their determination, you are entitled to have your benefits continued until a hearing is held by the SSA.[102]

Unless you are able to persuade the SSA that they are wrong in claiming that you have been overpaid, they will probably ask you to repay the benefits they claim you received improperly. The SSA usually attempts to recover overpaid benefits by reducing future SSI checks each month until the overpaid amount has been recovered.[103] However, you can ask the SSA to waive recovery of the overpaid amount.[104] As with Social Security benefits, waiver will be granted only if you establish that the error was not your fault and that recovery of the overpayment would either "defeat the purpose of the Supplemental Security Income program" or be "against equity and good conscience" or that the overpaid amount is so small as to be inefficient to recover.[105] (For a detailed discussion of these conditions, see chapter 1.) If you request a waiver within thirty days of your receipt of the notice of overpayment, you will receive your benefits pending the waiver determination, and you will have the opportunity for a personal conference.[106]

How much can the SSA take from my SSI benefits if I do not qualify for a waiver?

Beginning October 1984, the SSA is limited in the amount of adjustment or recovery of an SSI overpayment in any month to the lesser of: (1) the amount of the benefit for the month, or (2) an amount equal to 10 percent of the person's countable income (including SSI) for that month. There are, however, two exceptions: (1) the limitation does not apply where "fraud, willful misrepresentation, or concealment of material information" is involved; and (2) the limitation does not apply when the recipient requests "a different rate at which income may be withheld or recovered."

Fraud is interpreted to mean something more than "fault." In addition, the SSA must clearly notify claimants that the 10 percent rate of withholding is the norm and that a higher rate of repayment is not expected or required.[107]

Will the SSA hold me liable for an overpayment if my bank account or other assets exceed the resource limit?

Where your assets exceed the $1,900 (in 1988) limit by $50 or less, you will be deemed to be without fault for purposes of waiving the overpayment, unless the SSA finds that the failure to report the excess was "knowing and willful" on your part. This will help some SSI recipients who unknowingly permit their bank accounts to creep up over the limit.

Congress has indicated that when the individual's assets exceed the resource limit by more than $50, the existing Social Security Act provision on waiver may warrant a waiver of all or part of the resulting overpayment.[108]

Do I have to tell the SSA if my income changes?

Yes. You are required to report any changes in your income or living situation which may affect your eligibility for SSI or the amount of SSI benefits that you are receiving.[109] This report must be filed not later than ten days after the month in which the change of circumstances occurred.[110] Failure to make such a report can result in your being overpaid and can lead to an effort by the SSA to recover the overpayment.[111] The SSA also can impose a penalty of between $25 and $100 for failure to make a required report on time. The penalties are collected by reducing your SSI check in the amount of the penalty. The SSA will not collect the penalty if you have good cause for failing to report on time.[112] In addition, the SSA will redetermine every year whether you are still eligible for SSI.[113] The redetermination process requires you to fill out forms similar to the application forms you fill out when you first apply. The SSA may require you to fill out these forms more often than every year if they believe a change in circumstances has occurred which affects your benefits.[114]

Can a creditor attach my SSI checks?

No. Just as the Social Security Act forbids creditors from attaching Social Security benefits, a creditor is prohibited from attaching SSI benefits.[115] However, Congress has authorized a procedure under which state governments are repaid for interim assistance provided to you while your application for SSI was pending.

But before the SSA will send your first SSI check to your state, the SSA must have written authorization from you, and your state must have a agreement with the SSA to receive your first check. The state must pay you the balance from your first check in excess of its reimbursement within ten days, and it must provide you with an opportunity for a hearing if you disagree with its actions.[116]

Can I receive both Social Security and SSI?

Yes. In fact, over half of the persons receiving SSI also receive Social Security benefits. If your Social Security benefits are less (in 1988) than $374 (plus the state supplement, if any) per month for an individual or $552 (plus the state supplement, if any) per month for a couple, you can receive some SSI benefits.[117]

Can I receive both SSI and food stamps?

Yes. Except in California, Wisconsin, Minnesota (Hennepin

County), Ohio (Cuyahoga County), Oregon, Utah, Vermont, Virginia (Arlington County), and New York (Monroe County), it is possible to receive both food stamps and SSI. In addition, households in which all members are applicants for or recipients of SSI must be informed of the availability of food stamp benefits and assisted in making a simple application to participate in the food stamp program at the Social Security office. Finally, households containing only SSI recipients are automatically eligible for food stamps, with some exceptions.[118]

Can I receive both SSI and Medicaid?

Yes. A person can receive both SSI and Medicaid.[119] In fact, in many states a person who is eligible for SSI is automatically eligible for Medicaid. In other states, only some persons eligible for SSI are also eligible for Medicaid. This is explained in more detail in chapter 8.

Will the SSA notify me if it decides I am not eligible for benefits or if it decides to reduce, suspend, or terminate my SSI benefits?

Yes. The SSA is required by law to notify a person applying for SSI benefits of its decision on an application. If it decides that you are eligible for benefits, it will notify you of the amount it concludes you are entitled to receive.[120]

You also will be notified if the SSA decides to deny your application for SSI benefits.[121] If your application has been denied, the notice you receive must explain the reason why your application was denied and how you can appeal the denial of your application.[122]

If you are already receiving SSI benefits and the SSA decides to reduce, suspend, or terminate these benefits, it must send you a notice of that decision and of your right to a reconsideration or a hearing before the determination takes effect.[123] This notice must explain the reason for the decision and must explain how you can appeal.[124]

Can I appeal SSA decisions affecting my benefits?

Certainly. Almost all decisions by the SSA affecting your SSI benefits can be appealed[125] but some cannot. For example, a decision to deny emergency assistance or benefits as presumptively disabled prior to a final determination of disability cannot be appealed.[126] In addition, informal advice by an SSA employee that you are not eligible for SSI benefits cannot be appealed. For this reason, you should always insist upon filing a formal application for benefits.

How does the SSI appeals system work?

The system for SSI appeals is similar to the system explained in chapter 1 for appealing decisions concerning Social Security benefits. Likewise, many of the suggestions in that chapter on how to handle a Social Security appeal apply to the SSI process. However, because there are important differences between the two systems, a description of the SSI system follows.

Initial Determination. As with Social Security benefits, most decisions by the SSA affecting your SSI benefits are called "initial determinations." Included within the definition of initial determinations are decisions to grant or deny an application for benefits and decisions to reduce, suspend, or terminate benefits. As is true of Social Security benefits, you should appeal adverse initial determinations because if you do not, the determination will become final.[127]

Reconsideration. The first stage in the SSI appeals process is called "reconsideration," as in Social Security appeals. If you wish to appeal an adverse initial determination, you should file a request for a reconsideration within sixty days of receiving notice of the SSA's initial determination on your benefits.[128] This request should be in writing, either on an SSA form or by letter. You can send the request to any SSA district office. If you have requested a reconsideration, the SSA must acknowledge receipt of your request and—if appropriate—should schedule a conference within fifteen days of your request for reconsideration.[129]

The SSA has established three different methods of reconsideration. The first, called "case review," provides an opportunity for you to submit additional evidence of your eligibility for SSI (such as additional evidence that you are 65) and an opportunity to discuss your situation with an SSA employee, who will review your file and decide whether the initial determination concerning your benefits was correct.[130]

Another kind of conference available is called an "informal conference."[131] In an informal conference, you can bring witnesses to testify to your eligibility for SSI, and the SSA employee is required to keep a record of the conference and include it in your file. This employee will not have had anything to do with your case prior to your request for reconsideration.[132]

A third type of conference available is called a "formal conference."[133] In the formal conference you can subpoena documents and witnesses to help prove your eligibility for SSI, and you can cross-examine witnesses whose testimony is unfavorable to you. A record is kept of the formal conference and is made a part of your SSA file.[134]

The type of reconsideration method you are entitled to depends upon the basis for the initial determination affecting your right to benefits. If you have just applied for benefits and the initial determination was that you were not entitled to benefits, you may choose either a case review or an informal conference.[135] It is usually to your advantage to request an informal conference because of the additional rights available to you. However, if your application for SSI benefits was based on a claim that you are blind or disabled, and the denial of your application was based on a medical issue (i.e., that you are not blind or disabled), then the only form of reconsideration available to you is the case review.[136]

If you are appealing a decision to reduce, suspend, or terminate your SSI benefits, then you are entitled to choose case review, informal conference, or formal conference.[137] In addition, if you appeal any SSA determination to suspend, reduce, or terminate your SSI benefits (except for disability cessations based on medical factors—see below) within ten days of the receipt of the SSA notice, your benefits will be continued until a decision on such initial appeal is issued.[138] Your request for appeal should indicate that you want your benefits continued during the appeal. If you fail to state a preference as to the type of reconsideration, you will receive only a case review.

Can I appeal an unfavorable reconsideration determination?

Yes. If you are notified that the reconsideration determination upheld the earlier decision that you are not eligible for benefits or that your benefits are to be reduced, suspended, or terminated, you may appeal this determination by filing a written request for a hearing within sixty days of receiving the notice of the reconsideration determination.[139] This request should be sent to your local Social Security office. Unless you file such a request, the reconsideration determination will become final.[140]

SSI hearings are quite similar to hearings involving Social Security benefits. You should prepare for an SSI hearing in the same way that you would prepare for a hearing in connection with a claim for Social Security benefits.[141] The Social Security Act requires that a hearing decision be reached within ninety days of the date you requested it, except in disability cases for which there is no deadline.[142] However, it often takes longer than ninety days for a decision to be reached. If the delay in your case is unreasonable, you may be able to secure a court order for a prompt decision.[143] After a decision has been reached, you will receive written notice from the administrative law judge explaining what has been determined in your case.[144]

Can I appeal an unfavorable hearing decision on my SSI benefits?

Yes. If the decision by the administrative law judge is that you are not eligible for benefits or that your benefits should be reduced, suspended, or terminated, you can appeal this decision to the Appeals Council of the SSA.[145] Your appeal should be in writing and should be sent to the local SSA office or to the Appeals Council within sixty days of receiving the adverse hearing decision.[146] Unless such an appeal is filed, the decision of the hearing officer becomes final.[147] Appeals Council review in SSI cases proceeds in the same way as in Social Security cases. You will be notified in writing of the decision by the Appeals Council.[148]

Can I appeal a decision by the Appeals Council?

Yes. If you are dissatisfied with the Appeals Council's decision, you may appeal the decision by filing suit in a federal court within sixty days of receiving the adverse Appeals Council decision.[149] Judicial review of adverse SSI decisions is the same as in Social Security cases.

Will my benefits be continued while I appeal?

In some circumstances, yes. If your initial application for benefits is denied, you will not receive benefits until you have been successful in your appeal. For example, if your application is denied, but the denial is reversed at the reconsideration stage, you will receive benefits for the first time after the favorable reconsideration determination. However, these benefits will be retroactive to the first month in which you were eligible and had an application for benefits on file.

If you have been receiving SSI benefits and are notified that the SSA believes your benefits should be reduced, suspended, or terminated, you are entitled to continue to receive benefits until a reconsideration determination (or hearing decision in medical cessation cases) has been reached.[150] However, to continue to receive benefits pending a reconsideration determination, you must request reconsideration within ten days of being notified that the SSA intends to reduce, suspend, or terminate your benefits. If you send a notice to the SSA requesting reconsideration within the 10-day period, the SSA must continue to pay you benefits until it reaches a decision after the reconsideration conference or hearing.[151]

You can continue to appeal beyond the reconsideration, but your benefits will not continue during the remaining stages of appeal. If it is determined at one of the appeal stages that the unfavorable decision was erroneous, you will have your benefits restored for the future and will also receive a check containing back benefits for the months between the reconsideration determination or hearing decision and the time the favorable decision was reached on appeal.

What happens if my disability benefits are to be terminated because the SSA says that my medical condition has improved?

In disability cases where the SSA has determined that you are no longer disabled or blind because your medical condition has improved, you are entitled to a "face-to-face" reconsideration.[152] If you want your benefits continued during this appeal, you must file both your request for reconsideration and your request to have benefits continued within ten days of your receipt of the notice of termination.[153] If you miss this 10-day deadline or if you do not want your benefits continued, you have sixty days from your receipt of the notice of termination or reconsideration notice to request either a reconsideration or a hearing.[154] As with all SSI appeals, if you miss either the 10-day or 60-day deadline, you can show "good cause" to excuse your failure to file on time.[155]

Should I have my benefits continue while I appeal?

Usually, yes. It is almost always to your advantage to ask to have your benefits continue pending a reconsideration determination. If the SSA attempts to persuade you not to have your benefits continue pending reconsideration, you should *not* agree. The only disadvantage of insisting that your benefits be continued pending appeal is that if your appeal is unsuccessful, the benefits you receive between the time you were notified of the SSA's intention to cut off your benefits and the time of the reconsideration decision can be treated as an overpayment.[156] This means that the SSA may attempt to collect these benefits from you. The method for collecting these overpayments is the same as for collecting any overpayment.

What happens to the SSI benefits that the SSA owes me if I die before receiving them?

If you die before receiving the SSI benefits for which you applied, effective for benefits payable after 31 May 1986, these retroactive benefits will go to your spouse (regardless of whether he or she is also eligible for SSI). In the case of a disabled or blind child who has died, the retroactive benefits will go to the child's parent.[157]

NOTES

1. The legal authority for the Supplemental Security Income program is contained in Title XVI of the Social Security Act, 42 U.S.C. §§ 1381–1385 (1982). HHS regulations implementing the program are found in 20 C.F.R. § 416.101 *et seq.* (1987).

2. SSA Program Operations Manual System (POMS) §§ SI 01415.001, *et seq.*

3. 50 *Social Security Bulletin* 18 (May 1987).

4. 42 U.S.C. § 1382c(a)(1)(A) (1982).

5. 42 U.S.C. § 1382c(a)(2) (1982). The same definition of blindness is used for SSI as is used for Social Security Insurance benefits. However, a more liberal standard of blindness is used for persons who were eligible for aid to the blind benefits in Dec. 1973. 20 C.F.R. § 416.982 (1987).

6. 42 U.S.C. § 1382c(a)(3) (1982). Disability for purposes of eligibility for SSI benefits is largely the same as for eligibility for Social Security

benefits. However, a more liberal standard of disability is used for persons who were eligible for aid to the disabled benefits in Dec. 1973 and in at least one month prior to July 1973. 20 C.F.R. § 416.907 (1987).

7. 42 U.S.C. § 1382c(a)(1)(B) (1982). Persons not admitted for permanent residence but who have been granted official permission to reside in the United States indefinitely are also eligible for SSI. 20 C.F.R. § 416.1618 (1987); 52 Fed. Reg. 21939-21945 (June 10, 1987) (to be codified in 20 C.F.R. §§ 416.1615, .1618).

8. 20 C.F.R. § 416.120(c)(3) (1987).

9. Pub. L. No. 98-369, § 2611.

10. 42 U.S.C. § 1382b(a)(1) (1982); 20 C.F.R. § 416.1212 (1987).

11. 20 C.F.R. § 416.1212(c) (1987).

12. 20 C.F.R. § 416.1216(b) (1987). Equity value equals the fair market value of the item, minus any encumbrances.

13. 20 C.F.R. § 416.1216 (c) (1987).

14. 20 C.F.R. § 416.1218(b)(2) (1987).

15. *Id.*

16. 20 C.F.R. § 416.1230 (1987).

17. 20 C.F.R. §§ 416.1220–.1224 (1987); SSA POMS §§ SI 01140.001 *et seq.* (12/87). One court has struck down the $6000/6 percent rule. *See Interdependent Neighborhoods v. Petit*, 659 F. Supp. 1309 (D. Me. 1987) (case involved use of rule in Medicaid determinations).

18. 20 C.F.R. § 416.1232 (1987).

19. 20 C.F.R. § 416.1231 (1987): Pub. L. No. 100-203, § 9105 (Dec. 22, 1987), amending 42 U.S.C. § 1382b(d).

20. 42 U.S.C. § 1382b(c) (1982); 20 C.F.R. 416.1246 (1987); Pub. L. No. 100-203, § 9104 (Dec. 22, 1987), adding 42 U.S.C. § 1382b(c)(4).

21. Pub. L. No. 100-360, § 303(c), amending 42 U.S.C. § 1382b(c). *See also* 42 U.S.C.A. § 1396p(c) (1983); Deford, "Medicaid Liens, Recoveries, and Transfer of Assets After TEFRA," 18 *Clearinghouse Rev.* 134, 137–139 (June 1984).

22. 20 C.F.R. § 416.1201(a) (1987). *Cf.* 52 Fed. Reg. 31757–31762 (Aug. 24, 1987) (to be codified in 20 C.F.R. § 416.1240) (final rule) (undisposed property will be valued at CMV, unless the individual submits evidence establishing lower value); and Pub. L. No. 100-203, § 9103 (Dec. 22, 1987), amending 42 U.S.C. § 1382b(b) (an individual does not have to dispose of jointly held property if its sale would cause undue hardship, due to loss of housing, for the other owner[s]).

23. *See, e.g., Barker v. Mathews*, 427 F. Supp. 16 (E.D. Tenn. 1976).

24. SSA POMS §§ SI 01120.210, *et seq.* (Oct. 1985).

25. 20 C.F.R. § 416.1202 (1987). However, this rule applies only if you

and your spouse are living together. *Id.* In addition, the resources of a parent are deemed to an eligible child and the resources of an "essential person" likewise are deemed. 20 C.F.R. §§ 416.1202, .1203 (1987).

26. Pub. L. No. 100-203, § 9103 (Dec. 22, 1987), adding 42 U.S.C. § 1382b(b)(2); 52 Fed. Reg. 31757, 31762 (to be codified in 20 C.F.R. § 416.1240); 20 C.F.R. § 416.1240–.1244 (1987). SSI payments under this rule are called "conditional payments." First, you must agree in writing to sell enough of your "nonliquid" resources to bring yourself within the basic resources maximum. Second, you must agree to repay the government the difference between the SSI payments you have received from the time you agreed to sell the resources until the time of sale and the amount of SSI benefits you would have received during the same period had the proceeds from the sale been included as available at the beginning of such period. In effect, this will often amount to a repayment of the net proceeds of the sale minus any amount of the proceeds necessary to raise your available "nonexempt" resources up to the maximum allowed under the basic resources rule. The third condition is that the sale generally must be made within six months if real property is being sold or three months for all other types of property. The time period can be extended if there is a valid reason. *Id.* Under a new rule, effective Aug. 24, 1987, there is no ceiling on nonliquid resources (however, total includable liquid resources cannot exceed three times the monthly federal benefit rate) and conditional payments are permitted regardless of the amount of the nonliquid resource so long as the person agrees to attempt to sell it at current market value. 52 Fed. Red. 31757 (Aug. 24, 1987) (to be codified in 20 C.F.R. § 416.1240). In some cases, it may be better not to receive conditional payments. For example, where property can be easily disposed of, you may prefer to lower the total resources to within the maximums allowed by independently spending the sale proceeds, thereby enjoying a temporarily higher standard of living. Another possibility is to spend the excess resources on buying or establishing an excluded resource (*e.g.*, a burial account or fund or repairs on your home).

27. 20 C.F.R. § 416.1102 (1987).
28. 20 C.F.R. § 416.1102 (1987).
29. *Id.*
30. 20 C.F.R. § 416.1130 (1987).
31. 20 C.F.R. § 416.1110 (1987).
32. 20 C.F.R. § 416.1120 (1987).
33. 20 C.F.R. § 416.1121(a) (1987).

34. 20 C.F.R §§ 416.1121(b), (g) (1987).

35. 20 C.F.R § 416.1121(f) (1987).

36. 20 C.F.R. § 416.1110(a) (1987). However, payments in-kind for certain kinds of work, including work as a domestic or as a farmworker, are treated as unearned income. *Id.*; SSA POMS § SI 00830.280A (10/81).

37. SSA POMS § SI 00820.110C (10/81).

38. 20 C.F.R. § 416.1140 (1987). The presumed value actually is one-third of the maximum federal SSI payment plus $20. At present (1988) payment levels, this works out to the amounts specified in the text.

39. 20 C.F.R. § 416.1131 (1987).

40. *See, Hickman v. Bowen*, 803 F.2d 1377 (5th Cir. 1986) (an applicant can receive a loan of in-kind food and shelter while waiting for application to be approved).

41. 20 C.F.R. § 416.1131(a)(2) (1987).

42. 20 C.F.R. §§ 416.1132–.1133 (1987).

43. 42 U.S.C. § 1382a(b)(2) (1982); 20 C.F.R. § 416.1124(c)(12) 1987).

44. 20 C.F.R. § 416.1103(d) (1987).

45. 20 C.F.R. § 416.1124(c)(1) (1987).

46. 20 C.F.R. § 416.1103(a)(6) (1987).

47. 20 C.F.R. pt. 416, subpt. K, app. (1987).

48. 20 C.F.R. § 416.1124(c)(4) (1987).

49. 20 C.F.R. pt. 416, subpt. K, app. (1987).

50. 20 C.F.R. § 416.1124(c)(8) (1987).

51. 20 C.F.R. § 416.1103(a) (1987); *e.g.*, *Lapin v. Mathews*, 422 F. Supp. 1089 (D.D.C. 1976).

52. 20 C.F.R. § 416.1103(b) (1987).

53. 20 C.F.R. § 416.1103(c) (1987).

54. *Id.*

55. 20 C.F.R. § 416.1124(c)(2) (1987).

56. 20 C.F.R. pt. 416, subpt. K, app. (1987).

57. 20 C.F.R. §§ 416.1112(c)(1), 1124(c)(6) (1987).

58. 20 C.F.R. § 416.1103(b)(3) (1987).

59. 42 U.S.C.S. § 1382a(b)(4)(B)(13) (1985); 20 C.F.R. § 416.1157 (1987). This provision has now become permanent. *See*, Pub. L. No. 100-203, § 9101 (Dec. 22, 1987).

60. *See* 20 C.F.R. pt. 416, subpt. K, app. (1987).

61. 42 U.S.C. § 1382a(b)(4) (1982).

62. *Id.*

63. 20 C.F.R. § 416.1102 (1987). However, the income of a spouse or parent will be counted for eligible children and spouses, and the income of an "essential person" is counted. 20 C.F.R. §§ 416.220–.223, .1160–.1169 (1987).

64. 42 U.S.C. § 1382a(b) (1982).

65. 20 C.F.R. § 416.1163 (1987). For example, if you are applying for benefits but your wife is not, the determination of whether you are eligible for SSI will work as follows. Your income will be counted in the normal way—that is, the regular income exclusions will be utilized in determining your income. If your wife has any income, the SSA will determine how much of this income can be counted by applying slightly different exclusion rules than it normally uses to determine countable income. Once it has decided how much countable income she has, it will add this income to your countable income to determine whether you are eligible for SSI benefits. You will be eligible for benefits if your combined countable income does not exceed the maximum income couples are allowed to have. However, the amount of benefits you will receive will never be more than you would have received if your were living alone. The process of including the income of an ineligible spouse in counting how much income the eligible spouse has is called "deeming." *Id.*

66. 20 C.F.R. § 416.1163(d); *see also* example 3 (1987).

67. 42 U.S.C. § 1382j (1982); 20 C.F.R. § 416.1166a (1987).

68. 20 C.F.R. §§ 416.200, .203–.204, .410–.414, .420, .501–.503 (1987); *See* Pub. L. No. 97-35, § 2341, *amending* 42 U.S.C. § 1382(c); SSA POMS §§ SI A022002.000, *et seq.* (pt. 5) (1/82); SI A 00810.012 (1/83) (pt. 5).

69. 20 C.F.R. § 416.310 (1987).

70. *Cf.* 20 C.F.R. § 416.340 (1987). However, if you write or make an oral inquiry to the SSA expressing an intention to apply for SSI benefits, you will be treated as having applied as of the date of this first communication if you *then* complete an official application within sixty days of the SSA notice to file a formal application. *Id*; 20 C.F.R. § 416.345 (1987).

71. 20 C.F.R. § 416.325 (1987).

72. Pub. L. No. 97-248, § 181, *amending* 42 U.S.C. § 1382(c)(2); 20 C.F.R. §§ 416.330, .335, .421 (1987).

73. SSA POMS § SI 00501.510A (pt. 5) (6/83).

74. 20 C.F.R § 416.801–.806 (1987). However, the proof-of-age requirements for a person claiming to be at least 68 years old are relaxed. 20 C.F.R. § 416.806 (1987).

75. 20 C.F.R. § 416.901 (1987).

76. Pub. L. No. 98-369, 98 Stat. 494, the "Deficit Reduction Act of 1984", §§ 2651(a), (j); 42 U.S.C.S. § 1320b-7 (1985).

77. 20 C.F.R. § 416.345 (1987).

78. *See Braunstein v. Harris*, 498 F. Supp. 1301 (D.D.C. 1980) (Court found that the date claimant orally inquired about benefits and filed

for statement of earnings should be the date of application). *Cf. Schweiker v. Hanson*, 450 U.S. 785 (1981) (misinformation by SSA worker does not stop the SSA from requiring formal application to establish entitlement to benefits).

79. 42 C.F.R. § 435.911(a); 45 C.F.R. § 206.10(a)(3) (1986).

80. 20 C.F.R. § 416.210 (1987).

81. 20 C.F.R. § 416.806 (1987). If you later are determined not to be eligible for SSI, payments you received in the meantime are treated as overpayments. *Id.*

82. 20 C.F.R. §§ 416.931–.934 (1987).

83. 20 C.F.R. § 416.934 (1987); SSA POMS §§ DI 00404.210A, 2152.5 (pt. 4) (10/81); 17 *Clearinghouse Rev.* 416 (Aug./Sept. 1983).

84. 20 C.F.R. § 416.931 (1987).

85. 20 C.F.R. § 416.520 (1987); Pub. L. No. 100-203, § 9109 (Dec. 22, 1987), amending 42 U.S.C. § 1383(a)(4)(A).

86. 20 C.F.R. § 416.520(b)(3) (1987).

87. SSA POMS §§ SI E02004.100, *et seq.* (9/85); RS E02801.030, *et seq.* (8/85).

88. 42 U.S.C. § 1383(g)(1) (1982), as amended by Pub. L. No. 100-203, § 9110 (Dec. 22, 1987); 20 C.F.R. §§ 416.1901–.1922 (1987).

89. 20 C.F.R. §§ 416.1904–.1908 (1987).

90. 20 C.F.R. § 416.502 (1987).

91. 20 C.F.R. §§ 416.601–.665 (1987).

92. 42 U.S.C. § 1382(a)(2) (1982); 20 C.F.R. § 416.601(b)(1) (1987).

93. 42 U.S.C. § 1382(f) (1982); 20 C.F.R. 416.1603 (1987). The application of this provision to a former resident of Connecticut now residing in Puerto Rico was unsuccessfully challenged in *Torres v. Mathews*, 426 F. Supp. 1106 (D.P.R. 1977), *rev'd per curiam*, 435 U.S. 1 (1978). *See* SSA POMS §§ SI 01415.001, *et seq.*, for the charts of state supplements.

94. 42 U.S.C. § 1382(e)(1) (1982). Exactly what constitutes a public institution is unclear. Excluded are community residences with sixteen or fewer residents and educational or vocational training institutions. SSA POMS §§ SI 00520.100 *et seq.*; 20 C.F.R. §§ 416.201, .211 (1987); B. Lybarger & N. Onerheim, *An Advocate's Guide to Surviving the SSI System*, at 159–62 (Mass. Poverty Law Center, Inc. 1985) [Lybarger & Onerheim]. In addition, if you are a resident of a public emergency shelter for the homeless, you may be eligible for SSI benefits for any six months throughout which you reside in the shelter in any 9-month period. 42 U.S.C.S. § 1382(e) (1)(D) (1985), as amended by Pub. L. No. 100-203, § 9113 (Dec. 22, 1987); 20 C.F.R. §§ 416.201, .211(d) (1987).

95. 42 U.S.C. § 1382(e)(1)(B) (1982) as amended by Pub. L. No. 100-203,

§ 9119 (Dec. 22, 1987); 20 C.F.R. § 416.414 (1987).

96. Staff of Senate Comm. on Finance, 95th Cong., 1st Sess., the Supplemental Security Income Program 242, 247–52 (Comm. Print 1977).

97. 20 C.F.R. § 416.214 (1987).

98. 42 U.S.C. § 1382c(d)(2) (1982); 20 C.F.R. §§ 416.1806(c), .1826(c) (1987).

99. At least one suit has been filed attempting to speed up the process by which lost checks are replaced. *Moore v. Weinberger,* C.A. No. 75-2555-T (D. Mass. 1976), [1974–1976 Transfer Binder] 2 *Pov. L. Rep.* (CCH) ¶ 22,560. *See also* Lybarger & Onerheim, *supra* note 94, at 237–40.

100. 20 C.F.R. § 416.558 (1987).

101. 20 C.F.R. §§ 416.1401 *et seq.* (1987).

102. SSA POMS § GN 02220.035 (pt. 2) (1/82).

103. 20 C.F.R. § 416.570 (1987).

104. 20 C.F.R. § 416.558 (1987).

105. 20 C.F.R. § 416.550 (1987); SSA POMS § GN 02260.055 (pt. 2) (8/82).

106. SSA POMS §§ GN 02201.060 (pt. 2) (3/83), 02270.001–02270.020 (pt. 2) (3/83).

107. Pub. L. No. 98-369, § 2610 (to be codified at 42 U.S.C. § 1383(b)(1); H.R. Rep. No. 98-861, 98th Cong., 2d Sess. 1389, *reprinted in* [1984] 6B U.S. Code Cong. & Ad. News 751, 1383.

108. Pub. L. No. 98-369, § 2613 (to be codified at 42 U.S.C. § 1383(b)(3)). The conferees also address in report language the case where the person exceeds the assets limit by more than $50: "The managers recognize that there can be cases where large amounts of excess assets can exist in circumstances where it would be inappropriate to require full repayment of SSI benefits. However, the managers believe that such situations should be adequately provided for by an existing statutory provision which directs the Secretary to avoid penalizing indviduals who are without fault. *The Secretary is directed to review the regulations and procedures implementing this statutory provision to make any necessary changes to assure that a realistic assessment of the culpability of individuals is made.*" (emphasis added) H.R. Rep. No. 98-861, 98th Cong., 2d Sess. 1390, *reprinted in* [1984] 6B U.S. Code Cong. & Ad. News 751, 1384.

109. 20 C.F.R. §§ 416.704–.712 (1987).

110. 20 C.F.R. § 416.714(a) (1987); SSA POMS § SI 02301.400 D (pt. 5) (10/84).

111. *Cf.* 20 C.F.R. §§ 416.537–.538 (1987).

112. 20 C.F.R. §§ 416.724, .732 (1987).

113. 20 C.F.R. § 416.204 (1987).

114. 20 C.F.R. § 416.240, .714(b) (1987).

115. 42 U.S.C. § 1383(d)(1) (1982).

116. 42 U.S.C. § 1383(g)(1) (1982).

117. *See supra* notes 33 and 43.

118. 7 U.S.C. § 2015(g) (1982); the Food Security Act of 1985, Pub. L. No. 99-198, tit. XV, Subtit. A, §§ 1507, 1531, 99 Stat. 1567, 1582, *amending* 7 U.S.C. §§ 2014(a), 2020(i); 51 Fed. Reg. 28196, 28201– 28202 (Aug. 5, 1986) (to be codified in 7 C.F.R. §§ 273.2(j), .8(a), .9(a), .10(d)(7), (g)(1)(ii)) (interim rule); 7 C.F.R. § 273.2(k) (1986).

119. 42 U.S.C. § 1383c (1982).

120. 20 C.F.R. § 416.1404 (1987).

121. *Id.*

122. *Id.*

123. 20 C.F.R. §§ 416.1336(b), .1404(c) (1987).

124. 20 C.F.R. § 416.1404(b) (1987).

125. 20 C.F.R. § 416.1402 (1987).

126. 20 C.F.R. §§ 416.1403(a)(1), (2) (1987).

127. 20 C.F.R. § 416.1405 (1987).

128. 20 C.F.R. § 416.1409 (1987). You may be able to request a reconsideration later than sixty days after receiving notice of the initial determination if you have good cause for the delay. 20 C.F.R. § 416.1411 (1987).

129. 20 C.F.R. § 416.1413c(c) (1987).

130. 20 C.F.R. § 416.1413(a) (1987). This employee is not supposed to have had any previous connection with your case. 20 C.F.R. § 416.1420 (1987).

131. 20 C.F.R. § 416.1413(b) (1987).

132. 20 C.F.R. § 416.1420 (1987).

133. 20 C.F.R. § 416.1413(c) (1987).

134. 20 C.F.R. §§ 416.1413(c), .1420 (1987).

135. 20 C.F.R. § 416.1413a (1987); SSA POMS § GN 03110.070 (pt. 2) (9/83).

136. 20 C.F.R. § 416.1413a(b) (1987).

137. 20 C.F.R. § 416.1413b (1987).

138. *Id*; 20 C.F.R. § 416.1336(b) (1987). *See also* 51 Fed. Reg. 17057, 17066–17067 (May 8, 1986) (to be codified in 20 C.F.R. § 416.1380(d), (e)) (proposed rules).

139. 20 C.F.R. § 416.1433(b) (1987). An extension of time in which to request a hearing may be obtained for good cause. 20 C.F.R. §§ 416.1411, .1433(c) (1987).

140. 20 C.F.R. § 416.1421 (1987).

141. 20 C.F.R. §§ 416.1444–.1453 (1987).

142. 42 U.S.C. 1383(c)(2) (1982); 20 C.F.R. § 416.1453(b) (1987).

143. *See, e.g., Cockrum v. Califano*, 475 F. Supp. 1222 (D.D.C. 1979), *rem. on other grounds sub nom. Cockrum v. Harris*, 634 F.2d 1358 (D.C. Cir. 1980). *Cf. Heckler v. Day*, 104 S. Ct. 2249, 2258 n.33 (1984) (Classwide injunctive relief is improper, but individual relief may be available); *Barnett v. Bowen*, 665 F. Supp. 1096 (D. Vt. 1987) (class members entitled to notice informing them of reasons for delay, identity of SSA contact person, and the right to seek judicial relief if they feel that their requests for reconsideration and hearing have been unreasonably delayed).

144. 20 C.F.R. § 416.1453 (1987).

145. 20 C.F.R. § 416.1467 (1987).

146. 20 C.F.R. § 416.1468 (1987). An extension of time in which to appeal may be obtained for good cause. 20 C.F.R. §§ 416.1411, .1468(b) (1987).

147. 20 C.F.R. § 416.1455 (1987).

148. 20 C.F.R. § 416.1479 (1987).

149. 42 U.S.C. § 1383(c)(3) (1982). An extension of time in which to appeal may be obtained for good cause. 20 C.F.R. §§ 416.1411, .1482 (1987).

150. 20 C.F.R. § 416.1336(b) (1987). The only exceptions to this rule are when benefits are terminated because the recipient is dead, the recipient is receiving more than one check per month, or the amount received is impossibly high. In the latter two situations, you will continue to receive benefits but at a lower amount. 20 C.F.R. §§ 416.1336–.1337 (1987).

151. 20 C.F.R. § 416.1336(b) (1987); 51 Fed. Reg. 18611, 18619, 18620 (May 21, 1986) (to be codified in 20 C.F.R. §§ 416.966(c)(1), (d)(1)) (proposed rules).

152. Pub. L. No. 97-455, § 4 (codified in 42 U.S.C. § 405(b)(2)); 51 Fed. Reg. 288 (Jan. 3, 1986); 20 C.F.R. §§ 416.1414–.1418 (1987).

153. *See* 51 Fed. Reg. 18611, 18619 (May 21, 1986) (to be codified in 20 C.F.R. § 416.996(c)(1)) (proposed rules).

154. *Id.* at 18619, 18620 (to be codified in 20 C.F.R. §§ 416.996(c)(1), (d)(1)); 20 C.F.R. §§ 416.1409, .1433 (1987).

155. *Id.* at 18619, 18620 (to be codified in 20 C.F.R. §§ 416.996(c)(2), (d)(2)); 20 C.F.R. § 416.1411 (1987).

156. 20 C.F.R. § 416.537 (1987). *See also* 51 Fed. Reg. 18611, 18620 (1986) (to be codified in 20 C.F.R. § 416.996(f)) (proposed rules) ("Waiver of recovery of an overpayment resulting from continued benefits to you may be considered as long as the cessation determination was appealed in good faith.")

157. Pub. L. No. 99-643, § 8 (1986).

3

Disability Programs under Social Security and Supplemental Security Income

ELIGIBILITY

What disability programs does the Social Security Administration operate?

There are two distinct disability programs operated by the Social Security Administration.[1] One program is part of the Supplemental Security Income (SSI) program, an overview of which is presented in chapter 2 of this book. SSI pays benefits to disabled persons[2] provided that their countable income and resources are below a certain level.[3] The other disability program is the Social Security Disability Insurance Program, (Title II of the Social Security Act). It pays benefits to disabled workers, widows, widowers,[4] and their dependents provided the worker is fully insured.[5] An overview of the Social Security program can be found in chapter 1 of this book.

In some cases, an individual may qualify for disability benefits under both Social Security (SSA) and SSI. This would occur if the amount the individual disabled person received in her monthly Social Security check was below the income limits in her state for SSI, and she met the resource and other eligibility requirements for SSI.[6]

Is the definition of disability the same under both programs?

Generally, yes, although there are a number of exceptions. The definition of disability for both programs is an inability to "engage in any substantial gainful activity by reason of any medically determinable physical or mental impairment which can be expected to result in death or which has lasted or can be expected to last for a continuous period of not less than 12 months . . ."[7] The SSA definition continues: "An individual shall be determined to be under a disability only if his physical or mental impairment or impairments are of such severity that he is not only unable to do his previous work but cannot, considering his age, education, and work experience, engage in any other kind of substantial gainful work which exists in the national economy."[8] However, the definition of disability for widows, surviving divorced wives, widowers, or surviving divorced husbands is based on medical factors alone, and vocational factors (age, education, and prior work experience) are not considered. These individuals must also be found incapable of any gainful activity.[9] Because the definition of disability for widows, surviving divorced wives, widowers, and surviving divorced husbands sets forth a much more stringent standard, an individual who does not meet this definition may well qualify for disability benefits under the SSI program, Social Security disability, on her own account, or both.

I am 62 and disabled. For what benefits should I apply?

Generally, if you are unable to work, you should apply for Social Security disability benefits rather than early retirement. There are two reasons why this is so. First, your benefits are likely to be higher. The Social Security disability program will pay an individual the same benefits he would receive if he were to retire at age 65. In contrast, under the early retirement program, benefits are reduced by five-ninths of one percent for each month of retirement prior to one's 65th birthday.[10] Remember, however, that there are special earnings requirements that have to be met in order to receive Social Security disability benefits.[11] It is possible that a person may have enough quarters to qualify for early retirement but may not meet the special earnings requirements for Social Security disability benefits. Second, a person who receives Social Security disability benefits for a period of twenty-four (24) months, becomes eligible for Medicare benefits thereafter.[12] These medical insurance benefits are of great value—and could not otherwise be obtained until the individual reached 65 years of age.

In many states, the SSI program is tied directly to the state Medicaid program. An SSI recipient in such a state receives Medicaid coverage automatically. It is advisable, then, to apply for SSI benefits not because the amount of cash benefits is great but because Medicaid coverage can be very important for obtaining and paying for medical care.

With regard to disability benefits for widows, widowers, and surviving divorced spouses, there is an actuarial reduction, and a person can receive as low as 71.5 percent of the benefit she otherwise would receive if she waited until age 65 to take the benefit.[13]

How does the Social Security Administration determine whether an individual is disabled?

The Social Security Administration uses a step-by-step[14] process in determining whether an individual is disabled. The process is quite complicated, and you are strongly encouraged to seek legal assistance from advocates experienced in this area of law to assure that your case is analyzed properly.

Step 1: Are you engaged in "substantial gainful activity"? Simply stated, this step asks whether you are "working," and if so, whether the work you do qualifies as "substantial gainful activity" so as to show that you are not disabled. The criteria by which the SSA determines substantial gainful activity (SGA) are complex[15] but will be summarized briefly. SGA involves work activity for pay or profit requiring significant physical or mental activities.[16] Taking care of one's self, household chores, hobbies, therapy, school attendance, and club and social activities generally is not considered to be SGA.[17] The more you are able to do that which requires experience, skills, supervisory functions, and responsibility, the more likely your activity will be considered SGA.[18] In determining SGA, SSA will also consider how well you do your work, whether it is done under special conditions, and how long it takes you.[19]

A finding that you did *not* engage in SGA during a particular period does not address the question of your *ability* to engage in SGA. The SSA will examine all medical and vocational evidence to determine if an activity which is not SGA may show the ability to perform SGA. For example, a hobby such as cabinet making or miniature ship building may show the ability to engage in SGA even though you do not make money on the activity. If you are an employee, then the SSA considers the amount you earn in determining whether you are engaging in SGA. Simply stated, if you work and average less than $190 per month, the SSA generally will not consider your activity as SGA. If you work and average more than $300 a month, the SSA generally will consider that you have engaged in SGA.[20] (These

TABLE 3.
Flow Chart of How SSA Determines Disability

	Step 1: Is claimant engaged in Substantial Gainful Activity (SGA)?	YES BENEFITS DENIED
	NO	
	Step 2: Does claimant have an impairment lasting or expected to last at least 12 months or ending in death?	NO BENEFITS DENIED
	YES	
	Step 3: Does the impairment significantly limit the ability to work, i.e., is it severe?	NO BENEFITS DENIED
	YES	
BENEFITS YES AWARDED	Step 4: Does the impairment meet or equal a listing in Appendix 1?	
	NO	
	Step 5: Does the claimant have sufficient Residual Functional Capacity to return to past work?	YES BENEFITS DENIED
	NO	
BENEFITS NO AWARDED	Step 6: Is claimant able to do any Substantial Gainful Activity in the national economy?	YES BENEFITS DENIED
	NO	
BENEFITS YES AWARDED	Exception: Does the claimant's impairment prevent his/her customary exertional performance, and does (s)he have a marginal education with 35–40 years of work experience confined to unskilled arduous physical labor?	NO BENEFITS DENIED

Source: Amended excerpt from *Disability Practice Manual for Social Security and SSI Programs* (Legal Counsel for the Elderly, AARP, 1985), p. 28. This is a summary of requirements. See text for details.

dollar figures represent countable income and are in effect for 1988. There is a possibility the figures may increase in the future.) The presumption of SGA based on average monthly earnings can be rebutted by evidence showing that the work was not "substantial" even though it was considered "gainful" under the regulatory guidelines. Work must be *both* substantial and gainful to meet this test.

If you are self-employed, the SSA will consider such factors as your activities and their value to the business, the hours, skills, energy output, efficiency, and responsibilities of your activity, especially as compared to an unimpaired person engaging in the same type of activity. If you manage a business or spend more than forty-five hours a month in a management capacity, you probably will be considered as engaging in SGA.[21]

If the SSA determines that you are engaging in SGA, they will consider you *not* disabled, and they will not proceed with the later steps of the sequential evaluation process.

Step 2: Is your disability expected to last at least twelve months or result in death? If not, the SSA will determine that you are not disabled.

Step 3: Is your mental and/or physical disability so severe that your ability to perform basic work activities is limited or prevented? In this step, the SSA determines whether your impairment(s) are severe. To do so, the SSA must consider whether the combined effect of your impairment(s) is enough to meet this severity requirement.[22] Examples of basic work activities are walking, standing, sitting, lifting, pushing, pulling, reaching, carrying, handling, seeing, hearing, speaking, understanding, remembering and carrying out instructions, using judgment, and responding appropriately to supervision, coworkers, and changes in the work routine.[23] If the SSA finds that your impairment(s) are not severe, they will determine that you are not disabled.

In 1975, only 8.4 percent of applicants were denied disability on the basis of medical factors alone. By 1982, the percentage of claims that were denied on this basis had risen to 40.3 percent.[24] It appears that the SSA may be using this step as a "catch-all" basis to deny claims.

This step in the sequential evaluation process has been challenged in court cases throughout the country. Claimants have asserted that it is inconsistent with the Social Security Act in that it appears to be a determination on medical factors alone and does not consider key vocational factors such as age, education, and work experience. Five circuit courts agreed with this contention[25] while five other circuit courts[26] upheld the regulation by interpreting it as a *de minimis* threshold requirement for eligibility. As one court stated, "an impairment can be considered as not severe only if it is a slight abnormality which has such a minimal effect on the individual that it would not be expected to interfere with the individual's ability to work, irrespective of age, education, or work-experience."[27] The SSA responded to this litigation by issuing a ruling which appears to adopt a *de minimis* standard.[28] In 1987, the Supreme Court in *Bowen v. Yuckert*[29] ruled that the severe impairment regulations were consistent with the Social Security Act, but several justices expressed concerns about the way the regulations were being administered by the SSA. As a result of *Yuckert*, it appears that the SSA will have to apply a *de minimis* standard in the severity step. The most prudent course of action for claimants at this point is to make certain that their files at the SSA office contain detailed information concerning their ability to do basic work activities. In addition, claimants should seek professional legal assistance from individuals experienced in this area of law who will ascertain the status of the law and how best to proceed in claims where the severity step may pose an obstacle to obtaining benefits.

Step 4: Does your disability meet the requirements of the SSA's Listing of Impairments? The SSA has set forth in an appendix to its regulations an extensive list of impairments, divided into thirteen categories of body systems.[30] This Listing of Impairments is discussed in further detail below. But if an individual's impairment meets one of those on the Listing of Impairments or consists of a combination of impairments equivalent to a listed impairment or impairments,[31] the individual is found eligible for disability benefits. An applicant for disabled widow or disabled widower[32] benefits or for SSI disabled child benefits[33] must meet the requirements of the listings or the equivalent of the listings. Applicants not meeting these requirements will be found ineligible for these special disability benefits.

For all other applicants for SSI and Social Security disability benefits who do not meet the listings, the SSA proceeds to the next step in the evaluation process.

Step 5: Do you retain the ability to do past relevant work? In this step, the Social Security Administration gathers information about the type of work you have done in the last fifteen years. In analyzing your past relevant work, the SSA will pay particular attention to the exertional requirements of the jobs, the skill level of the jobs, the tools and machinery you used, the degree of responsibility involved, and whether you supervised other employees. If the SSA finds that you could return to your past work, disability benefits are denied. If you cannot return to your past work, the SSA proceeds to the next step.

Step 6: Are you able to do any substantial gainful activity (SGA) in the national economy?

Once you have shown you cannot return to past relevant work, the SSA must show what—if any—type of work you can do, in light of age, education, and prior work experience. Individuals whose impairments are primarily exertional in nature will have their cases analyzed in light of the "grid regulations" described below. Basically, the grids[34] are charts that use the factors of age and educational, exertional, and skill level and of a person's prior work experience to determine whether he or she is disabled. If the individual falls under one of the grids where there is a directed finding of "disabled," benefits will then be awarded. Likewise, if the grids are not applicable (typically cases involving mental impairments) but the individual's impairments prevent him or her from engaging in substantial gainful activity, benefits will also be awarded. On the other hand, if he is found not disabled on the basis of the grids, a finding of not disabled will be issued. The grids are not always applicable, nor does the SSA always apply them correctly.

There is an important exception to the step-by-step process outlined above. Individuals with a marginal education[35] (generally sixth grade or less) who have thirty-five years or more of arduous unskilled labor experience, and who—because of severe impairment(s)—cannot return to their former work, generally are considered to be disabled without further analysis of their claim.[36] Coalminers and certain types of construction laborers may fall into this category.

Throughout the sequential evaluation process must the Social Security Administration consider the combined effect of multiple impairments?

Yes. The Social Security Administration must consider the

combined effect of multiple impairments on your ability to work, and throughout the sequential evaluation process. It is important therefore to inform the Social Security Administration at all levels of the appeals process of all your impairments, the combined effect of those impairments, and medical documentation of the existence of those impairments.

What are the "listings"?

The "listings" refers to appendix 1[37] of the Social Security regulations which contains a "Listing of Impairments." Most disability applicants will have their claims evaluated in light of the listings. As indicated above, disabled widows, widowers, and disabled surviving divorced spouses must show that their impairments meet the listings or an equivalent of a listing or they will be found not disabled. For other individuals, failure to meet the requirements of the listings does *not* necessarily mean that their claims will be denied. Their claims will be analyzed in light of steps five and six explained above.

The listings were revised and updated in 1985.[38] The mental impairment listings have been revised and expanded substantially to bring the regulations more in line with current views for properly analyzing mental impairments.

Two sets of listings exist—one generally applies to individuals over age 18 (part A), the other to individuals under age 18 (part B).[39] Each set categorizes impairments into thirteen body systems. The thirteen systems are: (1) musculoskeletal system, (2) special senses and speech, (3) respiratory system, (4) cardiovascular system, (5) digestive system, (6) genito-urinary system, (7) hemic and lymphatic system, (8) skin, (9) endocrine system, (10) multiple body systems, (11) neurological, (12) mental disorders, (13) neoplastic diseases, malignant. (The listings for children have an additional category for growth impairment.)

Comparing an individual's impairments to the listings is a difficult and complex task for which it is advisable to seek professional medical and legal assistance to ensure that an appropriate analysis is done.

What are the "grids"?

The "grids" refer to another segment of the Social Security regulations formally entitled, "Medical-Vocational Guidelines."[40] The grids formalize the consideration of a claimant's age, education, and work experience which is required by the statutory definition of disability.

Before the grids were established, each claimant's individual circumstance had to be considered. These judgments were difficult and considerable variation in treatment resulted. The grids were issued to ease the decision-making process and to attempt to achieve uniformity in disability determinations, especially at the administrative law judge level.

In many cases, application of the grids will preclude the use of a vocational expert and arguably does not result in as individualized a determination as might be required by the Social Security Act. The Supreme Court, however, in *Heckler v. Campbell*,[41] held that the determination as to whether jobs exist that a person having the claimant's qualifications could perform is not a unique factual determination and can be resolved by rulemaking—specifically by use of the grids. Furthermore, the Supreme Court stated that the grid regulations are not inconsistent with the Social Security Act, especially since claimants have the opportunity to present evidence of their abilities as well as evidence that the guidelines do not apply to them.

The grids are three tables based upon a claimant's residual functional capacity (RFC) for work after his/her disability is considered. Once a claimant's RFC is determined to be limited to sedentary, light, or medium work, each RFC table organizes a claimant's age, education, and work experience into a series of rules which each direct a finding of disability or nondisability. These grids are fully used in a Social Security disability case wherein an individual has established that he is not able to return to his former work and that his impairments are primarily exertional.

For example, suppose Joe, aged 56 with an eighth grade education, was a furniture mover before injuring his back. Because of this severe impairment he is no longer able to do the lifting required by his past relevant work as a furniture mover. An evaluation by SSA would then have to be made as to the exertional level of work he is still capable of performing on a sustained basis. This medical determination is called his "residual functional capacity" or RFC. Assuming that Joe's past relevant work is categorized as "heavy" work,[42] the categories remaining are "medium,"[43] "light,"[44] "sedentary,"[45] and "very heavy."[46]

If Joe is found to be capable of performing medium work (which requires occasional lifting of up to 50 pounds and frequent lifting of up to 25 pounds), then the "medium work" table of the grids is applied. This table lists thirty-one rules covering all possible combinations of age, education, and skill level of an individual's past relevant work experience. With Joe's age (closely approaching advanced age), education (marginal), and prior work experience, rule number 203.01 would be applicable. This rule directs a finding of "disabled."[47]

A number of cautionary remarks should be made about the grids. First, they are to be rigidly applied only in cases where the impairments are primarily exertional in nature. Examples of nonexertional impairments are mental problems, sensory and skin problems, postural and manipulative limitations, pain, or environmental restrictions (e.g., an inability to tolerate dust or fumes).[48] The SSA frequently ignores nonexertional impairments; therefore an individual with such impairments should carefully and thoroughly document his or her case file concerning these areas. Second, the grids can be used to find nondisability only if the claimant's circumstances fit each factor completely. Thus, ability to perform less than a full range of sedentary work, for example, would preclude use of the grids. Such a situation would generally require that the SSA show, by means of a vocational expert, that there are jobs which exist in significant numbers in the national economy which the individual could perform. The SSA would need to show this in order to make an appropriate determination that such an individual is not disabled. Third, the grids become relevant only after one has established an inability to return to one's former type of work as a result of a severe medically determinable impairment(s). Fourth, the Social Security Administration may misapply the grid regulations or may use an inappropriate category. This may happen if the formal educational level or job title does not reflect the individual's true skill level. For example, a high school graduate who may not be able to read or write well should perhaps be more appropriately classified as an individual with a marginal educational level. Fifth, while there are eighty-two separate grid regulations, only sixteen lead to a finding of disabled (less than 20 percent). Generally speaking, the younger and/or the higher the skill level and educational attainment, the less likely the grids will help an individual obtain benefits.

As in the case of the listings, the proper application of the grids can be a complex matter. If you encounter difficulty in obtaining benefits as a result of the grids, you should seek professional legal assistance from individuals experienced in this area of law.

APPLICATIONS

How do I apply for Social Security and SSI disability benefits?

The application process for Social Security disability benefits is largely the same as for other types of Social Security and SSI benefits as described in chapter 1 and chapter 2 of this book, respectively. However, several special aspects of the disability application process require emphasis. You should take to the interview all the medical, hospital, and doctors' reports that you have concerning your condition. You will be asked questions about the nature of your former work, your hospitalizations, your medications, and your daily activities. Be as precise and detailed as you can be to ensure that the SSA will develop a complete record of your disability.

You also will be asked to sign a number of release forms to enable the SSA to retrieve your medical, clinic, and hospital records.

You should cooperate fully with the SSA to make sure that complete and up-to-date records and reports from doctors, hospitals, clinics, and other providers who have treated you are obtained by the SSA and placed in your SSA file. In this manner, the SSA has the documentation with which to make a fully informed and fair decision in your case. Many disability claims are denied primarily because information was not fully provided, and the SSA did not thoroughly seek out all the medical records and other available evidence.

At the end of the application interview, if you feel that the SSA still lacks a complete picture of your disabled condition, write on the application any additional information you think helpful. Furthermore, be as responsive as possible to the questions posed in the step-by-step analysis explained earlier.

When should I apply for Social Security or SSI disability benefits?

If you believe that you are disabled, you should apply immediately. Under the Social Security disability insurance program, you are entitled to up to twelve months retroactive benefits from the date you apply, assuming that you can establish that you were disabled during that time period. There is, however, a five-month waiting period from the date of the onset of the disability. Therefore, to get a full twelve months of retroactive benefits, you would have to show an onset date of seventeen months prior to the date of the application.[49] Recall also that entitlement to Social Security benefits requires meeting the special earnings requirements (the 20/40 test). In general, the further in the past you want to establish that you were disabled, the more difficult it becomes. Similarly, the longer you wait to apply without working, the more likely your insured status will expire. This can be an especially troublesome problem if your work history is sporadic (i.e., you do not have twenty covered quarters immediately preceding your stopping work).

Under the SSI program, there is no special earnings requirement, nor is there a five-month waiting period. There are, however, no benefits under SSI payable before the date of the application for benefits.

Are there any medical reports from my own doctor that might be helpful?

Yes. A complete, detailed, and current statement from your doctor is critical to establishing your eligibility for disability benefits. Ask your doctor for a letter detailing your condition. You may not be able to get as detailed a statement as might be ideal. Do not be discouraged. Do the best you can to obtain as current and detailed a statement as possible. Ideally, the letter should include an evaluation of your medical impairments and your capabilities, discussing issues such as:

- How long and how often has your doctor been treating you?
- What impairments does your doctor consider you to have?
- When did they start, how long will they last, and are they disabling?
- What are the symptoms of your impairments?
- What are the "signs" (anatomical, physiological, or psycho-

logical abnormalities demonstrable by medically acceptable clinical diagnostic techniques) of your impairments?
- What laboratory findings (e.g., x-rays, lab tests, electrophysiological tests) have been made in your case?
- What medication does your doctor prescribe for your condition? (Date, purpose, effectiveness, and side effects for each medication should be included).
- Whether, to what degree, and with what frequency you are likely to experience pain as a result of your condition.
- What incidents in your medical history relate to your present condition?
- What is the prognosis?
- Does your condition prevent you from doing your prior work?
- Would working adversely affect your impairment? Explain.
- Do your impairment(s) affect your ability to hear, speak, or see? Explain.
- In an eight-hour work day, for how long does the doctor feel you can sit, stand, or walk, and can you do these activities on a sustained basis (eight hours a day, five days a week, fifty weeks a year)?
- How much does the doctor feel you can lift and carry on a regular basis?
- Are your hands and feet impaired to the extent that you have difficulty with grasping, reaching, pushing, pulling, and manipulating or operating leg/foot controls?
- How frequently can you bend, squat, kneel, crawl, and reach above shoulder level?
- Would working conditions involving any of the following situations be contraindicated in light of your impairments?
  - unprotected heights
  - moving machinery
  - noise and vibration
  - extreme temperatures
- Are there any other aspects of your condition which adversely affect your physical capacity to work?

You may want to send your doctor a copy of the Listing of Impairments most appropriate to your condition. A skilled advocate trained in this area of law can help you refine and focus on questions to your doctor that will be most appropriate in your own case.

Will the Social Security office have all my other records?

Usually no. This is especially true if you have many different hospital and doctor records. A major reason that many claims are denied throughout the appeal process is that a careful and exhaustive culling of existing records has not been done. To avoid this situation, give the SSA complete and accurate information concerning doctors, hospitalizations, and clinics and emergency room treatments. You can assist in this process by telephoning, writing, or visiting the provider to gather all the relevant records. Where the records are voluminous, you can ask your treating physician to summarize segments of your medical records.

Will a letter from my employer help my disability claim?

Generally, a letter from your current or former employer can be very helpful. Since one of the steps in analyzing a disability case is to determine whether you can return to your former work,[50] a detailed letter from your former employer (especially in situations where you tried to go back to work and were unable to do the job) can be very helpful in showing your inability to return to your former work.

In many cases, you may find it impossible to obtain a letter from your employer. Do not be discouraged from applying or pursuing a claim just because you do not have such a letter. Certainly many if not most claims do not have the benefit of the insight that a letter from an employer can provide but are nevertheless successful claims. Likewise, you should not be intimidated by the large number of topics listed below which an employer might address. All the topics may not be appropriate to your situation. But if you are able to augment your file at the SSA with a letter from your employer, some of the topics important to a disability claim which your former employer might address are:

- a detailed description of your duties
- the amount of time you had to spend standing, walking, lifting, pushing, pulling, bending, and kneeling on your job

- the heaviest items you had to lift on a regular basis
- the tools, machines, processes, and raw materials you had to work with
- problems experienced on the job related to the disability (absenteeism, coworker assistance)
- an assessment as to whether you can do your former work given your present condition and a detailed explanation as to how this assessment was made.

If I am currently working in a sheltered workshop or a special work setting, what type of statement should I get from my employer?

To demonstrate to the SSA the nature of this special work setting, a letter from your current employer might cover such questions as:

- What reasons did he have for hiring you?
- How do you fit into the activities of the business?
- Who performed your duties before you were hired?
- How much time was spent on such duties?
- If you lost the job, what—if any—replacement would be made?
- What amount of time would the replacement spend on your duties?
- What is your rate of absenteeism?
- What type of work are you least able to perform because of your condition?
- Do you need unusual assistance or special supervision because of your medical condition?
- How does your performance compare to others whom your employer employs?
- Does your employer pay you more money because of past work, size of your family, friendship, familial relationship, or other factors not related to performance as opposed to what would be paid another employee for the same work?
- Does your employer consider your work to be worth substantially less than the amount paid? Explain. Give an estimate of the value of the services and how your employer arrived at the estimate.
- If your employer is retaining you on the payroll despite unsatisfactory work, what are your employer's reasons for doing so?

• Is your employer's establishment a sheltered workshop?

What do I do if I cannot obtain a letter from my employer?
If you cannot get a statement from your employer, you should submit to the Social Security Administration a detailed listing of your jobs over the past fifteen years. Describe specifically the duties involved. It is particularly important to detail the exertional demands of your past work. Be accurate in this description. You should not "puff up" your job especially with regard to supervisory responsibilities. An individual who is truly a supervisor of other employees is generally considered to possess a higher degree of skill than one who does not. Supervising skills are ones that are often transferable to other work environments. Hence, an individual who puffs up his job description by labelling himself a "boss" may be denied disability benefits because the SSA, relying on the erroneous job description, finds that the individual has skills transferable to other less strenuous jobs that the SSA considers him capable of performing. Furthermore, job titles such as "mechanic" or "nurse's aide" often are too broad to be helpful and can be misleading unless you describe precisely the nature of your duties.

What is an SSA "consultative examination"?
An SSA consultative examination is an examination performed by a doctor who is paid by the SSA. Generally, the SSA will order a consultative examination when they feel there is insufficient medical information about your condition.[51] When the SSA orders a consultative examination, you will be sent a notice of the name of the doctor, his or her address, and the time of the appointment. You should attend the consultative examination unless you have a good reason not to do so.[52]

Many claims are denied based on the consultative examiner's report. Often the consultative examiner's report contradicts the assessment by your own treating physician. There are a large number of court decisions concerning conflicts between the reports of consultative examiners and those of individuals' treating physicians.[53] The general rule is that the SSA should rely more heavily on the assessment of a treating physician, but there are a number of exceptions. For example, the consultative examiner may be a specialist in the particular area of medicine in which the individual's impairment(s) occur. And consultative reports are generally fairly detailed narratives typed on the doctors' stationery, often with a battery of test results to support the narrative report while in some instances, the treating physician's records are not clearly legible or consist of box checking on a preprinted form. Overbroad conclusions such as "I do not believe Mr. Jones can work" without narrative analyses and laboratory or clinical findings to support them are equally ineffective. Current detailed statements from the treating physician are therefore very important to obtain and add to the SSA file.

A number of precautions should be taken to reduce potential problems with consultative examinations. First, make sure that your own treating physician gives you or the SSA a complete, detailed report as outlined above. Second, ask in advance for the SSA to send you to your own doctor or to another doctor of your choice at the SSA's expense. If the SSA is reviewing your case and considering terminating your disability benefits, they are likely to honor such a request. Third, if you go to the SSA's consultative examination(s), document very carefully what happens. You should keep a record of the following information:

- how long the examination lasted
- what questions the doctor asked you
- who else you spoke with and for how long
- what tests the doctor performed
- what areas of your body were examined
- whether you thought the doctor had difficulty understanding you
- what were your reactions to the questions and tests performed (For example, did you experience any pain while performing range of motion tests?)

This information could be especially helpful to you at the hearing in the event that you received only a cursory consultative examination.

Does the SSA ever send an individual to a psychiatrist or psychologist for a consultative examination?

Yes. And although some people are ashamed or embarrassed to go to a psychiatrist or psychologist, these reports can be very helpful to a disability claim, especially in situations where the individual:

- has difficulty remembering recent events;
- has difficulty concentrating;
- is often depressed and has physical symptoms such as weight loss, difficulty sleeping, or thoughts of suicide;
- spends very little time with other people;
- has a problem with alcohol or other drugs;
- has a long history of inability to get along with others in a work setting;
- is in a lot of pain most of the time because of illness;
- is depressed frequently because of a disabling condition.

Aren't there any situations in which I could be so severely disabled that the SSA can presume that I am disabled?

Under the SSI program, there is such a provision.[54] Under this provision, if you meet all the other criteria for SSI eligibility, you can get SSI benefits for a period of up to three months if you meet any one of these criteria:

- amputation of two limbs
- amputation of a leg at the hip
- allegation of total deafness
- allegation of total blindness
- allegation of bedridden state due to a longstanding condition
- allegation of a stroke more than three months ago and continued marked difficulty in walking or using hand or arm
- allegation of cerebral palsy, muscular dystrophy, or muscular atrophy and marked difficulty in walking, speaking, or coordination of the hands or arms
- allegation of diabetes with amputation of the foot
- allegation of Down's syndrome
- allegation of severe mental deficiency made by another individual filing on behalf of an individual who is at least seven years of age
- allegation of Acquired Immune Deficiency Syndrome.

Further, if you are deemed eligible for payment under this provision and later found ineligible, you will not be considered to have been overpaid. For procedures to be followed to obtain benefits under this provision, turn to chapter 2 of this book.

APPEALS PROCEDURE

What are my appeal rights under the Social Security and SSI disability programs?

Generally, the appeal procedures for the disability programs are the same as described in chapters 1 and 2 of this book, with a few exceptions.

If the SSA decides to terminate your SSI or Social Security disability benefits, you may be eligible to continue monthly benefits while you appeal the termination decision, if you appeal within ten days of receiving the termination notice. You have a right to appeal within sixty days, but ten days insures continued receipt of benefits pending a redetermination. The SSA will presume that you receive the notice within five days from the date on the face of the notice. In order to be eligible for these benefits you must request in writing both (1) the appeal of the disability termination and (2) the continuation of your SSA/SSI disability benefits.

If you are unsuccessful in your appeal at the reconsideration level, you should again appeal within ten days and state in writing that you want to receive benefits through the ALJ hearing stage. Again, you have a right to appeal within sixty days, but appealing within ten days ensures continued receipt of benefits.

If you are found not disabled at the ALJ hearing level, you may still appeal that decision (within sixty days), but your benefits will be cut off. You will not be able to receive benefits beyond this point in the appeal process. However, if you win at a later appeal level, you will receive your benefits retroactive to the cut-off date.

There are two exceptions to this general rule for benefit payment pending appeal. If you are receiving Social Security benefits and are terminated for nonmedical reasons, you are *not* entitled to receive benefits pending appeal. Secondly, if you are receiving SSI disability benefits and are terminated for non-medical reasons, you are entitled to apply for continuing benefits while you appeal for a reconsideration, but if the claim is denied, you are *not* entitled to benefits pending the ALJ hearing appeal. Remember that under either program, you are entitled to benefits pending appeal if you are threatened with termination for *medical* reasons (i.e., the SSA believes your medical condition has improved). If you are unsuccessful in your appeal, you will incur an overpayment, but you will be able to request a waiver of any such overpayment of benefits.[55]

I was denied benefits initially and requested a reconsideration. What happens at the reconsideration level?

This is the first stage of the appeal process. At this stage, the SSA will probably send you a questionnaire asking:

- whether your condition has changed since you applied;
- what physical and mental limitations you have as a result of your condition;
- what restriction(s) your doctor(s) has placed on you as a result of your condition;
- what illnesses or injuries you have that are not already on record with the SSA;
- what physicians you have seen since you filed your claim;
- what treatment you have received since you filed your claim;
- what hospitalizations, clinic visits, nursing homes, or extended care facility stays you have had since you filed your claim;
- whether you have worked since you filed your claim;
- how your illness or injury affects your ability to care for your personal needs;
- what changes have occurred in your daily activities since you filed your claim.

You will also probably be asked to sign release forms so that the SSA can collect any additional medical records and other information that might be helpful. The SSA may also order that an additional examination(s) be done.

In cases involving termination of benefits, the Social Security Administration is implementing new reconsideration procedures under which an individual will have a face-to-face meeting with an SSA official as part of the reconsideration process.[56] Nevertheless, due to the SSA's failure to develop a complete record at reconsideration and due to the complexity of the regulations (especially on issues such as transferability of skills and appropriate use of the grids), many claimants are unsuccessful in having their initial determinations reversed upon reconsideration.

Persistence is often the key to a successful Social Security claim. Nowhere is that more important than in appealing adverse reconsideration decisions. This decision, issued to the claimant in the form of a written notice, normally contains a very brief statement as to why the SSA again denied the claim. Once you have received this notice, you can file for an administrative hearing before an administrative law judge—the best forum for you to make a thorough presentation of your claim before an impartial decisionmaker.

What happens after I make a request for a hearing?

First of all, you and your representative[57] will receive notice of the date and time of the hearing. This may take a number of months from the date of your request for a hearing. Generally, though, you will receive it at least two weeks before the hearing date.[58]

Prior to the hearing date, you will have an opportunity to review your file. You have the right to copies of all of the documents in the file.[59] If you have not already done so, you should go over the contents of your file carefully to make sure that all your medical records and doctors' reports are included. You should also read carefully what the consultative reports (if any) say about your condition. You might wish to take your consultative report(s) to your treating physician and ask her to send a letter to the SSA expressing her opinion on the contents of the consultative report(s). A trained advocate can provide you with assistance on all of these tasks. In addition, your file should contain a listing of all your jobs in the last fifteen years or so with descriptions of your duties on those jobs. Your file should also have a current listing of your medications, when they were first prescribed, who prescribed them, the purpose of the medication, and any side effects you experience as a result of this medication. If any of this information is not in your file, take immediate steps to make sure that it is included. If you are unable to gather some of these documents before the hearing, you can ask the judge to leave the record open for a week or two after the hearing to allow you to submit them at that time.

Should I obtain an attorney or paralegal to represent me at an SSA hearing?

Generally yes. A Social Security disability hearing is a fairly complex legal proceeding. While this chapter is intended as a general overview, it is not a substitute for experienced legal representation. To locate a legal representative, contact your local bar association or the legal aid or legal services program in your area. Because this is a specialized area of law, you should seek out a representative who is well versed in the intricacies of Social Security law. For more detailed information on how to secure an attorney, see chapter 1 of this book.

In the event that you are unable to obtain a legal representative, you should ask the ALJ to help you gather evidence in your case. The ALJ has a duty to develop the record fully and to conduct a full and fair hearing[60]—a duty which is heightened when an individual is unrepresented.[61] If you feel after the hearing that the ALJ did not fully develop the record, this may be the basis for a court remanding the case to the SSA.[62]

What questions are the ALJ and/or my legal representative likely to ask me at the hearing?

It is impossible to predict all the questions that are likely to be asked at a hearing. However, there are a number of questions that are asked at most hearings. These questions are intended to elicit answers that help the ALJ to analyze the claim in light of the sequential evaluation process described above. The general categories of the questions are: background information (age, education, training, family history), vocational history, medical problems, and daily activities. Some of the common questions in these areas are as follows.

- What is your name, address, age, marital status, living arrangement?
- Do you have to climb stairs to get to your apartment; how many times a day do you do this?
- What education and vocational or other specialized training have you had?
- Can you read, write, and do arithmetic?
- What jobs have you had?
- What specifically were the duties of your jobs?
- How much lifting, standing, walking, and bending did you have to do on your jobs?
- Did you supervise others on your jobs?
- Did you have difficulty getting along with others on your jobs?
- How long would it take for someone to learn your job?

- Did you have to fill our forms, reports, or other written documents on your former jobs?
- Did you hire and fire people?
- What are your illnesses, their duration and symptoms?
- What (if any) pain do you experience? Describe its location, intensity, duration, and frequency.
- What drugs do you take for your condition(s), how effective are they, and what side effects (if any) do you experience from these drugs?
- What doctors, clinics, hospitals have you visited, for how long, and for what conditions?
- What specific tasks of your former job(s) are you unable to do now?
- What limitations are there on your ability to walk, stand, sit, stretch, breathe, squat, push, pull, and lift?
- What is a typical day like for you?
- To what extent can you do household chores?
- Can you prepare your own meals?
- Do you drive your own car?
- How do you spend your time?
- How well do you sleep?
- What do your social activities consist of?
- What difficulty do you have in remembering things or carrying out instructions?

These questions are intended to give the judge the information needed to analyze properly whether you are disabled. If you are not represented, be certain that you give the judge specific and detailed information regarding:

- Any pain you experience. You should tell the judge where you experience the pain, how long it lasts, what it feels like, whether medication helps and to what degree, and how the pain interferes with your ability to work and perform basic activities. You should also, if possible, get documentation from your doctor concerning this pain and its cause.
- Any limitation you have in performing daily activities.
- The specific duties of your former work, and what you are not able to do now.
- The extent to which the medication you take interferes with your ability to work and perform daily activities.

- The extent to which your quitting your job(s) or changing jobs reflected your inability to perform adequately because of your disabilities.

It is important to provide all this information for your appeal at the hearing level because normally new evidence cannot be submitted after the hearing decision has been issued. If the new evidence is material to your claim, it may be possible to submit it after the hearing level if you are able to establish good cause for *not* submitting it at the hearing and if it relates to your condition prior to the date the hearing decision was issued.[63]

What is a "vocational expert"?

A vocational expert is a witness that the ALJ may call to attend an SSA disability hearing. The purpose of this witness is to provide expert testimony concerning whether there are jobs in significant numbers in the national economy which you are capable of performing. In conducting this analysis, the vocational expert must take into account your age, education, prior work experience, and medical conditions. If a vocational expert is going to be at your hearing, you are entitled to receive notice of this in writing; the notice you receive of the date and time of the hearing should also state whether a vocational expert will be present.

In many SSA disability hearings, a vocational expert is not present. But if one is, normally it will be because (1) there is an issue in your case regarding whether you have skills that can be transferred to other jobs; (2) there is an issue in your case involving nonexertional impairment(s) (for example, problems with hearing, seeing, remembering, or other mental problems); or (3) there is an issue involving whether you can perform the full range of work in a specific exertional category (such as medium or light work). The vocational expert can provide testimony on these issues and state—in response to hypothetical questions from the ALJ—the number and availability of jobs in the national economy which you can perform with your particular vocational background.

To cross-examine a vocational expert effectively generally requires professional legal assistance. Therefore, if a vocational expert is called to your hearing, you should seek the assistance of an attorney or paralegal experienced in this area of law.

What witnesses should I bring to my SSA disability hearing?

A witness can be helpful to you by testifying concerning areas such as your prior work, your overall health, and your daily activities. Typically, a witness is a friend or relative who knows you well and sees you frequently. Obviously, if your doctor or former employer can testify, that would be very helpful although this rarely happens. You should always know in advance what your witness can say about your condition, former employment, and daily activities. Generally, the testimony of the witness(es) is short and is based only on the witness' personal knowledge of you. Some situations in which a witness might be particularly helpful are:

- if you do not feel that you are very articulate about your condition or that you will have difficulty explaining to the judge all your medical problems;
- if you experience a great deal of pain;
- if you have a mental impairment of any type;
- if you have seizures;
- if you have had problems with alcohol or drugs.

What if my witness(es) cannot attend the hearing?

In most cases it is much better for your witness(es) to be at the hearing. If your witness or witnesses cannot attend the hearing, you can have them write statements and submit the statements to the ALJ. The statement should address these issues:

- why the witness could not be present at the hearing;
- what relationship the witness is to you (friend, neighbor, relative, former employer);
- how long the witness has known you;
- based on the witness' personal knowledge, the limitations imposed on you in light of your medical condition. (The more detail that can be provided here, the better, especially if he or she has observed any behavior of yours such as shaking, falling, or shortness of breath.).

The statement should be signed and dated. Ideally, this statement should be notarized, but this is not an absolute requirement.

What happens after the hearing?

Normally the ALJ will not make his decision at the close of the hearing but will usually send a written decision in a month or several months from the date of the hearing. If the hearing decision is favorable to you, and you have an SSI claim, you then will be asked to visit your local Social Security office. There an SSA claims worker will ask you questions regarding your income, resources, and living arrangement in order to verify whether you meet the financial eligibility criteria for SSI, to calculate any retroactive benefits (from the date of your SSI application) to which you are entitled, and to calculate the amount of SSI you are entitled to on a monthly basis. Assuming that you have provided the SSA with all the necessary information concerning your finances and your living arrangement, you then will receive a notice from the SSA telling you the amount of retroactive SSI benefits (if any) to which you are entitled and the amount of your monthly SSI benefits. If you believe the amounts are incorrect, you can of course appeal this decision.[64] Consult chapter 2 of this book concerning how appropriate benefit amounts are determined. After receiving a favorable decision involving Social Security disability, the SSA will send you an "award letter." This letter will tell you the amount of any retroactive benefits you are to receive and the amount you are to receive on a monthly basis.

RECEIVING BENEFITS

Once I start getting disability benefits are there any changes I need to report?

Yes. If you are receiving Social Security or SSI disability benefits, you should report any of the following situations to the SSA:

- if your medical condition improves to the point that you go back to work
- if you go back to work
- if you begin earning more money
- if you receive worker compensation or other public disability benefits
- if there is a death of a family member collecting on your account

If my medical condition improves, can the SSA cut off my disability benefits?

Generally, the SSA can cut off your disability benefits based on medical improvement only if your medical condition has improved to the point at which you are able to engage in substantial gainful activity. This relatively recent change in the law came as a result of pressure from many sources on the SSA to alter its policy with regard to terminating benefits. The SSA had taken the position that an individual must always be able to show that he or she is disabled, and the SSA could terminate an individual's benefits if they considered that person not disabled according to the sequential evaluation process addressed earlier in this chapter. Courts across the country ordered the SSA to apply a medical improvement standard under which the SSA would have to come forward with evidence that the individual's condition had improved since the SSA last reviewed the claim.[65] Congress—in response to public outcry and to court decisions—set forth certain conditions that would have to be met before benefits could be terminated in the Social Security Benefits Reform Act of 1984.[66] Final regulations on this new medical improvement standard were published by the SSA in December, 1985.[67] The process the SSA uses to determine whether they should terminate your benefits based on medical improvement is a complex step-by-step analysis briefly outlined below.[68]

Step One: Are you engaging in substantial gainful activity? This question is addressed above in the section of this chapter on eligibility. The same analysis is undertaken in these circumstances except that you can take advantage of a "trial work period,"[69] a period of time (usually nine months) in which you can attempt to go back to work without such an attempt having an adverse affect on your receipt of disability benefits. If the trial work period is over, and you are engaging in substantial gainful activity, then the SSA will find the disability to have ended. If not, the SSA proceeds to step two.

Step Two: Do your current impairments meet or equal the listings? Again, this question is the same as discussed above. An analysis of your condition is made in light of the Listing of Impairments.[70] If an individual's impairments meet or equal a listing, disability benefits continue. If not, the SSA proceeds to step three.

Step Three: Has there been medical improvement in your condition(s) since the time of the last review? This step involves a comparison of the severity of the medical impairments you demonstrated at the prior review of your claim as compared to their current severity. This step of the analysis compares only the impairments previously documented at a prior review and does not include new medical impairments which may have arisen subsequently. If there has been medical improvement based on this restricted comparison, the SSA proceeds to step four. At the time the SSA notifies you that they are reviewing your case, you should submit to the SSA any new medical evidence you have or can obtain concerning your condition. You should retain copies of all your medical records for yourself as well so that you have a complete record of your claim. If there has been no medical improvement, the SSA proceeds to step five.

Step Four: Is the medical improvement related to your ability to work? In this step, the SSA looks at the assessment done previously as to your residual functional capacity and—taking into account only those impairments listed previously—attempts to create a current assessment of your residual functional capacity.

This step is fraught with problems—particularly because the SSA is in many cases creating a fictional assessment not based on all the current impairments of an individual, but only on those existing at the time of the prior review. This procedure may well be subject to litigation in the future. Nevertheless if the SSA finds at this point that the medical improvement is related to your ability to work, it proceeds to step six. If not, it proceeds to step five.

Step Five: Do any of the group one or group two exceptions apply? There are certain exceptions to the medical improvement standard that are categorized in two groups. The exceptions in group one are as follows.

1. New medical evidence and a new assessment of an individual's residual functional capacity show not that an individual's medical condition has improved, but that the individual has been a beneficiary of advances in medical or vocational therapy or technology (related to the individual's ability to work) and can now perform substantial gainful activity.
2. The individual has not improved medically but has undergone vocational therapy (related to the individual's ability to work) and can now perform substantial gainful activity.

3. Because of new or improved diagnostic techniques or evaluations the individual's impairment or combination of impairments is not as disabling as it was considered to be at the time of the most recent prior decision and that *therefore* the individual is capable of engaging in substantial gainful activity.
4. There is substantial evidence that the prior determination was in error.[71]

The exceptions to the medical improvement standard categorized in group two are as follows:

1. The prior determination was fraudulently obtained.
2. The individual engaged in substantial gainful activity.
3. The SSA cannot locate the person.
4. The person without good cause fails to cooperate in a review.
5. The person without good cause fails to follow prescribed treatment.[72]

If one of the exceptions in group one applies, the SSA proceeds to step six. If one of the exceptions in group two applies, the SSA finds that there is no disability and proceeds to terminate benefits. If no exceptions apply, then benefits continue. Note that the exceptions in group two can be applied throughout the evaluation process, not only at step five.

Step Six: Do you have a severe impairment? If you do not meet this test, benefits are terminated. If your residual functional capacity assessment as described in step four shows significant limitation in your ability to do basic work activities, the SSA goes to step seven. If the answer to the question based on all impairments is yes, the SSA also proceeds to step seven.

Step Seven: Do you—based on all current impairments— have the residual functional capacity to return to your past relevant work?[73] This step is essentially the same as step five as discussed in the eligibility section of this chapter. Note that at this point, the SSA must consider your current impairments and not just those you had when you were previously determined to be disabled. Therefore, your task here is to explain and document with medical evidence any additional medical problems that have arisen since your prior review.

If it is determined—based on all current impairments—that

you can return to past relevant work, your benefits are terminated. If not, the SSA proceeds to step eight.

Step Eight: If you are unable to return to your past work, the SSA determines whether you can perform other work. This step is described in detail as step six in the eligibility section. At this step, your age, education, and prior work experience are factored into the process of determining whether you are disabled. If the SSA finds that you can perform other work, your benefits are terminated; if not, your benefits are continued.

Is the process described in the previous question the same process the SSA uses if I am receiving the special type of disability benefits described above for disabled widows, widowers, and surviving divorced spouses?

No. As noted above, the special disability benefits are obtainable only if you meet the conditions of the Listings of Impairments. This special disability program therefore pays benefits based on medical criteria alone. Therefore, the standard for medical improvement is different from the process explained in the previous question.[74] The process differs in that there is no severity step, the listing step comes before the medical improvement review, and inability to do past work or other substantial gainful activity is not part of the analysis. The process used in special disability benefits is described below.

Step One: Is the person engaging in substantial gainful activity? If the answer is yes and the trial work period is over, then SSA will find that your disability has ended.

Step Two: Has there been medical improvement in the conditions the person had at the time of the last review (based on the medical listings used at that time)? If the answer is yes, then go to step three. If the answer is no, go to step four.

Step Three: Is the medical improvement related to the person's ability to work? If the answer is yes, go to step five. If the answer is no, go to step four.

Step Four: If the answers to step two or step three were no, do any of the exceptions in group one or group two apply? (For more information on the exceptions turn to the previous question in this chapter.) If a group two exception applies, go to step five. If a group two exception applies, disability ends. If no exceptions apply, benefits continue.

Step Five: If the answer to step three or step four is yes, then

SSA determines whether the person's current impairment(s) meet or equal the current Listing of Impairments. If they do meet the current listings, benefits continue. If not, disability benefits end.

The SSA has sent me a notice telling me that they no longer consider me disabled. What do I do to contest this decision?

To contest the decision by the SSA, you should request a reconsideration as explained in the section of this chapter on appeals. It is extremely important that you appeal within ten days of your receipt of this notice *and*—within those same ten days— state in writing that you want your benefits continued during the appeal.[75] Ultimately of course, you can appeal any time within sixty days of the receipt of the notice, but receipt of benefits pending your review may be jeopardized.

There is now a procedure under which individuals in these medical cessation cases will be afforded a face-to-face reconsideration.[76] This means that you will have an opportunity to present your case before a disability hearing officer. This hearing generally will be held in an office of the state disability determination service rather than at a Social Security office. This face-to-face reconsideration hearing does not replace the hearing before an administrative law judge. You always have a right to a hearing before an administrative law judge if you appeal an adverse reconsideration decision. In this instance as well, you should request an appeal within ten days and state that you wish to receive benefits pending a hearing decision. Of course, here too you have a right to appeal within sixty days.

What rights do I have at my face-to-face reconsideration hearing?

You have a number of rights at your face-to-face reconsideration hearing.

1. You may request that the agency assist in obtaining pertinent evidence.[77]
2. You may request that the agency issue a subpoena to compel the production of evidence or testimony.[78]
3. You may have a representative who may be an attorney or other authorized individual.[79]
4. You or your authorized representative may review the evidence in your file either on the date of your hearing or at an earlier time at your request.[80]

5. You may present witnesses and question any witnesses at your hearing.[81]
6. You may waive your right to appear at the hearing.[82] (Generally, it is in your best interest *not* to waive your right to appear.)
7. You may ask to have the record left open for up to fifteen days after the hearing in order to submit additional evidence under certain circumstances.[83]
8. You have the right to review and comment on any additional evidence the agency obtains after the hearing. The agency must notify you in writing of this additional evidence and you will have ten days to respond.[84]
9. You have the right to a copy of a proposed reconsideration decision if it is one where the director "corrects the deficiency" in a hearing officer's proposed decision. You have a right to submit written comments before it is issued and a right to review your file and the proposed decision of the hearing examiner. You must submit your comments within ten days.[85]

If SSA finds that I am no longer disabled, what are some helpful points to keep in mind in appealing my case?

A few helpful points are:

1. Always appeal your case in a timely manner. If you want to receive benefits pending an appeal, request your appeal within ten days and state that you want benefits pending.

2. Review your file at the agency well in advance of the hearing. Go through each document carefully and make sure that SSA's records are thorough, complete, and up to date.

3. Always make sure that your file at SSA is current and complete. Gather all your recent medical records and reports and make sure that all your impairments are well documented in SSA's files.

4. Personally appear at the face-to-face reconsideration hearing. There you will be able to tell the decisionmaker about your condition and demonstrate why you are not capable of working.

If I lose at my face-to-face reconsideration hearing, what can I do?

You still have the right to request a hearing before an administrative law judge (ALJ). You can appeal an adverse hearing decision at the ALJ level to the Appeals Council, and then you can appeal to federal district court.

Is it really worth taking my disability case to federal court?
In many instances, yes. The number of Social Security cases that are reversed or remanded at the federal court level is very significant. In fact, your chances of success at that level of appeal are much greater than at the Appeals Council. There is a very large body of caselaw on the disability programs under SSI and OASDI.[86] The law is complex, and the procedures in federal court require the submission of briefs. At this level of the appeal process, it is essential to be represented by an attorney who is knowledgeable and experienced in the disability area.

At the federal court level, you will not have the opportunity to appear or testify before the judge. The court will decide the case based on the evidence already in the record, the briefs submitted by your attorney and the SSA's attorney, and (in some instances) oral argument by the attorneys. The scope of the review by the court is limited to determining whether there is substantial evidence to support the decision by the SSA. Substantial evidence is defined as "such relevant evidence as a reasonable mind might accept as adequate to support a conclusion."[87]

In determining whether there is substantial evidence to support the SSA's decision, there are numerous legal issues and potential legal errors that a federal court may consider. One general area that courts will examine very carefully is the manner in which the ALJ conducted the hearing, developed the record, and analyzed the case in his or her decision. This is especially true when the claimant is unrepresented. Other very common areas where legal error is found include proper assessment of pain or nonexertional impairments; appropriate consideration of the treating physician's opinion as opposed to the consultative physician's opinion; proper analysis of the claim in light of the medical listings, the medical vocational guidelines, or the substantial gainful activity criteria.[88]

What are some other common reasons for losing SSI or Social Security Disability benefits?
A person who—without good reason—fails to have a physical examination required by the SSA may lose benefits. The SSA

often sends recipients for a consultative examination at the SSA's expense. A recipient should submit to this examination unless he or she has good reason (such as illness, lack of notice, inaccurate information, a death or serious illness in the immediate family).[89]

If a treatment can restore your ability to work, then you must follow that treatment. The treatment must be prescribed (as opposed to merely suggested) and may be refused if there is good cause (such as in a surgical procedure that poses great risk). Failure to follow a prescribed treatment without good cause can result in the loss of benefits.[90] Furthermore, if you are considered disabled because you are an alcoholic or a drug addict, you can lose your benefits if you fail to comply with the terms, conditions, and requirements of your treatment.[91]

Finally, if you fail to provide the SSA with the information they need (e.g., medical or other evidence), you may lose your benefits.[92]

NOTES

1. 42 U.S.C. §§ 401–433 (1982 & Supp. III 1985) (Social Security Disability); 42 U.S.C. §§ 1381–1383c (1982 & Supp. III 1985) (Supplemental Security Income Program).
2. 42 U.S.C. §§ 1381(a) (1982 & Supp. III 1985).
3. 42 U.S.C. § 1382(d) (1982).
4. 42 U.S.C. § 423(a) (1982 & Supp. III 1985) (disability); 42 U.S.C. § 402(e)(1))B)(i) (1982 & Supp. III 1985) (widow's benefits); 42 U.S.C. § 402(f)(1)(B)(i) (1982 & Supp. III 1985) (widower's benefits).
5. 42 U.S.C. § 402(e)(1)(C)(i) (1982 & Supp. III 1985) (widow's insurance requirement); 42 U.S.C. § 402(f)(1)(C) (1982 & Supp. III 1985) (widower's insurance requirement).
6. 42 U.S.C. § 402(e)(1)(D) (1982 & Supp. III 1985) (widow's requirements); 42 U.S.C. § 402(f)(1)(D) (1982 & Supp. III 1985) (widower's requirements).
7. 42 U.S.C. § 423(d)(1) (1982 & Supp. III 1985). 42 U.S.C. § 1382c(a)(3)(A) (1982 & Supp. III 1985).
8. 42 U.S.C. § 423(d)(2)(A) (1982 & Supp. III 1985).
9. *Compare* 42 U.S.C. § 423(d)(2)(B) (1982 & Supp. III 1985) (disability definition for widow, surviving divorced wife, widower, and surviving divorced husband) *with* 42 U.S.C. § 423(d)(1)(A) (1982 & Supp. III 1985) (disability definition for all other individuals).

10. 42 U.S.C. § 402(q)(1) (1982 & Supp. III 1985).

11. See ch. 1 concerning the insured status requirements.

12. 42 U.S.C. § 426(b) (1982 & Supp. IV 1985).

13. 20 C.F.R. §§ 404.410(c)(1)–(2)(1987).

14. 20 C.F.R. § 404.1520(1987); 20 C.F.R. §§ 416.920(1987).

15. 20 C.F.R. §§ 404.1571–.1575(1987); 20 C.F.R. §§ 416.971–.975(1987).

16. 20 C.F.R. § 404.1572(a)(1987); 20 C.F.R. § 416.972(a)(1987).

17. 20 C.F.R. § 404.1572(c)(1987); 20 C.F.R. § 416.971(c)(1987).

18. 20 C.F.R. § 404.1573(a)(1987); 20 C.F.R. § 416.973(a)(1987).

19. 20 C.F.R. §§ 404.1573(b)–(e)(1987); 20 C.F.R. §§ 416.973(b)–(e) (1987).

20. 20 C.F.R. §§ 404.1574(b)(2)(vi), .1574(a)(3)(vi)(1987); 20 C.F.R. §§ 416.974(a)(2)(vi), .974(a)(3)(vi)(1987).

21. 20 C.F.R. § 404.1575(1987); 20 C.F.R. § 416.975(1987).

22. 20 C.F.R. § 404.1523(1987); 20 C.F.R. § 416.923(1987).

23. 20 C.F.R. § 404.1521(1987); 20 C.F.R. § 416.921(1987).

24. Background Material and Data on Major Programs within Jurisdiction of the Committee on Ways and Means: Report of the House Committee on Ways and Means, 98th Cong., 1st Sess. 79 (1983).

25. *Baeder v. Heckler*, 768 F.2d 547, 553 (3d Cir. 1985); *Johnson v. Heckler*, 769 F.2d 1202, 1213 (7th Cir. 1985); *Brown v. Heckler*, 786 F.2d 870, 873 (8th Cir. 1986); *Yuckert v. Heckler*, 774 F.2d 1365, 1370 (9th Cir. 1985); *rev'd sub nom. Bowen v. Yuckert*, 107 S. Ct. 2287 (1987), *Hansen v. Heckler*, 783 F.2d 170, 176 (10th Cir. 1986).

26. *See McDonald v. Secretary of Health and Human Servs.*, 795 F.2d 1118, 1123, 1125 (1st Cir. 1986); *Chico v. Schweiker* 710 F.2d 947, 954-55 n.10; (2d. Cir. 1983); *Evans v. Heckler*, 734 F.2d 1012, 1014 n.3 (4th Cir. 1984); *Stone v. Heckler*, 752 F.2d 1099, 1101 (5th Cir. 1985); *Salmi v. Secretary of Health and Human Servs.*, 774 F.2d 685, 691 (6th Cir. 1985).

27. *Brady v. Heckler*, 724 F.2d 914, 920 (11th Cir. 1984).

28. Social Security Ruling 85-28 (1985).

29. 107 S. Ct. 2287 (1987).

30. 20 C.F.R. pt. 404, Subpt. P, app. 1 (1987).

31. 20 C.F.R. § 404.1526(a) (1987); 20 C.F.R. § 416.926(a) (1987).

32. 20 C.F.R. § 404.1577 (1987).

33. 20 C.F.R. § 416.924 (1987).

34. 20 C.F.R. pt. 404, subpt. P, app. 2 (1987).

35. 20 C.F.R. § 404.1564(b)(2) (1987); 20 C.F.R. § 416.964(b)(2) (1987).

36. 20 C.F.R. § 404.1562 (1987); 20 C.F.R. § 416.962 (1987).

37. 20 C.F.R. pt. 404, subpt. P, app. 1 (1987).

38. 50 Fed. Reg. 35054-35070 (Aug. 28, 1985); *see also* 20 C.F.R. pt. 404, supt. P, app. 1 (1987).

39. 20 C.F.R. pt. 404, subpt. P, app. 1, pt. A, pt. B (1987).

40. 20 C.F.R. pt. 404, subpt. P, app. 2 (1987).

41. *Heckler v. Campbell* 461 U.S. 468 (1983).

42. 20 C.F.R. § 404.1567(d) (1987); 20 C.F.R. § 416.967(d) (1987).

43. 20 C.F.R. § 404.1567(c) (1987); 20 C.F.R. § 416.967(c) (1987).

44. 20 C.F.R. § 404.1567(b) (1987); 20 C.F.R. § 416.967(b) (1987).

45. 20 C.F.R. § 404.1567(a) (1987); 20 C.F.R. § 416.967(a) (1987).

46. 20 C.F.R. § 404.1567(e) (1987); 20 C.F.R. § 416.967(e) (1987).

47. 20 C.F.R. pt. 404, subpt. P, app. 2, table no. 3, rule 203.01 (1987).

48. 20 C.F.R. pt. 404, subpt. P, app. 2 § 200.00(e) (1987).

49. 20 C.F.R. § 404.320 (1987).

50. 20 C.F.R. § 404.1520(e) (1987); 20 C.F.R. § 416.920(e) (1987).

51. 20 C.F.R. § 404.1517 (1987); 20 C.F.R. § 416.912 (1987).

52. 20 C.F.R. § 404.1518 (1987); 20 C.F.R. § 416.918 (1987).

53. A few examples are: *Mitchell v. Schweiker*, 699 F.2d 185 (4th Cir. 1983); *Broadbent v. Harris*, 698 F.2d 407 (10th Cir. 1983); *Narrol v. Heckler*, 727 F.2d 1303 (D.C. Cir. 1984).

54. 20 C.F.R. §§ 416.931–.934 (1987).

55. 42 U.S.C. 1383(b)(1)(B) (Supp. III, 1985).

56. 42 U.S.C. § 405(b)(2) (1982 & Supp. III 1985).

57. It is highly recommended that you secure an attorney or paralegal to represent you at a hearing. The text is written, however, so that the reader who is not represented will know generally what steps need to be taken.

58. 20 C.F.R. § 404.938 (1987); 20 C.F.R. § 416.1438 (1987).

59. 20 C.F.R. § 401.405 (1987). The SSA experimented with a system in which a representative of the SSA would present the SSA's case at hearings reviewing reconsideration determinations. After this trial period the SSA decided not to proceed further with the adversarial experiment. 52 Fed. Reg. 17, 285 (May 7, 1987).

60. 20 C.F.R. § 404.944 (1987); 20 C.F.R. § 416.1444 (1987).

61. There are a large number of cases on this point as well. A few examples of some recent cases are: *Lashley v. Secretary of HHS*, 708 F.2d at 1048 (6th Cir. 1983); *Bluvband v. Heckler*, 730 F.2d 886 (2d Cir. 1984); *Early v. Heckler*, 743 F.2d 1002 (3rd Cir. 1984); *Kane v. Heckler*, 731 F.2d 1216 (5th Cir. 1984); *Narrol v. Heckler*, 727 F.2d 1303 (D.C. Cir. 1984).

62. *Id.*

63. 42 U.S.C. § 405(g) (1982) (concerning "good cause" requirement for court remand); 20 C.F.R. §§ 404.970, .976, .979, 416.1470, .1476, .1479 (1987) (concerning Appeals Council consideration of evidence).

64. 20 C.F.R. §§ 404.907–.981 (1987); 20 C.F.R. §§ 416.1407–.1491 (1987).

65. There are a large number of court decisions concerning the burden

of proof in medical cessation cases. *See, e.g., Parente v. Heckler*, 735 F.2d 743 (2d Cir. 1984); *Early v. Heckler*, 743 F.2d 1002 (3d Cir. 1984); *Dotson v. Schweiker*, 719 F.2d 80 (4th Cir. 1983).

66. 42 U.S.C. § 423(f) (1982 & Supp. III 1985).

67. 50 Fed. Reg. 50118–50147 (Dec. 6, 1985).

68. A much more detailed discussion of the medical improvement regulations can be found in an article entitled, "The New Medical Improvement Standard in Social Security and SSI Disability Cases," Mar. 1986, by Eileen P. Sweeney, National Senior Citizens Law Center, Suite 400, 2025 M St. N.W., Washington D.C. 20036.

69. *See supra* note 66.

70. *See supra* note 38 and accompanying text.

71. 20 C.F.R. § 404.1594 (d) 20 C.F.R. § 404.1579 (d) (1987); 20 C.F.R. § 416.994 (b) (3) (1987); 20 C.F.R. § 416.994 (c) (3) (1987).

72. 20 C.F.R. § 404.1594 (e) (1987); 20 C.F.R. § 404.1579 (e) (1987); 20 C.F.R. § 416.994(b)(4) (1987); 20 C.F.R. § 416.994(c)(4) (1987).

73. 20 C.F.R. § 404.1594(f)(7) (1987); 20 C.F.R. § 416.994(b)(5)(vii) (1987).

74. *See generally* 20 C.F.R. § 404.1579 (1987).

75. 20 C.F.R. § 416.1336(b) (1987).

76. 20 C.F.R. § 404.913–.921 (1987); 20 C.F.R. § 416.1413–.1421 (1987).

77. 20 C.F.R. § 404.916(b)(1) (1987); 20 C.F.R. § 416.1416(b)(1) (1987).

78. *Id.*

79. 20 C.F.R. § 404.916(b)(2) (1987); 20 C.F.R. § 416.1416(b)(2) (1987).

80. 20 C.F.R. § 404.916(b)(3) (1987); 20 C.F.R. § 416.1416(b)(3) (1987).

81. 20 C.F.R. § 404.916(b)(4) (1987); 20 C.F.R. § 416.1416(b)(4) (1987).

82. 20 C.F.R. § 404.916(b)(5) (1987); 20 C.F.R. § 416.1416(b)(5) (1987).

83. 20 C.F.R. § 404.916(e) (1987); 20 C.F.R. § 416.1416(e) (1987).

84. 20 C.F.R. § 404.916(f) (1987); 20 C.F.R. § 416.1416(f) (1987).

85. 20 C.F.R. § 404.918 (1987); 20 C.F.R. § 416.1418 (1987).

86. For examples of cases and common issues, see M. Schuster, *Disability Practice Manual for Social Security and SSI Programs* and its 1986–87 supplement; and app. 4D, *Recent Decisions in Disability Case Law* (Legal Counsel for the Elderly, AARP, 1985).

87. *Richardson v. Perales*, 402 U.S. 389 (1971).

88. *Supra* note 86.

89. 20 C.F.R. § 404.1518 (1987); 20 C.F.R. § 416.918 (1987).

90. 20 C.F.R. § 404.1530 (1987); 20 C.F.R. § 416.930 (1987).

91. 20 C.F.R. §§ 416.935–.939 (1987).

92. 20 C.F.R. § 404.1593, 1594(e); 20 C.F.R. § 416.993, 994(b)(4)(ii) (1987).

4

Civil Service and Railroad Pension Programs

CIVIL SERVICE RETIREMENT

What type of retirement benefits are available to employees of the federal government?

Since 1984 when newly hired federal workers were brought into the Social Security system for the first time, there have been major changes to the retirement system applicable to federal employees. One system is known as the Civil Service Retirement System (CSRS).[1] The other system is known as the Federal Employees' Retirement System (FERS).[2] CSRS, in general, covers federal employees hired prior to 1984; FERS covers all new federal employees hired after 31 December 1986. There are special rules applicable to certain employees hired or rehired between 1 January 1984 and 31 December 1986.[3] Also, all employees covered by CSRS have been given a limited opportunity to elect to be covered by FERS. Both programs co-exist under and—for the most part—are administered by the Office of Personnel Management (OPM).[4] The rules applicable to CSRS and FERS are complicated. For more detailed information concerning these programs you may consult the OPM or the personnel office of the agency for which you work or worked. Be aware that there are many questions concerning the proper interpretation of CSRS and FERS and that litigation may be necessary to resolve these questions. For this reason do not hesitate to seek legal assistance if you are denied benefits to which you believe yourself entitled.

What are the essential elements of CSRS?

CSRS is financed by mandatory payroll deductions and employing agency contributions. The employing agency obtains the funds that it is required to contribute through federal budget appropriation procedures. The employee's annuity (or pension) paid pursuant to CSRS is in lieu of Social Security benefits.

Annuities or lump sum benefits are payable under CSRS to employees or their survivors on the basis of age, years of service, and other criteria. Generally speaking, the amount of a CSRS annuity is based on the employee's average wage for the three consecutive years of highest pay and on his length of employment.[5] An alternative formula is permitted if it provides a higher annuity.[6]

To be eligible for CSRS benefits, an employee must have worked a specific number of years in a CSRS-covered job category. If an employee has made the required annual contributions, CSRS credit will generally be given for civilian government service and military service.[7] Unused sick leave days can also be counted in calculating length of service.[8] And there are provisions which enable some employees to receive additional CSRS credit by purchasing additional annuities or by making voluntary contributions for prior years of military or civilian service for which no contribution was made to CSRS.[9]

Depending on the length of federal employment, a person may be eligible for either of two types of CSRS annuities. Persons who have worked at least five years in a CSRS-covered position before leaving for a job outside the federal civil service system are eligible for a "deferred" annuity. A deferred annuity is not payable until the employee has attained the age of 62.[10] A second type of annuity is referred to as an "immediate" annuity. Immediate annuities are payable thirty days after voluntary retirement from federal employment to persons who qualify under a formula based on age and length of employment. Immediate annuities are available to persons who are age 62 and have five years of employment, age 60 and have twenty years of employment, or age 55 and have thirty years of employment.[11]

Within CSRS there are special retirement provisions for certain classes of employees such as law enforcement officers, fire fighters, and air-traffic controllers.[12] Also, for persons who leave federal employment under special circumstances, such as during a reduction of the work force, annuities can begin immediately if they have worked at least twenty-five years for the federal government or if they are 50 years of age and have twenty years of federal employment.[13] For certain persons leaving employment with the federal government for another job there is the option to receive a lump-sum payment of all accrued benefits in lieu of an annuity.[14] And lump-sum death benefits are payable when an employee or retiree dies without survivors or when a former employee dies before retirement.[15] Finally, CSRS has a Thrift Savings Plan option so that most employees can save up to 5 percent of their salary and receive a tax break.[16]

What are the essential elements of FERS?

FERS provides retirement benefits from three different sources: (1) a Basic Benefit Plan, (2) Social Security, and (3) the Thrift Savings Plan.

1. *Basic Benefit Plan* The Basic Benefit Plan is funded through contributions from federal employees and the federal government. To be eligible to receive the Basic Benefit Plan you must have at least five years of creditable civilian service with the federal government.[17] Survivor and disability benefits are available after eighteen months of creditable service.[18] Creditable civilian service generally includes federal civil service and military service for which a contribution has been paid.[19]

A person can retire with a Basic Benefit as soon as he reaches what is known as the "minimum retirement age" (MRA) and has ten years of creditable civilian service. The MRA is the first year in which you can receive benefits and varies according to the year in which you were born.[20] For example, for anyone born before 1948, the MRA is age 55. A person can also retire when his age and years of federal service match one of another set of retirement combinations—for example: for 5 years of service, benefits begin at age 62; for 20 years of service at 60 years of age; for 30 years of service at your MRA.[21] If at your MRA you have only 10 years of creditable civilian service, you can wait until age 62 for full benefits and get a "deferred" annuity, or you can begin receiving reduced benefits any time before age 62.[22] FERS provides a Special Retirement Supplement for those who retire after 30 years of service at their MRA and those who retire at age 60 after 20 or more years of service. This Special Retirement Supplement is paid until age 62 when a person is eligible for Social Security benefits; however, the amount of the Special Retirement Supplement may be reduced if the retiree's income is higher than an allowable amount.[23] FERS also permits withdrawal of contributions to the Basic Benefit Plan when an employee leaves federal employment.[24] If this option is exercised, that person will not be eligible to receive Basic Benefits based on service covered by the refund.

2. *Social Security* For purposes of FERS, "Social Security" means benefit payments provided to workers and their dependents who qualify as beneficiaries under Old-Age, Survivors, and Disability Insurance (OASDI) programs of the Social Security Act. The rules applicable to Social Security under FERS are the same as those applicable to any person receiving benefits under the Social Security Act.

3. *Thrift Savings Plan* The third part of the FERS package is a tax deferred savings plan. All federal employees covered by FERS are eligible to participate in the Thrift Savings Plan (usually within six to twelve months after hire).[25] The employing government agency automatically contributes an amount equal to 1 percent of the employee's pay to a savings account each pay period even if the employee does not contribute each pay period.[26] Additionally, if an employee chooses, he may contribute up to 10 percent of his pay to the savings plan through payroll deductions, and the government will match a portion of those savings according to a sliding schedule with a maximum match of 5 percent of the employee's salary.[27]

Funds may be withdrawn from the Thrift Savings Plan when the employee retires, becomes disabled, or leaves federal employment if at that time the employee's right to the FERS Basic Benefit Plan has become vested.[28] Depending upon length of service and age, an employee (or that employee's beneficiaries) may elect to receive savings in the form of an annuity or lump-sum payment or to roll it over into an Individual Retirement Account or similar plan.[29] In some circumstances, the employee may borrow from the savings plan account for serious financial needs such as the purchase of a home, medical expenses, educational expenses, and financial hardship.[30]

Are disability benefits provided under CSRS and FERS?

Yes. Both CSRS and FERS provide disability benefits; however, the disability benefits offered by the two plans differ in several respects. CSRS requires a minimum of five years employment in a CSRS-covered position to qualify for benefits,[31] while FERS requires only eighteen months of FERS-covered service to qualify for disability.[32] However, if a person applies for disability benefits under FERS that person must also apply for

Social Security disability insurance benefits or show that he is not eligible for those benefits.[33]

CSRS and FERS both use essentially the same definition of disability. To be found disabled under either system, an employee must be unable because of disease or injury to render useful and efficient service either in the employee's current position or in a vacant position in the same agency at the same grade or pay level for which that employee is qualified to render useful and efficient service.[34] In general, it is easier to establish disability under CSRS and FERS than to establish disability under Social Security.

Under CSRS, disability benefits will generally be equal to the employee's projected pension benefits at age 60 or to 40 percent of the employee's average salary for the three consecutive highest salary years.[35] Cost of living benefits will be added annually at the full rate of inflation.

Under FERS, in general, during the first year of disability an employee will be paid 60 percent of his average salary for the three consecutive highest salary years minus 100 percent of an approximation of any Social Security insurance benefit for which that person qualifies.[36] After the first year and until age 62, if a person remains disabled and does not qualify for Social Security, the FERS disability benefit will be 40 percent of average pay for the three consecutive highest salary years. If the disabled person qualifies for Social Security insurance benefits, the FERS disability benefits will be reduced by 60 percent of the initial Social Security benefit to which that person is entitled.[37] Cost of living benefits will be added annually although this benefit may be somewhat less than the rate of inflation.

Do CSRS and FERS provide for survivors' benefits?

Yes. Both CSRS and FERS provide for survivors' benefits. Under both CSRS and FERS, surviving spouses must meet certain requirements such as age and length of marriage (i.e., nine months unless death is due to accident) in order to qualify for benefits.[38] An election can be made to provide benefits for a spouse married after a federal employee has retired;[39] and, for a married retiree, the annuity is reduced in order to provide survivors' benefits for the employee's spouse unless the employee *and* the spouse waive this benefit.

CSRS survivors' benefits. If a federal employee covered by the CSRS program dies after completing eighteen months of covered service, that employee's surviving spouse is entitled to survivors' benefits.[40] In general, if an employee dies while working for the government, the employee's spouse will receive at least 55 percent of the employee's accrued benefit.[41] If a person dies while a CSRS retiree, an eligible spouse will be paid 55 percent of the amount the deceased retiree was receiving in benefits or a lesser amount that the retiree and spouse agreed on at the time of retirement.[42] The benefits to which eligible children of a deceased employee covered by CSRS will be entitled depend on how many children that employee had and whether or not the spouse is still living.[43]

FERS survivors' benefits. If a person dies as a federal civilian employee covered by FERS with at least eighteen months of FERS-covered employment, eligible survivors will receive benefits. If a person dies while a federal civilian employee with more than eighteen months of FERS-covered service but less than ten years of total service, an eligible spouse will receive a lump-sum payment of $15,000 plus the higher of either half of the deceased employee's annual salary at the time of death or half of the average pay for the three consecutive years of highest pay.[44] If the deceased employee had ten years of covered service, an eligible spouse will also receive an annuity equal to one-half of the accrued Basic Benefit Plan.[45] If an employee met the Social Security eligibility requirements at the time of death, his survivors may also be entitled to Social Security survivors' benefits. Under FERS, surviving children (of employees and retirees) will receive the amount of the total children's annuity payable under CSRS reduced by the amount of Social Security benefits those surviving children are paid.[46] If a person is an FERS retiree at the time of death, an eligible surviving spouse will be paid 50 percent of the annuity and possibly a Special Retirement Supplement.[47]

How do I apply for retirement benefits?

A federal employee who is eligible for retirement and who is applying for CSRS retirement benefits[48] may file an application for retirement with his or her department or agency within thirty days before, on, or any time after that employee reaches the requisite retirement age. A former federal employee who is eligible for retirement may file an application for retirement with the OPM within thirty days before, on, or after that former employee meets the requisite retirement age. An applicant for disability retirement must submit an application for retirement (and an application for an annuity) before separation from service or within one year after separation from service, but this time limit may be extended in the case of an employee who is found to be incompetent on the date of separation or within one year thereafter. An employee who is retiring on account of voluntary or involuntary separation from service may file an application for immediate or deferred annuity only after his separation from service or not more than thirty days before the covering date of his annuity. At this time it is not certain whether the foregoing rules are also applicable to FERS; therefore, the employing agency's personnel office or OPM should be consulted. Whether retiring or applying for an annuity under either CSRS or FERS, it is wise to check on the applicable rules and deadlines well before the application is submitted.

What if a federal employee or retiree has a problem with the federal employees' health benefits program?

The health benefits plan[49] is generally the group health insurance program applicable to federal employees, retirees, their families and survivors. The OPM contracts with various qualified group health insurance carriers (such as Blue Cross-Blue Shield) around the country for group health insurance plan coverage. Individual claims for payment or service are initially handled by the health benefits plan carrier in which the employee or retiree is enrolled.[50] If a claim (or portion of a claim) or a service is initially denied by a health benefits plan carrier, the carrier will reconsider its denial if a written request for reconsideration is made within one year of the denial.[51] Such a written request should set forth the reasons why the enrollee believes the denied claim or service should have been paid or provided. The plan carrier must affirm the denial in writing to the enrollee—setting out in detail the reasons—within thirty days after receipt of the request for reconsideration or pay or provide the claim or service within such time unless it specifically requests additional information reasonably necessary to a determination.[52] If a plan carrier affirms its denial of a claim or fails to respond to a written request for reconsideration within 30 days of the request or within 30 days after it receives requested additional information, the enrollee may make a written request to the OPM for a review of the plan carrier's decision.[53] A request for review will not be considered unless it is received by the OPM within 90 days of the date of the carrier's affirmation of the denial or unless the carrier fails to respond within 120 days after the date of the enrollee's timely request for reconsideration or the date the enrollee was notified of the carrier's requests for additional information.[54] Under some limited circumstances this time requirement can be extended by the OPM. In reviewing a claim denied by a plan carrier, the OPM may review copies of all original evidence and findings upon which the plan carrier denied the claim and any additional evidence (including an advisory opinion from an independent physician) it deems appropriate.[55] Within 30 days after all evidence requested by the OPM has been received, it must notify the enrollee and the plan carrier in writing of its findings upon review.[56]

A court action to recover on a claim for health benefits should be brought against the carrier of the health benefits plan. An action to review the legality of the OPM's regulations applicable to the health benefits plan or a decision made by the OPM should be brought against the OPM.[57] According to the applicable federal regulations, an enrollee's dispute of an OPM decision *solely* because the OPM concurs in a health plan carrier's denial of a claim is not a challenge to the legality of the OPM's decision; therefore, any subsequent litigation to recover on the claim should be brought against the carrier, not the OPM.[58]

Where can an employee or retiree obtain additional information about benefits?

Current employees should contact the personnel office of the agency for which they work. Retirees (or their survivors) can also contact the personnel office of the agency which formerly employed them or they can contact the OPM's Retirement Information Office in Washington D.C., (202) 632-7700, which gives advice and information to retirees or their representatives. Persons who have left federal employment and are now eligible for an annuity (if for example they are 62 years of age) can also contact the Retirement Information Office for information and application forms. The Retirement Information Office can be contacted to report the death of a retiree or someone receiving survivors' benefits. If the Retirement Information Office cannot handle a problem immediately, it will refer the matter to other divisions (such as an advisory services division which handles very technical problems and emergencies or the medical claims dispute division which will assist retirees in disputes regarding health insurance benefits). If you are not satisfied with the response received from the agency personnel office or from the OPM, you should consider appealing the decision and seek legal assistance at the earliest possible time.

RAILROAD RETIREMENT

Who is eligible for Railroad Retirement benefits?

The Railroad Retirement system covers nearly all types of railroad employment in the United States. Employees of railroad labor unions and consolidated railroad terminal stations are included in the plan, but employees of local or intercity street rail systems and employees of railroad lines that operate within the confines of a mine or industrial plant are not covered.[59] If certain vesting and work record requirements are met, the spouses and dependent survivors of these employees also may receive benefits.

What benefits are available under the Railroad Retirement program?

The Railroad Retirement program provides benefits similar to those available under Social Security. Specifically, it provides for retirement,[60] disability,[61] spouses,[62] survivors,[63] lump-sum death,[64] and supplemental annuity benefits.[65] In most respects eligibility for these benefits is determined by standards and procedures similar to those used to determine eligibility for Social Security benefits. Because of the similarities between the Social Security and Railroad Retirement programs, this chapter does not contain a comprehensive discussion of the Railroad Retirement program. Be aware, however, that some features of the Railroad Retirement program are unique and railroad retirees may encounter difficulties not experienced by beneficiaries of other programs.[66] In particular, because many railroad retirees or their spouses may also qualify for benefits from Social Security, the Civil Service Retirement system, or state public employee pension programs, processing delays are common and errors in eligibility determinations and benefit calculations occur frequently. For these reasons, if you are denied benefits, doubt the accuracy of calculations concerning your benefits, or experience other problems, do not hesitate to seek qualified legal assistance.

May I receive Railroad Retirement benefits if I also receive benefits from Social Security or another public program?

Many railroad employees have spent a portion of their lives working for nonrailroad employers, thereby earning quarters of coverage for Social Security or similar credits for benefits under the Civil Service Retirement or a state public employee retirement program. Similarly, a railroad retiree's spouse may have qualified for benefits under one of these programs as a result of his or her work. Or a railroad retiree or his or her spouse may be eligible for veterans benefits. And in addition to being eligible for benefits as a result of their own work, a railroad retiree and his or her spouse may qualify for spouses or dependents benefits.

May a railroad retiree and his or her spouse receive benefits from more than one program?

The answer to this question depends on the benefit for which there is dual eligibility and the date on which eligibility vested. In most cases, a railroad retiree and his or her spouse will not receive the full value of all of the benefits for which they qualify. Usually a person eligible for more than a single benefit either receives the higher of the benefits to which he or she is entitled or has one benefit set off against another and thus receives less than the sum of the benefits to which he or she is entitled.[67] An example of the former may occur when a person is eligible for Railroad Retirement benefits both as a survivor (as a child or parent) and as a spouse.[68] An example of the latter is when as a result of his or her own work a person is eligible for both Railroad Retirement and Social Security benefits.[69] There are a number of exceptions to the usual rule against full receipt of dual benefits, however, and some railroad retirees and their spouses are eligible to receive multiple benefits with little or no reduction.

For example, under the Railroad Retirement Act of 1974,[70] persons receiving Railroad Retirement and Social Security benefits on 1 January 1975 continue to receive dual benefits (called vested dual benefits). Eligibility for vested dual benefits also was extended to certain individuals who had not retired by 1 January 1975, but who had worked long enough to be fully qualified under both systems: those who (1) had a "current connection" to the industry (12 months of railroad service in the previous 30 months); (2) had 25 or more years of railroad service; (3) performed some railroad service in 1974; or (4) fully qualified for Social Security by the close of the year (prior to 1975) in which they left railroad employment.[71] Vested dual benefits are not available to individuals fully qualified on 1 January 1975 who lack these characteristics nor to individuals who lacked sufficient credits on 31 December 1974 to be fully qualified under both systems. Despite the harsh consequences of the act for some railroaders, the Act was sustained by the Supreme Court.[72]

Thus, while some railroad retirees and their spouses are eligible for unreduced dual benefits from Social Security and Railroad Retirement, most dual beneficiaries from these programs have their benefits reduced. Similarly, many dual beneficiaries from federal and state public retirement programs have their benefits reduced. But dual receipt of Veterans and Railroad Retirement benefits does not affect one's Railroad Retirement benefits. Railroad Retirement benefits are divided into two parts: Tier 1 benefits (calculated very similarly to Social Security benefits) and Tier 2 benefits (based solely on railroad service). Technically what occurs in many dual benefit cases is that the railroad retiree's Tier 1 benefit is reduced or eliminated due to his or her receipt of a benefit from one of these other programs. This, of course, can cause confusion and delay when application for benefits is first made. It also can result in errors and delay if an individual or couple's circumstances later change. Under or overpayment of one's Railroad Retirement benefits can occur as a result of changes in the size of one's Social Security benefit, for example, and divorce, the death of a spouse, or other change in a family's circumstances also can affect eligibility for benefits and payment levels. Similarly, postretirement employment by one spouse can affect the family's eligibility for benefits and payment levels.

Because of the legal and factual complexities and the frequent involvement of two or more bureaucracies in dual benefit cases, the possibility of error is high. If you are denied benefits to which you believe yourself entitled or if you believe an error has occurred in calculating your benefit, do not hesitate to appeal. You also should seek assistance from an attorney or other qualified representative.

How do I apply for Railroad Retirement benefits?

An application for benefits may be submitted at any office of the Railroad Retirement Board.[73] The process for applying for Railroad Retirement benefits, including the evidence needed to prove eligibility for benefits, is very similar to the process of applying for Social Security benefits described in chapter 1. Your application will be reviewed by the board's Bureau of Retirement Claims, which will notify you in writing of their decision on your application.[74]

If you wish to appeal the decision on your application or other decisions affecting your benefits, you must file a written request for reconsideration.[75] Ordinarily you have sixty days in which to file this request,[76] but if you are seeking reconsideration of a decision that you have been overpaid or are seeking waiver of recovery of an overpayment, your request must be received by the board within thirty days of the date the notice of overpayment was sent to you.[77] Most reconsiderations are written reviews of the initial decision, but in overpayment cases you may request an oral hearing, which will be conducted by a disinterested board employee who will report to the Director of Retirement Claims who will issue a written decision.[78]

Appeals from reconsiderations lie with the Bureau of Hearings and Appeals and must be filed in writing within sixty days of the date of the reconsideration decision.[79] The hearing is conducted by a referee and closely resembles a Social Security Administration hearing. The referee is to issue a decision within forty-five days if evidence was heard; otherwise within ninety days.[80] An appeal from the referee's decision lies with the Railroad Retirement Board itself. The appeal must be filed within sixty days of the referee's decision and the Board is to issue its decision within ninety days.[81] If you wish to appeal the Board's decision you may do so by filing an appeal within one year in one of three federal courts: the U.S. Court of Appeals in the area in which you reside; the U.S. Circuit Court of Appeals for the Seventh Circuit (in Chicago, Illinois) or in the U.S. Court of Appeals for the District of Columbia.[82]

NOTES

1. 5 U.S.C.A. § 8301 *et seq.* (1980 & West Supp. 1987); 5 C.F.R. § 831.101 *et seq.* (1987).
2. 5 U.S.C.A. § 8401 *et seq.* (1980 & West Supp. 1987); 5 C.F.R. § 841.401 *et seq.* (1987).
3. 5 U.S.C.A. § 8402 (1980 & West Supp. 1987); 5 C.F.R. § 842.104 (1987).
4. 5 U.S.C.A. §§ 8347, 8461 (1980 & West Supp. 1987).
5. 5 U.S.C.A. § 8339 (1980 & West Supp. 1987).
6. *Id.*
7. 5 U.S.C.A. § 8332 (1980 & West Supp. 1987); 5 C.F.R. §§ 831.301–.303 (1987).
8. 5 C.F.R. § 831.302 (1987).
9. 5 U.S.C.A. § 8334 (1980 & West Supp. 1987); 5 C.F.R. §§ 831.401–.402 (1987).
10. 5 U.S.C.A. § 8338(a) (1980 & West Supp. 1987).
11. 5 U.S.C.A. § 8336(a),(b),(f) (1980 & West Supp. 1987).
12. 5 U.S.C.A. § 8336(c),(e) (1980 & West Supp. 1987).
13. 5 U.S.C.A. § 8336(d) (1980 & West Supp. 1987); 5 C.F.R. § 831.504 (1987).
14. 5 U.S.C.A. § 8342 (1980 & West Supp. 1987); 5 C.F.R. §§ 831.2002–.2010 (1987).
15. 5 C.F.R. § 831.2003 (1987).
16. 5 U.S.C.A. § 8351 (1980 & West Supp. 1987).
17. 5 U.S.C.A. § 8410 (1980 & West Supp. 1987).
18. 5 U.S.C.A. §§ 8442(b), 8451(a) (1980 & West Supp. 1987).
19. 5 U.S.C.A. § 8411 (1980 & West Supp. 1987).
20. 5 U.S.C.A. § 8412(h) (1980 & West Supp. 1987).
21. 5 U.S.C.A. § 8412(a),(b),(c) (1980 & West Supp. 1987).
22. 5 U.S.C.A. §§ 8413, 8415(f) (1980 & West Supp. 1987).
23. 5 U.S.C.A. § 8421 (1980 & West Supp. 1987).
24. 5 U.S.C.A. § 8424 (1980 & West Supp. 1987).
25. 5 U.S.C.A. § 8432 (1980 & West Supp. 1987).
26. 5 U.S.C.A. § 8432(c)(1)(A) (1980 & West Supp. 1987).
27. 5 U.S.C.A. § 8432 (1980 & West Supp. 1987).
28. 5 U.S.C.A. § 8433 (1980 & West Supp. 1987).
29. 5 U.S.C.A. §§ 8433, 8434 (1980 & West Supp. 1987).
30. 5 U.S.C.A. § 8433 (1980 & West Supp. 1987).

31. 5 U.S.C.A. § 8337(a) (1980 & West Supp. 1987).
32. 5 U.S.C.A. § 8451(a) (1980 & West Supp. 1987).
33. *See* 5 U.S.C.A. § 8452(a) (1980 & West Supp. 1987).
34. 5 U.S.C.A. §§ 8337(a), 8451 (1980 & West Supp. 1987).
35. 5 U.S.C.A. § 8339(g) (1980 & West Supp. 1987).
36. 5 U.S.C.A. § 8452(a) (1980 & West Supp. 1987).
37. 5 U.S.C.A. § 8452 (1980 & West Supp. 1987).
38. 5 U.S.C.A. §§ 8341(a), 8441 (1980 & West Supp. 1987).
39. *See* 5 U.S.C.A. §§ 8341(b)(3), 8442(a)(2) (1980 & West Supp. 1987).
40. 5 U.S.C.A. § 8341(d) (1980 & West Supp. 1987).
41. *Id.*
42. 5 U.S.C.A. § 8341(b) (1980 & West Supp. 1987).
43. 5 U.S.C.A. § 8341(e) (1980 & West Supp. 1987).
44. 5 U.S.C.A. § 8442(b) (1980 & West Supp. 1987). The $15,000 lump sum payment will be adjusted annually according to a prescribed formula.
45. *Id.*
46. 5 U.S.C.A. § 8443 (1980 & West Supp. 1987).
47. 5 U.S.C.A. § 8442(a), (f) (1980 & West Supp. 1987).
48. 5 C.F.R. § 831.501 (1987).
49. 5 U.S.C.A. § 8901 *et seq.* (1980 & West Supp. 1987); 5 C.F.R. § 8901.101 *et seq.* (1987).
50. 5 C.F.R. § 890.105(a) (1987).
51. 5 C.F.R. § 890.105(b) (1987).
52. *Id.*
53. 5 C.F.R. § 890.105(d) (1987).
54. *Id.*
55. 5 C.F.R. § 890.105(d)(2) (1987).
56. 5 C.F.R. § 890.105(d)(4) (1987).
57. 5 C.F.R. § 890.107 (1987).
58. *Id.*
59. 20 C.F.R. §§ 202.1–.15; 203.1 (1986).
60. 45 U.S.C.A. § 231a(a)(1) (West 1986).
61. 45 U.S.C.A. § 231a(a)(1)(iv), (v) (West 1986).
62. 45 U.S.C.A. § 231a(c) (West 1986).
63. 45 U.S.C.A. § 231a(d)(1) (West 1986).
64. 45 U.S.C.A. § 231e (West 1986).
65. 45 U.S.C.A. § 231a(b)(1) (West 1986).
66. *See generally*, "The Railroad Retirement Act" in National Senior Citizens Law Center, *Representing Older Persons* (1985).
67. *See generally*, U.S. Railroad Retirement Board, *Railroad Retirement and Survivor Benefits for Railroad Workers and their Families* (1987) [Railroad Retirement Benefits].

68. 45 U.S.C.A. § 231a(h)(4) (West 1986); 20 C.F.R. § 216.90 (1986).
69. 45 U.S.C.A. § 231b(m) (West 1986).
70. Pub. L. No. 93-445, 88 Stat. 1305 (1974).
71. 45 U.S.C.A. § 231b(h) (West 1986). Technically the benefits of these individuals are reduced, then most of the reduction is restored. *Id*.
72. *US. Railroad Retirement Bd. v. Fritz*, 449 U.S. 166 (1980).
73. *See generally*, 20 C.F.R. § 217 (1986).
74. *Id*. at § 260.
75. *Id*. at § 260.3.
76. *Id*.
77. *Id*. at § 260.4.
78. *Id*.
79. *Id*. at § 260.5.
80. *Id*. at §§ 260.6,.7.
81. *Id*. at § 260.9.
82. 45 U.S.C.A. § 231g (West 1986).

5

Private Pensions

What is a pension?

The term "pension" describes an agreement or program under which an employer, an employee, a union, or all of these contribute money to a fund during an employee's working years to provide income for the worker after he retires.[1] Pension really involves three separate topics for consideration: pension plans, pension funds, and pension benefits. A pension plan is the agreement or program established by the employer, employee, or union. A pension fund is the collection of money contributed by these parties under the pension plan. And a pension benefit is the money from the pension fund that is paid to the worker (usually monthly) after retirement. In this chapter we use the term "pension" loosely, sometimes referring to pension benefits, sometimes to all three concepts—plan, fund, and benefits.

Pensions are many people's last hope for more than bare subsistence living after retirement since Social Security's average payment of $479 per month for all retired workers and $725 per month for a couple[2] is insufficient to provide a decent standard of living and because few retirees have adequate savings. Pensions are also important because they represent a form of deferred compensation for work done by employees. This was recognized long ago by a federal appellate court which affirmed the obligations of an employer to bargain with a union representing its employees over employee pensions.

> Suppose that a person seeking employment was offered a job by two companies equal in all respects except that one had a retirement and pension plan and that the other did not. We think it reasonable to assume an acceptance of the job with the company which had such plan. . . . [S]uch a pledge on the part of the company forms a part of the consideration for work performed, . . . [T]he pension thus promised would appear to be as much a part of his "wages" as the money paid him at the time of the rendition of his services.[3]

You should know that employers are not required to establish pension plans. Nor are they required to continue plans they have established. Most governments (federal, state, and local), however, and many private companies do provide pension plans. It is estimated that close to half of the private (nongovernmental) work-force is employed by companies that have pension plans.[4] In March 1985, private pensions for women age 65 and over averaged about $2,440 a year and for men age 65 and over, about $4,550 a year.[5] This chapter concentrates on the rights to receive a private pension.

What laws govern pension plans?

Although an employer does not have to establish a pension plan, if a plan is established, it must meet certain minimum standards. Most of these standards stem from the Employee Retirement Income Security Act (ERISA) enacted in September 1974.[6] ERISA cured many of the problems that had plagued the private pension system for years. Other problems, however, were not cured by ERISA and it is therefore important to understand that ERISA provides a complex set of guidelines that most private sector pension plans must follow.[7] It provides significant protections for workers who stop working for their employer after the effective date of the act.[8] ERISA is not retroactive, however, so it does nothing for workers who retired before the act went into effect. ERISA cured many of the problems that had plagued the private pension system for years, but because of a number of omissions and exceptions, some significant problems remain, even for those retiring after ERISA went into effect. It is therefore important to understand how ERISA works.

In addition to ERISA, a number of other laws regulate private pensions. These include the Labor Management Relations Act,[9] the Age Discrimination in Employment Act of 1967,[10] the Civil Rights Act of 1964,[11] and the Internal Revenue Code.[12]

Must my employer have a pension plan for all employees?

No. As previously mentioned, whether an employer has a pension plan for employees is the employer's decision. Also, an employer may have a pension plan covering some groups or categories of employees and not others. Although ERISA imposed many new requirements on employers maintaining pension plans, it left unchanged preexisting Internal Revenue Code provisions that allow employers to exclude certain categories of employees from pension plans. The code permits an employer to exclude a category of employees if the plan benefits a certain percentage of employees or if—by including some and excluding other categories of employees—the employer does not discriminate in favor of employees who are officers, shareholders, or highly paid.[13]

How can I participate in a pension plan?

Before ERISA, a pension plan could exclude large groups of employees from becoming plan members. Most commonly, these employees were not permitted to participate in the plan because they were "too old" or "too young" when they started to work under the plan or because they had not worked long enough for the employer. Older workers in department stores, for example, were often excluded from pension plans.

Under ERISA, participation in (or enrollment in) pension plans is regulated so that employees of a certain age who work a certain number of hours per year must be allowed to participate in any pension plan which covers them. The general rule now[14] is that any employee who (1) is at least 21 years old and (2) has worked for his or her employer at least one year must be allowed to participate.[15] There are exceptions to this rule, however, and different provisions may apply to you.[16]

It is important to note that being a plan participant does not, by itself, give you the right to receive a pension. It only means that you are a member of the plan and can earn credit toward a pension. In addition, remember that these requirements are the minimum required by law. Your employer may have more generous rules, allowing employees to participate in a pension plan as soon as they are hired, for example.

How does the one-year period of service required for participation work?

ERISA defines a year of service as a 12-month period that begins when the employee starts work and during which the employee has 1,000 hours of service.[17] Because of the 1,000 hour per 12-month period minimum service requirement, many part-time and seasonal employees previously excluded from plans are now receiving pension credit. One thousand hours equals about 6 months of full-time (40 hours per week) or 12 months of part-time (20 hours per week) work.

As an alternative to the 1,000-hour rule, plans may require employees to complete a continuous year of employment, beginning when the employee starts work, before an employee must be allowed to participate. If the plan uses this rule, continuous periods of full or part-time work must be counted. Absences from work of less than one year do not break your continuous service and must also be counted.[18]

Can older workers be kept from participating in pension plans?

Generally, no. However, certain plans, called "defined-benefit plans," have been permitted in the past to exclude employees who began work within five years of normal retirement age from participating in the plan.[19] Defined-benefit plans are those which provide a definite benefit for each employee at retirement. An example of a defined-benefit plan is one which promises a benefit of $5 a month per year of service to a retiring participant so that a retiree with 20 years of service would receive a benefit of $100 per month. But because of the rule permitting exclusion of employees beginning work within five years of their plan's normal retirement age (frequently 65), a worker hired four years before retirement might receive nothing. Starting in 1988, employees cannot be excluded from participating in a plan because they were hired within five years of the plan's normal retirement age. Employees can be required to complete 5 years of service, though, to have the right to a pension.[20] Many pension plans covering low-income workers are defined-benefit plans.[21]

What is benefit accrual?

Once a person has satisfied the requirements for participation in a pension plan, he or she begins to accumulate or accrue credits that will determine the amount of his or her pension benefits. Normally, the size of a person's pension is based largely on the number of years the person has worked after becoming a participant in the plan.[22] Under ERISA, a plan participant who has worked at least 1,000 hours during a year must be credited as having accrued at least some benefits that year. An employer is permitted by ERISA to require an employee to work more than 1,000 hours to obtain credit for a full year of accrued benefits, but credit for at least a partial year of accrued benefits must be given to a plan participant working at least 1,000 hours.[23]

ERISA limits defined-benefit plans from "backloading" benefits, or providing that you earn benefits at a faster rate during later years of work.[24] However, the law permits plans to use a benefit formula which provides full benefits only if you work until normal retirement age and which reduces benefits if you do not.[25]

What is vesting?

"Vesting" is an employee's legal right to receive a pension at retirement age. A pension "vests" after you have worked for a specified period of time for an employer that has a pension plan.

Vesting is different from benefit accrual, as can be seen from the following example. Joe Smith began working for Ford Motor Company when he was 30 years old. After working there full time for five years, he quit his job at Ford and went to work for General Motors. Because Joe worked more than the 1,000 hours per year while at Ford and because he was over 21 years old when he went to work there, he was a participant in Ford's pension plan after his first year. And he has four years of accrued pension benefits. Nevertheless, he may never receive these benefits. Why? Because a company can require a worker to be employed for ten years before his benefits vest. A worker who leaves before his benefits vest may never receive them. On the other hand, if Joe stayed at Ford for ten years (including his first year when he was not a participant in the plan), his benefits would vest, and he would receive them even though he quit Ford long before retirement age.

Before ERISA, plans could provide for extremely stringent vesting requirements or for none at all. Now ERISA attempts to remedy these problems by establishing minimum vesting rules and requiring that plans provide for vesting prior to retirement.[26] A plan is allowed to provide for a more generous vesting schedule, but through 1988 its vesting schedule must be at least as good as one of the three called for by ERISA—10-year, 100 percent vesting; 15-year, graded vesting; and the "rule of 45."[27] In addition, ERISA requires that an employee become 100 percent vested if the employee works up to the plan's normal retirement age, regardless of the number of years worked.[28]

The vesting rules are due to change in 1989, but the changes will only apply to employees working under the plan in 1989 when the new rules take effect. If you stop working under a plan before the new rules apply, the old vesting rules apply.

Starting in 1989, plans will be required to comply with one of two vesting rules: 5-year, 100 percent vesting; or 7-year, graded vesting. The 7-year rule will require that employees be 20 percent vested after completing 3 years of service, increasing 20 percent per year until the employee is 100 percent vested after completing 7 years of service.

Nevertheless, union-negotiated multiemployer pension plans may continue to use the 10-year, 100 percent rule.[29]

What is 10-year, 100 percent vesting?

The 10-year, 100 percent vesting formula is the formula most often used by medium- and large-sized employers.[30] Under this schedule, the plan must provide a 100 percent vested pension at retirement to an employee who has at least ten years of service.[31] In other words, under this schedule if Jean Jones quits after nine years, she will receive no pension. But if she quits after ten years, she will receive a pension. The amount of the pension will be based on the benefits she accrued during her nine years of service as a plan participant. If the plan is a defined-benefit plan paying $15[32] per month for each year of service, at retirement Jean will receive a pension of $135 per month. If she continues working for her employer, the amount of the pension she has a vested right to receive will be based on all the years she participated in her employer's plan. So if she works an additional ten years, her pension will be $285 per month.

Note that Jean received a pension of $135 (not $150) after ten years and $285 (rather than $300) after twenty years. This is because all years of service are counted for vesting purposes, but only years of participation are counted for benefit accrual purposes, that is, for determining the amount of benefits that will be paid. Since an employee normally will not be a plan participant until he or she has worked for one year, years of participation will differ from years of service.

What is graded vesting?

Under graded vesting, at least 25 percent of an employee's accrued benefits from employer contributions must be vested after five years of service. An additional 5 percent must be vested for each of the next five years of service; and again another 10 percent must be vested for each year of the third five-year period.[33] At fifteen years, the employee is fully vested. The operation of this schedule can be seen in table 4:

TABLE 4

Graded Vesting, by Years of Service and Nonforfeitable Percentage

Years of service	Nonforfeitable Percentage
5	25
6	30
7	35
8	40
9	45
10	50
11	60
12	70
13	80
14	90
15 or more	100

To illustrate the way graded vesting works, assume that Mary Green works for a company with a defined-benefit plan paying $15 per month at retirement for each year of service. If she worked for 15 years, her pension would be fully vested and she would receive $210 per month at retirement (100% × $15 × 14 years). If she left after only five years, she would receive a pension at retirement (whereas under 10-year, 100 percent vesting she would not). But her pension would be only 25 percent vested and would be only $15 per month (25% × $15 × 4 years). (Again remember that the first year of service is counted for vesting but not for accrual purposes.)

What is the "rule of 45"?

Under the "rule of 45," an employee with five years of service must be at least 50 percent vested when the sum of his age and years of service totals 45. For each additional year, the employee's vested percentage is increased by 10 percent so that not later than five years after meeting the threshold "45" requirement, the participant is 100 percent vested.[34] The option further provides that the participant who has completed at least ten years of service regardless of age must be 50 percent vested in accrued benefits at the end of the ten years and must be vested in an additional 10 percent for each of the next five years of service.[35] Most plans have not used this vesting rule, and it may not be used for current employees after the start of the 1989 plan year.

Can plans be made to provide more rapid vesting schedules than those just described?

Yes. The ERISA schedules are the minimum permitted by law. A plan can create a more generous vesting schedule. Indeed, many pension plans do have more generous vesting provisions, often as a result of collective bargaining between unions and employers. In addition, if the plan is top-heavy (i.e., where officers and owners have accumulated more than 60 percent of the benefits in the plan), the plan must provide participants with a minimum benefit each year and faster vesting.[36] Plans in small offices are the most likely to be top-heavy.

For each year a plan is top-heavy, you will accumulate a minimum benefit under a defined-benefit plan or a minimum contribution under a defined-contribution plan based on a percentage of your earnings.[37] In addition, in each top-heavy year, the plan must provide that employees have a 100 percent vested right to all accumulated benefits after three years of service or that employees have a 20 percent right to all benefits after two years of service, increasing 20 percent per year to 100 percent after six years.[38] These top-heavy rules generally apply to plan years which begin in 1984 and later. When a top-heavy plan stops being top-heavy, your vesting percentage cannot be reduced, and the quicker vesting rule may continue to apply.[39] Also, even if the plan is not top-heavy, if the Internal Revenue Service (IRS) determines that the rate of turnover for rank-and-file employees will be substantially greater than the turnover rate for highly compensated employees, the IRS can require that the plan provide for more rapid vesting of benefits and generally does require plans of small employers to comply with a 4-40 vesting formula.[40] Under this formula, employees must be 40 percent vested after four years of service, increasing by 5 percent per year to 50 percent after six years and then increasing 10 percent per year until the employee is 100 percent vested after eleven years.[41] Requiring 4-40 vesting is intended to prevent discrimination, so that rank-and-file workers are not forced to subsidize supervisory employees by higher turnover rates which result in pension forfeitures.

ERISA enhances the ability of workers to argue to the IRS that more generous vesting should be established by requiring that employees be notified of an employer's application for IRS approval of a pension plan and by giving employees an opportunity to comment on the application. ERISA also makes it illegal for your employer to retaliate against you because you exercised your legal rights or to dismiss you because he wants to prevent you from earning a pension.[42] You may have to go through the plan's appeals procedure before filing a lawsuit on this type of claim.[43]

How are years of service counted for the different vesting schedules?

For vesting purposes, the definition of a year of service is basically the same as for participation purposes. The general rule is that all years of service in which at least 1,000 hours are worked are to be counted.[44] As a result, plans may no longer disregard long periods of service because short breaks have occurred, but must recognize the aggregate of all years of service. There are some exceptions, however, and it is important to note that certain years of service before the enactment of ERISA may not count.[45]

Treasury Department regulations also allow plans to calculate years of service by counting continuous years of employment, instead of using the 1,000 hour rule.[46] For example, if you started work on 1 February 1978, you need to work through 31 January 1988 (ten full years) to complete ten years of service. If you miss work for less than twelve months, there is no break in your continuous service. You must be given vesting credit for all days you are paid or are entitled to be paid for working, including sick leave and vacation time. If you are laid off, you must be given vesting credit for one year after your date of layoff. If you are discharged, your vesting service stops accumulating. A federal court of appeals has upheld these regulations.[47]

What is a break in service?

Prior to ERISA, many pension plans had restrictive rules which prevented employees from receiving credit for all of the years they worked. Called break-in-service rules, these provisions dictated that an employee's service prior to a period of absence from work would be disregarded in computing pension benefits. For example, one woman worked for a firm for thirty years, with occasional layoffs for short periods of time, the longest being from May 1966 to May 1968. When she applied for a pension, she found that none of her service before 1968 counted toward retirement because her absence during 1966 through 1968 was over eighteen months. The employer took no account of the twenty-five years she had worked prior to the break.[48]

ERISA limits the ability of an employer to exclude some years of service in determining the amount of a pension, and whether the employee has a vested right to it. ERISA requires that a plan participant accumulate one half-year's worth of benefits for each year he or she works at least 1,000 hours. If an employee works between 500 and 1,000 hours during a year, the employer need not give the employee credit for accruing benefits, but the employer cannot declare that a break in service has occurred.[49] Only if an employee has worked 500 or fewer hours during the year can the employer declare that a break in service has occurred, thus potentially affecting credit for benefits accrued in past years.[50]

ERISA also protects workers by preventing pension plans from taking away credit for years worked before a break in service. Only if (1) you have five consecutive break years, and (2) the number of break years is greater than or equal to the number of years worked before the break, can you lose credit for years worked before the break.[51] For example, if you have seven years of credited service and are laid off for two years after which you return to work for your old employer, ERISA requires that you be given credit for the seven years of service you accumulated before being laid off. Only if you were laid off for seven or more years could your years of work prior to the break be disregarded. And your years of service prior to the break will be disregarded only if your benefits are not vested.[52] For employees with vested benefits, an employer may not disregard years of service before the break. When a break has occurred, however, an employee may be required to complete a year of service after returning to work before the prior years will be counted.[53] Once your benefits have been vested, they cannot be taken from you no matter how long you are away from your job.

Can I still get benefits from a pension plan if I leave my job and compete with my employer?

If you have met the requirements of one of the ERISA vesting schedules, you cannot lose your vested rights by competing with your employer. Benefits vested more quickly than required by ERISA may, however, be forfeited if the plan contains a no-competition clause.[54]

Can my employer deprive me of vested benefits by amending my pension plan?

Before ERISA, an employer was free to change the vesting schedule of a pension plan in a way that would deprive workers of vested benefits. Under ERISA this is illegal.[55] For example, an employer cannot switch from a plan under which an employee with eight years of service has partially vested benefits to a plan which requires all workers to be employed for ten years before any benefits vest. However, pre-ERISA amendments depriving workers of benefits are not outlawed by ERISA; only amendments after the effective date of ERISA are illegal.

ERISA prevents plan amendments from taking away an employee's vested right to receive his accumulated retirement benefit at normal retirement age. However, ERISA did not prevent employers from taking away an employee's options under the plan to receive benefits before normal retirement age, benefits in any form of payment other than a lifetime annuity beginning at normal retirement age, or special retirement benefits if the employee had not qualified for the option before the amendment.

Plan amendments (made after July 1984) cannot eliminate an existing form of payment for previously accumulated benefits. An amendment also cannot eliminate an employee's right to receive a special benefit that the employee presently has partially qualified for, as long as the employee later satisfies the pre-amendment eligibility requirements for the benefit.[56] Nevertheless, since a plan amendment can limit how benefits are accumulated in the future, the amendment can limit this right to the amount accumulated on the date of amendment. Supplements to pensions that are paid only until the employee becomes eligible for Social Security are not protected and may be eliminated by a plan amendment.[57] For example, the Retirement Equity Act (REA) requires plans which terminate after 30 July 1984 to provide employees with the right to take early retirement according to the terms of the plan before termination.[58] Before the REA, a terminating plan which provided that an employee could retire at 55 instead of 65 with either a full or reduced pension had only to provide employees not yet 55 with a full pension at 65. The REA now requires plans, if they terminate, to provide these early retirement benefits if the employee qualifies for them either before or after the plan terminates.

A plan may, however, limit the value of these early retirement benefits to the value of the benefits the employee has accumulated on the date the plan is amended. An amendment can change how benefits earned in the future may be taken. The REA makes no change in the law concerning the benefits the Pension Benefit Guaranty Corporation (PBGC) guarantees will be paid in case the plan terminates without the money to provide them.[59]

Will years of service accumulated while working for one employer be lost if the business is acquired by a new employer?

No, ERISA requires that all years of service with the "employer or employers maintaining the plan" must be counted. The result is that when a new employer continues an old plan — in the case of a merger, for example — years of service from the previous employer's period of control must be counted.[60] If the new employer does not continue the old employer's plan but instead uses his own plan, the old years might not be counted.[61]

How do I file a claim to receive a pension?

Before ERISA, a worker whose claim for a pension was denied often had no way to find out the reason for the denial, no procedure to appeal the denial, and no right to sue in court to obtain a pension. ERISA remedies this situation.

Under ERISA, all pension plans are required to have a procedure by which a plan participant can submit a claim to receive a pension.[62] ERISA requires that all participants be given a plan summary that explains the procedure to be followed by anyone filing a claim.[63] ERISA also requires that an appeal procedure be established, including the following provisions:

The plan must give you written notice of the decision on your claim for benefits within 90 days. The plan may have one 90 day extension if you are given written notice of the extension before the first 90 days are up.[64] If your claim is denied, the specific reasons for the denial must be stated, with specific reference to the plan provision on which the denial is based.[65] If no decision is reached within the permitted 90 or 180 day period, the claim will be treated as if denied, and you can proceed to appeal.[66] Appeals under ERISA are to be in writing.[67] You have 60 days, from notice that your claim was denied, in which to file an appeal.[68] In most plans, a decision on your appeal is to be reached within 120 days of the time your appeal is received.[69] The decision on appeal must be in writing and refer to the plan provisions on which it is based.[70] To assist your appeal, ERISA requires that plan administrators allow you to review important pension documents affecting your claim for benefits and to allow you to submit written material in support of your appeal.[71]

ERISA does not require plans to permit you to appear in person to support an appeal. In other words, no hearing is required, although the statute does require a "full and fair review."[72] One court has stated that for a review to be "full and fair," the plan must, at a minimum, tell on what evidence the initial denial of your claim was based, let you respond as to whether the evidence was accurate and reliable, and on review, consider the evidence you submit as well as the evidence used to deny the claim.[73]

ERISA also entitles you to go to either state or federal court to sue your pension plan if your claim for benefits is denied,[74] but you must go through the plan's claims and appeals procedure before filing a lawsuit.[75] ERISA does not specify what the court will consider while hearing your appeal. Courts generally consider "whether the Trustees of the plan have acted arbitrarily, capriciously or in bad faith." The court determines "whether the Trustees' decision is supported by substantial evidence and, if so, whether they have made an erroneous decision on a question of law."[76] This means the court, more likely than not, will defer to the plan trustees' determination of what the facts of the case are[77] or what the plan intends.[78] But the court will determine what the plan's legal obligations are and whether the plan has complied with those obligations. And the court will focus on the evidence the plan trustees considered and might not consider further evidence which was not submitted to them.[79]

Can I work and still receive my pension?

Generally, yes, but there are some exceptions. A person entitled to receive a pension generally will not lose his pension because he decides to open a business or go to work full or part time.[80] ERISA, however, does permit a pension plan to suspend payment of pension benefits after a participant reaches the plan's normal retirement age if a recipient returns to work for his former employer.[81] ERISA also permits the suspension of benefits to a recipient who was a participant in a multiemployer plan if the retiree returns to work in the same industry, trade, and geographical area covered by the pension plan.[82] But in either case, your benefits can be suspended only if you work forty or more hours per month.[83] Of course, you can contest a decision by your plan that you are working in the same industry, trade, or locality. This was done by a former maritime worker whose pension benefits were suspended when he accepted a job with the government. The court ruled that government service was not work in the same industry.[84] If you have not yet reached the plan's normal retirement age, ERISA's vesting rules do not prevent the plan from enforcing a plan rule suspending your pension until normal retirement age if you go back to work.[85]

Also, a multiemployer plan's trustees cannot adopt a rule taking away your right under the plan to receive a pension before normal retirement age because you also work for a nonunion employer unless there is proof that the rule was adopted to enhance the financial integrity of the plan or to benefit plan members.[86]

Can I receive both Social Security and a pension?

Yes, but a plan may provide pensions only to workers earning above a certain income[87] or may reduce pensions of all workers by part of the amount a worker will receive[88] as a Social Security benefit.[89] This is called "integrating" a pension plan with Social Security. Since Social Security payments are weighted in favor of lower income workers, pension integration can have the effect of substantially reducing or eliminating the pension benefits of these workers.[90] For example, a plan which reduces your pension benefits by part of what you will receive as a Social

Security benefit (called an "offset" plan) typically might provide that you will receive 1 percent of average final earnings, multiplied by your years of service, minus 50 percent of the Social Security benefit you will receive at age 65. If your average final earnings are $18,000 ($1,500/month), you have worked thirty years for your employer under the plan, and if your monthly social security benefit at age 65 would be $600, your monthly pension from the plan at normal retirement age would be: $1\% \times \$1,500 \times 30 - 50\% \times \$600 = \$150$ per month. ERISA, however, forbids a pension plan from reducing your pension because of cost-of-living increases in Social Security.[91]

Does ERISA protect my pension if my employer goes out of business or terminates my pension plan?

Yes, in part. Before ERISA, many workers lost their pensions because an employer went out of business or decided to discontinue its pension plan. While ERISA does not require that an employer have a pension plan nor that it continue to operate a plan already established, it does provide partial protection for workers whose pension plan is terminated. The principal protection offered by ERISA is an insurance program which guarantees the payment of *some* pension benefits to retirees if their defined-benefit pension plan is terminated. The Pension Benefit Guaranty Corporation (PBGC)[92] was established by ERISA; defined-benefit pension plans[93] (with very limited exceptions)[94] are required to pay insurance premiums to the PBGC. In return for these premiums, the PBGC guarantees that participants of defined-benefit plans will be paid at least some of their pension if their plan folds or is terminated.[95] Only participants in defined-benefit plans are protected;[96] participants in defined-contribution plans are not protected. Moreover, only vested benefits are guaranteed.[97] So participants in a defined-benefit plan whose benefits had not vested when the plan terminated are not protected either. And even those with vested benefits have no guarantee that they will receive all of their benefits.[98] For example, if the plan increased benefits within five years of plan termination, the increase is not fully insured.[99] Also, many pension plans pay death, medical, and disability benefits in addition to normal retirement benefits. ERISA requires the PBGC to guarantee only basic retirement benefits, so you may lose other kinds of benefits in the event your plan is terminated.[100]

ERISA places an upper limit, adjusted for inflation by formula, on the amount of basic benefits which are guaranteed. For plans terminating in 1985, this amount is $1,687.50 per month. For 1986, the amount is $1,789.77.[101] For 1987, the amount is $1,857.95.[102]

If your plan is a multiemployer plan (i.e., a plan negotiated by a union with more than one employer), additional rules will determine what your benefit is under the plan and how much of your benefit is insured if the plan becomes insolvent. For example, if your employer stops contributing to the plan, you may lose benefits which are based on your service before the employer began contributing to the plan.[103] If the plan is in financial difficulty, benefits established or increased under the plan in the last five years may be eliminated.[104] And if the plan becomes insolvent, only part of your basic benefit is insured by the PBGC. That part is calculated by considering (1) the first $5 per month for each year of service fully insured;[105] (2) only 75 percent (or possibly 65 percent) of the next $15 per month for each year of service insured;[106] (3) any amount above this not insured. For example, if your plan provides a benefit of $25 per month for each year of service, and you have 20 years of service, your accumulated benefit is $500 per month. The PBGC fully insures the first $5 for each of your 20 years of service, or fully insures the first $100. 75% (or 65%) of the next $15 for each of 20 years, or 75% (or 65%) of $300, or $225 (or $195) is also insured. The last $5 (times 20 years) is not insured. Thus, only $325 (or $295) of your benefit is insured. As with plans provided by a single employer, there are exceptions to this general rule.[107] However, the PBGC generally will insure your pension *fully* if, on 29 July 1980, you were receiving your pension or were vested and within thirty-six months of the plan's normal retirement age.[108]

Finally, if a single employer, defined-benefit pension plan terminates, after annuities are purchased from an insurance company to provide pensions for workers with vested rights, money left over in the plan must be used to provide pensions for workers with nonvested benefits.[109] ERISA also protects workers by stiffening the funding requirements for pension plans so that there will be more funds available to pay beneficiaries in case the plan is terminated.[110]

The address and telephone number of the Pension Benefit

Guaranty Corporation are: 2020 K Street, N.W., Washington, D.C., (202) 778-8800.

What rights do widows (and widowers) have to pensions?

Before ERISA, private pension plans did not have to offer benefits for widows. Those plans that did usually required the spouse to sign a form and agree to take a reduction in his or her own pension. Often the spouse simply never got around to signing the form, and despite good intentions, the widow received no pension benefits when the spouse died. ERISA made some important changes, and the Retirement Equity Act of 1984 (REA), amending ERISA, requires plans to provide a survivor's benefit if a spouse has a vested right to a pension and worked or was on paid leave on or after 23 August 1984.[111] Under the REA, a survivor's pension is protected once the worker becomes vested.[112] Whether the worker dies while still employed or after retirement, the worker's spouse will collect a survivor's pension unless he or she gives written consent to waive that survivor's pension.[113] The amount of the worker's pension is reduced at retirement to provide for the survivor's pension, which must be 50 percent of the reduced amount the worker receives or would have received had he lived to retirement age.[114]

Technically, the survivor's protection comes at two points: protection before the worker retires and protection at retirement. The worker's spouse can waive either of these protections. The plan must tell employees within three years of the plan year in which the employee turns 32[115] of their spouse's right to receive a survivor's benefit if, as a vested worker, he or she dies before retiring.[116] Nevertheless, even if the worker's spouse waives the protection at some point before the worker retires, he or she will automatically have the protection again once the worker retires and starts collecting a pension.[117] If the worker's spouse waives the protection at the time the worker retires, the plan can provide that this decision is irrevocable.

In general, a plan must begin paying the survivor's pension immediately if the worker died after reaching retirement age and, if the worker died before retiring, in the year the worker could have retired under the plan (usually age 55).[118] A basic survivor's pension must be paid for the survivor's life, even if the survivor remarries. A spouse will have a right to this survivor's benefit if he or she was married at least one year before the worker's pension started or before he died, whichever is earlier.[119]

If an employee was not working or on paid leave under the plan on or after 23 August 1984, the rules are more complex. Generally, if you worked under the plan between 1976 and 23 August 1984, had ten years of service, and have not started to receive your pension, you may elect that your spouse receive survivor's benefits if you die before starting to receive a pension.[120] The plan is required to have told you by 30 September 1985 of this right to elect survivor's benefits.[121] Also, if you worked under the plan on or after 2 September 1974 but left work before ERISA was first applied to the plan (generally, in 1976), and have not started to receive your pension, you may elect to provide your spouse with survivors' benefits if you die while receiving your pension.[122]

Before the Retirement Equity Act of 1984, ERISA did not require plans to provide survivors' benefits if workers earned pensions but died before retirement. To receive a survivor's pension, the plan had to have a provision allowing for early retirement,[123] the worker had to have reached that age or been within ten years of normal retirement (whichever came later)[124] and the worker had to sign a form agreeing to reduce his or her early retirement pension to provide for the survivor's pension.[125] Also before the REA, ERISA did not require plans to pay a spouse a survivor's benefit if the worker signed a form before starting to receive his pension, saying he did not want his pension reduced to provide for a survivor's benefit. If a person was working under a plan when ERISA was first applied to it and started to receive his pension before the 1985 plan year began, a surviving spouse will receive a benefit unless a worker signed such a form before starting to receive a pension.

How can I find out about my plan?

A pensioner is unable to enforce his right in a pension fund until he is aware what these rights are. Detailed reporting and disclosure requirements therefore form an important part of ERISA.

To what information is a participant or beneficiary of a plan entitled?

ERISA requires plan administrators to furnish all participants or beneficiaries with a summary of their pension plan within 90 days after he or she becomes a participant, or within 120 days after the plan is initiated.[126] This "summary plan description" is required to be written in a manner calculated to be understood by the average plan participant. And it must be sufficiently accurate and comprehensive to inform participants and beneficiaries of their rights and obligations under the plan.[127] The description must include the names and addresses of the administrator and trustees of the plan. It must outline the requirements for participation, benefit accrual, and vesting, as well as conditions that will result in forfeiture of benefits. And it must include the procedure to be followed in presenting claims for benefit and the remedies available when claims are denied.[128]

The summary plan description must be distributed every ten years or after five years if there are changes in the plan. Summaries of changes in the plan must be given to participants during the plan year after the plan year in which the change is adopted.[129] The law also requires that plan participants and beneficiaries be given a summary of the plan's annual financial report.[130] If your employer is not providing this information to you, contact the Office of Communications within the Department of Labor for assistance. The address and telephone number are: Room 5666, U.S. Department of Labor, Washington D.C. 20216; (202) 523-8921. The plan's annual financial report and summary plan description are on file in the Labor Department's Division of Public Disclosure and can be obtained from that office. That address is: Room N5507, U.S. Department of Labor, Washington, D.C. 20216. The telephone number is: (202) 523-8771.

To what additional information am I entitled?

Upon the written request of a plan participant, the administrator of the plan is required to furnish a statement saying whether the participant has earned the right to receive a pension at retirement age and what the amount of the pension would be as of the date of the statement. If benefits have not yet vested, the statement must indicate the earliest date when benefits will vest. A request, however, for information regarding accrued benefits can be made only once in every 12-month period.[131] If more than one employer makes contributions to your plan, however, you might not get a benefit statement until the Department of Labor issues rules requiring the plan to provide statements.[132]

In addition, plan administrators are required to make copies of the legal pension plan document, the latest detailed financial report, and the written instrument under which the plan was established or is operating available for examination.[133] Plan participants or beneficiaries are entitled to obtain copies of these documents upon written request and payment of reasonable copying costs.[134]

How can I be sure that the information I receive from a plan is sufficient?

Under ERISA, plan administrators are required to file with the Secretary of Labor a copy of information sent to participants. This includes copies of the summary plan description and summaries of modifications in the plan. Also, the law requires that a report summarizing all aspects of a plan's financial operations must be made annually to the Secretary of Labor and to the Internal Revenue Service.[135] In addition, the Secretary of Labor is empowered to request even more detailed information regarding operation of the plan.[136] If you have doubts about the information you are receiving about your plan, contact the Pension and Welfare Benefit Administration, U.S. Department of Labor, 200 Constitution Ave., N.W., Room N-5658, Washington, D.C. 20210, (202) 523-8776 or the Department of Labor office nearest you. The Department has offices in the following cities: Boston, Mass.; New York, N.Y.; Philadelphia, Penn.; Atlanta, Ga.; Fort Wright, Ken.; Detroit, Mich.; St. Louis, Mo.; Chicago, Ill.; Kansas City, Mo.; Dallas, Tex.; San Francisco, Calif.; Seattle, Wash.; and Los Angeles, Calif. Consult a phone directory for the address and telephone number of the office nearest you.

What standards of conduct regulate the investments of pension-plan assets?

Before ERISA, a major problem faced by participants and beneficiaries of pension plans was the irresponsible way in which the assets of the plan were managed. Pension-plan trustees, managers, and others sometimes used fund assets to benefit themselves and invested fund assets in real-estate deals and other high-risk schemes that often went broke.

Under ERISA, plan trustees and others who exercise control over the management of the plan or the disposition of its assets or who render investment advice for a fee are required to discharge their duties solely in the interest of plan participants and beneficiaries.[137] They also are required to use care, skill, and prudence in managing the plan's assets,[138] and they must minimize the risk of losses to the fund by diversifying their investment of fund assets.[139]

ERISA also prohibits these persons from engaging in a wide range of practices harmful to the fund, such as lending the fund's money to friends; borrowing money from the fund for their personal use; selling their own property to the fund; or buying property from the fund. In addition, a pension plan may not have more than 10 percent of the fair market value of its assets invested in the employer's stock or real property.[140] If you suspect that plan assets are being invested in violation of these rules, you should contact an office of the U.S. Department of Labor.

May I sue my plan for violations of ERISA?

Yes. One of the most important features of ERISA is the fact that it substantially strengthens the ability of plan participants, retirees, and the government to sue their pension plans. Under ERISA, participants and beneficiaries may bring lawsuits against plans and those who manage them to enforce rights created by ERISA and by their pension plan.[141] The actions available include the following.

1. Participants and beneficiaries may sue plan administrators who fail or refuse to comply with proper requests for information. Administrators may be personally liable to the participant or beneficiary for up to $100 per day from the date of the failure or refusal.[142] Any person who fails to furnish information or maintain records in accordance with the requirements of the law may be liable for a civil penalty of $10 for each employee with respect to whom the failure occurs.[143] And there may be criminal liability for willful violations of disclosure requirements: for violations by a private individual, the law provides for a $5,000 fine or imprisonment for not more than one year, or both; corporate violations may result in a fine of up to $100,000.[144]

2. Participants and beneficiaries may sue to recover benefits due, to enforce existing rights, or to clarify rights to future benefits under the terms of the plan.[145]
3. Suit may be brought against persons who have any discretionary control over the management of a plan for breach of their duties under ERISA and the plan.[146] The law provides that these people will be personally liable for restoration of any losses to the plan that result from a breach of their duties.[147]
4. Participants may sue to prevent any act which violates any provision of the law or to enforce any provision of the law or the plan.[148]
5. Participants also may request the secretary of labor to exercise his authority to enforce the participation or vesting provisions of ERISA.[149] And the secretary also may sue to prevent improper practices or to enforce ERISA or plan provisions.[150]
6. Finally, it is important to emphasize that under ERISA, courts may allow reasonable attorneys' fees and costs of the action to either party.[151] This provision may encourage plan participants to bring lawsuits to vindicate their rights by making it economically possible to obtain a lawyer to bring these suits. A worker who wins a law suit to recover benefits unlawfully denied by a pension plan will ordinarily be awarded an attorney's fee, unless such an award would be unjust.[152] However, a worker who brings a frivolous lawsuit could be required to pay the other side's attorney's fee.[153] If you believe the pension plan is not complying with its legal obligation either to provide you with information or benefits you are entitled to, you also can contact the Office of Technical Assistance within the Department of Labor (Room N5658, U.S. Department of Labor, Washington, D.C. 20216; (202) 523-8776).

Can sex discrimination in pension plans be challenged?
Yes. The federal courts have been consistent in holding that the Civil Rights Act of 1964, Title VII[154] applies to retirement funds.[155] The relevant provisions of Title VII[156] make it an

unlawful practice for an employer to discriminate against an employee on the basis of sex.[157]

Does the Age Discrimination in Employment Act of 1967 affect pension plans?

The Age Discrimination in Employment Act of 1967 (ADEA), passed seven years before ERISA, was generally not intended to regulate pension plans.[158] The act permitted employee benefit plans to make age distinctions where the cost of providing a benefit increased with an employee's age.[159] In 1979, the U.S. Department of Labor interpreted the 1978 amendments to the ADEA to permit plans to deny an employee benefits for service beyond the plan's normal retirement age.[160] This interpretation was withdrawn in 1987.[161] It is unclear how the ruling will affect employees previously denied credit by their plans for their service after normal retirement age. Effective for 1988 and after, however, an amendment to the ADEA will require plans to give employees credit for service after the plan's normal retirement age.[162]

An employee denied benefit credit under a pension plan for service before 1988 which is after the plan's normal retirement age, may choose to file a charge of age discrimination with the nearest office of the Equal Employment Opportunity Commission (EEOC). Prompt filing of a charge is necessary to protect your rights under the ADEA and to preserve your right to pursue your claim in court. Filing the charge does not guarantee that you will receive benefit credit for your past service.

What effect does the Labor-Management Relations Act have on enforcement of pension rights?

Section 301[163] of the Labor-Management Relations Act (LMRA) grants to federal courts the power to hear suits by and against labor organizations[164] to enforce collective-bargaining agreements, and it can be used in suits involving collectively bargained pension plans. Plans subject to section 301 are those administered solely by the employer.

Section 302 of the LMRA[165] also can be used to enforce the rights of plan participants; it applies only to pension funds that are jointly administered by an employer and a union.

To be successful in a case filed under sections 301 or 302, you must prove that the trustees of the pension fund have acted arbitrarily, capriciously, or in bad faith.[166] This is a difficult burden to bear, and most suits under these sections have been unsuccessful.[167] A notable recent exception is a case in which a federal court of appeals found that plan trustees acted arbitrarily and capriciously in 1970 when they decided to raise benefit levels two and a half times for employees who qualified for pensions but, at the same time, maintained their eligibility rules which had the effect of excluding 96 percent of employees from qualifying for a pension.[168]

The LMRA is less important to pension-plan participants now than it was before ERISA since, in most situations, ERISA provides better remedies than does the LMRA. Nevertheless, ERISA does not provide full relief in all situations, and a plan participant may still wish to sue under the LMRA. The court will apply the same standard in reviewing whether a plan trustee has complied with his obligations under either the LMRA or ERISA.[169] The court, however, will not review under either statute whether the terms of a union-negotiated pension plan, contained in a collective bargaining agreement, are fair and reasonable, as long as the terms are legal.[170] The court will, though, determine whether the trustees have acted arbitrarily or capriciously in interpreting or administering the plan.[171]

In a divorce action, do I have a right to share in my spouse's pension or retirement benefits?

Whether a husband or a wife has a right to receive any part of their spouse's private pension depends on state law. Most states consider retirement benefits to be part of the marital property divided at divorce.[172]

Another major factor considered by the courts is whether the pension has vested at the time of the divorce proceedings. If the pension has vested, the court is more likely to recognize the pension as property. If it has not vested, a court is less likely to consider pension benefits as marital property that can be divided.[173]

Upon divorcing, if a court-approved property settlement agreement or a court order gives you a share of your ex-spouse's pension, the Retirement Equity Act of 1984 requires the plan to pay you that share.[174] The plan will be required to obey the court order (called "qualified domestic relations order") only if the order clearly states (1) the plan that the order applies to; (2) the name and mailing address of the ex-spouse and of each person who will be receiving a share of that pension; and (3) how much the plan will pay to each person receiving a share, how the payments are to be made, and for how long the payments will continue.[175] You may receive your share as soon as your ex-spouse reaches the plan's earliest retirement age (typically 55), even if he does not apply for his pension until later.[176] And you may receive your share in any form that the plan uses to pay benefits.[177] The plan also must provide you with certain information, such as a copy of the plan, the summary plan booklet (including future notice of changes in the booklet), and the summary annual report.[178]

Before the REA, plans were not required to pay survivors' benefits to divorced spouses.[179] The REA allows a divorce court to order the plan to pay a spouse a survivor's pension.[180] If the divorce occurs after a worker has retired and signed away (the worker is no longer permitted, after 23 August 1984, to sign away survivor's protection for a spouse) survivors' protection for a spouse, the plan may object to being required to change the form of benefit once it starts to be paid. At least one court, however, has said the plan *can* be forced to pay a survivor's pension.[181]

Plans must honor "qualified" court orders issued on or after 1 January 1985 and orders which were issued before then if the plan is paying benefits required by the order on 1 January 1985.[182]

Does the Internal Revenue Code protect pensions?

Yes. All of the major substantive protections of ERISA are also part of the Internal Revenue Code (IRC).[183] The Internal Revenue Service has been given exclusive authority to interpret these provisions.[184] Despite the extensive role played by the IRC, it offers plan participants relatively few direct remedies, most of which have been discussed elsewhere in this chapter.

Can I establish my own pension plan?

Yes. An individual may deduct up to $2,000 per year from gross income to contribute to an Individual Retirement Account (IRA).[185] Workers and nonworking spouses may contribute up to $2,250 to a joint IRA. By doing this, the individual is allowed a deduction from gross income, with the above maximums, so that the individual receives the deduction whether he or she takes the standard deduction or itemizes. If a worker or spouse, however, is a participant in a retirement plan, and your income is over a certain amount ($25,000 if single, $40,000 if married), you may lose all or part of the tax deduction for your contribution to the IRA.[186] And if you contribute more than the allowed amount, some income tax disadvantages will result.[187] To find out more about Individual Retirement Accounts, contact the IRS or any financial institution.

NOTES

1. Profit sharing, certain employer-sponsored savings and stock bonus plans, and other plans are often referred to as pension plans. However, in this chapter, we are limiting our discussion to conventional pension plans, which are plans providing for the payment of definitely determinable benefits to employees after retirement for a period of years, usually for life. Pension benefits are not based on an employer's profits. While many pension plans provide that employees who become disabled are eligible to receive their vested pension benefits before reaching the plan's normal retirement age (typically age 65), pension plans are not required to do so.

2. *Social Security Bulletin, Annual Statistical Supplement, 1986,* tables 71, 92. United States Dep't. of Health and Human Services, Social Security Administration.

3. *Inland Steel Co. v. NLRB,* 170 F.2d 247, 253 (7th Cir. 1948), *cert. den.,* 336 U.S. 960 (1949).

4. "Designing a Retirement System For Federal Workers Covered by Social Security," Committee on Post Office and Civil Service, U.S. House of Representatives, Comm. Print 98-17, 98th Cong., 2d Sess., 229.

5. *March, 1985 Current Population Survey,* Current Population Reports, Series P-60, No. 149, Aug. 1985. United States Bureau of the Census, Income Branch. In addition to traditional pension plans, some employers maintain profit-sharing plans and other arrangements to which portions of ERISA may not apply. For example, the insurance provisions of ERISA do not apply to profit-sharing plans.

6. Employee Retirement Income Security Act of 1974, Pub. L. No. 93-406, Sept. 2, 1974, 88 Stat. 829 *et seq.,* 29 U.S.C. §§ 1001–1461 (1982). ERISA was amended by the Multi-employer Pension Plan Amendments Act of 1980 (MPPAA), Pub. L. No. 96-364, Sept. 26,

1980, 94 Stat. 1218 *et seq.*, The Retirement Equity Act of 1984 (REA), Pub. L. No. 98-397, Aug. 23, 1984, 98 Stat. 1426 *et seq.*, the Single Employer Pension Plan Amendments Act of 1986 (SEPPAA), Pub. L. No. 99-272, Apr. 7, 1986, Title XI; the Omnibus Budget Reconciliation Act of 1986, Pub. L. No. 99-509, Oct. 21, 1986, and the Tax Reform Act of 1986, Pub. L. No. 99-514, Oct. 22, 1986.

7. Governmental and church pension plans, as well as some other specialized types of pension plans are exempt from ERISA's requirements. 29 U.S.C. § 1003(b) (1982).

8. Different provisions of the act became effective at different times. Check with an office of the Dep't. of Labor to learn when each provision of the act went into effect. Write or call the Pension and Welfare Benefit Administration, U.S. Department of Labor, 200 Constitution Ave, N.W., Room N-5658, Washington, D.C. 20210, (202) 523-8776 for the Department of Labor office nearest you.

9. 29 U.S.C. §§ 141–97 (1982 & Supp. III 1985).

10. 29 U.S.C. §§ 621–34 (1982 & Supp. III 1985).

11. 42 U.S.C. § 2000e (1982).

12. 26 U.S.C. §§ 1–9042 (1982 & Supp. III 1985). The Internal Revenue Code was amended by the Tax Equity and Fiscal Responsibility Act of 1982 (TEFRA), Pub. L. No. 97-248, 96 Stat. 324 *et seq.* (1982), to require plans seeking tax advantages to give employees additional rights, and by the Consolidated Omnibus Budget Reconciliation Act of 1985 (COBRA), Pub. L. No. 99-272, Titles X and XI (1986); the Omnibus Budget Reconciliation Act of 1986, Pub. L. No. 99-509, and by the Tax Reform Act of 1986, Pub. L. No. 99-514 (1986).

13. 26 U.S.C. § 410(b) (1982), as amended by the Tax Reform Act of 1986, Pub. L. No. 99-514, § 1112(a).

14. ERISA originally permitted plans to exclude employees under age 25 from participating. Starting in 1985, for most plans, the Retirement Equity Act of 1984 only permits plans to exclude employees under age 21, 29 U.S.C. § 1001 (note) (Supp. III 1985); Pub. L. No. 98-397, § 302(a).

15. 29 U.S.C. § 1052(a)(1)(A) (Supp. III 1985).

16. Plans providing employees with fully vested rights to their subsequently accrued benefits after three years of service may require up to three years of service instead of one year for entry into the plan. The Tax Reform Act of 1986, Pub. L. No. 99-514, § 1113(e)(3), reduces this three-year waiting period to two years, starting in 1989. 29 U.S.C. § 1052(a)(1)(B)(i) (1982). Under this variation, the age-21 requirement would remain in force. Plans maintained exclusively for educational institutions may substitute age 26 for age 21 if they provide for 100 percent vesting after one year of service. 29 U.S.C. § 1052(a)(1)(B)(ii) (Supp. III 1985).

17. All hours that the employee is paid or entitled to be paid must be counted (such as for sick leave or vacation time). 29 C.F.R. § 2530.200b–2(a) (1986); 29 U.S.C. §§ 1052(a)(3)(A), (C) (1982). Once employees have completed the initial 1,000 hours of service, plans must provide for them to begin participation on the first day of the following plan year or six months after they have satisfied the service requirement, whichever is earlier. 29 U.S.C. § 1052(a)(4) (1982).

18. If a plan uses this "elapsed time" rule, additional rules require the plan to count certain time during layoffs toward satisfying the one-year requirement. 26 C.F.R. § 1.410(a)–7(c) (1986). The rule does not require work to be full-time. The rule requires that periods of full- or part-time work be counted.

19. 29 U.S.C. §§ 1052(a)(2)(A),(B) (1982).

20. ERISA § 202(a)(2), as amended by the Omnibus Budget Reconciliation Act of 1986, § 9203(a)(1).

21. Classification of a pension plan as a defined-benefit plan also has important consequences for funding and benefit guarantee purposes. This will be discussed later in this chapter. *See also* 29 U.S.C. § 1002(35) (1982).

22. Pension benefits can be computed in two different ways. One, already discussed, is the defined-benefit plan. The other is the defined-contribution plan. "In a defined-contribution plan, the employer contributes a specified amount to the employee's account for each year of service. Unlike the defined-benefit plan, the retirement benefit is not fixed, but varies with the amount of such contributions and the performance of the plan's investments during the employee's career. The accrued benefit under a defined-contribution plan is merely the balance in the individual's account at any given time." Preminger, Jennings, & Alexander, "What Do You Get with the Gold Watch? An Analysis of the Employee Retirement Income Security Act of 1974," 17 *Ariz. L. Rev.* 424, 437 (1975). *See also* 29 U.S.C. §§ 1002(34),(35) (1982); *Nachman Corp. v. PBGC*, 446 U.S. 359 (1980).

23. 29 U.S.C. § 1054(b)(3) (Supp. III 1985); 29 C.F.R. § 2530.204 (1986).

24. 29 U.S.C. § 1054(b)(1) (1982). While you might earn larger benefits during later years because a uniform rate is applied to your higher earnings, the rate at which you earn benefits (as a percentage of earnings) must be fairly uniform during your work years. If the plan uses this "fractional" rule to calculate your benefits and if you leave the plan before your normal retirement age, benefits you would be entitled to *if* you had worked until normal retirement age are multiplied by the fraction: total years of plan participation/total years you would have participated if you had worked until normal retirement age.

25. 29 U.S.C. § 1054(b)(1)(C) (1982).

26. Nevertheless, if a plan does not provide for early retirement, ERISA does not give employees the right to receive their vested pension benefits before normal retirement age. *Johnson v. Franco*, 727 F.2d 442 (5th Cir. 1984); *Hernandez v. Southern Nevada Culinary and Bartenders Pension Trust*, 662 F.2d 617 (9th Cir. 1981). ERISA also does not require a pension plan to pay benefits in a lump sum, but some plans do. The higher the interest rate used by the plan to calculate the lump-sum value of your benefit, the less you get. IRS rules require the plan to say what interest rate they are using. Revenue Ruling 79-90, IRB 1979-11, p. 11. To calculate the lump-sum value of your benefit, a plan may not use an interest rate higher than the rate used by the Pension Benefit Guaranty Corp. to value benefits when a plan terminates. If that amount is over $25,000, the plan may then use an interest rate which is 120 percent of the PBGC rate in determining how much you actually receive. This rule generally applies to lump sums distributed after 1984. ERISA § 203(e), 29 U.S.C. § 1053(e) (Supp. III 1985), as amended by the Tax Reform Act of 1986, § 1139.

27. As indicated later in this chapter, some plans are required to have more stringent vesting.

28. 29 U.S.C. § 1053(a) (1982).

29. The Tax Reform Act of 1986, § 1113.

30. 86 percent of employees in medium- and large-sized firms participate in pension plans with ten-year vesting. "Employee Benefits in Medium and Large Sized Firms, 1985," United States Dep't. of Labor, Bureau of Labor Statistics, Bulletin 2262, July, 1986, Table 63. Smaller employers frequently use the 4-40 vesting formula to protect against violating an IRS rule which prohibits paying disproportionately higher benefits to higher paid employees. *See* note 41.

31. 29 U.S.C. § 1053(a)(2)(A) (1982).

32. Defined-benefit pension plans providing flat dollar pension benefits average $15/month per year of service in companies with at least 100 employees. "Employee Benefits in Medium and Large Sized Firms," Bureau of Labor Statistics, U.S. Dep't. of Labor, Bulletin 2262, July, 1986, p. 49.

33. 29 U.S.C. § 1053(a)(2)(B) (1982).

34. 29 U.S.C. § 1053(a)(2)(C)(i) (1982).

35. 29 U.S.C. § 1053(a)(2)(C)(ii) (1982).

36. 26 U.S.C. §§ 416(g),(i) (1982 & Supp. III 1985). These requirements were added to the Internal Revenue Code by the Tax Equity and Fiscal Responsibility Act of 1982 (TEFRA).

37. 26 U.S.C. § 416(c) (1982 & Supp. III 1985).

38. 26 U.S.C. § 416(b) (1982).

39. 26 C.F.R. § 1.416-1 (Q + A V-7) (1988).

40. Rev. Proc. 75-49, 1975-2 C.B. 584, *modified by* Rev. Proc. 76-11, 1976-1 C.B. 550.

41. Rev. Rul. 302, 1968-1 C. B. 163. The IRS, however, is directed by the ERISA House Conference Report not to require a vesting schedule more stringent than 40 percent after four years with 5 percent for the next two years, followed by 10 percent for the next four years. H.R. Rep. No. 1280, 93d Cong., 2d Sess. 276–77 (1974). Prior to ERISA, the IRS could require a plan to provide fully vested rights after a reasonable waiting period if necessary to combat the anticipated discrimination.

42. 29 U.S.C. § 1140 (1982).

43. *Mason v. Continental Group, Inc.*, 763 F.2d 1219 (11th Cir. 1985); *cert. den.* 106 S. Ct. 863 (1985); *Kross v. Western Electric Co.*, 701 F.2d 1238 (7th Cir. 1983); *contra, Amaro v. Continental Can, Inc.*, 724 F.2d 747 (9th Cir. 1984).

44. 29 U.S.C. § 1053(b)(1) (Supp. III 1985). Plans are also permitted to give vesting credit for years worked before the employer(s) began contributing to the plan. When more than one employer begins contributing to the plan, the plan can reserve the right to cancel this "past service credit" if that employer subsequently withdraws from the plan. 26 U.S.C. § 411(a)(3)(E) (1982), added by the Multiemployer Pension Plan Amendments Act of 1980 Pub. L. No. 96-364, § 206.

45. *Id.* Years of service in which an employee fails to contribute to a plan requiring employee contributions and years of service in which an employer does not maintain a plan may be disregarded. 29 U.S.C. § 1053(b)(1)(B),(C), (1982). Years of service before age 18 also may be disregarded, except that plans adopting the rule-of-45 schedule may not disregard years of service before age 25 during which the employee was a participant. 29 U.S.C. § 1053(b)(1)(A) (Supp. III 1985). ERISA required plans to count an employee's years of service after age 22 for vesting purposes. The REA amends ERISA to require plans to count years of service after age 18.

46. 26 C.F.R. § 1.410(a)–7(d) (1986). A plan using this "elapsed time" method of counting service must add together nonsuccessive periods of service and give you credit for interruptions in employment of less than one year, 26 C.F.R. § 1.410(a)–7(d)(1) (1986); and give you up to 12 months additional credit if you are laid off or placed on a leave of absence. 26 C.F.R. §§ 1.410(a)–7(a)(3),(b)(2) (1986).

47. *Swaida v. IBM Retirement Plan*, 728 F.2d 159 (2d Cir.) *cert. den.* 469 U.S. 874 (1984).

48. R. Nader & K. Blackwell, *You and Your Pension* (1973).

49. 29 U.S.C. § 1052(b) (1982 & Supp. III 1985); 29 C.F.R § 2530.204 (1986).

50. 29 U.S.C. § 1053(b)(3)(A), (B) (Supp. III 1985).
51. 29 U.S.C. §§ 1052(b)(4), 1053(b)(3)(D) (Supp. III 1985). Int. Rev. Code of 1954, §§ 410(a)(5)(D), 411(a)(6)(D). The plan may require a full year of service after the break before crediting years of service prior to the break. 29 U.S.C. §§ 1052(b)(3), 1053(b)(3)(B) (1982); Int. Rev. Code of 1954, §§ 410(a)(5)(C), 411(a)(6)(B).
52. After 1984, a worker who takes a year off from work because she is pregnant or because he or she cares for a newly born or adopted child cannot be charged with a break-in-service for that one year. In other words, whatever the length of the break, it will be reduced by one year if leave is taken for these reasons. 29 U.S.C. §§ 1052(b)(5), 1053(b)(3)(E) (Supp. III 1985). A plan negotiated by a union may wait until the agreement in effect on Aug. 23, 1984 terminates but only until Jan. 1, 1987 to comply with this rule and the five-year-break rule. These rules are amendments to ERISA added by the Retirement Equity Act of 1984. 29 U.S.C § 1001 (note) (Supp. III 1985). The rule that breaks-in-service be at least five years before you lose credit, added by the REA, will not restore pre-break years of credit lost before the rule applies.
53. 29 U.S.C. § 1052(b)(3) (1982), 1053(b)(3)(B) (1982).
54. *Noell v. American Design Profit Sharing Plan*, 764 F.2d 827 (11th Cir. 1985); *Hepple v. Roberts & Dybdahl, Inc. Profit Sharing Plan*, 622 F.2d 962 (8th Cir. 1980); *Hummell v. S. E. Rykoff & Co.*, 634 F.2d 446 (9th Cir. 1980).
55. 29 U.S.C. § 1053(c)(1)(A) (1982).
56. 29 U.S.C. § 1054(g)(2) (Supp. III 1985); Pub. L. No. 98-397, § 301(a)(2), 98 Stat. 451.
57. 130 Cong. Rec. S9671, S9679-80 (daily ed. Aug. 2, 1984) (S. Rep. on H.R. 4280, 98th Cong., 2d Sess.).
58. 29 U.S.C. § 1054(g)(2) (Supp. III 1985); Pub. L. No. 98-397, § 301(a)(2), 98 Stat. 1451.
59. 130 Cong. Rec. S9742 (daily ed. Aug. 6, 1984) (remarks of Sen. Dole); 130 Cong. Rec. H8756 (daily ed. Aug. 9, 1984) (remarks of Rep. Clay).
60. 29 U.S.C. § 1053(b)(1) (Supp. III 1985). Similarly, plans must provide that participants will be entitled to receive benefits equal to or greater than the benefits they would have been entitled to receive immediately before the merger had the plan been terminated. 29 U.S.C. § 1058 (1982).
61. ERISA § 1015, 26 U.S.C. § 414(a)(2) (1982), provides that service for a former owner, under a new owner's plan shall, to the extent provided by the Treasury Department regulations, be treated as service for the new owner. To date, the Treasury Department has not issued any regulations under this provision. *See Phillips v. Amoco Oil Co.*, 799 F.2d 1464 (11th Cir. 1986), *cert den.*, 107 S. Ct. 1893 (1987).

62. 29 U.S.C. § 1022(b) (1982). *See generally* Pillsbury, "Employee Benefit Plan Claims Under ERISA," 8 *Journal of Pension Planning and Compliance* 49 (1982).

63. *Id.*

64. 29 U.S.C. § 1133 (1982); 29 C.F.R. § 2560.503–1(e)(3) (1986).

65. 29 C.F.R. § 2560.503–1(f)(1,2) (1986).

66. 29 C.F.R. § 2560.503–1(e)(2) (1986).

67. 29 C.F.R. § 2560.503–1(g)(1) (1986).

68. 29 C.F.R. § 2560.503–1(g)(3) (1986).

69. 29 C.F.R. § 2560.503–1(h)(1) (1986).

70. 29 C.F.R. § 2560.503–1(h)(3) (1986).

71. 29 C.F.R. § 2560.503–1(g)(1) (1986).

72. 29 U.S.C. § 1133 (1982).

73. *Grossmuller v. UAW*, 715 F.2d 853 (3d Cir. 1983).

74. 29 U.S.C. § 1132(e) (1982).

75. *Mason v. Continental Group, Inc.*, 763 F.2d 1219 (11th Cir.) *cert. den.* 106 S. Ct. 863 (1985) *Amato v. Bernard*, 618 F.2d 559 (9th Cir. 1980).

76. *Short v. Central States Pension Fund*, 729 F.2d 567, 571 (8th Cir. 1984).

77. *But see Maggard v. O'Connell*, 671 F.2d 568 (D.C. Cir. 1982), where the court did not accept the plan trustees' decision concerning what the facts were because both the process and the evidence establishing the facts of the case were not adequate.

78. "Where both the trustees of a pension fund and a rejected applicant offer rational, though conflicting, interpretations of plan provisions, the trustees' interpretation must be allowed to control." *Miles v. New York State Teamsters Conference Pension and Retirement Fund Employee Benefit Plan*, 698 F.2d 593, 601 (2d Cir.), *cert. den.*, 464 U.S. 829 (1983).

79. *See, e.g., Short v. Central States Pension Fund*, 729 F.2d 567 (8th Cir. 1984); *Wardle v. Central States Pension Fund*, 627 F.2d 820 (7th Cir. 1980), *cert. den.*, 449 U.S. 1112 (1981); *Carter v. Central States Pension Fund*, 656 F.2d 575 (10th Cir. 1981).

80. *Riley v. MEBA Pension Trust*, 570 F.2d 406 (2d Cir. 1977).

81. 29 U.S.C. § 1053(a)(3)(B)(i) (1982); 29 C.F.R. § 2530.203–3(c)(1) (1986).

82. 29 U.S.C. § 1053(a)(3)(B)(ii) (1982); 29 C.F.R. § 2530. 203–3(c)(2) (1986).

83. 29 C.F.R. § 2530.203–3(c)(1,2) (1986).

84. *Riley v. MEBA Pension Trust*, 570 F.2d 409–13 (2d Cir. 1977); 586 F.2d 968 (2d Cir. 1978). These rules limiting when the plan can suspend your pension only apply to plans that employers contribute to. If the plan is run by a union and funded entirely by employee contributions, these limitations do not apply. 29 U.S.C. § 1051(4) (1982).

85. *Geib v. N.Y. Teamster's Pension Fund*, 758 F.2d 973 (3d Cir. 1985); *Johnson v. Franco*, 727 F.2d 442 (5th Cir. 1984).

86. *Chambless v. Masters, Mates, and Pilots Pension Plan*, 772 F.2d 1032 (2d Cir. 1985), *cert. den.*, 106 S. Ct. 1994 (1985); *Deak v. Masters, Mates, and Pilots Pension Plan*, 821 F.2d 572 (11th Cir. 1987).

87. For your service during and after 1989, a plan may subtract only up to 50 percent of the pension benefit you accumulate because of the amount of your Social Security benefit. For service before 1989, the 50 percent cap does not apply, and pension benefits for some lower paid workers for these years could legally be wiped out because of the amount of their Social Security benefit. Internal Revenue Code § 401(1)(4)(B), as amended by the Tax Reform Act of 1986, 1111(a). The permissible cut-off point is determined by the Internal Revenue Service under a complex formula based on the part of your Social Security benefits attributable to employer contributions. *See* Schulz and Leavitt, *Pension Integration: Concepts, Issues, and Proposals*, Employee Benefits Research Institute, 1983, pp. 5–6. *See generally* Rev. Rul. 71-446, 1971-2 C.B. 187.

88. Pension plans are permitted to estimate a participant's Social Security benefits in calculating their pensions but then must recalculate benefits based on actual Social Security payments once the participant begins receiving Social Security, at the request of the participant. Rev. Rul. 84-45, 1984-1 C.B. 115; *Dameron v. Sinai Hospital of Baltimore, Inc.* 626 F. Supp. 1012, (D. Md., 1986) *aff'd*, 815 F.2d 975 (4th Cir. 1987).

89. 26 U.S.C. § 401(a)(5)(1982); 26 C.F.R.§ 1.411(c)(4) (1986). *See generally Alessi v. Raybestos-Manhatten, Inc.*, 451 U.S. 504 (1981). 56 percent of all plan participants in medium- and large-sized companies are in plans which are "integrated" with Social Security. "Employee Benefits in Medium and Large Firms, 1984," United States Dep't. of Labor, Bureau of Labor Statistics, Bulletin 2237 (1985), p. 11.

90. The fairness of pension integration formulas is currently in controversy. *See Schulz and Leavitt, supra* note 87; "The Case of the Disappearing Pension," Pension Rights Center, 1984.

91. 29 U.S.C. § 1056(b) (1982).

92. 29 U.S.C. § 1302(a). PBGC is a unit within the Dep't. of Labor.

93. 29 U.S.C. § 1321(a),(b) (1982). Defined-benefit plans were defined earlier in this chapter. *See* text accompanying note 19, *supra*.

94. One exception is an employer providing professional services which has a plan covering twenty-five or fewer active participants.

95. 29 U.S.C. § 1321(b)(13) (1982); 29 U.S.C. § 1306 (1982); 29 U.S.C. § 1322 (1982). Termination is defined by 29 U.S.C. § 1341–43 (1982). Events causing termination include the failure of the plan to meet ERISA funding requirements, the inability of the plan to pay benefits when due, and a significant reduction in the number of plan participants. *Id.*

96. Disputes have arisen between PBGC and pension plans over whether the plan is a defined-benefit or defined-contribution plan. PBGC has sought to protect workers by finding a plan to be a defined-benefit plan where the status of the plan is unclear. *Connolly v. PBGC*, 419 F. Supp. 737 (C.D. Cal. 1976) *rev'd* 581 F.2d 729 (9th Cir. 1978), *cert. den.*, 440 U.S. 935 (1979); *on remand*, No. 84-1555 (C.D. Cal., May 1, 1984), *aff'd*, 106 S. Ct. 1018 (1986).

97. 29 U.S.C. § 1322 (1982).

98. 29 U.S.C. § 1322(b) (1982).

99. 29 U.S.C. § 1322(b) (1982).

100. *Id.*

101. PBGC News Release, Nov. 21, 1985.

102. PBGC News Release, 87-4, Nov. 17, 1986.

103. 29 U.S.C. § 1053(a)(3)(E) (1982).

104. 29 U.S.C. § 1425(a)(1); 26 U.S.C. § 418D(a)(1) (1982).

105. 29 U.S.C. § 1322a(c)(1) (1982).

106. 29 U.S.C. § 1322a(c)(2) (1982).

107. 29 U.S.C. § 1322a (1982).

108. 29 U.S.C. § 1322a(h) (1982).

109. 29 U.S.C. § 1344(a)(6) (1982).

110. 29 U.S.C. §§ 1081–86 (1982). The Single Employer Pension Plan Amendments Act of 1986, Pub. L. No. 99-272, Title XI, 100 Stat. 82, Apr. 7, 1986, requires a pension plan to have sufficient assets to provide for all pension benefits promised to employees before an employer who is not in financial difficulty will be permitted to terminate the plan. 29 U.S.C. §§ 1341(b)(1), (b)(2)(A)(i) (1982), as amended by Pub. L. No. 99-272, § 11008. Generally, if an employer files a request after Dec. 31, 1985 to terminate a plan, the plan must comply with this requirement. Pub. L. No. 99-272, § 11019(a). *See also* PBGC transition rules, 51 Fed. Reg. 12489 (Apr. 10, 1986).

111. 29 U.S.C. § 1055(a) (Supp. III 1985), 29 U.S.C. § 1001 (note) (Supp. III 1985); Pub. L. No. 98-397, § 303(c).

112. 29 U.S.C. § 1055(a) (Supp. III 1985).

113. 29 U.S.C. § 1055(c)(2) (Supp. III 1985).

114. 29 U.S.C. § 1055(d) (Supp. III 1985).

115. 29 U.S.C. § 1055(c)(3)(B) (Supp. III 1985).

116. 50 Fed. Reg. 29,371 (1985), Proposed Reg. 26 C.F.R. § 1.401-11T (Q & A 30).

117. 29 U.S.C. § 1055(c) (Supp. III 1985).

118. 29 U.S.C. § 1055(e)(1) (Supp. III 1985).

119. 29 U.S.C. § 1055(f) (Supp. III 1985).

120. 29 U.S.C. § 1001 (note) (Supp. III 1985); Pub. L. No. 98-397, § 303(e)(2) (1984).

121. 50 Fed. Reg. 29,371 (1985), codified as 26 C.F.R. § 1.401(a)-11T (Q & A 28).

122. 29 U.S.C. § 1001 (note) (Supp. III 1985); Pub. L. No. 98-397, § 303(c)(1) (1984).

123. Employee Retirement Income Security Act of 1974, Pub. L. No. 93-406, § 205(b), (c)(1); 88 Stat. 862 (1974).

124. Employee Retirement Income Security Act of 1974, Pub. L. No. 93-406, § 205(c)(1); 88 Stat. 862 (1974).

125. *Id.*

126. 29 U.S.C. § 1024(b)(1) (1982).

127. 29 U.S.C. § 1022(a)(1) (1982). One court has stated in passing that plan descriptions should note deficiencies as well as describe benefits of the plan. *See Johnson v. Central States, Southeast and Southwest Areas Pension Fund*, 513 F.2d 1173 (10th Cir. 1975).

128. 29 U.S.C. § 1022(b) (1982). Although ERISA does not require that plans give participants the legal plan document, and few do, many plans take the position that it is this document—not the summary plan description given to participants—that controls if they are different. One federal court of appeals has held that a participant was justified in relying on a reasonably clear and literal interpretation of a summary plan description to determine his rights to a pension, even if the summary was inconsistent with the plan document. *McKnight v. Southern Life and Health Insurance Co.*, 758 F.2d 1566 (11th Cir. 1985). Another court of appeals, however, has stated that a participant must show that he acted in reliance on the summary or would be significantly prejudiced if the summary was not applied. *Govoni v. Bricklayers Local 5 Pension Fund*, 732 F.2d 250 (1st Cir. 1984).

129. 29 U.S.C. § 1024(b)(1) (1982).

130. 29 U.S.C. §§ 1024(a), (b) (1982).

131. 29 U.S.C. §§ 1025(a), (b) (1982).

132. 29 U.S.C. § 1025(d) (1982).

133. 29 U.S.C. § 1024(b)(2) (1982).

134. 29 U.S.C. § 1024(b)(3) (1982).

135. 29 U.S.C. §§ 1021(b)(1), 1024(a)(1) (1982).

136. 29 U.S.C. § 1024(a)(1) (1982). As an additional safeguard, ERISA requires most plans to engage an independent accountant, who is empowered to examine plan records as necessary to determine whether the financial statements required in the annual report are presented fairly and consistently. The accountant must also determine whether the summary information distributed to participants is presented fairly. 29 U.S.C. § 1023(a)(3)(A) (1982).

137. 29 U.S.C. § 1104(a)(1)(A) (1982). These individuals are called fiduciaries. *Id.*

138. 29 U.S.C. § 1104(a)(1)(B) (1982).
139. 29 U.S.C. § 1104(a)(1)(C) (1982). Pension plan assets are the nation's largest single source of capital. In 1985, they were estimated at $1 trillion. Ippolito, Pensions, *Economics & Public Policy* (1985) at table 1-1.
140. 29 U.S.C. §§ 1106, 1107 (1982).
141. 29 U.S.C. § 1132(a) (1982). The act further provides that federal district courts shall have jurisdiction, without respect to jurisdictional amounts or diversity requirements, to redress grievances under the new law. 29 U.S.C. § 1132(f) (1982). The General Accounting Office estimates that the Labor Department can monitor only 1 percent of plans.
142. 29 U.S.C. §§ 1132(a)(1)(A), 1132(c) (1982).
143. 29 U.S.C. § 1059(b) (1982).
144. 29 U.S.C. § 1131 (1982).
145. 29 U.S.C. § 1132(a)(1)(B) (1982). If you are attempting to obtain benefits or enforce your rights under the terms of the plan, you may bring a lawsuit in state or federal court. If you are claiming, however, that the plan has violated legal obligations imposed by ERISA, you must file the lawsuit in federal court. 29 U.S.C. § 1132(e)(1) (1982). In either case, all claims relating to the plan will be decided by federal law under ERISA. State law will not apply. 29 U.S.C. § 1144(a) (1982); *Shaw v. Delta Air Lines*, 463 U.S. 85 (1983).
146. 29 U.S.C. § 1132(a)(2) (1982).
147. 29 U.S.C. § 1109(a) (1982). *See Massachusetts Mutual Life Ins. Co. v. Russell*, 473 U.S. 134 (1985). In addition, a fiduciary may be held liable, under certain conditions, for the breach of duty of a cofiduciary. *See* 29 U.S.C § 1105 (1982).
148. 29 U.S.C. § 1132(a)(3) (1982).
149. 29 U.S.C. § 1132(b)(2) (1982).
150. 29 U.S.C. § 1132(a)(5) (1982). Moreover, in order to determine whether a violation has occurred, the secretary of labor is empowered to launch investigations into the administration of plans. 29 U.S.C. § 1134(a) (1982).
151. 29 U.S.C. § 1132(g)(1) (1982).
152. *Smith v. CMTA-IAM Pension Trust*, 746 F.2d 587 (9th Cir. 1984); *Landro v. Glendenning Motorways, Inc.*, 625 F.2d 1344 (8th Cir. 1980).
153. *Bittner v. Sadoff & Rudoy Industries*, 728 F.2d 820 (7th Cir. 1984). A worker, however, who reasonably brings a lawsuit to recover benefits should ordinarily not be punished by having to pay an opponent's attorney's fee. *Marquardt v. North American Car Corp.*, 652 F.2d 715 (7th Cir. 1981).
154. 42 U.S.C. § 2000(e)(2) (1982).

155. *Burtmess v. Drewrys, U.S.A., Inc.*, 444 F.2d 1186 (7th Cir.), *cert. denied*, 404 U.S. 939 (1971).

156. 42 U.S.C. § 2000(e)(2)(a)(1) (1982).

157. *Arizona Governing Comm. for Deferred Comp. Plans v. Norris*, 463 U.S. 1073 (1983); *City of Los Angeles, Dep't. of Water & Power v. Manhart*, 435 U.S. 702 (1978).

158. *United Air Lines, Inc., v. McMann*, 434 U.S. 192 (1977).

159. *EEOC v. Westinghouse Electric Corp.*, 725 F.2d 211 (3d Cir. 1983), *cert. den.*, 469 U.S. 820 (1984).

160. 29 C.F.R. § 860.120(f)(1)(iv)(B) (1986).

161. *See American Assn. of Retired Persons v. EEOC*, 823 F.2d 600 (D.C. Cir., 1987); *see also* 29 C.F.R. § 1625.10 (1987).

162. 29 U.S.C. § 623(i), as amended by the Omnibus Budget Reconciliation Act of 1986, Pub. L. No. 99-509 § 9201, 100 Stat. 1973.

163. 29 U.S.C. § 185 (1982).

164. Even though the act speaks of suits only by and against labor organizations, courts have allowed the employee to sue in his own name. *Sheeran v. General Electric Co.*, 593 F.2d 93 (9th Cir.), *cert. den.*, 444 U.S. 868 (1979).

165. 29 U.S.C. § 186 (1982).

166. *Manes v. Williams*, 513 F.2d 1264 (8th Cir. 1975).

167. *E.g.*, *Craig v. Bemis Company*, 517 F.2d 677 (5th Cir. 1975).

168. *Ponce v. Construction Laborers Pension Trust for So. Cal.*, 774 F.2d 1401 (9th Cir. 1985).

169. *Harm v. Bay Area Pipe Trades Pension Fund*, 701 F.2d 1301 (9th Cir. 1983).

170. *UMW Health and Retirement Funds v. Robinson*, 455 U.S. 562 (1982).

171. *Hurn v. Plumbing, Heating and Piping Industry Trust*, 648 F.2d 1252 (9th Cir. 1981).

172. "Your Pension Rights at Divorce: What Women Need to Know," Women's Legal Defense Fund, Pension Rights Center, 1983.

173. *Compare Barba v. Barba*, 486 A.2d 928 (N.J. Sup. Ct. 1985) (nonvested interest not a marital asset) *with Hagerman v. Hagerman*, 682 S.W.2d 28 (Mo. App. 1984) (nonvested interest is marital asset).

174. 29 U.S.C. § 1056(d)(3)(A) (Supp. III 1985).

175. 29 U.S.C. § 1056(d)(3)(C) (Supp. III 1985).

176. 29 U.S.C. § 1056(d)(3)(E) (Supp. III 1985).

177. 29 U.S.C. § 1056(d)(3)(D,E) (Supp. III 1985).

178. 29 U.S.C. § 1056(d)(3)(J) (Supp. III 1985).

179. Employee Retirement Income Security Act of 1974, Pub. L. No. 93-406, § 205(d), 88 Stat. 863. ERISA only required plans to pay survivors' benefits to spouses married for one full year before the worker died. This rule still applies to workers who started to receive

pensions before the 1985 plan year started or who were not working or on paid leave under the plan on or after Aug. 23, 1984.

180. 29 U.S.C. § 1056(d)(3)(F) (Supp. III 1985).

181. *Allison v. Allison*, 234 Cal. Rptr. 671 (Cal. App. 2 Dist. 1987).

182. 29 U.S.C. § 1001 (note) (Supp. III 1985); Pub. L. No. 98-397 § 303(d).

183. The Treasury Department estimates that in 1986, it will lose $55 billion in revenue from tax breaks given to pension plans. *Special Analyses: Budget of the United States Government, Fiscal Year 1986*, Executive Office of the President, Office of Management and Budget, 1985, p. G-46. This is the largest of all federal tax subsidies.

184. ERISA Reorganization Plan 4, Executive Order 12108, 43 Fed. Reg. 47,713 (1978).

185. Int. Rev. Code of 1954, § 219.

186. Internal Revenue Code § 219, as amended by the Tax Reform Act of 1986, § 1101.

187. Int. Rev. Code of 1986, § 4973.

6

Age Discrimination in Employment

Age discrimination in employment is prohibited by statutes in a majority of our states as well as the District of Columbia. These statutes, however, vary in the age range of the protected class, the types of employment activities prohibited, and the remedies available to victims of age discrimination.[1] The absence of a national approach to the issue of age discrimination in employment had led to only limited success in challenging this problem.

Prior to 1964, the United States government had done little to remedy age discrimination in employment. However, Congress—in adopting Title VII of the Civil Rights Act of 1964, which prohibited discrimination based on race, color, religion, sex or national origin—included in the statute a section requiring the secretary of labor to report to Congress on the problem of age discrimination in employment. Section 715 of Title VII required the secretary to include in this report "recommendations for legislation to prevent arbitrary discrimination in employment because of age. . . ."[2] This report, which found that age discrimination in employment was a persistent and widespread problem, concluded that: "The elimination of arbitrary age limits on employment will proceed much more rapidly if the Federal Government declares clearly and unequivocally, and implements as far as practicable, a national policy with respect to hiring on the basis of ability rather than age."[3]

In 1967, Congress finally took a broad approach to the problem of age discrimination in employment when it enacted the Age Discrimination in Employment Act of 1967 (ADEA).[4] While responsibility for enforcement of the ADEA originally fell to the secretary of labor, Congress transferred this authority to the Equal Employment Opportunity Commission (EEOC) in 1979.[5]

Is age discrimination in employment illegal?

It is unlawful under many state statues as well as the federal ADEA to discriminate on the basis of age in employment decisions. The stated purpose of the ADEA is "to promote the employment of older persons based on their ability rather than age" and "to prohibit arbitrary age discrimination in employment."[6] Because the ADEA, as originally enacted, did not apply to state and local governmental units,[7] constitutional challenges to age limits in public sector jobs were important in the early 1970s. In 1974, Congress amended the act to cover these governmental units.[8] The leading case in this area involved a challenge to the state of Massachusetts' mandatory retirement age of 50 for state troopers, *Massachusetts Board of Retirement v. Murgia*.[9] The Supreme Court in *Murgia* rejected the claim that age-based employment classifications required special judicial scrutiny under the Equal Protection Clause of the Fourteenth Amendment to the United States Constitution. The Court upheld the state's mandatory retirement age. Subsequent constitutional challenges to age limitations in public sector employment have been equally unsuccessful.[10]

The ADEA prohibits covered employers from discriminating against job applicants and employees in a wide range of employment actions, including hiring, promotion, training, demotion, lay off, fringe benefits, and discharge.[11] The act also makes it illegal for employment agencies to discriminate on the basis of age in employment referrals.[12] It is illegal for labor organizations to discriminate against their members on the basis of age or to attempt to cause an employer to violate the ADEA.[13] The ADEA also prohibits age-based employment advertising[14] as well as retaliation against individuals who have opposed violations of the act.[15]

Who is protected by the ADEA?

The ADEA, as originally enacted in 1967, protected individuals who were between the ages of 40 and 65.[16] In 1978, Congress amended the act to protect individuals who were between the ages of 40 and 70.[17] In 1986, Congress further expanded the ADEA's protections to cover all individuals over the age of 40.[18] Protection for federal employees also begins at age 40 and has no upper age limit.[19] The act applies to both applicants for employment[20] and employees of any employer covered by the law. In 1984, Congress amended the ADEA to include U.S. citizens employed by a United States employer or by a foreign company controlled by a United States employer in a workplace located in a foreign country.[21]

There are a number of exemptions to the act's protections.

State and local governments, until 31 December 1993, under certain conditions, can enforce hiring and retirement age limits for law enforcement officers and firefighters which otherwise would violate the ADEA.[22] And the ban on mandatory retirement does not apply to tenured faculty until 31 December 1993.[23] Prior to 1 January 1994, individuals who are serving under a contract of unlimited tenure at an institution of higher education can be retired at age 70.[24] Elected state and local officials and the non-civil service staff, as well as employees on the policy-making level are not protected by the act.[25] Employees who are working in executive or high policy-making positions and who would retire with benefits equal to at least $44,000 per annum may be involuntarily retired once they have reached age 65.[26] Finally, the act prohibits discrimination among those protected by the act (40 and older) which would favor younger protected age group members. Thus, if an employer discriminates against a 50-year-old in favor of a 40-year-old or a 30-year-old, the ADEA is applicable.[27] But, if the employer discriminates against a 35-year-old in favor of a 25-year-old, the ADEA is inapplicable.

Victims of age discrimination in employment need to understand the differences in protections offered by the ADEA and by the state statutes. While the ADEA protects those 40 and older from a broad range of age-based employment discrimination, a particular state's statute may protect a wider range of people or may prohibit only particular age-based conduct.[28] And the ADEA does not preempt state or local laws or regulations prohibiting age discrimination in employment.[29] In addition, there is a developing body of law, based on common-law contract and tort theories, that provides a basis for additional arguments that can be used to challenge age discrimination in employment.[30] Other courts have recognized a "covenant of good faith and fair dealing" applicable to certain employment relationships.[31]

Most importantly, those wishing to pursue an age discrimination claim under the ADEA need to carefully examine their own state's law prohibiting age discrimination in employment. Victims of age discrimination in employment should determine whether their state: (1) has a law prohibiting age discrimination in employment; and, (2) whether it has an agency to enforce such a law. The Supreme Court has held that when both these conditions are met, a claimant must resort to the state administrative proceeding before bringing an ADEA lawsuit.[32]

Who is subject to the ADEA?

The ADEA covers the activities of employers, employment agencies, and labor organizations. Employers subject to the act are those engaged in an industry affecting interstate commerce and who have twenty or more employees for each working day in each of twenty or more calendar weeks in the current or preceding calendar year.[33] In 1974, Congress amended the ADEA to include state and local governmental units in its definition of employers,[34] and the Supreme Court has upheld the ADEA's application to state and local governments.[35] Employment agencies are defined by the act to include any person or agent of such person who regularly seeks to procure employees for an entity meeting the ADEA's definition of employer.[36] To be covered by the ADEA, a labor organization must have at least twenty-five members or maintain a hiring hall to procure employment opportunities for employees.[37] It is uncertain whether the ADEA's prohibitions against discriminatory age limits applies to apprenticeship programs.[38]

How can age discrimination be proven?

The easiest way to make out a case of age discrimination is with evidence showing that the employer explicitly relied on the age of the applicant or employee in making a decision. For instance, if an employer's personnel manual provided that no person under 21 or over 50 would be hired and an employer rejected a 54-year-old applicant solely because of his age, a clear-cut case of age discrimination is evident.[39] Even without evidence of such overt discrimination, it may be possible to establish the employer's state of mind by demonstrating instances of overt age discrimination in other, but similar, circumstances, such as a company promoting a "younger image."[40]

But the basic question that arises is what an individual must show in court to prove that he or she is a victim of discrimination. The first step in proving discrimination is establishing a *prima facie* case. For example, if a 50-year-old applicant for a truck-driver job could show that he was rejected because of his age, a *prima facie* case of discrimination is established. If an individual fails to make out a *prima facie* case, he or she loses even if the other side offers no evidence at all.

"Disparate treatment" discrimination involves intentional, less favorable treatment of members of a protected class (i.e., those 40 years of age or older) from those not part of the protected class (i.e., those under 40). Thus, an employer's refusal to offer training to employees over 40 could constitute disparate treatment discrimination. In a disparate treatment case in which there is no direct evidence of discrimination, once a *prima facie* case is established, the burden shifts to the employer to produce a legitimate, nondiscriminatory reason for its action. For example, the employer who offered training only to those under 40 might assert, as a defense, that only those under 40 applied for the training. The ultimate burden of proving discrimination, therefore, remains with the individual claiming discrimination.[41]

The standard for a *prima facie* showing of discrimination set out in *McDonnell Douglas Corp. v. Green*,[42] an employment discrimination case brought under Title VII, has influenced ADEA cases. *McDonnell Douglas* provides that a plaintiff establishes a *prima facie* wrongful denial of hiring case by showing: (1) he is a member of the protected class; (2) he applied and was qualified for the job; (3) despite his qualifications, he was rejected; and, (4) after his rejection, the employer continued to seek applications with the plaintiff's qualification. A majority of courts have adopted *McDonnell Douglas* in ADEA cases, sometimes modifying the test to fit the particular facts of the case.[43] Other courts have questioned the application of *McDonnell Douglas* to ADEA cases.[44]

As a result of the broad range of age claims being litigated, including company- or plant-wide reduction-in-force cases, courts have had to adopt more flexible standards than those contained in the four-part *McDonnell Douglas* test.[45] Thus, in several reduction-in-force cases, the fourth part of the test (the employer sought to hire with the plaintiff's qualifications) has been eliminated.[46] In addition, some courts have held that when the plaintiff introduces direct or circumstantial evidence of discriminatory intent, the *McDonnell Douglas* standards need not be met.[47]

Can there be age discrimination even if age is not the only explanation for the employer's conduct?

Yes, there can be, if at least one of the bases of the employer's conduct is discriminatory. In a number of cases, the issue has arisen as to the true reason for an employer's action. If the court finds that the only reason for an employer's conduct was something other than age, such as the employee's inadequate job performance[48] or chronic tardiness,[49] no case of age discrimination exists. Conversely, if the employer's response to the employee's claim of age discrimination is shown to be no more than an excuse or pretext for discrimination (e.g., the reason given for termination is employee incompetence when the employer's desire to hire "younger and new people" constitutes the real motivation),[50] there is again no issue of multiple motives. The employee has proven age discrimination.

The difficulty arises when an employer seems to have acted with mixed motives, one of which is the age of an employee. However, it seems unlikely that the courts will require employees to prove that employers were motivated solely by age for employees to prevail in age discrimination cases. The majority of courts that have confronted this issue have found discrimination if age was a determining factor in decisionmaking, that is, one that made a difference with respect to the outcome.[51] A less accepted approach is to hold that the ADEA has been violated if age played *any* role in the decisionmaking process.[52]

Can there be age discrimination if the employer's action is based not on age, but on some "neutral" criterion that has a disproportionately adverse impact on older workers?

Yes. Two theories of liability have been recognized by the courts in employment cases involving the ADEA as well as Title VII—disparate treatment and disparate impact. Disparate treatment, which has already been discussed, involves claims of intentional discrimination.[53] Disparate impact claims involve systemic or institutional discrimination by employment policies which, while appearing neutral, have a greater negative effect on protected class members.[54] For example, a police department's policy of not hiring any police officer with more than two years of experience, a policy neutral in appearance, would have a more negative effect on those 40 and older than those under 40. Both of these theories of discrimination were originally developed under Title VII, the statute on which the ADEA's prohibitions are based.[55] While there has never been a question of intentional discrimination or disparate treatment being unlawful under the ADEA, there has been some controversy over the application of disparate impact analysis to ADEA cases.[56]

A problem that arises is that some employment practices that may disproportionately exclude older persons from employment are lawful. Thus, job-related employment qualifications that include a certain level of physical fitness may eliminate more older than younger people from job opportunities. Such provisions may be valid under the ADEA which allows employers to act on "reasonable factors other than age."[57]

In other situations, however, employers' actions have been found to violate the ADEA because of their disparate impact on older persons. For example, a school board's decision not to hire teachers with more than five years of teaching experience was held unlawful.[58] In that case, the court held that statistical evidence showing a correlation of years of experience and membership in the protected age group (40 to 70) sufficiently established the disparate impact required for proving age discrimination. In another case, a court considered whether an employee should be allowed to offer evidence that his employer selected him for a demotion because he received higher pay due to his seniority.[59] In that case, the court said that discrimination based on factors, such as seniority, that have an adverse impact on older employees violates the ADEA.[60] In a third case, former employees of Western Union asserted that they had been selected for furlough in a reduction-in-force action because of age-related factors.[61] While the former employees did not win, the court recognized that disparate impact analysis can be applied in such cases. In yet another case, an employer sought to justify its selection of employees for discharge on the grounds that those individuals lacked the special electronics training most needed by the company. The court held that such discharges constituted an unlawful practice since the employer had encouraged younger employees to participate in training, and older employees had not been available for training because of busy work schedules.[62] Courts also have held it unlawful for employers to deny transfers to employees on the grounds that they are approaching a mandatory retirement age[63] or to discharge older workers because younger employees offer the company more promise or potential.[64] These cases make it clear that maintaining age-based barriers to employment opportunities as well as intentional discrimination against individuals because of their age is unlawful.

What defenses are required of an employer, employment agency, or labor organization that has been accused of age discrimination?

The type of proof required of a defendant (i.e., employer, employment agency, or labor organization) to win an age discrimination in employment case depends on the type of evidence the plaintiff or victim of discrimination presents in establishing a *prima facie* case of age discrimination. If the plaintiff establishes a *prima facie* case using the *McDonnell Douglas* formula, the burden of production falls on the defendant to "articulate some legitimate, non-discriminatory reason" for its alleged discriminatory action.[65] This articulation requirement simply shifts the burden of production (or of going forward with evidence), and it does not shift the burden of persuasion. The burden of persuasion in such cases always rests with the plaintiff or victim of discrimination.[66]

In cases in which the plaintiff establishes a pattern or practice of discrimination (cases generally founded on statistics), the defendant must demonstrate that the plaintiff's proof is either inaccurate or insignificant.[67] When there is strong, direct evidence of discrimination—as in the case of an employee who can prove he was told he was being discharged because of his age—the defendant can only rebut this claim of discrimination by proving by a preponderance of evidence that the same decision would have been reached despite the presence of the age factor.[68] Less compelling direct evidence of discrimination does not justify shifting the burden of proof to the defendant.[69]

The ADEA sets forth five statutory defenses to a claim of age discrimination. Congress, in establishing the ADEA, and the federal agencies responsible for enforcing it, have recognized that certain practices of employers, employment agencies, and labor organizations should be lawful. These defenses are: bona fide occupational qualification (BFOQ),[70] reasonable factor other than age (RFOA),[71] employee benefit plan,[72] discharge or discipline for good cause,[73] and good faith reliance.

The RFOA and good cause defenses have been viewed simply as denials of a plaintiff's prima facie case.[74] The BFOQ, employee benefits plan, and good faith reliance defenses, in contrast, admit disparate treatment but seek to avoid liability by affirmative defense. Thus, an employer asserting these defenses has the burden of proving the affirmative defense by a preponderance of the evidence to avoid liability. The "good faith reliance" defense[75] provides that when an employer pleads and proves that its actions, which are alleged to be discriminatory, were taken "in good faith in conformity with and in reliance on any written administrative regulation, order, ruling, approval, or interpretation, of the . . . [Equal Employment Opportunity Commission],"[76] it cannot be held to have violated the ADEA.[77]

1. *The bona fide occupational qualification (BFOQ) defense.* The ADEA permits discrimination "where age is a bona fide occupational qualification reasonably necessary to the normal operation of the particular business."[78] There has been considerable litigation concerning this bona fide occupational qualification (BFOQ) defense and its application.

In June 1985, the Supreme Court adopted a two-pronged test for weighing a BFOQ defense.[79] First, an employer must show that the job qualifications it has established are reasonably necessary to the essence of its business. Second, the employer must have a factual basis for believing that either all or substantially all of the persons over the age limit cannot perform the job safely and efficiently or that it is impossible or highly impractical to assess fitness on an individualized basis.

Employers have had mixed success in asserting the BFOQ defense. While some courts have struck down maximum hiring age limits for jobs involving the public safety (e.g., police, firefighters, pilots),[80] other courts have upheld similar age limitations.[81] Courts also have split on the legality of mandatory retirement ages for employees in public safety jobs.[82] The varied results in these cases are due to the different facts presented in each case and the degree of scrutiny applied by the courts in evaluating the BFOQ defense.

In 1986, Congress passed the Age Discrimination in Employment Amendments,[83] which made several significant changes in the ADEA. The amendments expanded the act's protections by lifting the "age 70 cap," so that it protected all workers 40 and older. The amendments, however, also created a seven-year exemption for law enforcement and fire departments which allows them to enforce hiring or retirement age limits that were in effect on 3 March 1983.[84] This amendment will decrease substantially the number of cases in which employers will raise the BFOQ defense because most BFOQ cases have involved such public safety departments.

2. *The reasonable factor other than age defense.* The ADEA permits age discrimination when the differentiation is based on a "reasonable factor other than age" (RFOA).[85] Factors other than age that may be considered reasonable include physical fitness requirements, production standards, or validated tests. When, however, an employment practice, such as a test, has an adverse effect on people protected by the ADEA (those 40 or older), it will be lawful only if the employer can prove it is a "business necessity."[86] An employee's misconduct,[87] inability to communicate with management, and disrespect for management[88] as well as an employer's lack of work for an individual in light of his or her skills[89] have all been held lawful as "reasonable factors other than age." The "business necessity" test is met if an employer can prove that the challenged practice is "significantly related to successful job performance."[90] The defense is unavailable when an employment practice uses age as a limiting criterion (e.g., maximum hiring or mandatory retirement age limits).[91]

3. *The bona fide employee benefit plan defense.* The ADEA permits an employer to "observe the terms of any bona fide employee benefit plan such as a retirement, pension, or insurance plan" as long as the plan is not a subterfuge to evade the purposes of the act. Congress, however, amended the ADEA in 1978 to make it clear that no such employee benefit plan shall require or permit the involuntary retirement of an employee under age 70 on the basis of age.[92]

The purpose of the employee benefit plan defense is to take into account the increased cost of providing certain benefits to older workers. The defense allows employers to reduce benefits, such as retirement, pension, or insurance benefits, so long as the cost incurred by the employer on behalf of the older worker is equal to that incurred on behalf of the younger worker. As a result, employers will not be discouraged from hiring older workers because of the increased cost of providing such benefits.[93]

An employer seeking to use the employee benefit plan defense must prove that (1) the plan is bona fide; (2) it is not a subterfuge to evade the ADEA; and (3) the action taken against the employee was based on observing the terms of the plan. While a court has held that a plan is bona fide as long as it exists and pays benefits,[94] other courts have examined carefully whether a particular "plan" fits within this defense. Thus, one court held that a lay-off benefit plan, which does not have age-related cost factors but provides benefits based only on length of service, cannot be used to deny lay-off benefits to employees on the grounds that they are eligible for retirement.[95] The court reasoned the eligibility for retirement is too closely linked to age to be a valid justification.[96] Another court held that an employer's severance pay plan that excludes those eligible for retirement benefits from a one-time ad hoc cash payment was not a "bona fide" plan because it was not part of a coordinated benefit plan.[97] The pension plan defense also has been held inapplicable to an accrued sick leave pay policy.[98]

4. *The discharge or discipline for good cause defense.* The ADEA provides that employees can be disciplined or discharged for good cause.[99] An individual's being within the age group protected by the ADEA (40 or older) does not prevent an employer from disciplining or discharging the individual when "good cause" for such action exists. Good cause for terminations has been found in cases in which employers discharged employees for repeated tardiness[100] or poor performance.[101]

5. *The good faith reliance defense.* In addition to these four statutory defenses, the ADEA has incorporated a fifth from the Portal-to-Portal Act.[102] This defense provides that if an employer can prove that in taking an action that is challenged as discriminatory, he acted in good faith and in conformity with "any written administrative regulation, order, ruling, approval or interpretation,"[103] he will not be subject to any liability or punishment. The EEOC has established a procedure for obtaining opinion letters that could provide a basis for this defense.[104]

Are "help wanted" advertisements that specifically exclude or discourage those 40 and older from applying unlawful?

Employment advertisements that specifically exclude or discourage individuals protected by the ADEA from applying are generally unlawful.[105] However, such age-based advertising is lawful when the employer can prove that age is a bona fide occupational qualification.[106]

The general standard for reviewing help wanted advertisements is that employers and employment agencies may solicit job applicants among particular age groups, so long as the solicitation does not state or imply that only persons within those age groups are acceptable for employment. Thus, such terms as "excellent first job," "recent graduates," "returning veterans," and the like have been held nondiscriminatory when the employer is simply appealing to particular groups of potential applicants.[107] An advertisement, however, that states or implies that only young people need apply or limits individual positions to "recent graduates" or to persons "one or two years out of college," is impermissibly discriminatory.[108]

Use of the word "young" in help-wanted advertisements generally has been condemned by the courts[109] and sometimes is expressly forbidden by controlling statutes or rules.[110] The word "girl," because it is generally understood to imply youth, has likewise met judicial disapproval.[111] However, use of the word "junior," (e.g., junior executive,) has been viewed simply as stating the scope of employment duties nondiscriminatorily, rather than implying an intent to hire only young people.[112]

If I believe I have been the subject of age discrimination, how do I make an official complaint?

To assure that your rights are protected fully, take two actions immediately. First, file a charge of discrimination with the Equal Employment Opportunity Commission (EEOC) within 180 days of the discriminatory act.[113] The charge should provide the name of the discriminating party or parties (i.e., employer, employment agency, or labor organization), the specific type of discrimination involved (e.g., hiring, training, denial of benefits), and the facts that form the basis of the charge.[114] While it is possible to file a charge by letter or by phone,[115] it may be to your advantage to visit one of the EEOC offices in person. Second, if your state has a law prohibiting age discrimination in employment and an agency in charge of administering that law, also file the charge with your state agency. If you are unsure what agency to contact, your local EEOC office or state department of labor or employment services can advise you.

After filing a charge with the EEOC, you must wait at least sixty days before filing a lawsuit.[116] But it is important to file your lawsuit within two years of the discriminatory act to avoid having the suit dismissed as untimely.[117] However, the time limits for filing a charge may be waived by the courts under certain conditions. And while it is extremely important to be timely in filing with the EEOC or appropriate state agency, your failure to do so will not absolutely bar a lawsuit under certain limited circumstances.[118]

EEOC offices are located in the following cities: Albuquerque, NM; Atlanta, GA; Baltimore, MD; Birmingham, AL; Boston, MA; Buffalo, NY; Charlotte, NC; Chicago, IL; Cincinnati, OH; Cleveland, OH; Dallas, TX; Denver, CO; Detroit, MI; El Paso, TX; Fresno, CA; Greensboro, NC; Greenville, SC; Houston, TX; Indianapolis, IN; Jackson, MS; Kansas City, MO; Little Rock, AR; Los Angeles, CA; Louisville, KY; Memphis, TN; Miami, FL; Milwaukee, WI; Minneapolis, MN; Nashville, TN; Newark, NJ; New Orleans, LA; New York, NY; Norfolk, VA; Oakland, CA; Oklahoma City, OK; Philadelphia, PA; Phoenix, AZ; Pittsburgh, PA; Raleigh, NC; Richmond, VA; San Antonio, TX; San Diego, CA; San Francisco, CA; San Jose, CA; Seattle, WA; St. Louis, MO; Tampa, FL; and Washington, D.C. Consult a phone directory for the address and phone number of the office nearest you.

What should I include in the charge filed with the EEOC?
The basic purposes of the charge are to provide the EEOC with sufficient information, to notify the prospective defendant (i.e., the party that allegedly discriminated) of the charge, and to allow the EEOC the opportunity to resolve the alleged unlawful practice informally.[119] If you give the EEOC a detailed account of all the important information relating to your charge, the agency will be able to evaluate more fully your claim of discrimination. To the degree the information is available, you should include the following in your charge:

1. Your name, address, and telephone number;
2. The name, address, and telephone number of the party that discriminated against you (employer, employment agency, labor organization);
3. Who did or said what, when, and where;
4. All the circumstances—dates, participants, witnesses, etc.
5. Reasons the employer, employment agency, or labor organization gave for their actions and/or statement; and
6. Reasons you believe the above actions were taken and statements were made.

In addition, to the degree they are available and have a bearing on your charge, you should provide the EEOC with contracts, policy and procedure manuals, letters (such as applications, commendations, promotions, transfers, terminations), or any other documents that relate to your charge. You also should indicate the relief you seek (e.g., reinstatement, backpay, lost seniority, lost health benefits).

Can the EEOC investigate a claim of age discrimination without a formal charge?

The EEOC does not need to have a "charging party" in order to investigate a claim of age discrimination under the ADEA. The agency can act on any information concerning an alleged violation of the ADEA. In addition, the EEOC can, on its own, conduct an investigation of employers, employment agencies, and labor organizations.[120]

As a result, an employee who does not want to be identified to his employer as having filed a charge can take one of two steps to have the discriminatory conduct investigated. First, an individual can file a "complaint" rather than a charge, indicating that he does not want to have his claim disclosed to his employer. The identity of the complainant will not be revealed to the employer without the complainant's written consent or a court order.[121] Secondly, an individual can provide information concerning the possible ADEA violation directly to the EEOC. The EEOC can then conduct, on its own initiative, a directed investigation of the challenged practice.[122] The ability of the EEOC to conduct such directed investigations without a charging party, greatly expands its ability to enforce the ADEA. Agencies that refer older individuals for employment, for example, might notice that a particular employer that is hiring has failed to hire the older applicants the agency has referred. Such information, if provided to the EEOC, could be the basis for a directed investigation and a possible lawsuit alleging discrimination in hiring.

Why must someone give the EEOC notice of their age discrimination claim before bringing an age discrimination suit, and what happens during the waiting periods after filing the federal charge and/or state complaint?

The purposes of the notice requirement and waiting periods

are to provide time for the EEOC to attempt to resolve the dispute by "conciliation, conference, and persuasion";[123] to avoid litigation; to alert the EEOC to potential cases of widespread importance; and to alert employers of the charges against them on a timely basis.[124]

The ADEA and most state statutes make conciliation efforts an absolute requirement; the EEOC or the appropriate state agency must make efforts to settle the matter without litigation or other formal proceedings.[125] Most of the state statutes[126] also provide that all discussion during conciliation conferences are strictly confidential although there is no such requirement expressed in the ADEA.

If the discrimination complaint cannot be settled by conciliation, what then?

Under the ADEA, the discrimination victim may bring a suit sixty days after filing a charge of age discrimination.[127] The EEOC also is authorized to bring a suit in its own name or on behalf of the discrimination victim.[128] A suit by the EEOC—if it precedes the private suit—forecloses any suits by private parties.[129] An ADEA suit also supersedes any state proceedings then pending.[130]

Under many state antidiscrimination statutes, the next step after conciliation is a formal adversary proceeding. A hearing before the appropriate administrative agency may be the only state remedy available,[131] but the discrimination victim may have the option to sue directly in state court, bypassing the administrative process.[132] At state administrative hearings, the state agency itself may present the case against the alleged violator;[133] or the discrimination victim may do so on his own behalf; or the state agency may have the option of hearing a presentation by its legal staff,[134] the victim, or both.[135] In some states, the agency's legal staff or the state attorney general may bring suit directly (bypassing the administrative process)[136] on behalf of the discrimination victim.

The type of relief available to victims of age discrimination in employment depends in part on the statute under which the age claim is brought. For example, the ADEA provides liquidated or double damages for willful violations but does not provide damages for pain and suffering. Some state laws, on the other hand, do provide damages for pain and suffering. As a result, it is important to consider what relief is most appropriate in a particular case before deciding whether to litigate an age case under state law or the ADEA.

How soon must a lawsuit be started under the ADEA?

Generally, a lawsuit must be filed within two years of the discriminatory act or practice.[137] If, however, a violation is "willful," the action can be brought within three years.[138] The Supreme Court has held that for a violation to be "willful," it must be shown that the employer knew or showed disregard as to whether its conduct violated the ADEA.[139]

Can an individual be part of a class action under the ADEA?

A class action is a lawsuit in which one or more individuals may sue as a representative or representatives of a group of individuals sharing a common interest in the matter that is being litigated. Under Title VII of the Civil Rights Act of 1964—which prohibits discrimination based on race, sex, national origin, or religion— class actions have been used to challenge patterns of discrimination. For example, if an employer refused to hire women, one or two women could bring a lawsuit on behalf of all women denied employment because the employer did not hire women.

Traditional class-action lawsuits used in Title VII cases are not available in ADEA cases. Group actions in ADEA cases are covered by the "opt-in" procedures of the Fair Labor Standards Act (FLSA).[140] The primary difference between ADEA group actions and traditional class actions is that each ADEA plaintiff must consent personally to join the action, and those who do not "opt-in" are not bound by the judgment.[141]

Participation in ADEA and FLSA group actions has been facilitated by a number of courts. Some courts have approved notice being given of an existing lawsuit and offering potential class members the opportunity to join in by filing written consent.[142] In addition, it has been held that each "opt-in" plaintiff doesn't have to fulfill the EEOC or state agency charge filing requirements as long as those requirements are met by a "representative" plaintiff within applicable time limits.[143] As a result, an individual who may have missed the 180- or 300-day time limit for filing an ADEA charge, which is ordinarily a prerequisite for a suit, may still be able to join in a pending action without filing a charge.

Can an employee who has signed a document saying he will not sue his employer later sue for age discrimination?

Employers sometimes require employees to sign a statement saying that the employee will not sue the employer before the employer will give the employee a benefit, such as severance pay or pension benefits. If you think that you are a victim of age discrimination, you should not sign such a release or waiver without first discussing the matter with an attorney. Signing such a release may bar you from suing your employer for any form of discrimination, including age discrimination.[144]

Can someone who has his ADEA discrimination charge processed by a state agency then bring an ADEA suit in federal court?

If an individual has an ADEA charge processed by a state fair employment agency, and the agency determination is ruled on by a state court, a subsequent ADEA suit in federal court may be barred.[145] One court even held that a state court decision, upholding a state tenure review board's determination that a teacher was not terminated because of her age, is grounds for dismissing a separately filed federal court ADEA suit.[146] As a result, an individual who wishes to raise an age discrimination claim may be forced to choose the forum in which he wants to have his age claim heard since pursuing a claim through a state administrative process may result in being barred from later pursuing one under the ADEA.

What relief is available for victims of age discrimination in employment?

The basic principle underlying an analysis of appropriate remedies in an age discrimination case brought under the ADEA is that the victims of age discrimination should "be restored to the economic position they would have occupied but for the intervening unlawful conduct of employers."[147] The type of remedy which is appropriate depends upon the facts of the particular case. Thus, an individual who was unlawfully terminated should be entitled to reinstatement, back pay, retroactive seniority (where appropriate), and work-related and other benefits lost due to the termination.

The ADEA authorizes the courts "to grant such legal or equitable relief as may be appropriate to effectuate the purposes of this Act."[148] Those purposes are "to promote employment of older persons based on their ability rather than age" and "to prohibit arbitrary age discrimination in employment."[149] The courts may grant—among other forms of relief—judgments compelling employment, reinstatement or promotion or judgments enforcing liability for amounts owing as a result of violations of the act such as back pay for wrongfully discharged employees.[150] Under state statutes,[151] typical remedies include hiring, reinstatement, promotion, restoration or admission to labor union membership, back pay and benefits, and appropriate injunctive relief. The following is a more complete discussion of the forms of relief available to victims of age discrimination.

Back Pay. The victim of discrimination should be "made whole"—that is, compensated for all wages and other monetary benefits lost as a result of the discrimination. If an employer has violated the ADEA by refusing to hire an individual, that individual should be compensated for all the wages he or she would have received from the date of wrongful denial of employment until the time he or she is actually hired by the employer (less any wages earned at another job).[152] If an individual has been unlawfully discharged, he or she would be awarded all wages lost until the time of reinstatement by that employer (less any wages earned at another job).[153] In addition to monetary damages, the victims of discrimination should also be awarded any other monetary benefits that would have accrued during the period (e.g., increased pension benefits). The principle of "making the victim of discrimination whole," of course, indicates that the employer is only required to compensate the victim for *actual* losses (unless liquidated damages, punitive damages, or damages for pain and suffering are awarded).

If the victim finds other employment prior to trial, his back pay award will be reduced by the amount of wages earned,[154] so long as such earnings would not have been available if the victim had been working for the employer (e.g., earnings from after-hours, part-time employment would not be subtracted from the award).[155] Other items that have been held to reduce back pay awards include severance pay, layoff allowances, and accrued vacation pay.[156] The courts have split on whether unemployment compensation benefits and pension benefits should be deducted from back pay awards.[157]

One who has been denied a job or terminated must attempt to find another comparable job in order to receive back pay.[158] Courts have held that this requirement does not require that individual to accept lesser types of employment.[159] However, a court has held that where an employee refused an offer of a comparable job in another town, with the employer paying moving expenses, the employee was not entitled to back pay.[160]

Do not assume that a court will award back pay just because you have been denied employment or fired because of your age. You should make a record of your effort to find other employment. This record should include: copies of all job applications or help-wanted advertisements to which you responded, a list of all job-related telephone calls or interviews including the date and name of the person to whom you spoke, and copies of all letters you have written or received in your effort to find work.

Hiring. The courts have the authority to require employers to hire victims of discrimination. In a number of cases, however, the courts have not specifically required that individuals be hired, but have held that they be given the same opportunity to compete as younger job applicants.[161]

Reinstatement or Front Pay. Courts have the authority under the ADEA to provide equitable relief,[162] including reinstatement.[163] Where possible, the victim of discrimination should be reinstated to his or her original position held at the time of dismissal.[164] Courts, however, may find reinstatement inappropriate under certain circumstances. For example, one court held reinstatement inappropriate where it would result in displacing an innocent employee.[165]

Awarding front pay where reinstatement has been denied has found support in the courts.[166] Front pay is computed in a way similar to back pay. It consists of the loss of future earnings, offset by probable future employment, and reducing the difference to its present value.[167] If a court finds that an employer has violated the ADEA but that reinstatement is inappropriate, the victim of discrimination should be compensated for the loss of future earnings. Front pay awards are important for several reasons. The potential for an award of front pay encourages employers to reinstate wrongfully terminated employees. It also ensures that victims of discrimination receive compensation for wages they would have earned but for their former employer's discrimination. At least one court, however, has held that if the employee refuses reinstatement, such refusal should waive any claim to front pay.[168] Since the purpose of the ADEA is the continued employment of older persons, it has been held that reinstatement is the preferred remedy.[169]

Promotion. The ADEA specifically provides that the courts have authority to grant "judgments compelling . . . promotion. . . ."[170] Individuals wrongfully denied promotions have obtained court orders requiring employers to promote them.[171] Courts have discretion whether to order equitable relief, such as a promotion, in particular cases.

Fringe Benefits. Fringe benefits to employees are just as real and measurable as lost wages. As a result, courts have awarded victims of age discrimination a variety of fringe benefits to make them whole. The types of fringe benefits that have been awarded include: pension benefits,[172] health benefits,[173] insurance benefits,[174] sick leave,[175] and seniority rights.[176]

Liquidated Damages. The ADEA provides that where a violation is willful, the victim of discrimination is entitled to "liquidated damages" or statutory double damages.[177] The United States Supreme Court, in a case involving a challenge of the Trans World Airlines (TWA) mandatory retirement policy, set forth the standard for determining whether an employer's violation of the ADEA is "willful."[178] The court held that a violation is "willful" when the employer "knew or showed reckless disregard" as to whether the ADEA prohibited the employer's conduct.[179] The court noted that TWA had met with its lawyers to determine whether its mandatory retirement policy was lawful and modified its policy to comply with the TWA attorneys' understanding of the ADEA's requirements. The Court concluded that since TWA had acted reasonably and in good faith in attempting to determine whether its policy violated the ADEA, the violation was not willful and, therefore, an award of liquidate damages not appropriate.

Pain and Suffering. A victim of age discrimination, particularly an individual who has been forcibly retired, can suffer severe emotional distress. This emotional stress, in turn, may lead to medical problems.[180] While the majority of federal courts that have considered the issue of awarding damages for pain and suffering under the ADEA have denied such awards,[181] many state laws prohibiting age discrimination in employment provide for such damages.[182]

If an individual has been subjected to pain and suffering as a result of age discrimination and the applicable state statute provides damages for such injury, it may be best to bring a lawsuit under the state statute. While some federal courts have allowed individuals to combine state law claims for pain and suffering with an ADEA lawsuit in federal court,[183] other courts have not allowed such claims.[184]

Preliminary Injunctions. If an employee is about to be retired or has recently been retired, the employee can go into federal court and ask a judge to forbid his employer from retiring him. The ADEA authorizes a court to order employment or re-employment of an individual.[185] Preliminary injunctions also can be used to prevent an individual from being retired rather than laid off[186] and to prevent retaliation against an individual for filing a charge of age discrimination with the EEOC.[187]

In determining whether to grant a preliminary injunction, courts must weigh the following factors: (1) whether the employee has shown that irreparable harm will result if the injunction is not granted, (2) the probability that the employee will be able to prove his case of discrimination at the time of the trial, (3) whether the employer will suffer harm if the injunction is granted, and (4) whether the public interest is served by granting the injunction.[188]

It should be recognized that the burden of putting together enough information to prove the probability of success at trial and establishing "irreparable harm" in a case may be substantial. As a result, the decision regarding whether to seek preliminary relief should be weighed carefully.

Attorney's Fees and Costs. In addition to the relief discussed above, the ADEA provides for an award of attorney's fees and costs to a victim of age discrimination who successfully litigates an age discrimination claim.[189] However, several recent Supreme Court decisions have placed significant limitations on the availability of such relief.[190]

NOTES

1. For a summary of state statutory provisions prohibiting age discrimination in employment, see H. Eglit, *Age Discrimination* 20-1 to 20-10 (1981). For an analysis of the substance of some of these statutes, see C. Edelman & I. Siegler, *Federal ADEA Law: Slowing Down the Golden Watch*, 59–67, 293–328 (1978 & Supp. 1980).

2. 42 U.S.C. § 2000e–14 (1964).

3. Report of the Secretary of Labor to Congress Under Section 715 of the Civil Rights Act of 1964, The Older American Worker — Age Discrimination in Employment (June 1965).

4. 29 U.S.C. § 621 *et seq.* (1967).

5. Reorganization Plan No. 1 of 1978, § 2, 43 Fed. Reg. 19807 (1978). Congress subsequently ratified this transfer of enforcement authority. Act of Oct. 19, 1984, Pub. L. No. 98-532, 98 Stat. 2705 (1985).

6. 29 U.S.C. § 621(b) (1982).

7. Pub. L. No. 90-202, 81 Stat. 605 (1967).

8. Pub. L. No. 93-259, 88 Stat. 74 (1974) (codified at 29 U.S.C. § 630(b) (1982)). As amended in 1974, the ADEA exempted elected officials and their personal staff, policy-making appointees, or an immediate adviser with respect to the exercise of the constitutional or legal powers of the office. 29 U.S.C. § 630(f) (1982).

9. 427 U.S. 307 (1976). The Supreme Court in *Murgia* applied the rational basis test to the age limit challenged. The Court, by its silence, rejected the position that age-based employment classifications constitute an irrebutable presumption in violation of the Due Process Clause of the Fourteenth Amendment. For the Due Process Clause of the Fifth Amendment (federal government) or the Due Process of the Fourteenth Amendment (state or local government) to apply, there must be some governmental action.

10. For examples of other unsuccessful constitutional challenges, see, e.g., *Vance v. Bradley*, 440 U.S. 93 (1979) (mandatory retirement age of 60 for foreign service officers not a violation of the Equal Protection Clause of the Fifth Amendment); *Alford v. City of Lubbock*, 664 F.2d 1263 (5th Cir.), *cert. denied*, 456 U.S. 975 (1982) (not unconstitutional to deny employees hired after age 50 the right to participate in state retirement system).

11. 29 U.S.C. § 623(a) (1982).

12. 29 U.S.C. § 623(b) (1982).

13. 29 U.S.C. § 623(c) (1982).

14. 29 U.S.C. § 623(e) (1982). EEOC Guidelines, 29 C.F.R. § 1625.4 (1986).

15. 29 U.S.C. § 623(d) (1982).

16. Pub. L. No. 90-202, § 12, 81 Stat. 607 (1967).

17. Pub. L. No. 95-256, § 3, 92 Stat. 189 (1978).

18. Pub. L. No. 99-592, 100 Stat. 3342, 3344 (1986). The Age Discrimination in Employment Amendments of 1986 amended section 12 of the ADEA, 29 U.S.C. §§ 631(a) by removing the age 70 cap from the ADEA's protections. For most individuals, the expansion of the ADEA's protections to those 70 and older began on Jan. 1, 1987. Pub. L. No. 99-592, § 7(a). For employees covered by collective bargaining agreements, the expansion of the ADEA's protections to those 70 or older does not take effect until expiration of their collective bargaining agreement or Jan. 1, 1990, whichever occurs first.

19. 29 U.S.C. § 633a(a) (1982). Federal law, however, does allow the imposition of hiring age maximums and mandatory retirement ages for certain classes of federal workers, such as law enforcement officers, firefighters, and air traffic controllers.

20. *See, e.g., Hahn v. City of Buffalo*, 770 F.2d 12, 15 (2d Cir. 1985).

21. Act of Oct. 9, 1984, Pub. L. No. 98-459, codified in 29 U.S.C. §§ 623(h) and 630(f)(Supp. III 1985). *See, e.g.*, Street, "Application of U.S. Fair Employment Laws to Transnational Employers in the United States and Abroad, 19 *N.Y.U. J. of Int'l. L. & Pol.* 357 (1987).

22. *See* 29 U.S.C.A. §§ 623(i); 630(j); 630(k) (West Supp. 1987), as amended by Pub. L. No. 99-592. To fall within this seven year exemption (Jan. 1, 1987 to Dec. 31, 1993), the hiring or retirement age limit must be an age limit that was, pursuant to state or local law, in effect on Mar. 3, 1983 and must be part of a bona fide hiring or retirement plan which was not a subterfuge to evade the ADEA.

23. 29 U.S.C.A. § 631(d)(1986), added by Pub. L. No. 99-592.

24. *See* note 23.

25. 29 U.S.C. § 630(f) (Supp. III 1985).

26. 29 U.S.C. §§ 631(c)(1), (c)(2)(1982 & Supp. III 1985), as amended 1984.

27. *See* 29 C.F.R. § 1625.2 (1986).

28. *See, e.g.*, Human Rights Act of Minnesota, § 363.01, subdivision 28 (1985) (protects those over the age of majority (18) from age discrimination in employment).

29. *See, e.g.*, 29 U.S.C. § 633(a)(1982); 29 C.F.R. § 860.120(g) (1986) (Dep't. of Labor, which originally enforced ADEA, stated that the ADEA did not preempt state law.)

30. For a discussion of limitations on the "employment at will" doctrine, see *Annotation, Modern Status of Rule That Employer May Discharge At-Will Employee for Any Reason*, 12 A.L.R. 4th 544 (1982).

31. *See, e.g., Cancellier v. Federated Dep't. Stores*, 672 F.2d 1312 (9th Cir.), *cert. denied*, 459 U.S. 859 (1982) (applying California law); *Rees*

     v. Bank Bldg. and Equip. Corp., 332 F.2d 548 (7th Cir.), *cert. denied*, 379 U.S. 932 (1964) (applying Missouri law).

32. *Oscar Mayer v. Evans*, 441 U.S. 750 (1979).

33. 29 U.S.C. § 630(b) (1982). While it has been held that part-time employees are added to the number of full-time workers in determining coverage—*Thurber v. Jack Reilly's, Inc.*, 717 F.2d 633 (1st Cir.), *cert. denied*, 466 U.S. 904, (1984) (Title VII case)—it has been held that independent contractors do not count in determining coverage. *Copley v. Morality in Media, Inc.*, 25 Empl. Prac. Dec. (CCH), ¶ 31,570 (S.D.N.Y. 1981) (Title VII). Similarly, it has been held that directors of corporations and unpaid officers not participating in corporate affairs should not be counted. *Zimmerman v. North Am. Signal Co.*, 704 F.2d 347 (7th Cir. 1983) (ADEA); *McGraw v. Warren County Oil Co.*, 707 F.2d 990 (8th Cir. 1983) (ADEA).

34. 29 U.S.C. § 630(b) (1982). The federal government is also a covered employer. 29 U.S.C. § 633a(1982).

35. *Equal Employment Opportunity Commission v. Wyoming*, 460 U.S. 226 (1983).

36. 29 U.S.C. § 630(c)(1982).

37. 29 U.S.C. § 630(e)(1982).

38. The Dep't. of Labor originally adopted and the EEOC subsequently has ratified an interpretive guideline that provided that the ADEA was not applicable to age restrictions on entry into bona fide apprenticeship programs. 29 C.F.R. § 860.106 (1986). However, this guideline was held in *Quinn v. New York State Elec. and Gas Corporation*, 569 F. Supp. 655 (N.D.N.Y. 1983), *summary judgment granted*, 621 F. Supp. 1086 (N.D.N.Y. 1985), to be "inconsistent with the language, purpose and history of the ADEA." *Id.* at 656. The EEOC reaffirmed the apprenticeship exemption after *Quinn*. 52 Fed. Reg. 33809 (Sept. 8, 1987).

39. *Hodgson v. Poole Truck Line, Inc.*, 4 Fair Empl. Prac. Cas. (BNA) 265 (S.D. Ala. 1972). *See also Hodgson v. First Federal Sav. & Loan Ass'n.*, 455 F.2d 818 (5th Cir. 1972) (interviewer's notes said "too old for teller").

40. *Rose v. National Cash Register Corp.*, 703 F.2d 225 (6th Cir.), *cert. denied*, 464 U.S. 929 (1983).

41. *Texas Dep't. of Community Affairs v. Burdine*, 450 U.S. 248 (1981).

42. 411 U.S. 792 (1972); *See also* Note, "Allocation of Proof in ADEA Cases: A Critique of the Prima Facie Case Approach," 4 *Industrial Relations L.J.* 90 (1980) (discussing the standard of proof requirements established by the Supreme Court for Title VII cases which has been adopted by most courts in ADEA litigation).

43. *See, e.g., LaMontagne v. American Convenience Products, Inc.*, 750 F.2d 1405, 1409 n. 1 (7th Cir. 1984); *Douglas v. Anderson*, 656 F.2d 528 (9th Cir. 1981); *Loeb v. Textron, Inc.*, 600 F.2d 1003 (1st Cir. 1979); *Wilson v. Sealtest Foods Div. of Kraftco Corp*, 501 F.2d 84 (5th Cir. 1974).

44. *See, e.g., Sahadi v. Reynolds Chemical*, 636 F.2d 1116 (6th Cir. 1980); *Pace v. Southern Railway System*, 701 F.2d 1383 (11th Cir. 1983), *cert. denied*, 464 U.S. 1018 (1984).

45. *See* discussion of *McDonnell Douglas* test in *Blackwell v. Sun Elec. Corp*, 696 F.2d 1176 (6th Cir. 1983). *See* Comment, "Should McDonnell Douglas Apply in ADEA Cases?," 15 *U. Tol. L. Rev.* 1202 (1984) (the *McDonnell Douglas* formula should be limited in reduction-in-force cases).

46. *See e.g., Massarsky v. General Motors Corp.*, 706 F.2d 111, 118 n. 13 (3rd Cir.) *cert. denied*, 464 U.S. 937 (1983); *McCuen v. Home Ins. Co.*, 633 F.2d 1150 (5th Cir. 1981).

47. *See, e.g., Hagelthorn v. Kennecott Corp.*, 710 F.2d 76 (2d Cir. 1983); *Stanojev v. Ebasco Services, Inc.*, 643 F.2d 914 (2d Cir. 1981). *See also* Note, "Civil Rights Use of Direct Evidence to Establish a Prima Facie Case of Discrimination Under the ADEA Obviates the Need to Make an Independent Showing of Pretext," 18 *Wake Forest L. Rev.* 59 (1982) (advocating that if circumstantial evidence is used, the pretext burden must be met at some stage in the trial and if direct evidence is used, the pretext rebuttal is superfluous).

48. *Havelick v. Julius Wile & Sons Co.*, 445 F. Supp. 919 (S.D.N.Y. 1978).

49. *Bishop v. Jelleff Associates*, 398 F. Supp. 579 (D.D.C. 1974).

50. *Brennan v. Reynolds & Co.*, 367 F. Supp. 440 (N.D. Ill. 1973).

51. *See, e.g., EEOC v. University of Oklahoma*, 774 F.2d 999, 1002 (10th Cir.), *cert. denied*, 106 S. Ct. 1637 (1986) ("age made a difference"); *Ackerman v. Diamond Shamrock*, 670 F.2d 66, 70 (6th Cir. 1982) ("ultimate issue was whether age was a factor in a decision of an employer to terminate an ADEA claimant and whether the age of the claimant made a difference in determining whether he was to be retained or discharged"); *Sahadi v. Reynolds Chem.*, 636 F.2d 1116, 1117 (6th Cir. 1980) ("age would not have to be the sole reason, but only a contributing factor in connection with the discharge").

52. *See, e.g., Brennan v. Ace Hardware Corp.*, 362 F. Supp. 1156 (D. Neb. 1973), *aff'd*, 495 F.2d 368 (8th Cir. 1974) (lower court held for employer on procedural grounds, and was affirmed on that basis but lower court applied an "a factor" test in dealing with the merits).

53. *See McDonnell Douglas Corp. v. Green*, 411 U.S. 792 (1972). *See*

also Liddle, "Disparate Treatment Claims Under ADEA: "The Negative Impact of *McDonnell Douglas v. Green*," 5 *Employee Relations L.J.* 549 (1980).

54. *Griggs v. Duke Power Co.*, 401 U.S. 424 (1971) (requirement of a high school diploma or passing intelligence test found not to be job related and to have an unlawful disparate impact on blacks); *Dothard v. Rawlinson*, 433 U.S. 321 (1977) (*Griggs* disparate impact analysis applied to sex discrimination claims).

55. The "prohibitions of the ADEA were derived *in haec verba* from Title VII . . ." *Lorillard v. Pons*, 434 U.S. 575, 584 (1978).

56. *See* Note, "Age Discrimination and the Disparate Impact Analysis," 34 *Stan. L. Rev.* 837 (1982).

57. 29 U.S.C. § 623(f)(1)(Supp. III 1985).

58. *Geller v. Markham*, 635 F.2d 1027 (2d Cir. 1980), *cert. denied*, 451 U.S. 945 (1981). A majority of the United States Courts of Appeals have also held that disparate impact theory applies to the ADEA. *See, e.g., EEOC v. Borden's, Inc.*, 724 F.2d 1390 (9th Cir. 1984) (severance pay policy requiring all employees eligible for early retirement to forego severance pay violates ADEA).

59. *Dace v. ACF Industries, Inc.*, 722 F.2d 374 (8th Cir. 1983), *supplemented* 40 Fair Empl. Prac. Cas. (BNA) 1604 (8th Cir. 1984).

60. *Id.* at 378, citing with approval *Leftwich v. Harris-Stowe State College*, 702 F.2d 686 (8th Cir. 1983) (discharging older workers on the basis that they earn higher salaries violates the ADEA).

61. *Allison v. Western Union Tele. Co.*, 680 F.2d 1318 (11th Cir. 1982).

62. *Coates v. National Cash Register Co.*, 433 F. Supp. 655 (W.D. Va. 1977).

63. *Stone v. Western Air Lines, Inc.*, 544 F. Supp. 33 (C.D. Cal. 1981).

64. *Hays v. Republic Steel Corp.*, 12 Fair Empl. Proc. Cas. (BNA) 1640 (N.D. Ala. 1974), *modified on other grounds*, 531 F.2d 1307 (5th Cir. 1976).

65. *Texas Dep't. of Community Affairs v. Burdine*, 450 U.S. 248, 253 (1981).

66. *Id.*

67. *International Brotherhood of Teamsters v. United States*, 431 U.S. 324, 360 (1977).

68. *See, e.g., Buckley v. Hospital Corp. of Am., Inc.*, 758 F.2d 1525 (11th Cir. 1985).

69. *See, e.g., Zebedeo v. Martin E. Segal Co., Inc.*, 582 F. Supp. 1394 (D. Conn. 1984).

70. 29 U.S.C. § 623(f)(1)(1982).

71. *Id.*

72. 29 U.S.C. § 623(f)(2)(1982).

73. 29 U.S.C. § 623(f)(3)(1982).

74. The RFOA defense can, under certain circumstances, be construed as an affirmative defense on which the defendant bears the burden of proof. *See* "The Age Discrimination in Employment Act's Forgotten Affirmative Defense: The Reasonable Factor Other Than Age Exception," 66 *Boston Univ. L. Rev.* 155 (1986).

75. Section 7(e) of the ADEA incorporates § 10 of the Portal-to-Portal Act (29 U.S.C. § 259) which creates the statutory "good faith reliance" defense.

76. 29 U.S.C. § 259(a) (1982).

77. The Equal Employment Opportunity Commission, in 1983, issued regulations pertaining to § 10 of the Portal-to-Portal Act. (29 C.F.R. § 1626.18 (1984).

78. 29 U.S.C. § 623(f)(1)(1982).

79. *Western Air Lines, Inc. v. Criswell*, 472 U.S. 400 (1985).

80. *See, e.g.*, Hahn v. City of Buffalo, *supra* note 20 (hiring age of 29 for police officers unlawful); *EEOC v. County of Los Angeles*, 706 F.2d 1039 (9th Cir. 1983), *cert. denied*, 464 U.S. 1073 (1984) (maximum hiring age of 35 for entry level position in sheriff department and fire department, helicopter pilot unlawful); *Smallwood v. United Airlines, Inc.*, 661 F.2d 303 (4th Cir. 1981), *cert. denied* 456 U.S. 1007 (1982) (maximum hiring age of 35 for police unlawful).

81. *See, e.g.*, *Hodgson v. Greyhound Lines, Inc.*, 499 F.2d 859 (7th Cir. 1974), *cert. denied sub nom, Brennan v. Greyhound Lines, Inc.*, 419 U.S. 1122 (1975) (maximum hiring age of 35 for bus drivers does not violate ADEA); *EEOC v. Missouri State Highway Patrol*, 748 F.2d 447 (8th Cir. 1984), *cert. denied*, 474 U.S. 828 (1985) (maximum hiring age of 32 for patrol officers and radio operators and mandatory retirement age of 60 for patrol officers does not violate ADEA).

82. *See, e.g.*, *EEOC v. Missouri State Highway Patrol*, *supra* note 81 (Mandatory retirement age of 60 for state highway patrol lawful); *Heiar v. Crawford County*, 746 F.2d 1190 (7th Cir. 1984), *cert. denied*, 472 U.S. 1027 (1985) (mandatory retirement age of 55 for police officers held unlawful); *Western Airlines v. Criswell*, 472 U.S. 400 (1985) (denying pilots opportunity to down-bid to flight engineer position at age 60 violates the ADEA); *EEOC v. Com. of Pa.*, 829 F.2d 392 (3d Cir.), *cert. denied*, 108 S. Ct. 1109 (1988) (no BFOQ defense established for age 60 mandatory retirement since state failed to develop, implement, and enforce minimum fitness standards).

83. Pub. L. No. 99-592, § 2, 100 Stat. 3342 (1986).

84. Pub. L. No. 99-592, §§ 3, 4, and 5, 100 Stat. 3342 (1986). The

amendments also created a seven-year exemption which allows institutions of higher education to mandatorily retire tenured faculty at age 70.

85. *See generally*, Eglit, *Age Discrimination*, *supra* note 4, § 16.31 ("The Reasonable Factor Other Than Age Exception").

86. 29 C.F.R. § 1625.7(d)(1986).

87. *Hanslovan v. Pennsylvania Mines Corp.*, 603 F. Supp. 464 (W.D. Pa. 1985).

88. *LaMontagne v. American Convenience Prods., Inc.*, 750 F.2d 1405 (7th Cir. 1984).

89. *West v. Fred Wright Constr. Co.* 756 F.2d 31 (6th Cir. 1985).

90. *Griggs v. Duke Power Co.*, 401 U.S. 424, 426 (1971).

91. 29 C.F.R. § 1625.7(c) (1986). *See, e.g.*, *Marshall v. Goodyear Tire and Rubber Co.*, 22 Fair Empl. Prac. Cas. (BNA) 775 (W.D. Tenn. 1979).

92. 29 U.S.C. § 623(f)(2)(1982).

93. *See* Comments, Amendment to Interpretative Bulletin, 44 Fed. Reg. 30,648 (1979); 29 C.F.R. pt. 1625.10 (1987).

94. *EEOC v. Home Insurance Co.*, 672 F.2d 252 (2d Cir. 1982).

95. *See, e.g.*, *EEOC v. Westinghouse Electric Corp.*, 725 F.2d 211 (3d Cir. 1983), *cert. denied*, 105 S. Ct. 92 (1984).

96. *Id.* at 222.

97. *EEOC v. Borden's, Inc.*, *supra* note 58.

98. *Alford v. City of Lubbock*, *supra* note 10.

99. 29 U.S.C. § 623(f)(3)(1982).

100. *Stringfellow v. Monsanto Co.*, 320 F. Supp. 440 (N.D. Ill. 1973).

101. *See, e.g.*, *Anderson v. Viking Pump Div., Houdaille Industries, Inc.*, 545 F.2d 1127 (8th Cir. 1976); *Havelick v. Julius Wile Sons & Co.*, *supra* note 48.

102. 29 U.S.C. § 259 (1982).

103. *Id.*

104. 29 C.F.R. § 1626.18 (1986).

105. 29 U.S.C. § 623(e) (1982).

106. The federal regulations pertaining to "help wanted" advertisement can be found at 29 C.F.R. § 1625.4 (1986).

107. *Brennan v. Approved Personnel Services, Inc.*, 8 Empl. Prac. Dec. (CCH) ¶ 9810 (M.D.N.C. 1974), *rev'd sub nom. Hodgson v. Approved Personnel Services, Inc.*, 529 F.2d 760 (4th Cir. 1975); *Brennan v. Paragon Employment Agency, Inc.*, 356 F. Supp. 286 (S.D.N.Y. 1973), *aff'd. without opinion*, 489 F.2d 752 (2d Cir. 1974).

108. *Brennan v. Approved Personnel Services, Inc.*, *supra* note 107; *Brennan v. C/M Mobile, Inc.*, 8 Empl. Prac. Dec. (CCH) ¶ 9532 (S.D. Ala. 1974).

109. *Hodgson v. First Federal Savings & Loan Assn.*, *supra* note 39. *Cf. Hodgson v. Western Textile Co.*, 7 Empl. Prac. Dec. (CCH) ¶ 9383 (N.D. Ill. 1974).

110. *See, e.g.*, Connecticut Commission Civil Rights Rule 371-2a, (1972) 3 Empl. Prac. Guide (CCH) ¶ 21.276.

111. *Hodgson v. Career Counselors Int'l., Inc.*, 5 Fair Empl. Prac. Cas. (BNA) 129 (ND Ill. 1972). *Cf. Hodgson v. Western Textile Co.*, 7 Empl. Prac. Dec. (CCH) ¶ 9383 (N.D. Ill. 1974).

112. *Brennan v. Approved Personnel Services, Inc.*, *supra* note 107.

113. Most courts have held that the 180-day time period for filing is not jurisdictional and is subject to tolling. *See, e.g.*, cases cited in 29 Am. Jur., *Trials*, chapter 1 at 38, note 22 (1982). It is also important to note that if you file a charge with a state referral agency within 180 days of the discriminatory act, you can file a charge with the EEOC within 300 days.

114. For a more complete discussion of the EEOC regulations on the form and content of a charge of age discrimination, see 29 C.F.R. §§ 1626.6, 1626.8 (1986).

115. 29 C.F.R. § 1626.7 (1986).

116. 29 U.S.C. § 626(d) (1982). However, if you are seeking to prevent future unlawful employment discrimination (*e.g.*, mandatory retirement), you may be able to get the EEOC to complete its processing of the case to allow you to go into court in less than 60 days. See Sheeders, "Procedural Complexity of the ADEA—An Age Old Problem," 18 *Duq. L. Rev.* 241 (1980) (discusses the policies and purpose of the 60-day waiting period).

117. The ADEA, 29 U.S.C. § 626(e) (1982), incorporates the limitation periods contained in the Portal-to-Portal Act 29 U.S.C. § 255 (1982). The statute of limitations in ADEA case is two years, unless the violation is willful. The limitations period for willful violations is three years. These limitations periods can be tolled, for purposes of EEOC litigation, for up to a year during the time the EEOC, after determining a respondent (employer, employment agency, or labor organization) has violated the ADEA, attempts to conciliate the case. 29 U.S.C. § 626(e) (1982).

118. *See, e.g.*, *Dartt v. Shell Oil Co.*, 539 F.2d 1256 (10th Cir. 1976), *aff'd by an equally divided court*, 434 U.S. 99 (1977) (filing 36 days after 180 days had elapsed where individual had sought and relied upon legal advice, had not been informed until 180 days that she had to file to preserve her rights and there was no indication of any prejudice to the defendant-employer from the 36-day delay); *Charlier v. S. C. Johnson & Sons. Inc.*, 556 F.2d 761 (5th Cir. 1977) (delay

in start of statutory time period at least until the victims know or should have known about their statutory rights).

119. Conference Report to Accompany H.R. 5383, H.R. Rep. No. 95-950, 95th Cong., 2d Sess. 12 (1978).

120. 29 C.F.R. pt. 1626.4 (1986).

121. *Id.*

122. *See supra* note 120.

123. 29 U.S.C. § 626(b) (1982).

124. 29 U.S.C. § 626(d) (1982).

125. Conciliation is a prerequisite to any ADEA suit. *See Brennan v. Ace Hardware Corp., Supra* note 52 (upholding a district court judgment for the defendant-employer on grounds of insufficient conciliation efforts).

126. *See, e.g.,* CAL. LABOR CODE § 1421 (West 1971); N.J. STAT. ANN. § 10:5-14, (West Supp. 1986); DEL. CODE ANN. tit. 19 § 712(c) (1984); N.Y. EXEC. LAW § 297.3a (McKinney Supp. 1986).

127. 29 U.S.C. § 626(d) (1982).

128. 29 U.S.C. § 626(b) (1982).

129. 29 U.S.C. § 626(c) (1982).

130. 29 U.S.C. § 633(a) (1982).

131. *See, e.g.,* CONN. GEN. STAT. ANN. §§ 46a-84 (West Supp. 1986).

132. *See, e.g.,* N.Y. EXEC. LAW § 297.9 (McKinney Supp. 1986).

133. *Supra* note 131.

134. *See, e.g.,* DEL. CODE ANN. tit. 19 § 712(f) (1984).

135. *See, e.g.,* N.J. STAT. § 10:5-16 (West Supp. 1985).

136. *See, e.g.,* N.J. STAT. § 10:5-14.1 (West Supp. 1985).

137. 29 U.S.C. § 626(e), incorporating § 6 of the Portal-to-Portal Act of 1947, 29 U.S.C. § 255 (1984).

138. *Id.*

139. *McLaughlin v. Richland Shoe Co.,* 108 S. Ct. 1677 (1988).

140. 29 U.S.C. § 216(b).

141. *See, e.g., Woods v. New York Life Ins. Co.,* 686 F.2d 578 (7th Cir. 1982); *Kinney Shoe Corp. v. Vorhes,* 564 F.2d 859 (9th Cir. 1977); *LaChapelle v. Owens-Illinois, Inc.,* 513 F.2d 286 (5th Cir. 1975).

142. *See, e.g., Woods supra* note 141; *Braunstein v. E. Photo Lab., Inc.* 600 F.2d 335 (2d Cir.), *cert. denied,* 441 U.S. 944 (1979).

143. *See, e.g., Bean v. Crocker Nat'l. Bank,* 600 F.2d 754 (9th Cir. 1979); *Mistretta v. Sandia Corp.,* 639 F.2d 588 (10th Cir. 1980).

144. *See, e.g., Runyan v. National Cash Register Corp.,* 787 F.2d 1039 (6th Cir.), *cert. denied,* U.S. 107 S. Ct. 178 (1986).

145. *See Kremer v. Chemical Const. Corp.,* 456 U.S. 461 (1982) (federal district court required to give preclusive effect to state court

judgment upholding state administrative agency's rejection of employment discrimination claim; discrimination complaint filed in federal court therefore dismissed).

146. *See, e.g., Cooper v. Oak Park School. Dist.*, 624 F. Supp. 515 (E.D. Mich. 1986).

147. *Rodriguez v. Taylor*, 569 F.2d 1231, 1238 (3d Cir. 1977), *cert. denied*, 436 U.S. 913 (1978).

148. 29 U.S.C. § 626(b) (1982), incorporating FLSA § 16, 29 U.S.C. § 216 (1982).

149. 29 U.S.C. § 621(b) (1982).

150. For a discussion of damages available under the ADEA, see vol. 29 Am. Jur. *Trials*, chapter 1, "Age Discrimination in Employment Action under ADEA" and specifically § V. "Remedies in Court Actions," 50–72.

151. *See, e.g.*, Alaska Stat. § 18.80.130 (1974) (amended 1975); CAL. LABOR CODE § 1426 (West 1971); CONN. GEN. STAT. § 31-127 (1972) (amended 1974, 1975, 1976); N.J. STAT. ANN. § 10:5-17 (1976); N.Y. EXEC. LAW § 297-4c (McKinney 1972) (amended 1974, 1977).

152. *Rodriguez v. Taylor, supra* note 147 (rejected job applicant who prevails in ADEA case entitled to back pay in amount they would have earned but for discrimination, less wages actually earned from other employment that could not have been performed at the same time as the job sought).

153. *Bishop v. Jelleff Assoc., Inc., supra* note 49.

154. *Id.*

155. *Laugeson v. Anaconda, supra* note 51.

156. *Id.; Equal Employment Opportunity Commission v. Sandia Corp.*, 639 F.2d 600 (10th Cir. 1980).

157. *See, e.g., EEOC v. United Airlines*, 575 F. Supp. 309 (N.D. Ill. 1983), *modified on other grounds*, 755 F.2d 94 (7th Cir. 1985) (back pay reduced by amount received in pension benefits but not unemployment compensation benefits); *Equal Employment Commission v. Sandia, supra* note 156 (unemployment compensation should not be offset against back pay); *see also* "Annot. Offsetting Unemployment Benefits Received Against Award for Backpay in Employment Discrimination Actions," 66 A.L.R. Fed. 880 (1984).

158. *Laugeson v. Anaconda, supra* note 51.

159. *Schulner v. Jack Eckerd Corp.*, 572 F. Supp. 56 (S.D. Fla.) *aff'd*, 706 F.2d 1113 (11th cir. 1983).

160. *Cowen v. Standard Brands, Inc.*, 572 F. Supp. 1576 (N.D. Ala. 1983).

161. *See, e.g., Hahn v. City of Buffalo, supra* note 20. *Smallwood v. United Airlines, supra* note 80.

162. 29 U.S.C. § 626(b) (1982). *See also* Note, "Front Pay: A Necessary Alternative to Reinstatement under the Age Discrimination Act," 3 *Fordham L. Rev.* 579 (1984) ("There May be Factors that Preclude Reinstatement and Make the Alternative Remedy of Front Pay Appropriate").

163. *See EEOC v. Sandia Corp.*, 639 F.2d 600, 627-28 (10th Cir. 1980); *Duffy v. Wheeling Pittsburgh Steel Corp.*, 738 F.2d 1393 (3d Cir. 1984), *cert. denied*, 469 U.S. 1087 (1984).

164. *See, e.g., Coates v. National Cash Register Co.*, *supra* note 62.

165. *Spagnuolo v. Whirlpool Corp.*, 717 F.2d 114 (4th Cir. 1983). *See also Houghton v. McDonnell Douglas Corp.*, 627 F.2d 858, 866–67 (8th Cir. 1980), *rev'd*, 716 F.2d 526 (8th Cir. 1983); *Kiel v. Goodyear Tire and Rubber Co.*, 575 F. Supp. 847 (N.D. Ohio 1983), *aff'd mem.*, 762 F.2d 1008 (6th Cir. 1985).

166. *Whittlesey v. Union Carbide Corp.*, 742 F.2d 724 (2d Cir. 1984); *EEOC v. Prudential Federal Savings and Loan*, 741 F.2d 1225 (10th Cir. 1984), *vacated*, 469 U.S. 1134 (1985), *later op.*, 763 F.2d 1166 (10th Cir.), *cert. denied*, 106 S. Ct. 312 (1985), *Gibson v. Mohawk Rubber Co.*, 695 F.2d 1093, 1100 (8th Cir. 1982) and *Naton v. Bank of California*, 649 F.2d 691, 700 (9th Cir. 1981).

167. *Loeb v. Textron, Inc.*, *supra* note 43.

168. *Monroe v. Penn-Dixie Cement Corp.*, 335 F. Supp. 231 (N.D. Ga. 1971).

169. *Blim v. Western Elec. Co., Inc.*, 731 F.2d 1473 (10th Cir.) *cert. denied sub nom. A.T. & T. Technologies, Inc. v. Blim*, 469 U.S. 874 (1984).

170. 29 U.S.C. § 626(b) (1982).

171. *See, e.g., DeFries v. Haarhues*, 488 F. Supp. 1037 (C.D. Ill. 1980); *Jones v. Cleland*, 466 F. Supp. 34 (N.D. Ala.), *aff'd without opinion*, 619 F.2d 82 (5th Cir. 1980).

172. *Loeb v. Textron, Inc.*, *supra* note 43.

173. *Blackwell v. Sun Electric Corp.*, 696 F.2d 1176 (6th Cir. 1983). For a further discussion, see Smith & Legette, "Recent Issues in Litigation Under the Age Discrimination in Employment Act," 41 *Ohio St. L.J.*, 349, 369 (1980).

174. *Mistretta v. Sandia Corp.*, *supra* note 143.

175. *Alford v. City of Lubbock*, *supra* note 10.

176. *Spagnuolo v. Whirlpool Corp.*, *supra* note 165.

177. 29 U.S.C. § 626(b) (1982).

178. *Trans World Airlines, Inc. v. Thurston*, 469 U.S. 111 (1985).

179. *Id.* at 128–29, 105 S. Ct. at 625–26. *See also* Walters & Pursell, "Emotional Distress: The Battle over a New Tort Under Age Discrimination Continues," 30 *Lab. L.J.* 667 (1979); Note, "Liqui-

dated Damages and Statute of Limitations Under the Willful Statement of the FLSA and ADEA: Repercussions of *Trans World Airlines, Inc. v. Thurston*," 24 *Washburn L.J.* 516 (1985) (discusses the new standard for "willful" adopted by the Supreme Court).

180. Tanay, "Work Deprivation Depression," 8 *Psychiatric J. Ottawa* 139 (1983).

181. *See, e.g., Slatin v. Stanford Research Institute*, 590 F.2d 1292 (4th Cir. 1979); *Vasquez v. Eastern Air Lines, Inc.*, 579 F.2d 107 (1st Cir. 1978); *Dean v. American Sec. Ins. Co.*, 559 F.2d 1036 (5th Cir. 1977), *cert. denied*, 434 U.S. 1066 (1978). *See* Note, "Damages in Age Discrimination Cases: A Closer Look," 17 *U. Rich. L. Rev.* 573, 580–82 (1983) ("Compensatory Damages for Pain and Suffering Should be Allowed").

182. *See, e.g.*, "Washington's State Law Against Discrimination," WASH. REV. CODE. ANN. § 49. 60. 10 *et seq.* (West 1982).

183. *Kelly v. American Standard, Inc.*, 640 F.2d 974 (9th Cir. 1981); *Selbst v. Touche Ross & Co.*, 587 F. Supp. 1015 (S.D.N.Y. 1984).

184. *Alveari v. American Int'l. Group, Inc.*, 590 F. Supp. 228 (S.D.N.Y. 1984); *Kempe v. Prince Gardner, Inc.*, 569 F. Supp. 779 (E.D. Mo. 1983).

185. 29 U.S.C. § 626(b) (1982). *See Hodgson v. Approved Personnel Services, Inc., supra* note 107.

186. *EEOC v. Chrysler Corp.*, 546 F. Supp. 54 (E.D. Mich. 1982), *aff'd*, 733 F.2d 1183 (6th Cir. 1984).

187. *EEOC v. U.S. Steel Corp.*, 583 F. Supp. 1357 (W.D. Pa. 1984).

188. 11 J. Wright & Miller, *Federal Practice and Procedure*, § 2948, at 427 (1975).

189. Section 16(b) of the FLSA, which provides that a court shall allow reasonable attorney fees and costs to be paid to the prevailing plaintiff by the defendant, is incorporated by reference into the ADEA by 29 U.S.C. § 626(b) (1982).

190. *See Crawford Fitting Co. v. J. T. Gibbons, Inc.*, 107 S. Ct. 2494 (1987) (limiting award of expert witness fees to a maximum of $30 per day); *Pennsylvania v. Delaware Valley Citizens' Council*, 107 S. Ct. 3078 (1987) (enhancement of lodestar for risk of nonpayment limited to exceptional cases).

PART TWO
The Right to Health Care

Adequate health care is vital to older persons. Poor health frequently accompanies advancing age, and older persons often require considerably more health care than do other segments of the population. Medicare, available on the basis of age, and Medicaid, available to those who are poor, are the principal public programs of medical assistance for older persons. While these programs enable many older persons to obtain needed health services, significant deficiencies in these programs diminish their effectiveness in responding to the health care needs of older persons. Medicare primarily pays for some costs of acute care and physician services but provides little help with the costs of chronic health problems and long-term care. Serious administrative and procedural problems make the program difficult to understand and utilize effectively. Soaring health care costs have led to program cutbacks and further cuts are threatened.

Medicaid is of critical importance to the elderly poor, but because it is administered partly by the states, its benefits are distributed unevenly. In some states, benefits are comprehensive while in others, few benefits are available. And the eligibility requirements for Medicaid are so restrictive that many older persons find themselves unable to pay for medical expenses and ineligible for Medicaid. Like Medicare, Medicaid is complex, and significant administrative problems cause difficulties for program beneficiaries.

More than one million older persons reside in nursing homes. The last decade has seen significant strides in improving the quality of life for residents of nursing homes—a number of states have enacted laws to protect nursing home residents. And state and federal efforts to enforce nursing home requirements are improving. But problems remain. Some nursing homes continue to be deficient, and enforcement continues to be uncoordinated and underfunded. Some persons, particularly Medicaid recipients and heavy-care patients, continue to have problems gaining access to nursing homes while adequate alternatives to institutional long-term care remain poorly coordinated and regulated and underfinanced. The important subject of nursing homes is discussed in Chapter 9.

7

Medicare

The health care needs of older persons are greater than those of any other segment of the society of the United States. The population of our country is aging, with the most rapid growth occurring in the 75- to 85-year old age group.

Despite annual expenditures of nearly $70 billion, Medicare has failed to provide adequate health care insurance to its 30 million subscribers. Prior to Medicare, the elderly spent a lower percentage of their income on health care needs than do today's Medicare beneficiaries.[1] The 1965 promise that Medicare would relieve the elderly of the burden of medical expenses has not been fulfilled. Proof lies in the realities of rising deductibles, copayments, and premiums and in the extensive list of services not covered under the program. But elderly and disabled Medicare recipients face a foe even more formidable than rising health care costs and inadequate legislative solutions: the Health Care Financing Administration (HCFA). HCFA, which administers the nationwide Medicare program, appears dedicated to restricting Medicare coverage and has campaigned to shift medical care costs to patients and other third party payers such as Medicaid. These efforts threaten already inadequate Medicare coverage.

What is Medicare?

Medicare, enacted in 1965, is now the principal health care insurance for nearly 30 million persons who are 65 or older or are disabled.[2] Medicare is not a welfare program. Unlike Medicaid, the other major public medical program, eligibility for Medicare has nothing to do with financial need. It is funded by Federal Insurance Contributions Act (FICA) payroll deductions and by some premiums paid by participants.

The Medicare program consists of two parts—hospital insurance (Part A) and supplementary medical insurance (Part B). Part A covers primarily the cost of hospital, skilled nursing facility, home health, and hospice care and is available to most recipients without payment of premiums. Part B covers many other health care expenses, such as physician services, diagnostic tests, and the use of medical equipment. Enrollment in Part B is optional and is purchased by paying a monthly premium, which usually is deducted automatically from one's Social Security check. Both Part A and Part B require payment of deductibles and copayments. Medicare does not always cover the full bill and certainly does not cover all possible medical needs.

How is the Medicare program administered?

The United States Department of Health and Human Services (HHS) has overall responsibility for the administration of the Medicare program. Within HHS is the Health Care Financing Administration (HCFA), which has direct responsibility for the administration of Medicare and Medicaid. The HCFA has offices in Baltimore and Washington D.C. with regional branches throughout the country. The Social Security Administration participates in the operation of Medicare by accepting applications for enrollment and by providing information concerning Medicare.

The day-to-day administration and operation of the Medicare program is handled through private insurance companies that have contracted with the government. For Part A, these companies (called fiscal intermediaries) process initial determinations on coverage, as well as the first stage of the appeals process.[3] Under Part B, these companies (called carriers) process all Medicare Part B claims through the hearing officer stage of the appeals process.[4] A final participant in Medicare administration is the peer review organization (PRO).[5] PROs are contractors with the Medicare program who have the responsibility of making many medical determinations in hospitals, including the appropriateness of admission and continued stays. PROs also are authorized to review other medical decisions concerning Medicare.

HOSPITAL INSURANCE: PART A

Who is eligible for Part A benefits?

There are four basic ways to qualify for Medicare.[6] The largest group of those who are eligible qualify by having reached age 65 and being entitled to receive either Social Security, or Railroad Retirement benefits.[7] Disabled persons of any age who have received Social Security or Railroad disability benefits for twenty-four months also are eligible. Eligibility begins with the twenty-fifth month. It is not necessary that the disability benefits be paid in consecutive months.[8] Persons with end-stage renal disease who require dialysis treatment or a kidney transplant are also eligible. There are different waiting periods for coverage depending upon the type of treatment received for the kidney disease.[9] A final eligible group is made up of persons over age 65 (called voluntary enrollees) who are ineligible for either Social Security or Railroad Retirement but purchase Medicare coverage by payment of a monthly premium. That amount is determined annually and, in 1988, is $234 per month. Mandatory enrollment in Medicare Part B is a prerequisite to receiving coverage as a voluntary enrollee in Medicare Part A.[10]

How do I apply for Part A benefits?

Enrollment is automatic for most eligible persons. An application for Social Security or Railroad Retirement benefits also is considered an application for Medicare. For those younger than 65 who are receiving Social Security or Railroad Retirement benefits, a Medicare card will be sent prior to the month eligibility begins. The same is true for people who are receiving disability benefits. Their enrollment will be established automatically after benefits have been received for twenty-four months.[11]

If a person is eligible for (but not receiving) retirement benefits, a written application must be filed.[12] Usually, this is the case of an individual who continues to work over age 65 but needs Medicare for health insurance coverage. Persons with end-stage renal disease[13] and voluntary enrollees must also enroll by written application.[14]

There are two enrollment periods: the initial[15] and the general.[16] The initial enrollment period begins with the third month prior to your 65th birthday and continues for the three months following. If you miss the initial enrollment, you must wait until the annual general enrollment period: January 1 to March 31. Coverage for those enrolled during the general enrollment period begins on July 1 of that calendar year.

To obtain full Medicare eligibility, you should enroll prior to the month in which you reach 65. Benefits can begin with the first day of the month. Otherwise, the day of entitlement will be delayed.

If a person misses the initial enrollment period and files a late application, a 10 percent penalty on the premium costs is imposed for a period equal to the number of full years that have elapsed since the initial enrollment period.[17] However, if enrollment is late as a result of error, misrepresentation, or inaction by the Medicare administration, relief may be available to correct the mistake. Enrollees should always keep a record of when and who they contacted at the Social Security office.

For those working over age 65, individuals with employer-based health insurance, and those whose spouses have such insurance, a special enrollment period begins with the month in which employer-based insurance no longer is available.[18] As a result, the working aged are excepted from the premium penalty payment.[19]

Will Medicare pay for all my hospital and nursing-home bills?

No. Although Medicare is the primary health insurance of the elderly and disabled, it leaves many gaps in coverage. These gaps are explained in later sections. Some (but not all) of these gaps can be filled through supplemental health insurance. Today, Medicare is used primarily for short term hospital stays and physician's services. Long-term nursing-home care and care for the chronically ill is very limited. Likewise, many necessary medical services, such as eyeglasses and hearing aids, are not covered at all.

What services are covered by Medicare Part A?

Under Part A of Medicare, payment is available for four services:[20] (1) inpatient hospital services, (2) inpatient care in a nursing home that is classified as a "skilled nursing facility," (3) home health services, and (4) hospice care. Each of these services is subject to limitations, which can include deductibles, copayments, and length of care.

What hospital services are covered by Part A?

Most of the services provided by a hospital will be covered by Medicare Part A. Medicare will pay for a semiprivate room; meals; most nursing services; most drugs, medical supplies, and equipment; x-rays and lab tests; charges for operating and recovery rooms; and the cost of intensive care.[21] A private room is covered only if the patient's condition requires isolation or if no semiprivate beds are available. Medicare Part A does not pay for private duty nurses or personal convenience items such as television or a telephone. Remember that physician's bills are generally covered under Medicare Part B rather than Part A.

What coverage conditions are imposed on the receipt of inpatient hospital services?

Medicare will help pay for inpatient hospital care only if (1) the hospital participates in the Medicare program;[22] (2) a doctor has certified the need for the prescribed care for the treatment of an illness or injury;[23] (3) the care needed can be provided only in a hospital;[24] and (4) the hospitalization is not determined to be medically unnecessary by the utilization review committee of the hospital or by the peer review organization.[25] If these conditions have been met, Medicare covers up to ninety days of hospital care per spell of illness, for services provided through 31 December 1988, subject to the following deductibles and copayments in 1988: (1) $540 first day deductible per spell of illness;[26] (2) three-pint blood deductible;[27] (3) $135 per day copayment from the sixty-first through the ninetieth day of care;[28] (4) $270 per day co-insurance for each lifetime reserve day. As a result of the Medicare Catastrophic Coverage Act of 1988, major changes in the hospital benefit take effect on 1 January 1989. These changes include: (1) allowance of unlimited coverage for days of inpatient hospital services; (2) application of a single, annual deductible; (3) elimination of all copayments; and (4) elimination of the "spell of illness" requirement.[29]

What is a "spell of illness"?

Medicare coverage for hospital and skilled nursing facility services rendered before 31 December 1988 is limited by a concept called a "spell of illness."[30] The terminology is somewhat misleading since a "spell of illness" is not directly related to a particular illness. Instead, it is better understood as a "benefit period." The spell of illness controls when deductibles and copayments are due and when benefits are exhausted.

A spell of illness begins the first day a patient enters a hospital as a Medicare Part A beneficiary. It ends sixty days after the patient has stopped receiving inpatient services in a hospital or skilled nursing facility.[31]

What if more than ninety days of inpatient hospital services are needed within one spell of illness?

Under the system in effect until 31 December 1988, Medicare offers an individual sixty lifetime reserve days beyond the ninety days allowable for coverage in a spell of illness.[32] Utilization of reserve days is automatic. In 1988, for each day utilized there is a copayment of $270. Once a lifetime reserve day is used, it cannot be replaced.

You may elect not to use your lifetime reserve days. To do so, notify the Health Care Financing Administration in writing prior to receipt of services. In some cases, election not to use lifetime reserve days may be accepted if made within ninety days following discharge. You may change your mind at any time and begin to draw on your reserve days by notifying the HCFA of your decision. Because Medicare will pay for an unlimited number of days in a hospital beginning on 1 January 1989, lifetime reserve days are not needed for services rendered after that date and the concept is eliminated effective in 1989.

What hospital coverage problems might a Medicare patient face?

The primary problems faced by hospital patients relate to the hospital payment system adopted by Congress for Medicare in 1981. Called the "diagnostic related group (DRG) method," this system pays a hospital a fixed fee for each Medicare patient admitted with a particular diagnosis.[33] As a result of this system, hospitals are discharging patients earlier than in the past, often before the patient is fully recovered or even if the patient has nobody to assist him or her at home. But the process available to protect patients from premature discharge has been improving.

There are very important rights to advance notice and appeal that all patients should be aware of before making any decision to leave hospital care. First, the hospital cannot charge a patient for care or discharge him or her until the third day following the day they give the patient *written* notice of the lapse of Medicare coverage.[34]

Second, a patient can appeal immediately to the peer review organization (PRO),[35] a separate group of doctors and nurses who are paid by Medicare to review medical decisions. The hospital cannot charge a patient for care until the PRO issues its decision. A patient's best advocate at this stage is his or her doctor. Therefore, the patient should keep the doctor informed of what is being determined by Medicare and the hospital.

Which skilled nursing facility services are covered by Part A?
The vast majority of patients residing in skilled nursing facilities do not receive Medicare coverage for their stay. If a patient does meet the conditions of coverage for skilled nursing facility care, Medicare will pay for most nursing home services.[36] A semiprivate room; meals; regular nursing services; physical, speech, and occupational therapy, and other rehabilitation services; drugs and supplies provided by the facility; and medical equipment are all covered. Medicare will not pay for personal convenience items, private duty nurses, or doctor services. While the list of services that could be covered is extensive, the difficulty lies in meeting the conditions for coverage.

What limitations are imposed on the receipt of skilled nursing facility services?
Medicare will pay for skilled nursing facility services only if the patient requires daily skilled nursing or rehabilitation services, which, as a practical matter, must be provided on an inpatient basis at a skilled nursing facility.

In addition to the overall standard for coverage, several technical limitations are imposed.

1. The skilled nursing facility must be a participating provider of services under the Medicare program.[37]
2. The patient must have been in a hospital for at least three consecutive days before being transferred to the skilled nursing facility.[38] This limitation does not apply to services rendered after 31 December 1988.
3. Admission to the skilled nursing facility must occur within thirty days of being discharged from the hospital (some exceptions).[39]
4. The care must be required for a condition for which the patient was hospitalized or one which arose in the nursing facility while being treated for a condition related to hospitalization.[40]
5. The attending physician must certify that skilled nursing facility care is needed on a daily basis.[41]

If these conditions are met, Medicare may cover up to one hundred days of skilled nursing facility care for each spell of illness for services provided through 31 December 1988, subject to the following conditions (in 1988, $67.50 per day).[42] The total cost is borne by Part A for the first twenty days. Thereafter, the patient is responsible for paying some of the costs of these services. Beginning 1 January 1989, the Medicare Catastrophic Coverage Act of 1988 extends the number of days of skilled nursing facility services to 150 per calendar year and shifts the copayment requirement to the first eight days at a rate of 20% of the national average daily reasonable cost of these services (about $20.50 per day in 1989). The Act eliminates the three day prior hospitalization and spell of illness requirements.[43]

On what basis are skilled nursing facility claims usually denied?

HCFA's interpretation of the law on the skilled nursing facility benefit has led to severe cutbacks in coverage. The administration has focused primarily on the definition of "skilled" care and the requirement that "as a practical matter" care must be required on an inpatient basis at a skilled nursing facility. In reviewing skilled nursing facility claims, the Medicare administration frequently denies coverage on the basis that the patient requires only custodial (not skilled) care or that the care is not reasonable and necessary.

Medicare denials of skilled nursing facility care should be appealed using the appeals process described below. Advocates often obtain reversals of coverage denials through the administrative appeals process.

What is the difference between "skilled" and "custodial" care?

Skilled care is care which must be provided by a professional in order to ensure the effectiveness of the treatment and the medical safety of the patient.[44] In contrast, custodial care consists primarily of personal care services offered for the convenience of the patient or the patient's family.[45]

While not all patients in skilled nursing facilities are entitled to Medicare coverage, a substantial number have been classified as custodial care patients when they actually are receiving daily skilled services. Skilled nursing services include injections, tube feeding, care of bed sores, and the use of medical gases. Also included are observation and monitoring of a patient's unstable condition and any patient care plan in which the complexity of the personal care services requires management or evaluation by a skilled professional.

Often, patients who require daily physical therapy because of a hip fracture or a stroke have been denied Medicare coverage or have had coverage cut short on the basis that their care is custodial. Skilled rehabilitation services exist where the professional judgment of the physical therapist is essential to proper delivery of services and planning of the treatment. Where therapeutic progress is being made, continuous judgments are rendered by the skilled therapist.

A person's doctor and medical care providers are the key figures in determining whether skilled care is required. Their opinions should be well-stated and rationalized in the medical records using the language found in the Medicare regulations. Simple, conclusory statements will not suffice.

What does the "as a practical matter" condition of coverage mean?

In Congress' judgment, not everyone who requires daily skilled services requires inpatient care at a skilled nursing facility. Other treatment, such as care in an intermediate care facility or home care might be available to meet patients' needs. The "practical matter" test looks to the availability and feasibility of these alternatives.[46]

In deciding whether alternative treatment exists, cost is also considered. For example, if it were more expensive to provide home care services to a patient, then skilled nursing facility placement would be the most practical way of delivering medical care. Evidence on the relative costs of home care and nursing-home care can be obtained from providers of these services or the state health department. Furthermore, in considering alternative types of care, the patient or his advocate should make sure that nursing home records indicate any obstacles to health care presented in the home or another setting. For example, it would be important to document that an individual lives alone in a second floor apartment with access only by stairs if that individual has fractured a hip and cannot walk or climb stairs. Similarly, it would be important to document any attempt to find a nursing-home bed in an intermediate care facility if a person was rejected because of being too sick for such care.

What home health services are covered under Part A?

In 1980, the Medicare program was amended to improve Medicare coverage of home care services to the elderly and disabled. Effective 1 July 1981, Medicare covers an unlimited number of home health visits provided the conditions of coverage are met. There are no deductibles, and the only coinsurance requirement applies to durable medical equipment, for which the patient shares 20 percent of the cost.[47]

If the conditions for coverage are met, Medicare will pay for part-time skilled nursing care; physical, occupational, and speech therapy; medical social services; part-time services of a home health aide; and medical equipment. Transportation, meals on wheels, and homemaker services are not covered.[48]

What conditions of coverage are imposed on the receipt of home health services?

Medicare Part A will pay for home health care only if (1) the patient is confined to his or her home; (2) the patient requires intermittent skilled nursing care or physical or speech therapy; (3) a physician certifies that the patient needs the prescribed home health care; and (4) the home health services are provided directly by or under arrangements with a Medicare participating home health agency.[49]

What obstacles can be expected to the home health benefit?

The HCFA appears unhappy with the Congressional expansion of the home health benefit. As a result, it has interpreted the conditions of coverage restrictively. It frequently issues policy interpretations reducing the benefit's availability. Some examples follow.

As with the skilled nursing facility benefit, a person might be denied coverage because services required (such as therapy or nursing services) are determined not to be "skilled." As is explained in the next section, the HCFA also reduces coverage through its interpretation of the "intermittent care" requirement.[50]

Finally, an increasing number of coverage denials have been based on the "confined to home" requirement. This is true despite the law's fairly liberal definition of this provision. A patient is homebound if she is incapable of leaving home on a sustained basis to receive medical care, without the use of assistive devices (such as a wheelchair or walker) or the help of another person.[51]

A person denied coverage for home health services for one of these reasons should appeal the denial through the appeals process described later in this chapter. It is likely that Medicare's decision will not be very specific; in fact, it may not make a great deal of sense. These are fairly normal circumstances for Medicare today, and an appeal may be necessary to obtain a sensible, accurate decision.

What is considered "part-time or intermittent" care?

The Medicare administration considers "part-time or intermittent" care to be care which is not provided on a daily basis for an indefinite term.[52] Daily care (i.e., seven days a week) will be covered when the need for such care is clearly temporary. Medicare pays for up to eight hours a day, seven days a week skilled or home health aide care in unusual circumstances.

Normally, Medicare will try to claim that part-time or intermittent means two or three times a week for one to three hours per visit. This is wrong. So long as care is not needed on a daily basis indefinitely, part-time care which is medically necessary should be covered by Medicare.

The second interpretation of the part-time care or intermittent care requirement, which has been accepted by many administrative law judges across the country, is that part-time care should be distinguished from intermittent care.[53] Under this interpretation, daily part-time health aide services required indefinitely can be covered. Medicare coverage is available regardless of whether the patient is acutely ill or chronically ill and whether care is necessary for a long or a short term.[54]

What hospice services are covered under Part A?

The hospice benefit is a relatively new Medicare benefit. When the conditions for coverage are met, hospice services—including inpatient care, visiting nurse services, home health aide care, respite care (temporary inpatient or home care as a substitute for family care), and prescription drugs—can be covered.[55] The only copayments required of beneficiaries are a maximum of five dollars for each prescription drug and up to 5 percent of the cost of respite care.[56]

What limitations are imposed on the receipt of hospice services?

Part A will pay for necessary hospice services provided that the patient has been certified by his or her physician as terminally ill. Medicare considers patients to be terminally ill if they have a predicted life expectancy of less than six months.[57]

To qualify, a patient must make an *election* for hospice care which then limits the patient's option to obtain Medicare coverage for medical treatment of the terminal illness outside of the hospice program.

Through 1988 Medicare coverage for hospice care is limited to three coverage periods: the first two periods are for ninety days; the third period for thirty days. Effective 1 January 1989 hospice care can last longer than 210 days. Finally, the patient must receive the care from a Medicare participating hospice program.[58] Relatively few hospice programs have been certified as Medicare providers as a result of inflexible participation requirements and payment levels.

SUPPLEMENTARY MEDICAL INSURANCE: PART B

Who is eligible for Part B coverage?

Part B benefits are available to persons aged 65 and over and to certain disabled persons regardless of their financial circumstances. Applicants must be either U.S. citizens or aliens admitted for permanent residency status who have resided in the U.S. for at least five years.[59] The categories of eligibility for Medicare Part B are identical to those for Medicare Part A.

Medicare Part B is available through payment of a monthly premium[60] which, in 1988, is $24.80. An individual may enroll in Medicare Part B without being enrolled in Part A, but voluntary enrollees in Part A must enroll in Medicare Part B.

How do I enroll?

Enrollment in Medicare Part B is automatic for those who are entitled to Part A benefits. To decline this coverage, you must file a notice with the Social Security Administration. Enrollment in Part A and Part B should take place during the initial enrollment period in order to maximize the entitlement for benefits. Separate Medicare enrollment is unnecessary for those whose eligibility is based on their entitlement and receipt of Social Security or Railroad Retirement benefits. The application and enrollment procedures are comparable to those outlined for Medicare Part A.[61]

Medicare enrollment may be terminated and reinstated only one time. After a second termination, you no longer are eligible to enroll for Medicare Part B coverage.[62]

When does coverage begin?

Coverage begins no earlier than the month of your 65th birthday if your basis of eligibility is age-related.[63] To obtain Medicare coverage at that time, you must enroll sometime during the three months preceding the month of your 65th birthday. Later enrollment during the initial enrollment period leads to delayed eligibility.[64] Any enrollment during the general enrollment period (January 1 to March 31) results in coverage beginning on July 1 of that year.

How much are the premiums?

The amount of the premium is determined annually by the Secretary of Health and Human Services for the period beginning January 1. For 1988, the premium is $24.80 per month. The current premium amount is intended to cover 25 percent of program costs. The remainder of program costs are covered through the Medicare Trust fund and general tax revenues.

The Medicare Catastrophic Coverage Act of 1988 significantly alters the premiums that will be charged for Medicare Part B beginning in 1989.[65] The new law continues the general annual increases but adds a "flat monthly premium" to help pay for the Act's catastrophic coverage and prescription drug benefits. In 1989 this additional premium will add $4.00 to Part B monthly premiums, rising to an additional $10.20 per month in 1993. The Act also establishes a "supplemental premium" to be financed by additional income tax payments by Medicare beneficiaries. Based on a person's federal income tax liability, the premium cannot exceed $800 in 1989, rising to $1,050 in 1993.

Premiums are deducted automatically from Social Security disability or retirement benefits. Direct payment is required when Social Security benefits are not received.[66] Direct payment generally is made quarterly, but alternative arrangements can be made depending on an individual's financial circumstances.[67]

Some people have their Part B premiums paid through special state buy-in provisions, under which the Part B premiums of Medicare recipients who are eligible for Medicaid are paid by their home state.[68] The determination of whether to participate in such a buy-in agreement is made by each state and cannot be requested if the state has no such provision.

What services are covered by Part B?

Part B covered services include most medical care necessary as a supplement to Part A institutional services, particularly physicians' services and medical equipment. Not all services important to the elderly are covered.

Covered Services:[69]

1. physicians' services
2. services and supplies, including drugs and biologicals which cannot be self-administered, furnished incidental to physicians' services
3. diagnostic x-ray tests, diagnostic laboratory tests, and other diagnostic tests
4. x-ray therapy, radium therapy, and radioactive isotope therapy
5. surgical dressings and splints, casts, and other devices used for fractures and dislocations
6. rental or purchase of durable medical equipment
7. prosthetic devices
8. leg, arm, back, and neck braces and artificial legs, arms, and eyes
9. ambulance services
10. outpatient hospital diagnostic services
11. outpatient physical therapy
12. outpatient speech pathology
13. rural health clinic services

14. institutional and home dialysis services, supplies, and equipment
15. ambulatory surgical center services
16. pneumococcal and hepatitis-B vaccinations
17. home health services
18. immunosuppressive drugs for transplant patients
19. occupational therapy
20. mammography screening (effective 1 January 1990)
21. respite care for up to 80 hours (effective 1 January 1990)
22. influenza vaccine (contingent effective date)
23. certified nurse-midwife services
24. therapeutic shoes for patients with severe diabetic disease (contingent effective date)

Excluded Services:[70]

1. prescription drugs which do not require administration by a physician (covered after 1 January 1991 with a high deductible and copay)
2. routine physical checkups
3. eyeglasses or contact lenses, in most cases
4. eye examinations for purposes of prescribing, fitting, or changing eyeglasses or contact lenses
5. hearing aids
6. most immunizations, except as noted above
7. orthopedic shoes
8. custodial care
9. cosmetic surgery
10. most dental services
11. personal comfort items
12. routine foot care

Are prescription drugs covered under Medicare?

Inpatient drugs and drugs that cannot be self-administered are covered. In addition, beginning 1 January 1990 a new prescription drug benefit will be phased into Medicare.[71] In 1990 Medicare will cover home intravenous (IV) therapy drugs and extend coverage for certain immunosuppressive drugs used in organ transplants. Starting in 1991 Medicare will cover all other outpatient prescription drugs. The costs of providing this coverage are likely to be high, however, so Congress has imposed significant annual deductibles and copayments. In 1991, for example, the deductible is $600 and the coinsurance for most drugs is 50% of the approved charge.

In addition to the drug benefit, home IV drug therapy will be covered by Part B beginning in 1990. Essentially all of the services needed for home IV therapy—nursing, pharmacy, and related services—will be covered without deductible or coinsurance.

Does Part B pay all costs for covered services?

No. For nearly all Part B covered services, Medicare pays only 80 percent of the reasonable charge or reasonable cost. The beneficiary participates in the cost of covered services in three ways:[72] first, the annual deductible; second, 20 percent coinsurance on most services; and third, the difference or gap between the actual charge for the medical care and the Medicare's approved rate of payment.

In 1988, the annual deductible is $75. This deductible is met by submitting claims for coverable services. Medicare will keep a record of the deductible status and provide notice each time there is an update. The deductible is met on the basis of the approved, rather than the actual, charge for services.

Effective 1 January 1990, the Medicare Catastrophic Coverage Act of 1988 sets an annual limit on out-of-pocket expenses under Part B.[73] The upper limit is $1,370 in 1990 and thereafter will vary depending on the rate of inflation. The following expenses are counted in determining whether the limit has been reached: the annual Part B deductible, the 20% Part B coinsurance, and the three pint blood deductible. Not counted is any amount you pay above Medicare's "reasonable charge" for a service. Once you have reached the annual limit, Medicare will pay 100% of the "reasonable charge" for your Part B services.

What physician services are paid by Part B?

Medicare's payment for physician services includes coverage of most care provided by a medical doctor and *some* care provided by chiropractors, dentists, podiatrists, and osteopaths.[74] The physicians' services can be provided in the home, office, hospital, or nursing home. Direct patient care, such as surgery and consultation services, can be covered.

There are important limitations on the payment for "physician's services" which are provided by other than medical doctors. For example, the services of a dentist are covered only in matters related to an injury to the jaw or supporting structures. Routine dental care is not covered.

How much will Medicare pay for doctors' services?

Part B pays for 80 percent of the "reasonable charge" for doctors' services.[75] The reasonable charge is the lowest of (a) the physician's actual charge; (b) the customary charge of that physician for the same service; or (c) the prevailing rate among all physicians providing that service within the locality.[76]

There is usually a large gap (currently 25 percent on average) between Medicare's approved charge and the physician's actual charge. This does not mean that your physician is overcharging; rather it is a result of Medicare's "reasonable charge formula," which does not adequately account for changes in physician prices.

Currently, most physicians are restricted in their authority to increase their charges to Medicare patients. Only physicians who have agreed with HHS to accept assignments in all cases (participating physicians) can increase their charges without restriction.[77]

Medicare reimbursement for physician services has been confusing and inequitable. The only relief from the confusion occurs when a patient is fortunate enough to locate a participating physician.

What outpatient hospital services are covered by Part B?

Part B will help pay for services in an emergency room or outpatient clinic; diagnostic laboratory and x-ray tests billed by the hospital; medical supplies like splints, etc.; and drugs that cannot be self-administered.[78] With the exception of outpatient laboratory tests, Medicare pays 80 percent of the approved charge. As with all Part B services, the $75 deductible must be met before any payment will be made.

What physical or speech therapy is covered by Part B?

Medically reasonable and necessary services of a physical or speech therapist are covered by Medicare Part B, subject to the $75 deductible and the 80 percent limitation. These services can be provided in the physician's office, on an outpatient basis in a hospital or skilled nursing facility, or through a home health agency.[79]

If the patient receives physical therapy services from a Medicare approved independent physical therapist, Medicare benefits are limited to coverage of $500 of services in any year. The deductible and 80 percent limitation also apply.[80] To date, independent speech pathology services are not covered.

What home health services are covered under Part B?

The Part B home health services benefit is identical to the Part A benefit described earlier[81] and is not subject to the annual Part B deductible. Part B home health services are available to those enrollees not participating in Part A. The limitations under Medicare Part B are the same as those applied under Medicare Part A.[82]

What problems exist in Medicare Part B benefits?

With a massive insurance program, particularly one run by the federal government, numerous problems are to be expected. Conditions and limitations are imposed on nearly every item covered under Medicare Part B. The most frequently experienced problem involves the "reasonable charge" calculation.[83] The individual's only weapon against reasonable charge reductions is the physician's acceptance of a Medicare assignment explained below.

Another common problem occurs with Medicare coverage for durable medical equipment. There are no pre-purchase authorizations, so the individual who buys or rents the equipment and waits for Medicare's decision risks a denial. Durable medical equipment is equipment which must be able to withstand use, is primarily and customarily designed for medical purposes, and is generally not useful in the absence of injury or illness.[84] Medical equipment is covered only if it is used in the home. Medicare limits payment for medical equipment to either rental or purchase, whichever is more economical.

The chances of Medicare coverage can be improved if the individual obtains from the equipment supplier a copy of the coverage requirements for the particular equipment. These requirements should be reviewed and passed on to the physician for a prescription written in the language of the coverage requirements and indicating that the individual meets the coverage standards.

These problems represent only a sampling of the numerous obstacles to Part B benefits. Denials of coverage often are issued simply because of inadequate information. On other occasions, denials are the result of the many technicalities of coverage. The best protection in any Medicare Part B problem area is to have the physician or supplier accept a Medicare assignment (charging and billing agreement) of the claims. If the claim is then denied because the item or service was found to be not medically necessary, Medicare law allows for a waiver of the patient's liability. And remember, there is also the right to appeal.

Administration of Medicare

Is it necessary to submit bills to Medicare in order for payment to be made under Part A?

No. Under Part A (hospital insurance program), the provider of services submits a claim for Medicare payment.[85] Medicare will send the claimant a Medicare Claim Determination, which will indicate the services provided and the coverage determination. These notices should be retained in case of a later dispute with the provider of services or with Medicare.

If a provider thinks that a particular form of care is not covered under the Medicare program, the provider may not submit a claim to Medicare. However, the patient may insist that the provider submit the claim. Then, if the claim is denied, the result is a formal determination that can be appealed.

Is it necessary to submit bills to Medicare in order for payment to be made under Part B?

Frequently yes. The answer depends on whether the provider of medical services has accepted an assignment of the claim. When the provider of medical services has not accepted assignment, the patient must submit the bill to the Medicare carrier.[86] This includes bills for services rendered by physicians, therapists, and others, as well as claims for medical equipment and diagnostic tests. When the services were provided by a hospital, nursing home, or home health agency, the provider generally will submit the Part B claim to Medicare and be paid directly. In other circumstances, the provider of the medical services has the option to accept a Medicare assignment and to file a direct claim.[87]

In seeking Part B reimbursement, the patient must submit a claim form and attach a copy of the medical bill. It is extremely helpful if the bill is itemized and contains details of the actual services provided since claims are frequently rejected for insufficient information.

What is a Medicare assignment?

The Medicare program offers an option to providers of Part B services. Doctors, for example, can agree to bill Medicare directly for services they provide and then receive direct payment.[88] By agreeing to accept assignment, the doctor also agrees not to charge more than the Medicare-approved charge. With an assignment, the patient is responsible only for payment of the $75 deductible and the 20 percent that Medicare does not pay. The difference between the approved charge and the actual charge would not have to be paid. Medicare has instituted a system of "participating physicians."[89] A participating physician registers with Medicare and agrees to accept assignment in all cases for a full calendar year beginning January 1. Medicare publishes a list of these doctors which is available at most Social Security Offices and at the carrier's office. Doctors are catalogued according to specialty and location. Doctors who do not register as participating physicians may accept assignments on a case by case basis. Patients should request doctors to accept assignment.

Why do many doctors refuse assignment for Part B claims?

Doctors' incomes are reduced by accepting assignment because they receive no more than the Medicare-approved charge (which is usually 25 percent less than the actual charge). In addition, accepting assignment requires the completion of Medicare forms by doctor's office staff, so doctors blame the paperwork for their refusal to accept assignments.

How are claimants informed about Medicare Part B decisions?

Each time a claim is submitted for medical services to the Medicare Part B carrier, an Explanation of Medicare Benefits (EOMB) is issued. The explanation identifies the medical service provided, the date on which it was provided, and the decision reached regarding payment. If payment is not made in full, a brief explanation of the reason for the coverage denial or charge reduction is provided. The EOMB has been improved in format and substance as a result of litigation complaining that Medicare beneficiaries could not understand the notices and were not informed as to the reason for the coverage determination.[90]

The EOMB also provides information regarding the status of $75 annual deductible and explains the rights of appeal. Claimants should read and retain the Explanation of Medicare Benefits. It will be needed for submittal of a claim to other health insurance a claimant may have, and it serves as a record of the claimant's deductible status under Part B.

Who is responsible for providing explanation of nonpayment of Part B benefits?

Carriers are required to provide answers to Medicare beneficiaries who have questions about Part B benefits and claims. Each carrier is required to have a toll-free telephone number and a walk-in service to handle inquiries. Guidelines require the carriers to respond fully within a short time to any question. This means that not only must the carrier answer the telephone promptly, but also must quickly provide an answer to the question.[91]

Why does Medicare refuse to pay for services that are not "reasonable and necessary?"

The Social Security Act forbids Medicare payments, under Part A or Part B, for any services which are not "reasonable and necessary for the diagnosis and treatment of illness or injury."[92] In determining whether services are "reasonable and necessary," Medicare will look to such factors as the length of stay in an institution, the level of care required at that institution, the frequency of physician visits, and whether medical equipment ordered is intended to meet a medical need. The decision as to whether a particular treatment is "reasonable and necessary" is often a matter of judgment. Medicare's judgments on this issue are often incorrect.

Will Medicare pay for custodial care?

No. Medicare law specifically prohibits payment for custodial care.[93] However, neither the statute nor the regulations define custodial care clearly. The HCFA regulations define custodial care as care which does not meet the definition of skilled care.[94]

The courts generally have defined custodial care to be care for the convenience of the patient or the patient's family.[95] For example, a patient will be considered as receiving custodial care if the only reason the patient is admitted to the nursing facility is that the family is unable to provide personal care services for the patient.

Adverse custodial care decisions should be appealed. The HCFA's use of the custodial care exclusion has greatly reduced the value of the Part A skilled nursing facility benefit. But many Medicare beneficiaries who have challenged these decisions have prevailed and have been awarded benefits.

Who decides whether medical services are reasonable and necessary and whether or not they are custodial?

There are several participants in the decision-making process. First, the provider of services (i.e., hospital or nursing home) must decide whether services required by a patient meet Medicare coverage standards. If the provider feels the services are not reasonable and necessary, a Medicare claim will not be submitted, and no formal determination will be issued.

Hospitals and nursing homes also have utilization-review committees (URC), which are composed of doctors and other medical personnel who review admissions and continued stays to determine whether the patient requires the level of care offered by the facility.[96] Although a URC decision is not a formal decision by the Medicare program,[97] it will lead to a termination of Medicare benefits. Medicare payment is prohibited when the URC finds that continued care is not medically necessary.[98] Since the URC must consult with the patient's doctor before reaching its decision, it might be advantageous for the patient or his or her advocate to talk to the physician before the consultation and to be informed of when the URC will be considering his or her case.

Medicare intermediaries also may be involved in determining whether medical care is reasonable and necessary or whether it is custodial.[99] The intermediary will assume this responsibility in all hospital and nursing home cases except where a peer review organization is operating.

The HCFA independently contracts with peer review organizations (PRO) to perform the task of determining whether care provided to patients is reasonable and necessary.[100] A PRO can deny Medicare coverage for an admission to a hospital or nursing home. A PRO can also deny continued coverage for a patient in a hospital or skilled nursing facility. Presently, PROs are involved primarily with hospital coverage decisions, with a few PROs contracting to do decision making on the skilled nursing facility benefit as well.

What options are available if I disagree with a Medicare decision?

Too few. The appeals system provides inadequate opportunities to challenge an adverse decision prior to financial liability for care. Patients often leave a facility or decline further treatment after being informed their treatment is not covered by Medicare. The ability to challenge an adverse decision depends upon the source of that decision.

If the provider of services has decided that a patient's care is not medically necessary and therefore outside of Medicare coverage, his or her rights are limited. Where a PRO oversees the decision-making process, the patient can turn to the PRO for a formal determination.[101] A PRO will make an early decision regarding coverage rights, but it is not obligated to make a decision until the provider has submitted a bill.

If the provider has rendered a decision and there is no PRO, the only remaining alternative is to turn to the intermediary and demand that the provider submit a claim. This mechanism is of little benefit, since it takes weeks for the intermediary to review a claim and issue a decision. The patient will be obligated to pay bills incurred in the meantime.

Where the URC is the source of the coverage denial, there is no direct right of appeal. The patient must wait for a formal determination from the intermediary before filing an appeal. However, it is possible to informally ask the physician to request that the URC reconsider its decision. The physician may present her views to the URC before it reaches a final determination.[102] If the physician did not take this opportunity prior to the URC's decision, it is possible to reopen the case.

A patient's best advocate is her physician. If the doctor can provide sufficient information, documentation, and rationale regarding care, Medicare coverage may be granted.

When is the patient notified whether services are found to be reasonable and necessary?

The first notice regarding a finding that medical care is not reasonable and necessary probably will come from the provider of services.[103] Under a provision of the law known as the "waiver of liability," the provider of services is required to notify a patient at or before the time that such medical services are considered to be not reasonable and necessary. This notice can be provided either at or prior to admission or during a stay at a facility. The provider's notice is not a formal determination of noncoverage by Medicare and is not appealable.

The provider of services also might inform the patient that, in the opinion of the URC, her care is not medically reasonable and necessary. If the URC has concluded that a patient's care is not covered by Medicare, the provider cannot charge him or her for services until the fourth day following the date the facility was notified by the URC of noncoverage.[104] In a prospective payment/DRG hospital case, a facility cannot charge a beneficiary for care until the third day following the date of written notice of noncoverage.[105]

The PRO also is a likely source of patient notice, primarily in hospital-care cases. When a PRO determines that a patient is not entitled to Medicare coverage for a hospital stay, it must provide written notice to the patient, physician, hospital, and fiscal intermediary.[106] The notice must contain reasons for the denial, the effective date of the notice, and information concerning rights of appeal. A PRO can grant up to two grace days for discharge planning when the provider of services did not have reason to know that services were not covered.[107]

Finally, notice of noncoverage may come from the Medicare fiscal intermediary.[108] The intermediary will issue denials of coverage based on medical necessity only where there is no PRO. In all other cases, the intermediary could issue such notice at any time to the patient. In most cases, where the intermediary notice is the first one received by the patient, that notice is retroactive in its application.

Am I liable for services found to be not reasonable or necessary?

Possibly. The final answer depends on both the source and timing of notice that services are not covered by Medicare.

Under Medicare's waiver of liability provision, a patient is responsible for paying for unnecessary medical services or for services regarded as custodial only if he could reasonably be expected to know that the services were not covered by Medicare.[109] Under Medicare regulations, a patient is reasonably expected to know that services were not covered by Medicare only if he was so informed in writing. Therefore, retroactive coverage denials usually result in waiver of liability protection. The waiver of liability provision applies to all Part A claims and to those Part B claims for which a provider has accepted an assignment.

While at first glance the waiver of liability seems to offer patients great protection, its operation presents several problems. First, the waiver of liability system, as it works for providers of health care, serves to encourage providers to deny Medicare coverage and to avoid submitting a Medicare claim. This is because providers are threatened with shifted liability, i.e., they pay for the care if they submit a claim and Medicare denies payment. However, providers can avoid liability if they deny coverage and do not submit a claim. Second, if a patient has paid for care and is entitled to waiver protection, he or she must submit a Request for Indemnification to Medicare. Forms are available from Medicare and Social Security offices. Patients must take this extra step or they will not get the benefits of the waiver of liability provision.

APPEALS OF MEDICARE DETERMINATIONS

Most (but not all) decisions involving Medicare can be appealed. The appeal route depends upon the nature and the source of the denial. Only formal determinations from Medicare or its contractors (i.e., fiscal intermediaries, PROs, and carriers) can be appealed. If a provider of services has issued a denial notice and failed to submit a claim to Medicare, there is no right of appeal. For this reason, it is important to insist that a provider submit a claim to Medicare so that an appealable determination is rendered. There are various categories of appeals.

Eligibility Appeals

Eligibility determinations for Medicare Part A or Part B may be appealed.[110] Eligibility determinations are issued by the

Social Security Administration, and appeals are filed with them. The system is similar to that for the Social Security program. Before filing a formal appeal, a claimant may discuss the decision in an informal manner at the local Social Security Administration (SSA) office. The SSA can correct clear errors of fact at this stage. If the claimant is unsuccessful, a formal appeal can be filed at the SSA office. The first stage of appeal is known as a "reconsideration," which is a paper review of the file.[111] Additional evidence may be submitted, but there is no face-to-face hearing.

If the reconsideration determination is unfavorable, the claimant may request a hearing before a Social Security administrative law judge. This can be done through the local SSA office. At the hearing, testimony may be heard, evidence introduced, and witnesses cross-examined.[112] If the judge's decision is unfavorable, the next step is to file an appeal with the SSA Appeals Council. The last resort is to file suit in federal court.

PRO Decisions

Where the decision whether to pay for a Part A claim is made by the peer review organization, the initial challenge must be directed to the PRO.

The first stage of the PRO appeal is known as a "reconsideration."[113] A reconsideration should be requested in writing and filed at the office of the PRO or of the Social Security Administration or Railroad Retirement Board.[114] At reconsideration, a PRO will consider issues regarding level of care, medical necessity, and appropriateness of care.[115] Waiver of liability questions follow the non-PRO appeals route described below. Determinations regarding grace days cannot be appealed.

At a PRO reconsideration, a claimant has the opportunity to obtain and submit information but cannot review the record of the PRO initial deliberation or obtain information regarding the identity of the reviewers.[116] The reconsideration determination is issued by a peer reviewer,[117] i.e., an M.D., osteopath, or dentist. However, there is no requirement for review by a specialist in the area of the patient's diagnosis.

A person may request an expedited reconsideration if the PRO has denied coverage prior to admission to the facility or if it is a continued stay denial and the person remains in the facility.

An expedited reconsideration request must be filed within three days of the denial and only at the PRO office.[118] A PRO must issue its reconsideration determination within three days if the individual is still a patient or is awaiting admission.[119] Skilled nursing facility patients are entitled to decisions within ten days of an expedited reconsideration.[120] In all other cases, the PRO must issue a decision with thirty days.[121] That decision must be in writing and must present detailed reasons for the conclusion. After reconsideration, the patient has a right of appeal to an administrative law judge (ALJ).[122] The ALJ hearing allows the patient to present evidence and cross-examine any witnesses. To qualify for an ALJ hearing on a PRO appeal, there must be at least $200 in controversy. If the judge's decision is not favorable, there is a right of appeal to the Appeals Council and, if there is at least $2,000 in controversy, to federal district court.[123]

Non-PRO Part A Appeals

The first stage of the appeals process is, again, a reconsideration.[124] A reconsideration request should be made in writing to the intermediary that issued the initial determination. In an intermediary reconsideration, an in-house paper review is performed by an employee other than the one who issued the initial determination. Additional evidence may be submitted, but there is no right to an oral hearing.

Following a reconsideration determination, patients are entitled to a hearing before an administrative law judge if the amount in controversy exceeds $100.[125] A hearing request can be filed with the intermediary or a local SSA office. As with the PRO hearing, there is a right to present evidence and to cross-examine witnesses. An ALJ may utilize the services of a medical consultant who would issue an independent expert opinion which the ALJ will consider in reaching his decision. ALJs are required to provide free copies of the evidence if requested by the claimant or the claimant's representative. The hearing is an informal process—strict rules of evidence do not apply. It is also the best opportunity for the reversal of a Medicare denial since the attending physician's opinion is entitled to special weight and since the ALJ relies on law rather than Medicare policy manuals. The ALJ issues a written decision after the hearing.

Beyond the ALJ hearing, there is a right to an Appeals Council review[126] and also to a federal district court review if the matter in controversy exceeds $1000.[127] It is advisable to obtain legal representation for cases that go to federal court.

Part B Coverage Appeals

The Part B appeals system has undergone a major change with the Omnibus Budget Reconciliation Act (OBRA) of 1986. For services furnished before 1 January 1987, there are only two appeals steps with no judicial review.[128] For services furnished after 1 January 1987, there are limited rights to an ALJ hearing and judicial review.[129]

A review is the first step.[130] A written request must be filed with the carrier or at an SSA office. The review is performed in-house by the Medicare carrier, and the patient has the opportunity to present additional evidence.

For services provided before 1 January 1987, the final step in the Part B appeals process is a hearing before a carrier-appointed hearing officer.[131] The right to this hearing is limited to matters in which at least $100 is in controversy, and claims may be aggregated to reach the $100 threshold. The hearing officers are not employees of the carrier, but are independent contractors under the carrier's supervision and control. To obtain a hearing, a written request must be filed with the carrier or at an SSA office.

With the OBRA of 1986, several major changes in appeal rights were enacted into law. For Part B services provided after 1 January 1987, an ALJ hearing is available where the amount in controversy exceeds $500 and judicial review where the controversy exceeds $1000 in value. Claims between $100 and $500 are under the jurisdiction of a Part B hearing officer.[132]

While these amendments represent legislative victories for Medicare beneficiaries, the amendments are not without limitations. First, matters which are considered "national coverage determinations" cannot be reviewed by an ALJ, and such determinations cannot be invalidated based upon a violation of the Administrative Procedure Act (APA) or the Freedom of Information Act (FOIA).[133] The APA and FOIA require publication of and an opportunity for public comment on many government policies. Second, a court may not invalidate a national coverage determination without giving Medicare a second chance to prove its case.

And matters are complicated by a lack of definition as to what constitutes a "national coverage determination." Finally, challenges to the method of determining the amount of payment are precluded with respect to policies issued before 1 January 1981. This amendment appears to address the opening of a jurisdictional door by the Supreme Court[134] where the challenged "method of payment" involved classifying family physicians outside of a specialty status, thereby leading to reduced Medicare reimbursement.

What are the time limits for filing a Medicare appeal?

For eligibility, PRO, and non-PRO Part A appeals, an appeal must be filed within sixty days from receipt of the previous determination.[135] This sixty-day time period applies to each stage of the appeal: reconsideration, hearing, Appeals Council, and federal district court review. Expedited reconsideration requests on PRO appeals must be filed within three days of the initial determination.[136] In the absence of contrary evidence, the notice is presumed received within five days of its mailing.[137] It is possible to obtain an extension of time upon a showing of good cause for delay.[138] Age and infirmity usually are sufficient reasons for an extended appeal time.

With all Part B appeals, a six-month appeal time period applies at both the review and hearing stage. Good cause extensions are available.[139]

Is the Medicare appeals system adequate?

No. As in other government programs, Congress has attempted to strike a balance between the rights of individuals and the public interest. In Medicare appeals, the patient's right to Medicare coverage is weighed against the administration's interest in efficiency and in reducing costs.

The primary shortcoming in the Medicare appeals system is the lack of any right to appeal *prior* to the termination of Medicare coverage.[140] This means that a patient must risk paying for the care while awaiting an appeal decision and hoping for a reversal. Patients often are unwilling to risk having to pay for expensive hospital, nursing home, or home care so leave rather than stay and file a Medicare claim.

Another major problem with the system is the absence of time guidelines on the issuance of appeal determinations. While Medicare intermediaries are encouraged to process reconsideration determinations within 90 days, administrative law judges often take more than 200 days to issue hearing decisions. If a patient utilizes only these two steps in the appeals process, it could be a year before a decision is issued. Only PRO appeals must be issued within certain time guidelines. Unfortunately, the Supreme Court has not supported arguments that the Constitution requires that time guidelines be set for hearings and reconsiderations.[141]

Despite these shortcomings, the Part A and Part B appeals systems afford Medicare beneficiaries a good opportunity to correct erroneous, illegal, and improper coverage decisions. Advocates nationally report a high percentage of favorable ALJ and district court decisions.

What should a claimant do to win a Medicare appeal?

The answer to this question depends, of course, on the issue on appeal. If eligibility is disputed, it is important to introduce evidence establishing the claimant's right to participate in Medicare. For example, to establish age, records of birth, confirmation, or marriage can be introduced. Regardless of the issue on appeal, it is important to make certain that all facts of the case including all medical records are presented and that the case is reviewed within the guidelines of the law. It is not necessary to be a lawyer to win a Medicare appeal. The basic information on Medicare law needed to win an appeal is contained in this chapter.

The best source of expert evidence to support a Medicare appeal is the claimant's physician. The attending physician's opinion is given special weight in Medicare appeals, since he or she knows more about the claimant's medical needs than the party who is reviewing the medical records. Any appeal concerning a custodial care or medical necessity denial should be supported by a written, detailed statement by the claimant's doctor regarding the need for the care. The doctor must state what care is needed and the reasons for the particular level of care. If the doctor appears hesitant to cooperate, the patient might consider preparing a statement for his or her signature.

Adequate preparation is essential for a successful challenge to an adverse medical decision. An appeal is a good opportunity to obtain a fair determination based on the law. When in doubt about a Medicare claim determination, appeal.

Where can I find more information about Medicare?

If you are dissatisfied with a Medicare decision or need general information about Medicare, begin at the Social Security Office. For more information about Part A, you can contact the fiscal intermediary. For Part B, you can call the Medicare carrier. In addition, many legal service agencies and social service organizations have acted as Medicare advocates and can provide information and offer assistance. A partial list of these organizations is available in appendix D.

The Social Security Administration and Medicare carriers and intermediaries such as Blue Cross/Blue Shield may also have printed information. For example, a booklet *Your Medicare Handbook* is available and free at Social Security district offices. You should know, however, that the *Handbook* discusses Medicare in a simplified way. While it serves as a handy guide, it is not sufficiently detailed to provide a full understanding of Medicare.

Several detailed publications which can be of great assistance in getting to know your rights under Medicare are available. *Medicare: Obtaining Your Full Benefits* is a four volume set available from the Legal Counsel for the Elderly in Washington D.C. Prepared in cooperation with the American Association of Retired Persons (AARP), the set is available from many AARP chapters. An extensive three volume set of materials entitled the *Medicare and Medicaid Guide* is available from Commerce Clearing House. These volumes are updated regularly and are available in many law libraries. A thorough guide for Medicare advocates is contained in the *Social Security Practice Guide* (Matthew Bender), also available in law libraries.

If I have Medicare, is it necessary also to carry private health insurance?

As with all insurance, health insurance is a balance of risks. If you are healthy and anticipate no medical needs, then you might wish to risk having only Medicare. However, increased medical needs often come with age. And Medicare is not comprehensive—it does not meet all the health care needs of the elderly.

A variety of health insurance policies are available to supplement Medicare. Some supplement Medicare directly by paying Medicare's deductibles and coinsurances. Others (known as indemnity policies) provide set payments for each day in a hospital. Still others—major medical policies which frequently are available only to people as a retirement benefit—provide fairly good comprehensive coverage.

What types of health care coverage are offered under a Medicare supplement plan?

Most policies agree to pay the copayment not covered by Medicare. Still others will also pay the hospital and Part B deductibles. Finally, some policies include coverage for additional types of health care such as out-of-hospital prescription drugs, only partially covered by Medicare. New policies designed to cover the costs of long-term nursing home care are also being marketed.

Purchasing Medicare supplemental insurance involves difficult choices. Always compare carefully before buying a Medicare supplemental policy. Be aware of the gaps in Medicare coverage such as deductibles, coinsurances, and non-covered items. See what supplemental coverage insurance provides and always compare the costs of competing insurance policies. Generally, it is better to buy a single policy covering your needs rather than a series of policies.

The revisions in Medicare resulting from the Medicare Catastrophic Coverage Act of 1988 will have a large effect on Medicare supplemental policies. As a result, the Act requires insurance companies to inform policyholders of the effect of the Act on their policies. The Act also strengthens state and federal regulation of Medicare supplemental policies by, among other things, requiring enhanced standards for such policies and by establishing a 30-day free-look period in which policies can be returned for a full refund. Check with your state insurance commission and the HCFA to learn more about the requirements that these policies must meet.

NOTES

1. Special Comm. On Aging, 98th Cong., 2d Sess., Prospects For Medicare's Hospital Insurance Trust Fund 17, (Comm. Print 1983).
2. 42 U.S.C.A. § 1395 *et seq.* (West 1983 & Supp. 1987). *See generally Soc. Security Bull.*, June 1986, at 15.
3. 42 U.S.C.A. § 1395h (West 1983 & Supp. 1987).

4. 42 U.S.C.A. § 1395u(a) (West Supp. 1987).

5. 42 U.S.C.A. §§ 1320c-l; 1320c-3 (West 1983 & Supp. 1987).

6. 42 U.S.C.A. § 426 (West 1983 & Supp. 1987); 42 U.S.C.A. §§ 1395i-2(a); 1395c (West 1983 & Supp. 1987) 42 C.F.R. §§ 408.5 (p. A), 405.205, 405.206 (p. B) (1986).

7. 42 U.S.C.A. § 426(a) (West 1983 & Supp. 1987); 42 C.F.R. § 408.10 (1986).

8. 42 U.S.C.A. § 426(b) (West 1983 & Supp. 1987); 42 C.F.R. § 408.12 (1986).

9. 42 U.S.C.A. § 426-1 (West 1983 & Supp 1987); 42 U.S.C.A. § 1395rr(a) (West Supp. 1987); 42 C.F.R. § 408.13. (1986).

10. 42 U.S.C.A. § 1395i-2(a) (West 1983); 42 C.F.R. § 408.20. (1986).

11. 42 C.F.R. § 405.210(b) (1986); 42 C.F.R. § 408.6(b) (1986).

12. 42 C.F.R. § 408.6(c) (1986).

13. 42 C.F.R. § 408.13(d) (1986).

14. 42 C.F.R. §§ 408.6(d); 408.21 (1986).

15. 42 U.S.C.A. § 426 (West Supp. 1987); 42 U.S.C.A. § 1395i-2 (West 1983 & Supp. 1987); 42 C.F.R. § 408.6 (1986).

16. 42 C.F.R. § 408.21(c) (1986).

17. 42 U.S.C.A. § 1395r(b) (West Supp. 1987); 42 C.F.R. § 408.22(c) (1986); Comprehensive Omnibus Budget Reconciliation Act of 1985 (COBRA), Pub. L. No. 99-272, § 9124, 100 Stat. 282 (1986).

18. 42 U.S.C.A. § 1395p(i) (West Supp. 1987).

19. 42 U.S.C.A. § 1395r(b) (West Supp. 1987).

20. 42 U.S.C. § 1395d(a) (1983).

21. 42 U.S.C.A. §§ 1395d(a)(l); 1935x(b) (West 1983); 42 C.F.R. § 409.10 (1986).

22. 42 U.S.C.A. § 1395f(a) (West Supp. 1987); 42 C.F.R. 405 sub. J. (1986).

23. 42 U.S.C.A. § 1395f(a)(3) (West Supp. 1987).

24. 42 U.S.C.A. § 1395y(a)(l) (West 1983 & Supp. 1987).

25. 42 U.S.C.A. § 1395f(6) (West Supp. 1987); 42 U.S.C.A. § 1320c-3 (West 1983 & Supp. 1987).

26. 42 C.F.R. § 409.82 (1986); 51 Fed. Reg. 42007 (Nov. 20, 1986).

27. 42 C.F.R. § 409.87 (1986); 51 Fed. Reg. 42007 (Nov. 20, 1986).

28. 42 C.F.R. § 409.83 (1986); 51 Fed. Reg. 42007 (Nov. 20, 1986).

29. Medicare Catastrophic Coverage Act of 1988, Pub. L. No. 100-360 §§ 101, 102, 102 Stat. 683, 684–86 (1988).

30. *See* 42 U.S.C.A. § 1935d(a)(1), (2) (West 1983).

31. 42 U.S.C.A. § 1395x(a) (West 1983); 42 C.F.R. § 409.60 (1986).

32. 42 U.S.C. §§ 1395d(a), (b) (West 1983); 42 C.F.R. § 409.65 (1986).

33. 42 U.S.C.A. § 1395ww (West Supp. 1987).

34. 42 C.F.R. § 412.42 (1986).

35. Comprehensive Budget Reconciliation Act of 1985 (COBRA), Pub. L. No. 97-272, § 9351, 100 Stat. 282 (1986).

36. 42 U.S.C. §§ 1395(a)(2)(A); 1395x(h) (West 1987); 42 C.F.R. § 409.20 (1985).

37. 42 U.S.C.A. § 1395f(a) (West Supp. 1987).

38. 42 U.S.C.A. § 1395x(i) (West 1983) amended by P.L. No. 100-360, § 104(a)(2) (1988).

39. *Id.*

40. 42 U.S.C.A. § 1395f(a)(2)(B) (West Supp. 1987); 42 C.F.R. § 409.31 (1985).

41. 42 U.S.C.A. § 1395f(a)(2)(B) (West Supp. 1987); 42 C.F.R. § 405.1632. (1985).

42. 42 U.S.C.A. § 1395d(a)(2)(A) (West 1983); 42 U.S.C.A. § 1395e(a)(3) (West 1983); 42 C.F.R. § 409.85 (1986).

43. Pub. L. No. 100-360, § § 101, 102 (1988).

44. 42 C.F.R. § 409.32. (1986).

45. 42 C.F.R. § 405.310(g) (1986); 42 C.F.R. § 409.33(d) (1986).

46. 42 C.F.R. § 409.35 (1986); *see also Pilsums v. Harris*, [1981 Transfer Binder] Medicare & Medicaid Guide (CCH) ¶ 30, 908 (D. Conn. Feb. 11, 1981).

47. 42 U.S.C.A. § 1395d(a)(3), 1395 (k) (West 1983 & Supp. 1987).

48. 42 U.S.C.A. § 1395x(m) (West 1983 & Supp. 1987); 42 C.F.R. § 409.40 (1986).

49. 42 U.S.C.A. § 1395f(a)(2)(C) (West Supp. 1987); 42 C.F.R. § 409.42 (1986).

50. Health Care Financing Admin., Health Ins. Man., HIM-13 § 3119.6 discussed and cited in 1 Medicare & Medicaid Guide (CCH) ¶ 1448.01 (1986).

51. Pub. L. No. 100–203, § 4024 (1987), amending 42 U.S.C. § 1395f(a)(2)(C); *See also* Health Care Financing Admin., Health Ins. Man., HIM-13 § 3120.4 discussed and cited in 1 Medicare & Medicaid Guide (CCH) ¶ 1414 (1986).

52. *Supra* note 50.

53. *See* 42 U.S.C. § 1395x(m)(4); Dombi, "The Miller Case: A Cooperative Effort in Pursuing Patient Rights." *Caring*, Oct. 1984.

54. Health Care Financing Admin., Health Ins. Man., HIM-11 § 204 discussed and cited in 1 Medicare & Medicaid Guide (CCH) ¶ 1448 (1986).

55. 42 U.S.C.A. §§ 1395d(a)(4); 1395x(dd)(1) (West 1983 & Supp. 1987).

56. 42 U.S.C.A. § 1395e(a)(4)(A) (West 1983).

57. 42 U.S.C.A. § 1395x(dd)(3)(A) (West 1983).

58. 42 U.S.C. §§ 1395f(a)(7), 1395x(dd), amended by Pub. L. No. 100-360 §§ 101, 104(d)(2)(C) (1988).

59. 42 U.S.C. § 1395o (West 1983); *see also Mathews v. Diaz*, 426 U.S. 67 (1976).

60. 42 U.S.C.A. § 1395r (1983 West Supp. 1987).

61. 42 U.S.C.A. §§ 1395p(a), 1395p(d), 1395p(e), (West Supp. 1987); 42 C.F.R. § 405.210 (1986).

62. 42 C.F.R. § 405.214(c) (1986).

63. *See* 42 U.S.C.A. § 1395q(a)(2) (West 1983).

64. 42 U.S.C.A. § 1395q(a)(2) (West 1983); 42 C.F.R. § 405.221 (1986).

65. Pub. L. No. 100-360, §§ 111, 211 (1988).

66. 42 C.F.R. § 405.904(a) (1986).

67. 42 C.F.R. § 405.908 (1986).

68. 42 U.S.C. § 1395v, amended by Pub. L. No. 100-360, § 301 (1988).

69. 42 U.S.C.A. §§ 1395k (West 1983 & Supp. 1987); 1395x(s) (West 1983 & Supp. 1987); 42 C.F.R. § 405.231 (1986); *see also* Pub. L. No. 100-360, §§ 205, 206 (1988).

70. 42 U.S.C.A. § 1395y (West 1983 & Supp. 1987); 42 C.F.R. §§ 405.232, 405.310 (1986).

71. Pub. L. No. 100-360, §§ 202, 203 (1988).

72. 42 U.S.C.A. §§ 1395l(a), (b), 1395u(b)(J)(B) (West 1983 & Supp. 1987); 42 C.F.R. § 405.245 (1987).

73. Pub. L. No. 100-360, § 201 (1988).

74. 42 U.S.C.A. §§ 1395x(q); 1395x(r) (West Supp. 1987); 42 C.F.R. § 405.232a (1986).

75. 42 U.S.C.A. § 1395l(a) (West Supp. 1987).

76. *See* 42 U.S.C.A. § 1395u(b)(3)(B). (West Supp. 1987).

77. *See* 42 U.S.C.A. §§ 1395u(b)(4); 1395u(j) (West Supp. 1987); COBRA, *supra* note 17, § 9301.

78. 42 U.S.C.A. §§ 1395k(a); 1395x(s) (West 1983 & Supp. 1987); 42 C.F.R. § 405.231 (1986).

79. 42 U.S.C.A. §§ 1395k(a)(2)(c), 1395x(s)(2)(D) (West 1983); 42 C.F.R. §§ 405.232(e), 405.232(j) (1986).

80. 42 U.S.C.A. § 1395l(g) (West 1983).

81. *See* 42 U.S.C.A. §§ 1395d(a)(3), 1395k(a)(2)(A) (West 1983 & Supp. 1987); 1395x(s) (West 1983 & Supp. 1987).

82. *See* 42 U.S.C.A. §§ 1395(a)(1)(D), 1395n(a)(2)(A) (West 1983 & Supp. 1987).

83. 42 U.S.C.A. § 1395u(b)(3)(G) (West Supp. 1987).

84. 42 U.S.C.A. § 1395x(n) (West Supp. 1987); 42 C.F.R. § 405.514(b) (1986).

85. 42 U.S.C.A. § 1395cc (West Supp. 1987); 42 C.F.R. § 405.1667 (1986).

86. 42 C.F.R. § 405.1672(b) (1986).

87. 42 C.F.R. § 405.1675 (1986).

88. 42 C.F.R. § 405.1675(a)(1)(i) (1986).

89. 42 U.S.C.A. § 1395u(h) (West Supp. 1987).

90. *Gray Panthers v. Schweiker*, 652 F.2d 146 (D.C. Cir. 1981) (*reversed district court decision and remanded*), 716 F.2d 23 (D.C. Cir. 1983) (*remanded for further consideration*). For a discussion of the settlement concerning notice with respect to Part B claims and the procedure, see the discussion contained in *Gray Panthers v. Bowen*, [1987-1] Medicare & Medicaid Guide (CCH), ¶ 35,932, at 12,693–94 (Dec. 1, 1986).

91. 3 Medicare & Medicaid Guide (CCH), ¶ 13,400 (1986).

92. 42 U.S.C.A. § 1395y(a)(1) (West Supp. 1987); 42 C.F.R. § 405.310(k) (1986).

93. 42 U.S.C.A. § 1395y(a)(9) (West 1983); 42 C.F.R. § 405.310(g) (1986).

94. 42 C.F.R. § 405.310(g) (1986).

95. *Hayner v. Weinberger*, 382 F. Supp. 762 (E.D.N.Y. 1974); *Ridgely v. Secretary of Health, Education, and Welfare*, 475 F.2d 1222, 1223 n.3 (4th Cir. 1973); *Samuels v. Weinberger*, 379 F. Supp 120, 123 (S.D. Ohio 1973); *Pilsums v. Harris* [1981 Transfer Binder] Medicare & Medicaid Guide (CCH) ¶ 30, 908 (D. Conn. Feb. 11, 1981).

96. 42 U.S.C. § 1395x(k) (West 1983); 42 C.F.R. § 405.1035 (1986).

97. 42 C.F.R. § 405.706 (1986).

98. 42 U.S.C.A. § 1395f(a)(6) (West Supp. 1987).

99. 42 U.S.C.A. § 1395h. (West 1983 & Supp. 1987).

100. 42 U.S.C.A. § 1320c-3 (West 1983 & Supp. 1987).

101. 42 U.S.C.A. § 1320c-3(a) (West 1983).

102. 42 C.F.R. § 405.1035(g)(2) (1986); 42 C.F.R. § 405.1137(e)(2) (1986).

103. 42 C.F.R. § 405.195 (1986).

104. 42 U.S.C.A. § 1395f(a)(6) (West Supp. 1987).

105. 42 C.F.R. § 412.42(c)(3) (1986).

106. 42 C.F.R. §§ 466.94(a)(1) (1986).

107. 42 C.F.R. § 466.70(d) (1986).

108. 42 C.F.R. § 405.702 (1986).

109. 42 U.S.C.A. § 1395pp (West 1983); 42 C.F.R. § 405.330 (1986).

110. 42 U.S.C.A. § 1395ff(b)(1)(A) (West Supp. 1987); 42 C.F.R. § 405.704(a) (1986).

111. 42 C.F.R. § 405.710 (1986).

112. 42 C.F.R. § 405.720 (1986).

113. 42 U.S.C.A. § 1320c-4 (West 1983); 42 C.F.R. § 473.16 (1986).

114. 42 C.F.R. § 473.18 (1986).

115. 42 C.F.R. § 473.14 (1986).

116. 42 C.F.R. § 473.24 (1986).

117. 42 C.F.R. § 473.28 (1986).

118. 42 C.F.R. § 473.20(c) (1986).

119. 42 C.F.R. § 473.32(a)(1) (1986).
120. 42 C.F.R. § 473.32(a)(2) (1986).
121. 42 C.F.R. § 473.32(a)(3) (1986).
122. 42 C.F.R. § 473.40 (1986).
123. 42 C.F.R. § 473.46 (1986).
124. 42 C.F.R. § 405.710 (1986).
125. 42 U.S.C.A. § 1395ff(b)(2) (West Supp. 1987); 42 C.F.R. § 405.720 (1986).
126. 42 C.F.R. § 405.724; 20 C.F.R. § 404.967 (1986).
127. 42 U.S.C.A. § 1395ff(b)(2) (West 1983); 42 C.F.R. § 405.730 (1986).
128. 42 U.S.C. § 1395u(b)(3)(C) (West 1983); 42 C.F.R. 405 (subpt. H) (1986).
129. Omnibus Budget Reconciliation Act of 1986 (OBRA), Pub. L. No. 99-509, § 9341, 100 Stat. 1874 (1986).
130. 42 C.F.R. §§ 405.807–12 (1986).
131. 42 C.F.R. § 405.820–35 (1986).
132. Omnibus Budget Reconciliation Act of 1986 (OBRA), Pub. L. No. 99-509, § 9341, 100 Stat. 1874 (1986).
133. 5 U.S.C.A. §§ 551–706 (1983).
134. *Bowen v. Michigan Academy of Family Physicians*, 476 U.S. 667 (1986).
135. 42 U.S.C.A. § 405(g) (West 1983); 42 C.F.R. §§ 405.711, .722, .724, .730; 473.20(a), .42(b); 20 C.F.R. § 404.967 (1986).
136. 42 C.F.R. § 473 20(c) (1986).
137. 42 C.F.R. §§ 405.711, .722 (1986).
138. 42 C.F.R. §§ 405.712; 473.22; 20 C.F.R. § 404.933(c) (1986).
139. 42 C.F.R. §§ 405.807(c), .820(d) (1986).
140. *But see Martinez v. Bowen* [1987 Transfer Binder] Medicare & Medicaid Guide (CCH), ¶ 35,940 (D.N.M. Oct. 14, 1986).
141. *Heckler v. Day*, 467 U.S. 104 (1984).
142. 42 U.S.C.A. § 1395ss (West 1983 & Supp. 1987); 42 C.F.R. § 403.200ff (1986).

8
Medicaid

What is Medicaid?

Medicaid is a program of medical assistance to needy people, operated jointly by the state and federal governments.[1] Unlike Medicare, which is available regardless of financial need to any person 65 or older and to certain disabled individuals, Medicaid is available only to individuals with limited income and assets. In 1986, 22.4 million people received Medicaid benefits, of whom 3.4 million were older persons.

The Medicaid program is operated by state governments under guidelines established by the federal government. The cost of Medicaid is shared by the states and federal government, with the latter paying between 50 and 78 percent of the Medicaid bill in each state. At present, the total cost of the Medicaid program is $40.9 billion annually, with the federal government paying about $22.5 billion.

All the states plus Puerto Rico, the Virgin Islands, Guam, and the District of Columbia, now participate in Medicaid. Arizona has a limited program.[2] However, because of the joint (state-federal) nature of the Medicaid program, enormous variation exists among the states as to the eligibility requirements, benefits available, and other program features. Due to this variation, it is impossible to describe in detail the Medicaid program available in every state. Thus, this chapter is simply an overview of the Medicaid program. For a complete description of the Medicaid program in your state, contact the local Medicaid agency or the Social Security Administration.

What services are available through Medicaid?

Medicaid pays for many, but not all, medical services. Exactly which services are available depends on the state where you reside and the basis of your eligibility for Medicaid. Some states provide a broad range of services, while others provide relatively few. Two groups of people are eligible for Medicaid—the categorically needy and the medically needy.

To be categorically needy you must meet your state's definition of need. In most states, persons eligible for Supplemental Security Income (SSI) are considered categorically needy and are eligible for Medicaid. Some states, however, use income and resource standards for the categorically needy that are more restrictive than those under SSI.[3] In these states only those persons poor enough to meet these more restrictive standards are eligible for Medicaid as categorically needy.

The medically needy are aged (65 or older), blind, or disabled persons unable to meet the cost of their medical care, who have income or assets exceeding the limits for categorical eligibility. In many states they also are eligible for Medicaid.[4]

The services available from Medicaid are listed and described below. Federal law requires all states participating in Medicaid to provide the categorically needy with the following services: inpatient hospital services, outpatient hospital services, laboratory and X-ray services, skilled nursing facility services, the services of physicians, and home health services.[5] Federal rules also require payment for necessary transportation costs of Medicaid recipients to their providers of medical services.

The remaining services listed below are optional; states may, but need not, provide these additional services to the categorically needy and to the medically needy. States electing to serve the medically needy must provide to the elderly, as a minimum, ambulatory services for individuals entitled to institutional services and home health services to any person entitled to skilled nursing facility services.[6] In actual practice, however, most states with medically needy programs provide the medically needy with the same services as those which the categorically needy receive.[7]

Inpatient Hospital Care. If you are hospitalized, Medicaid will pay the cost of a semiprivate room, doctors' fees, laboratory tests, X-rays, and other services ordinarily furnished by the hospital to its patients.[8] For Medicaid to pay for hospital care, your hospitalization must have been ordered by a physician or dentist, and the hospital must be licensed by the state and approved for participation in Medicaid.[9]

Outpatient Hospital Services. Most hospitals have outpatient clinics in which services are available to persons who do not need to be hospitalized. Medicaid will pay for services rendered to outpatients under the direction of a physician so long as the services are needed and so long as the hospital is licensed and approved for participation in Medicaid.[10]

Laboratory and X-Ray Services. Medicaid will pay for laboratory tests and X-rays ordered by a physician, whether in a hospital, a doctor's office, a laboratory, or some other outside facility.[11]

Care in a Skilled Nursing Facility. Medicaid will pay for services rendered by a skilled nursing facility licensed by the state and approved for participation in Medicaid, if your doctor determines that you need those services.[12] Continued need for these services will be redetermined periodically.[13]

Physicians' Services. Medicaid will pay for the cost of services provided by a medical doctor or a doctor of osteopathy.[14] These services are covered by Medicaid whether provided in your home, a doctor's office, a hospital, or a nursing home.[15]

Home Health Services. Medicaid will pay for health services that are provided in your home,[16] pursuant to your doctor's orders.[17] Your doctor must provide a written plan of care that is reviewed every sixty days.[18] Health care services may include part-time nursing, aide services, medical supplies, equipment and appliances, physical therapy, occupational therapy, speech pathology, and audiology services.[19]

Transportation. Another important service provided by Medicaid is payment of transportation costs for Medicaid recipients to and from doctors' offices or medical facilities.[20]

The following services are optional under federal law. Your state may or may not pay for these services.

Care in an Intermediate Care Facility. Medicaid may pay for services rendered to you by an intermediate care facility licensed by the state and approved for participation in Medicaid.[21] Your continued need for these services will be redetermined periodically.

Services of State-licensed Practitioners. Medicaid may (but need not) pay for services rendered to you by chiropractors, optometrists, and other persons who are not medical doctors but who are licensed by the state to provide medical services.[22]

Private Duty Nurses. Medicaid may cover the cost of a private duty nurse if such nursing care is ordered by your doctor.[23] This is true whether the private duty nurse serves you in your own home, in a hospital, or in a nursing home.[24]

Clinic Services. Medicaid may pay for services provided to you by a medical clinic not associated with a hospital.[25]

Dental Services. Dental services, in some states, are paid for by Medicaid.[26]

Physical Therapy. Physical and occupational therapy, as well as speech, hearing, and other kinds of therapy, may be paid for by Medicaid when prescribed by a physician.[27]

Drugs, Dentures, Prosthetic Devices, and Eyeglasses. If your doctor prescribes drugs for you to take or if you need dentures, prosthetic devices, or eyeglasses, Medicaid may pay for these items.[28]

Care in a Mental Hospital or Institution for Tuberculosis. If you are 65 or older, Medicaid may pay for services rendered by a mental hospital or by an institution for tuberculosis.[29]

Emergency Hospital Services. Medicaid may pay for emergency hospital services rendered to you that are necessary to prevent your death or serious impairment to your life, even if the hospital providing the services is not participating in the Medicaid program.[30]

Personal Care Services in Your Home. Medicaid may pay for personal care services rendered to you, such as services by a housekeeper, if these services are prescribed by a doctor and are supervised by a registered nurse.[31]

Home and Community Based Services. To reduce Medicaid nursing home costs, states may offer (under a waiver of statutory requirements) home and community based services to individuals who would otherwise have to be institutionalized. These services may include, but are not restricted to, adult day care services, habilitation services, respite care, chore services, etc.[32]

Hospice Care. Medicaid may offer hospice care to terminally ill persons who elect such care.[33]

Respiratory Care Services. Medicaid may offer respiratory care services to ventilator dependent persons under some circumstances.[34]

How do I apply for Medicaid?

Application for Medicaid is accomplished by submitting a written application to the state agency designated to handle Medicaid applications, usually the Department of Social Services or Public Welfare.[35] In some states, you also can apply at a Social Security office. If you are uncertain where to apply, you can find out by contacting a local welfare agency. You will be asked to furnish proof of your age, income and resources, and residency (such as rent receipts, utility bills). If you own a car, take your car registration, and if you own property, take your tax assessment notice or tax receipt. If you are applying as medically needy, you should take any unpaid medical bills and any receipts for medical expenses paid within the last three months.

If you need assistance in applying for Medicaid, a friend or other person may contact the Medicaid agency on your behalf or go with you to the agency to help you apply, but in most cases you must sign an application yourself.[36] If you are unable to do so, you can authorize someone else to sign the application for you.[37] The Medicaid agency is obliged to help you apply for Medicaid benefits and should send a worker to your home if you are homebound and unable to go to the office yourself. If you are hospitalized or in a nursing home, the institution's social-work staff will possibly help you apply.

Federal law requires that Medicaid applications be acted upon within sixty days of the date the application was filed for persons applying as a result of disability[38] and within forty-five days of the date of the application for all other persons.[39] This requirement means that you should receive written notification of the acceptance or rejection of your Medicaid application within these time limits. If not, you are entitled to seek a hearing before the Medicaid agency to have the department's failure to act reviewed.[40]

If your application is approved, Medicaid will pay for medical services you received in the three months prior to the month of application[41] *if* (1) you meet the eligibility criteria during the three-month period, (2) the bills were not used to meet your spend-down (the amount of medical expenses you must incur to bring you down to your state's medically needy level), (3) the bills will not be paid by another health insurance, and (4) the provider of the medical services accepts Medicaid. Once approved, the state will redetermine your financial eligibility for Medicaid at least once a year,[42] and you are required to notify the state of any change in your circumstances which may affect your eligibility for Medicaid.[43]

Who is eligible for Medicaid?

Eligibility for Medicaid is based upon poverty, but not all low-income persons are eligible for Medicaid. To be eligible for Medicaid, your income and assets must be lower than levels established by the state in which you reside. These levels vary from state to state. In most states, persons who qualify for cash assistance from the Supplemental Security Income program for the aged (65 or older), blind, and disabled (SSI) are eligible automatically for Medicaid.[44] Some states, however, use stricter income and asset limitations in determining Medicaid eligibility.[45]

Effective 1 July 1987, Section 9402 of the Omnibus Budget Reconciliation Act of 1986 (OBRA) gave states the option to expand their Medicaid categorically needy program to cover person with incomes up to federal poverty guidelines who are 65 and over or disabled. In 1988, the poverty guidelines are $480.85 per month for an individual and $644.17 per month for a couple. States choosing this option must offer the same benefits provided to other categorically needy recipients. Costs incurred for medical care are not counted in determining eligibility.

Persons eligible for Medicaid because they meet the SSI standard of need or the stricter state standards are called categorically needy individuals.[46] Federal law requires each state participating in Medicaid to provide coverage for the categorically needy but not for the medically needy. However, a state may opt to provide coverage for the medically needy (aged, blind, or disabled persons whose resources or income disqualifies them from categorical eligibility but who are unable to pay their medical expenses).[47] Currently, thirty-six states and the District of Columbia provide Medicaid to the medically needy.[48]

How much income can I have and still be eligible for Medicaid?

Because the states contribute to the costs of Medicaid, eligibility standards vary from state to state. The allowable income level depends upon where you live, the basis of your eligibility for Medicaid, the number of persons in your family, and other factors.

One rule that applies to all Medicaid applicants is that to be counted as income in determining your eligibility for Medicaid, income must be "actually available" to you.[49] Thus, a state welfare department cannot properly consider as income money which theoretically is yours but which is actually unavailable to you. For example, the state of New York used to count money paid for Social Security taxes as income until a court ruled that this was improper since such money was not actually available to the person seeking Medicaid.[50]

Many states use Supplemental Security Income eligibility rules to determine eligibility for Medicaid. These rules are described in detail in the chapter on Supplemental Security Income.[51] In states that do not use SSI standards for Medicaid eligibility, different rules may apply. To find out what income is included in determining your eligibility in these states, contact the state Medicaid agency.

What assets can I own and still be eligible for Medicaid?

As with the rules for the amount of income you can have, the rules governing what assets you can have are complex and vary from state to state. Many states use SSI eligibility rules for determining Medicaid eligibility.[52] These standards are more liberal than most state welfare rules. Some of the things that the SSI rules permit you to have include a house, regardless of its value,[53] an automobile with a value of up to $4,500, cash and other liquid assets totaling more (in 1988) than $1,900 for an individual or $2,850 for a couple[54] and up to $1,500 set aside for each spouse's burial expenses.[55]

In states that maintain their own standards of Medicaid eligibility, rules governing the amount of property that may be held are always complex and frequently very stringent. For example, most states allow you to maintain a house as a homestead (family home) without losing Medicaid eligibility, but in some states your home is exempt only if its value does not exceed a certain limit. Most states also allow you to have household goods without counting the value of these goods against your Medicaid eligibility. States also permit you to have a limited amount of personal property and cash that will not count against you for determining your eligibility for Medicaid, but complicated rules govern what property is considered and how the property is valued for purposes of determining Medicaid eligibility.[56]

One problem you should keep in mind if you are considering applying for Medicaid is a federal law which allows (and in some cases *requires*) that you be denied Medicaid if you transfer or sell property for less than fair market value before you apply for Medicaid. Prior to 1 July 1988 states were permitted to deny Medicaid to persons transferring property within two years of applying for Medicaid.[57] Not all states exercised this option and federal law imposed limits on those states that did so. The Medicare Catastrophic Coverage Act of 1988 *requires* states to penalize any institutionalized Medicaid applicant who after 1 July 1988 has transferred any asset (including a home) for less than fair market value within thirty months of applying for Medicaid. If a state finds that such a transfer has occurred, it must deny Medicaid eligibility for as many months as are required to spend the uncompensated value of the transferred asset on nursing home care. (The penalty cannot exceed 30 months).[58] Transfer of a home is not penalized if the transfer is to (1) your spouse; (2) your dependent or disabled child; (3) a sibling with equity interest who resided in your home for one year before your institutionalization; (4) your son or daughter who had lived in your home for two years prior to your institutionalization and had cared for you. Also no transfer of any asset will be penalized if (1) transferred to your spouse or disabled child; (2) "satisfactory showing" is made that you intended to dispose of the asset at fair market value or for a purpose other than to qualify for Medicaid; or (3) your state determines denial of Medicaid would be an undue hardship.[59]

In 1986 Congress amended the Social Security Act to close what Congress regarded as a loophole under which "affluent" persons were obtaining Medicaid eligibility. The law authorizes states to count as an available resource (or as income) money or property held in a trust for the benefit of an applicant for Medicaid if the money or property could be distributed to the beneficiary under the terms of the trust. States are permitted to waive this rule if "undue hardship" would result.[60]

These complex federal rules governing transfer of assets create serious problems for older persons who may wish to transfer property for reasons totally unconnected with their desire to be eligible for Medicaid. If you plan to dispose of your assets, be very careful to do so in a way that does not jeopardize your eligibility for Medicaid and consult an attorney familiar with these requirements before making such a transfer. If your application for Medicaid is denied because of a recent property transfer, you can appeal the denial.

What income can I have and be eligible as medically needy?

Many states provide coverage to the "medically needy"—persons who are not eligible for cash assistance such as SSI because their incomes are too high, but who have high medical or long term care expenses. Although the rules governing eligibility for the medically needy are complex and often misunderstood, you should apply for Medicaid if your state has a medically needy program, if you are at least 65 or blind or disabled, and if you have high medical bills that you are unable to pay.

Your eligibility will be determined by whether your medical expenses equal or exceed the amount of your income over your state's medically needy income level (MNIL).[61] When you apply for Medicaid, you will receive notice that you are over-income and be advised of the amount you are over-income. This is your "spend-down" amount. Your Medicaid agency will subtract your incurred medical expenses from the amount you are over-income to determine if you are eligible as medically needy.[62] This is called "spending-down." The period during which an applicant must spend-down his or her excess income is called the budget period, usually three to six months for persons living at home and one month for institutionalized persons.[63] The following is an example of how excess income (spend-down amount) is calculated.

Mr. Brown has a monthly income of $500 from Social Security. The medically needy income level for his state is

$360 per month. His state has a six-month budget period. His spend-down amount is:

$ 500	Social Security income
− 20	general income exclusion
$ 480	
× 6	
$ 2880	total income for six month budget period
− 2160	6 times state's $360 medically needy income level
$ 720	spend-down amount

Mr. Brown will have to have incurred or paid $720 in medical expenses before he can qualify for Medicaid. He will have to repeat this spend-down every six months.

In meeting a spend-down amount, your medical bills need not actually have been paid so long as they were incurred and you are currently liable for the expenses. You can count very old bills as long as you still owe them. You can also count *paid* bills which are less than three months old. Federal law permits any legitimate medical expenses, whether covered by your state Medicaid plan or not, to be counted. Thus, expenses such as medical insurance premiums, prescription and over-the-counter-drugs, eyeglasses, transportation to providers, most dental expenses, and so on can be counted in determining whether you have spent-down to a level to be eligible for Medicaid. Remember, the bills must be your responsibility and not subject to payment by a third party such as Medicare, private health insurance, a friend or relative (unless by a financially responsible relative). When payment by a third party has been made, any amount which remains your responsibility can be used to meet your spend-down (for example, the 20 percent of your medical bill that Medicare does not pay). Your resources also must meet your state's standards.[64]

Medicaid will not pay for the bills used in the spend-down process, but the bills can make you eligible for a Medicaid card that will pay your other medical bills for the period of your eligibility.

If you do not understand how your Medicaid spend-down was computed or you think that your state has improperly denied your Medicaid application, do not hesitate to appeal the denial

and/or seek legal help in interpreting your spend-down requirements and in advising you of your appeal rights.[65]

**Can a state count income or assets belonging to my relatives
in determining whether I am eligible for Medicaid?**

Under federal law a state should not count the income or
assets of any relative except those of your spouse.[66] A husband
does have the obligation to support a wife and vice versa. The
rule requiring that your spouse's income and assets be counted
in determining your eligibility for Medicaid is called "deeming." The rule treats the income and assets of your spouse as
available to you. As a result, not only are your own income and
assets counted by the state in determining whether you are
eligible for Medicaid, the income and assets of your spouse are
likewise counted.[67]

These deeming rules can cause great hardship, resulting in
denial of Medicaid eligibility in situations where Medicaid
assistance is badly needed. An example is where one spouse
needs nursing-home care, often costing $1,500 to $3,000 per
month. The Medicare program and private health insurance
provide little coverage for the costs of long-term care, particularly nursing-home costs. Thus, until recently, before the institutionalized spouse could qualify for Medicaid assistance, a
couple had to deplete their life savings on the nursing-home
costs of the institutionalized spouse, leaving the community
spouse very little on which to live. The only other alternative
was to legally separate or divorce in order to obtain a court-
ordered division of their resources.

This unconscionable situation prompted a number of law suits
and led HHS to amend the deeming rule to partially alleviate the
problem which arises when one spouse is institutionalized and
applies for Medicaid.[68] Federal Medicaid regulations prohibit
states from counting the income and resources of the community
spouse if the spouses have "ceased to live together" and if only one
of them applies for Medicaid. This means that the state, when
evaluating the institutionalized spouse's application for Medicaid,
must stop counting the income and resources of the noninstitu-
tionalized spouse beginning with the month after the month in
which they are separated. Only the income and resources actually
contributed to the applicant spouse can be counted. An example

of this circumstance is the story of Sam and Sarah.

Sam and Sarah have been married for forty-five years. Sam's income from his government pension is $2,000 a month. Sarah, who stayed home to raise their children, receives only $250 a month in Social Security benefits. They own their home as tenants by the entirety. All other assets are in Sam's name; however their combined "countable" assets do not exceed the state Medicaid resource limit for a couple.

In January, Sarah enters a nursing home. She applies for Medicaid in January. Sam does not apply for Medicaid. In January all of Sam's income and resources are deemed available to Sarah and she is not eligible for Medicaid in January. However, in February, deeming stops and Sarah is then eligible for Medicaid.

If both you and your spouse apply for Medicaid, and one of you is in an institution, deeming of income will cease with the month after the month you stop living together, but resources are counted for six months after the month you are separated. If you and your wife stop living together for any reason other than institutionalization, your income and resources are counted as available to each other for purposes of Medicaid eligibility for the month you become separated and six months thereafter. If this causes loss of eligibility for Medicaid as a couple, then the state should only consider income and resources that are actually contributed.[69] If you are applying for Medicaid as medically needy, federal rules require that your spouse's income and resources be counted if actually contributed and allow your spouse's income and resources to be considered available to you even though not actually contributed.[70]

Despite the partial relief offered by the rules just described, the impoverishment of spouses of nursing-home residents continued to be a problem for many older persons, particularly for couples most of whose assets and income are in the name of the institutionalized spouse. In such cases, these resources were required to be spent on nursing-home care, leaving the community spouse without enough on which to live. In the Medicare Catastrophic Coverage Act of 1988, Congress responded to this situation by altering Medicaid asset and income rules to provide more income and assets for the community spouse. Beginning 30 September 1989, the spouse of an institutionalized Medicaid recipient is entitled to retain from the couple's income a monthly allowance of at least 122% of the federal poverty level for a couple ($786 in 1988), rising to 150% by 1992. If the community spouse's shelter costs (rent or mortgage, taxes, insurance and utilities) exceed 30% of her monthly allowance, she is entitled to retain an excess shelter allowance to cover these costs. Her total allowance cannot exceed $1500 (in 1989), except by order of a court or fair hearing. To the extent that income is owned by the community spouse, it is not deemed available to the institutionalized spouse.[71]

The Act also alters the way in which a couple's assets are allocated for purposes of determining whether the institutionalized spouse is eligible for Medicaid. Beginning 30 September 1989 a couple's nonexempt assets will be pooled (regardless of who formally owns them) and the community spouse may retain the higher of $12,000 (up to $60,000 at state option) or half the couple's nonexempt assets (but not more than $60,000). If the community spouse can demonstrate that she needs additional assets to raise her income to the monthly allowance described above, a court or fair hearing can so order.[72]

You can see that the Medicaid rules governing these matters are extremely complex. Consult a lawyer familiar with Medicaid law if you experience any of these problems.

Can my application for Medicaid be denied because I am not a citizen?

Any person who is a U.S. citizen, an alien lawfully admitted for permanent residence in the United States, or permanently residing in the United States under color of law is eligible to apply for Medicaid.[73] An alien not thus admitted to the United States may have his or her application denied for that reason.

Can my Medicaid application be denied because of where I live?

No. Although states can limit Medicaid to persons who are residents of the state, a state cannot deny Medicaid to you simply because you recently arrived in the state or because you own property in another state. The critical question is whether you have moved to the state with an intention of making your home there. If you satisfy this requirement, you should not be denied eligibility because of where you live.[74] If your application for Medicaid is denied because you recently moved to a state or county, you should challenge the denial by requesting a hearing and ultimately by going to court if necessary.[75]

Does residence in a mental hospital or public institution affect Medicaid eligibility?

Yes. Medicaid will not pay for the cost of providing care to a resident of a public or private mental hospital unless the resident is younger than 22 or at least 65. Similarly, Medicaid will not pay for the cost of caring for a resident of a public institution (a nonmedical facility owned or controlled by the government).[76]

What rights do I have if my application for Medicaid is denied or my benefits are reduced or terminated?

Under federal law you are entitled to timely and adequate notice of any decision affecting your Medicaid benefits. This means that you are entitled to written notice from the government stating what action it intends to take, the reasons for the proposed action, the legal basis for the action, an explanation of your right to appeal the action, and an explanation of how you can have your benefits continued until your appeal is heard.[77] You are entitled to receive this notice as soon as the government decides to take the action, and, if you are already receiving benefits, this notice should be mailed to you at least ten days before the government intends for the action to take place.[78] With a few minor exceptions, these rules apply to any action the government takes that affects your benefits adversely.[79] The rules apply, then, when the government fails to act on your application for Medicaid within the period required, when the government denies your application for benefits, when the government refuses to pay for medical services you have incurred, and when it decides you are no longer eligible for Medicaid.[80]

Federal law also requires that you be given a "fair hearing" at which you can contest the government's decision to reduce or terminate your Medicaid, or their failure to process your application in a reasonable amount of time, or any other agency action you believe to be wrong.[81] You can obtain this hearing by submitting a written request to the government within ninety days of the date of the government's decision, informing them that you would like a hearing to contest their decision.[82] If you have a good reason for missing the deadline, you can ask in writing for more time.[83] If you request the hearing within ten days of receiving notice, in most cases you are entitled to have your benefits continued until a decision is rendered after the hearing.[84] In some states, you can also have your benefits reinstated if you request the hearing within ten days after the effective date of the government's decision.[85]

A conference generally can be requested or may be scheduled before your hearing to see if your problem can be solved without a hearing. If you are not satisfied with the results of the conference, you still have the right to a hearing.

The hearing will be held before a state official who decides whether the government's decision is correct. You are entitled to have a friend, social worker, lawyer, or other representative assist you at the hearing.[86] You are also entitled to testify at the hearing yourself and to have other persons testify on your behalf, and you can cross-examine any witnesses the government presents at the hearing. In addition, you are entitled to examine the government's file on your case to help you prepare for the hearings.[87] The hearing must be held at a location which is convenient to you, and, if you are in a nursing home or are homebound, you may insist that the hearing be held at the institution or in your home.[88] You are also entitled to reimbursement for transportation to and from the hearing.[89] If the hearing involves medical issues, you may be able to obtain a medical examination at government expense to assist you in your case.[90]

The hearing will be something like a trial in court. The government officer hearing the case acts like a judge, and the government may be represented by an attorney. For this reason, it is very helpful for you to have a representative at the hearing, especially a lawyer or paralegal.

The government is required to reach a decision after your hearing. The decision must be rendered within ninety days of your request for a hearing, must be in writing, and must contain a statement of the decision and the reasons for the decision.[91] If the decision upholds the government's earlier decision affecting your benefits, you are entitled to notice of how you can appeal this decision further.[92]

Will Medicaid pay for all my medical bills?

No. Medicaid will not pay for all your medical expenses. To be paid by Medicaid, the services you receive must be covered by the Medicaid plan in the state in which you reside. As mentioned earlier, some state plans cover an extensive range of services, while others cover relatively few services.

Even if the service you receive is covered by Medicaid in your state, it still may not be paid by Medicaid. To be paid by Medicaid, the following requirements also must be met. The service generally must have been prescribed by a doctor or other licensed medical practitioner, and, in most cases, it must have been provided by a medical provider approved by and participating in Medicaid.[93] Additionally, in the case of some medical services such as hospitalization or care in a nursing home, your need for the service must have been confirmed by a committee of doctors and other health professionals created to review whether patients really need the medical services they are receiving.[94] Further, some states require *prior* authorization by the state Medicaid agency before Medicaid will pay for certain medical services, such as plastic surgery.[95] Finally, Medicaid will pay only what it regards as a reasonable charge for services you receive.[96] However, your provider must accept the amount as payment in full.[97] A provider may not bill you for the remainder, if any. Sometimes a provider will bill a patient for an amount over the Medicaid payment. In such a case, if you are sued by a provider, you can assert as a defense that the provider must accept the Medicaid payment as payment in full.

Medicaid will pay for out-of-state services needed in the case of a medical emergency or when your health would be endangered by returning to your resident state.[98] Furthermore, if you believe that you need a particular service and are told that Medicaid will not pay for it, do not hesitate to seek legal advice. You may be able to persuade the Medicaid agency to pay for the service through the appeals process.

Will Medicaid cost me anything?

It may, but not if you receive SSI and need a mandatory service. Whether a Medicaid recipient will have to pay anything for covered medical services depends on the rules of his state.[99] Federal law permits states to impose cost sharing by charging an enrollment fee or monthly premium of all medically needy Medicaid recipients.[100] An enrollment fee is a nominal sum of money that is required at the time of enrollment in Medicaid. A premium is a monthly fee, related to one's income, that may be required from the medically needy, regardless of whether services are received during a month. However, a state may *not* require categorically needy persons to pay either an enrollment fee or a premium.[101]

States also are permitted to charge copayments, coinsurance, and deductibles.[102] A copayment is an amount or percentage of the cost of a Medicaid service. For example, a state may require a two-dollar copayment for eyeglasses, or a fifty cent copayment for each prescription filled. A deductible is a fixed sum that a person who receives a Medicaid service must pay before Medicaid will pay the rest of the cost. Coinsurance is an amount imposed on payments for services. Copayments, deductibles, and coinsurance can be required of both medically needy and categorically needy recipients, with a few exceptions, for any services provided.[103] States are specifically prohibited from imposing copayments for necessary emergency care provided in hospital emergency rooms.[104] And federal law limits the amount a state can charge for copayments, coinsurance, and deductibles[105] and for enrollment fees and premiums.[106]

May I go to any doctor or hospital and have the bill paid by Medicaid?

No. Unless the provider from whom you receive medical care has been certified as eligible to receive payment from Medicaid and is willing to participate in Medicaid, you will be personally responsible for paying the cost of the medical treatment.[107] Therefore, it is important to find out if a doctor or hospital participates in Medicaid before receiving any medical services.

In many states, you may select any provider who is certified as eligible to receive Medicaid payments and who is willing to accept Medicaid patients.[108] You do *not* have to go to the cheapest provider. You have the right to choose the best physician or medical facility participating in the Medicaid program.

Recent changes in the Medicaid law, however, now enable states to obtain waivers to limit the freedom of Medicaid recipients to choose their health care providers.[109] Some states have requested and received waivers to begin cost containment plans, such as enrolling Medicaid recipients in health maintenance organizations, limiting recipients to one doctor, or using competitive bidding for certain services.[110]

If a provider participates in Medicaid, can it charge a Medicaid patient for services that are paid by Medicaid?

No. It is illegal for an enrolled doctor, hospital, or other provider to charge a Medicaid recipient any additional fee for services for which Medicaid has paid. Payment by Medicaid for services rendered is full payment for the services.[111] Several cases have relied upon this rule to forbid a provider from trying to bill a patient directly for services provided to the patient when the patient was eligible for Medicaid.[112]

Who receives the Medicaid payment?

Medicaid payments are usually sent directly to the doctor, hospital, or other provider of services. Rarely are they sent to a Medicaid recipient, even when the recipient has paid the doctor or other provider for covered services. For this reason, do not pay a medical provider directly in the hope you will be reimbursed by Medicaid. Instead, have the provider bill Medicaid directly. There are occasional exceptions to this rule when Medicaid recipients are reimbursed for medical expenses they have incurred.[113]

Retroactive reimbursement to Medicaid recipients can come up in several situations. The first is the case of a person who is denied Medicaid unlawfully. When this incorrect action is overturned, the person is entitled to retroactive reimbursement to the date the incorrect action was taken.[114] Second is the case of a person who has been found eligible for a three-month retroactive period of Medicaid coverage prior to the date of application. If the person incurred medical expenses during the retroactive period and these expenses have not been paid, the providers can then bill the Medicaid agency. The ban on direct payment to Medicaid recipients, however, has led to a different reimbursement procedure when the Medicaid recipient has paid for medical expenses during the three-month retroactive period. In accordance with a Health Care Financing Administration (HCFA) directive, the state is responsible only if the provider *voluntarily* refunds the recipient's earlier payment and then bills the Medicaid agency for the services rendered.[115] Because the Medicaid rate is lower than the private pay rate, however, providers are reluctant to make such refunds. One court recently addressed this inequity by ordering that "where vendors who regularly participate in the Medicaid program have extended medical supplies and received full payment from eligible applicants in the retroactive period, the state must compel those providers to refund the amounts paid and accept payment by the state as a condition of further participation."[116]

Can I participate in both Medicare and Medicaid?

Yes. If you are eligible for Medicare, you can also receive Medicaid benefits if you meet the Medicaid eligibility requirements in your state.[117] This can occur, for example, when your Social Security benefits are low enough that you are also eligible for Supplemental Security Income.

Receiving both Medicare and Medicaid can help you. For example, Medicaid will pay for some medical services that are not covered by Medicare. In most states, Medicaid will pay the monthly premium charged by Medicare for Medicare Part B benefits. Starting 1 January 1989, the new Medicare Catastrophic Coverage Act of 1988 requires state Medicaid programs (except for certain states where special rules apply) to pay the Medicare premiums, coinsurance, and deductibles for both the regular Medicare program and the new catastrophic insurance for Medicare recipients who have Medicaid. To be phased in over four years, the buy-in requirement will apply to those at or below 85% of the federal poverty level in 1989, rising to 100% in 1992.[118]

Does a private health insurance policy have any effect on Medicaid eligibility?

No. You may have any amount of private health insurance and still be eligible for Medicaid. In fact, the cost of your health insurance is a medical expense and can be deducted from your income in order to qualify you for Medicaid as medically needy.[119]

However, if you receive medical assistance that is covered by both Medicaid and private health insurance, you will be required to exhaust your private health insurance benefits before Medicaid will make any payments.[120] If Medicaid has already paid the bill, the state must seek reimbursement from your health insurance company. It cannot seek reimbursement from you unless your insurance company paid its benefits directly to you before the state sought its recovery.[121]

What is utilization control?

To assure that the money spent on medical care is not paying for unnecessary services, the federal government requires states to organize utilization-control systems that seek to ensure that medical care and services are of good quality and that treatment paid for by Medicaid is necessary.[122] Typical utilization-control methods are prior authorization of certain services and limitations on the length of time that a person may receive a service.[123] A particularly harsh method of utilization control is a review of the necessity of a service after it has been given. This type of utilization review may result in a decision by a state not to reimburse a provider for services that have been supplied.

If a utilization-review committee's decision results in a denial of Medicaid payment for services already rendered to you or for services which you believe to be necessary, you can appeal the denial. See chapter 9 on nursing homes for information on how the appeals system—defective as it is—works.

Can I be required to repay Medicaid for the costs of benefits that I have received?

Medicaid law does allow states, in limited circumstances, to recover benefits paid on behalf of a person 65 or older, or a person of any age who is receiving Medicaid in a nursing home or other long-term care medical institution. A lien can be placed on the real property of a Medicaid recipient in an institution who cannot be expected to return home. A lien is the right to sell a person's property to cover payment that has been made or will be made for a person's care. A lien cannot be placed on a person's home if a spouse; a minor, blind, or disabled child; or a brother or sister who partially owns the house resides there.[124] Before a lien is placed on your home, you must be notified and given an opportunity for a hearing[125] and your state must prove that you cannot reasonably be expected to be discharged to return home.[126]

If you die, your state may make a claim against your estate, including your home, for Medicaid paid after your 65th birthday. However, your state cannot make a claim until after the death of your surviving spouse or surviving minor, blind, or disabled child.[127] Also, no recovery can be made based on a lien that was placed on your home if you have a surviving spouse, surviving minor, blind, or disabled child, or brother or sister living in the home who has an "equity interest" in the home, or a son or daughter living in the home who provided care to you before you entered the institution.[128] Any lien put on your home will be removed if you leave the institution to return home.[129]

You can be required to pay incorrectly paid benefits, and in this case, a state can place a lien against your property following a court judgment.[130] An example of incorrectly paid benefits would be if you received Medicaid while you had assets in excess of allowable limits.

In addition, courts have held that a state may sue a Medicaid recipient to recover Medicaid benefits paid on the recipient's behalf when the recipient has successfully sued a person who injured him or her.[131] This situation usually arises when a Medicaid recipient has been hospitalized following an automobile accident. After the hospital bills are paid by Medicaid, a court may award the recipient damages for the accident which include compensation for the recipient's medical expenses. Under these circumstances, some courts have allowed the state to sue the recipient to recover the portion of the damage award which was designed to compensate the recipient for his or her medical expenses.

What can a recipient do if a state eliminates or reduces its Medicaid program?

Although they are not required to do so, all states—except Arizona, which has a limited program—now participate in Medicaid. And even though many states are finding that the costs of running the program are increasing, these states are unlikely to drop the program altogether, for they need federal financing to ease the burden of their obligation to help the needy. A number of states, however, have begun to try to cut costs by adopting more stringent eligibility requirements to obtain Medicaid, by reducing services available under Medicaid, by requiring Medicaid recipients to pay for a portion of the care, and by imposing other measures aimed at reducing costs.

If your state has announced plans to cut back on Medicaid, you should join with consumer groups, labor unions, physician and health-provider associations, as well as other groups interested in health care, to persuade the state not to reduce Medicaid services.[132] An attempt should be made to persuade the state to impose administrative controls to reduce costs in ways other than reducing services to needy Medicaid recipients. For example, unnecessary surgery; fraud by hospitals, nursing homes, and other health-care providers; overutilization of hospital and nursing-home care rather than cheaper forms of treatment; and bad management by the state Medicaid agency all contribute to high Medicaid costs.

One of the most common cost cutting measures is an attempt to contract with private insurers for a set price to pay for all care for Medicaid recipients. Whatever is left over is the insurer's profit and a part may, by the terms of the contract, be returned to the state. States desiring such contracts must seek a federal waiver and must prove to HHS that access to services by Medicaid recipients will not be impaired. Advocates can oppose these waivers by making their voices heard at HHS.

Lawsuits have challenged Medicaid cutbacks as violating federal requirements that a state Medicaid program "must be sufficient in amount, duration and scope as to reasonably achieve [its] purpose."[133] Some cutbacks have been struck down by courts as in violation of these requirements.[134] For example, when Kentucky issued a regulation limiting transportation of Medicaid recipients to four trips per month, a court ruled that any regulation that limited transportation for necessary medical treatment is contrary to federal statutes and therefore invalid.[135]

NOTES

1. Title XIX of the Social Security Act established the Medicaid program in 1965. The Congressional enactments that form the Medicaid program are contained in 42 U.S.C. § 1396(a)–(q) (1982 & Supp. III 1985). Federal regulations pertaining to Medicaid are in 42 C.F.R. Parts 430–499 (1987).

2. Arizona established an alternative to the conventional Medicaid program, the Arizona Health Care Cost Containment System (AHCCCS), which became effective Oct. 1, 1982. AHCCCS began as a three-year demonstration project, in which Arizona obtained waivers that enabled it to exclude certain Medicaid requirements, such as skilled nursing facility, home health, family planning, and nurse midwife services.

   AHCCCS is designed primarily to secure health care on a prepaid, per capita risk basis under contracts awarded to qualified bidders, but also pays some contractors on a fee-for-services basis when risk-based contracts are impractical. Under AHCCCS, Arizona receives federal financial support for the services it provides to categorically needy people who would qualify for Medicaid in any other state. 3 Medicare & Medicaid Guide (CCH) ¶ 15,554 (1985).

3. 42 C.F.R. § 435.1(d) (1987). The Social Security Amendments of 1972 (Pub. L. No. 92-603, Oct. 30, 1972), which established the federal Supplemental Security Income program (SSI), made it optional for states to provide Medicaid to all SSI recipients. *See* 42 C.F.R. § 435.1(a)–(d) for an overview of Medicaid eligibility as affected by the 1972 amendment. *See* 42 C.F.R. § 435.1(e) for a brief explanation of Medicaid eligibility as affected by the Omnibus Budget Reconciliation Act of 1981, Pub. L. No. 97-35, 95 Stat. 357 (1981).

4. 42 C.F.R. § 435.1(b)(3) (1987). The Omnibus Budget Reconciliation Act of 1981 (OBRA) enables states to restrict eligibility under the medically needy category. *Id.* at § 435.1(e).

5. *Id.* at § 440.210; 42 U.S.C. § 1396d(a) (1982 & Supp.III 1985).

6. 42 C.F.R. § 440.220(b), (c) (1987).

7. As of Oct. 1, 1985, of the 34 states plus the District of Columbia that have medically needy programs, 24 and the District of Columbia provide the same services to both the categorically needy and the medically needy. *Medical Services State by State*, (Oct. 1985) Office of Intergovernmental Affairs, Health Care Financing Administration, HCFA Pub. No. 02155-86. Since Oct. 1985, Florida and New Jersey have added medically needy programs.

8. 42 C.F.R. § 440.10(a)(1) (1987).

9. *Id.* at § 440.10(a)(2)(3).

10. *Id.* at § 440.20(a). Where state law enables nurse practitioners or physician assistants to provide primary health care, Medicaid may cover these costs and the supplies furnished as an incident to such care; it may also cover the cost of part-time or visiting nurses. *Id.* at § 440.20(b)(3), (4).

11. *Id.* at § 440.30.

12. *Id.* at § 440.40(a).

13. 42 U.S.C. § 1396b(i)(4) (1982 & Supp.III 1985).

14. 42 C.F.R. § 440.50 (1987).

15. *Id.*

16. "Home" does not include hospitals, nursing facilities, or most intermediate care facilities. *Id.* at § 440.70(c).

17. *Id.* at § 440.70(a).

18. *Id.*

19. *Id.* at § 440.70(b).

20. *Id.* at §§ 431.53, 440.170(a). Section 431.53 requires states with a Medicaid plan to pay transportation costs to and from providers. If other

arrangements are necessary to assure transportation, direct payment is allowed to the Medicaid recipient. Section 440.170(a) states that payment must be to a third party (the transportation provider), except as permitted under § 431.53. Such payment is usually through issuance of bus tokens or taxi vouchers.

21. *Id.* at § 440.150(a).
22. *Id.* at § 440.60.
23. *Id.* at § 440.80(b).
24. *Id.* at § 440.80(c).
25. *Id.* at § 440.90.
26. *Id.* at § 440.100.
27. *Id.* at § 440.110.
28. *Id.* at § 440.120.
29. *Id.* at § 440.140.
30. *Id.* at § 440.170(e).
31. *Id.* at § 440.170(f). Subsection f provides the following definition for "personal care services": "services prescribed by a physician in accordance with the recipient's plan of treatment."
32. 42 U.S.C. § 1396n(c) (1982 & Supp. III 1985); 42 C.F.R. § 440.180, pt. 441, sub. G (1987). Pt. 441, sub. G describes what a state Medicaid agency must do to obtain a waiver.
33. 42 U.S.C. § 1396d(a)(18), added by the Consolidated Omnibus Budget Reconciliation Act of 1985 (COBRA), Pub. L. No. 99-272, § 9505(a)(1) (1986).
34. 42 U.S.C. § 1396d(a)(20), added by the Omnibus Budget Reconciliation Act of 1986 (OBRA of 1986), Pub. L. No. 99-509, § 9408(c)(1) (1986).
35. 42 C.F.R. § 435.907 (1987). Section 431.10(b) requires each state to specify a single state agency to administer or supervise Medicaid in the state. Five states have designated the health department; twenty-two the welfare department; twenty an umbrella agency; and three states have named other agencies (the office of the governor in Alabama and an independent agency/commission in Georgia and Mississippi). *Analysis of State Medicaid Program Characteristics, 1984*, at 130, Health Care Financing Administration (March 1985).
36. 42 C.F.R. § 435.908 (1987).
37. *Id.* at § 435.907.
38. *Id.* at § 435.911(a)(1).
39. *Id.* at § 435.911(a)(2).
40. *Id.* at § 431.220(a)(1); 42 U.S.C. § 1396a(a)(3) (1982 & Supp. III 1985); *Edelman v. Jordan*, 415 U.S. 651 (1974). In *Edelman* the Supreme Court ruled that the courts may not order the state to pay welfare recipients back benefits. *See also Green v. Mansour*, 106 S. Ct. 423 (1986).

41. 42 C.F.R. § 435.914(a) (1987); 42 U.S.C. § 1396a(a)(34) (1982 & Supp. III 1985). The bills must be for services of a type covered by your state Medicaid plan. 42 C.F.R. at § 435.914(a)(1). Section 435.914(a)(2) adds "regardless of whether the individual is alive when application for Medicaid is made."

42. *Id.* at § 435.916(a).

43. *Id.* at § 435.916(b).

44. Alabama, Alaska, Arkansas, California, Colorado, Delaware, District of Columbia, Florida, Georgia, Idaho, Iowa, Kansas, Kentucky, Louisiana, Maine, Maryland, Massachusetts, Michigan, Mississippi, Montana, Nevada, New Jersey, New Mexico, New York, Oregon, Pennsylvania, Rhode Island, South Carolina, South Dakota, Tennessee, Texas, Vermont, Washington, West Virginia, Wisconsin, and Wyoming. *Analysis of State Medicaid Program Characteristics, 1984*, p. 16, Health Care Financing Administration (Mar. 1985).

45. Connecticut, Hawaii, Illinois, Indiana, Minnesota, Missouri, Nebraska, New Hampshire, North Carolina, North Dakota, Ohio, Oklahoma, Utah, Virginia. *Id.*

46. 42 C.F.R. §§ 435.100–.136 (1987). Federal regulations list groups of persons who must be included in state Medicaid plans as categorically needy persons. *Id.* at 435.210–211. Federal regulations include additional groups, called the "optional categorically needy," which the states may choose to include in their Medicaid plans.

47. *Id.* at § 435.300–.340.

48. Arkansas, California, Connecticut, District of Columbia, Florida, Georgia, Hawaii, Illinois, Iowa, Kansas, Kentucky, Louisiana, Maine, Maryland, Massachusetts, Michigan, Minnesota, Montana, Nebraska, New Hampshire, New Jersey, New York, North Carolina, North Dakota, Oklahoma, Oregon, Pennsylvania, Rhode Island, South Carolina, Tennessee, Texas, Utah, Vermont, Virginia, Washington, West Virginia, and Wisconsin.

49. 42 U.S.C. § 1396a(a)(17)(B) (1982 & Supp. III 1985).

50. *Dumbleton v. Reed*, 40 N.Y.2d 586, 357 N.E.2d 363, 388 N.Y.S.2d 893 (1976); *See generally* National Health Law Program, *An Advocates Guide to the Medically Needy Program*, at 38 (1985).

51. *See* 20. C.F.R. §§ 416.1112, .1124 (1987).

52. *Id.* at §§ 416.1210, 416.1212 (1987).

53. *Id.* at §§ 416.1210(c), 416.1218(b)(2) (1987). Your car will not be counted at all if it is (1) for transportation to get medical treatment, (2) for transportation to employment, or (3) modified for the handicapped. *Id.* at § 416.1218(b)(1) (1987).

54. *Id.* at § 416.1205 (1987). This SSI rule treats individuals who live with ineligible spouses the same as those who live with eligible

spouses. The rule also provides for an increase in the resource limits. The limit for individuals increases by $100 each year so that in 1988, it will be $1,900 and in 1989, $2,000; the limit for couples increases by $150 each year so that in 1988 it will be $2,850 and in 1989, $3,000. *Id.* at § 416.1205(c).

55. *Id.* at §§ 416.1210(1), 416.1231. Also recall that § 416.1124(c)(9) provides that any interest earned on these "burial funds" is excluded from income.

56. In *Harris v. Lukhard*, 733 F.2d 1075 (4th Cir. 1984), the court held that "(2) unsalability provision of Virginia's procedure fulfilled requirement of an articulate standard by providing that ownership of real property of a value over limiting amount would not preclude eligibility if property could not be sold after a reasonable effort for sale had been made or if sale would involve unreasonable loss."

57. 42 U.S.C. § 1396p(c)(1)–(2) (1982 & Supp. III 1985); 20 C.F.R. § 416.1246 (1987). *See generally* Deford, "Medicaid Liens, Recoveries and Transfer of Assets after TEFRA," 18 *Clearinghouse Rev.* 134 (1984).

58. Pub. L. No. 100-360, § 303(b), 102 Stat. 683, 760–61 (1988), amending 42 U.S.C. § 1396p.

59. *Id.*

60. 42 U.S.C. § 1396a(k), amended by COBRA, § 9506.

61. States are required to set a medically needy level that is between the highest amount payable under the Aid to Families with Dependent Children (AFDC) program and 133 percent of this level. 42 C.F.R. § 435.811 (1987); 42 U.S.C. § 1396b(f) (1982 & Supp. III 1985).

62. 42 C.F.R. § 435.831(c) (1987).

63. 42 C.F.R. § 435.831 (1987). The greatest obstacle to taking advantage of the medically needy program is that many states calculate the spend-down on a six-month basis. There has been litigation over this method of computing spend-down. The U.S. Supreme Court decided the issue in 1986, ruling that Massachusetts's adoption of a six-month medical expense spend-down period when determining Medicaid eligibility did not violate federal Medicaid laws. *Atkins v. Rivera*, 106 S. Ct. 2456 (1986). In some states, institutionalized persons may anticipate their projected expenses in order to qualify for Medicaid. *Williams v. St. Clair*, 610 F.2d 1244 (5th Cir. 1980).

64. 42 C.F.R. § 435.831, .845 (1987).

65. For a discussion of medically needy programs, see Wulsin, "Adopting a Medically Needy Program," 18 *Clearinghouse Rev.* 841 (Dec. 1984); National Health Law Program, *An Advocate's Guide to the Medically Needy Program* (1985); National Health Law Program,

An Advocate's Guide to the Medicaid Program (1985); Bonnyman and Robertson, "Making the Medicaid Spend-Down Program Work: A Partnership of Community Education and Administrative Advocacy," 18 *Clearinghouse Rev.* 105 (June 1987).

66. 42 C.F.R. § 435.602 (1987); 42 U.S.C. § 1396a(a)(17)(D) (1982 & Supp. III 1985). A recent HHS Medicaid policy transmittal advised states that they can require adult family members to contribute to the cost of nursing-home care received by their relatives, if there is a state statute of general applicability—that is, a state law concerning family financial responsibility, which is not restricted to Medicaid recipients only. Georgia, Virginia, Indiana, and Idaho have such enabling legislation. National Health Law Program, "Health Care for the Poor During 1983: A time of Reassessment and Transition," 17 *Clearinghouse Rev.* 977, 979 n.21 (1984).

67. 42 C.F.R. § 435.723(b) (1987).

68. *See Schweiker v. Gray Panthers*, 453 U.S. 34 (1981); *Herweg v. Ray*, 455 U.S. 265 (1982).

69. 42 C.F.R. § 435.723 (1987).

70. *Id.* at § 435.822(b).

71. Pub. L. No. 100-360, § 303(a), 102 Stat. 683, 754-60 (1988).

72. *Id. See also Purser v. Rahm*, 104 Wash. 2d 159, 702 P.2d 1196 (1985), *cert. dismissed*, 107 S.Ct. 8 (1987); *In the matter of Rose Septuagenarian v. David Septuagenarian*, 126 Misc. 2d 699, 483 N.Y.S.2d 932 (Fam. Ct. 1984); *Dept. of Health of the State of California vs. Secretary of HHS*, 823 F.2d 323 (9th Cir. 1987): Mitchell, "Spousal Impoverishment: Medicaid Burdens on the At-Home Spouse of a Nursing Home Resident," 20 *Clearinghouse Rev.* 358 (1986).

73. 42 C.F.R. § 435.402 (1987).

74. *Id.* at § 435.403. Because the critical issue in determining residence is the "intention" to make a particular state one's home, such things as voter registration, payment of local taxes, length of presence in the state, a state driver's license, rent receipts, mortgage payment books, change of address, etc., may be important sources of proof of residency.

75. *See Corr. v. Westchester County Dep't. of Social Services*, 33 N.Y.2d 111, 305 N.E.2d 483, 350 N.Y.S.2d 401 (1973). *See also Hutchings v. Brezenoff*, 95 A.D.2d 554, 467 N.Y.S.2d 382 (1983); *In re Casey v. Lavine*, 54 A.D.2d 250, 388 N.Y.S.2d 159 (1976); *In re Ruiz v. Lavine*, 49 A.D.2d 1, 370 N.Y.S.2d 710 (1975).

76. 42 C.F.R. § 435.1008(a) (1987).

77. *Id.* at § 431.210.

78. *Id.* at § 431.211.

79. *Id.* at § 431.213, 431.214 list the few exceptions from the advance notice rule. For example, in cases of suspected fraudulent receipt of benefits the agency need give only five days notice of its intent to reduce or terminate benefits. *Id.* at § 431.214(a).

80. There is substantial case law establishing that recipients who lose SSI or AFDC benefits should not be terminated automatically from Medicaid. Instead, a state should redetermine *ex parte* whether the recipient might be eligible for Medicaid on some other basis (such as medically needy). *See Crippen v. Kheder*, 741 F.2d 102 (6th Cir. 1984); *Massachusetts Ass'n. of Older Americans v. Sharp*, 700 F.2d 749 (1st Cir. 1983); *Stenson v. Blum*, 476 F. Supp. 1311 (S.D.N.Y. 1979), *aff'd* 628 F.2d 1345 (2d Cir. 1980), *cert. den.* 449 U.S. 885 (1980).

81. 42 C.F.R. § 431.220(a) (1987). *See Goldberg v. Kelly*, 397 U.S. 254 (1970) (landmark case that affirmed a recipient's right to a hearing).

82. 42 C.F.R. § 431.221(d) (1987).

83. *See, e.g.*, 20 C.F.R. § 416.1411 (1987) (dealing with requests for review under SSI program).

84. 42 C.F.R. § 431.230(a) (1987).

85. *Id.* at § 431.231(a).

86. *Id.* at § 431.206(b)(3). *See also* 45 C.F.R. § 213.23 (1987), which lists rights given claimants at hearings.

87. 42 C.F.R. § 431.242 (1987).

88. *See Id.* at § 431.240(a)(1).

89. *Id.* at § 431.250(f)(1).

90. *Id.* at § 431.240(b).

91. *Id.* at § 431.244(d)–(f).

92. *Id.* at § 431.245.

93. *Id.* at § 431.107: 42 U.S.C. § 1396a(a)(27) (1982 & Supp. III 1985). The Medicaid Act contains no requirement that hospitals participate in the Medicaid program. However, hospitals that have accepted federal construction funds under the federal Hill-Burton program are required, as of 1979, to participate indefinitely in the Medicaid program. 42 C.F.R. § 124.603(c)(1)(ii) (1987). *See American Hospital Ass'n v. Schweiker*, 721 F.2d 170 (7th Cir. 1983).

94. 42 C.F.R. § 456.101 (1987).

95. 42 U.S.C. § 1396a(a)(19)(A)(1982 & Supp. III 1985). *See Kessler v. Blum*, 591 F. Supp. 1013 (S.D.N.Y. 1984) (Court analyzes prior approval requirements generally).

96. *Id.* 42 U.S.C. § 1396(a)(13)(A) (1982 & Supp. III 1985). States may establish Medicaid payment rates that are "reasonable and adequate to meet the costs which must be incurred by efficiently and economically operated facilities."

97. 42 C.F.R. § 447.15 (1987).

98. *Id.* at § 431.52(b)(1)(i),(ii). Payment will also be made if, based on medical advice, the needed medical services are more readily available in another state or Medicaid recipients in a particular locality usually use the medical resources in another state. *Id.* at 431.52(b)(1)(iii), (iv).

99. *See id.* at § 447.50; 42 U.S.C. § 1396o (1982 & Supp. III 1985).

100. 42 C.F.R. § 447.51(b) (1987).

101. *Id.* at § 447.51(a).

102. *Id.* at § 447.53.

103. *Id.* at § 447.53(b). This section lists exclusions from cost sharing. For example, nursing-home residents are exempt from cost-sharing requirements. *Id.* at § 447.53(b)(3). Even if copayments are charged, a physician or hospital participating in the Medicaid program cannot deny care because the charge is not paid up front; however, you can be billed for the services.

104. *Id.* at § 447.53(b)(4).

105. *Id.* at § 447.54(a),(b). The requirement that cost-sharing charges must be nominal may be waived by HHS for nonemergency services provided in a hospital emergency room under certain conditions.

106. *Id.* at § 447.52(a),(b).

107. *Id.* at § 431.51(b),(c). However, in an emergency you can go to an uncertified or nonparticipating provider. 42 U.S.C. § 1395f(d)(1) (1982 & Supp. III 1985).

108. 42 C.F.R. § 431.51 (1987); 42 U.S.C. § 1396a(a)(23) (1982 & Supp. III 1985).

109. *See generally* 42 U.S.C. § 1396n (1982 & Supp. III 1985).

110. As of Mar. 1984, 42 freedom-of-choice waivers had been submitted by 19 states; 27 of the waiver applications had been approved, mostly for primary care case management (i.e., limiting recipients to one provider such as an internist or family practitioner from a selected list who is then responsible for the delivery of all non-emergency care provided to the Medicaid recipient). *Analysis of State Medicaid Program Characteristics, 1984*, p. 136, Health Care Financing Administration (Mar. 1985). For an analysis of freedom-of-choice limitations, see Dallek & Wulsin, "Limits on Medicaid Patients' Rights to Choose Their Own Doctors and Hospitals," 17 *Clearinghouse Rev.* 280 (1983).

111. 42 C.F.R. § 447.15 (1987). 42 U.S.C. § 1396h(d) (1982 & Supp. III 1985) makes it a felony for a provider to willfully and knowingly charge fees for what Medicaid has already covered.

112. *Cohen ex rel Cohen v. Quern*, 608 F. Supp. 1324 (N.D. Ill. 1984); *Sparks v. Sawaya*, 9 Ohio App. 2d 275, 459 N.E.2d 901 (Ohio App.

1983); *Samuel v. California Dep't. of Health Services*, 570 F.Supp. 566 (N.D. Cal. 1983).

113. 42 C.F.R. §§ 447.10, 447.25 (1987); 42 U.S.C. § 1396a(a)(32) (1982 & Supp. III 1985).

114. 42 C.F.R. § 431.246 (1987). *See also In re Schwartz v. Toia*, 68 A.D.2d 890, 414 N.Y.S.2d 23 (1979); *In re Lawrence v. Lavine*, 50 A.D.2d 734, 375 N.Y.S.2d 587 (1975).

115. Medical Assistance Manual, §§ 3-10.9-00 construed in 1 Medicare and Medicaid Guide (CCH) ¶ 14,703 (17) (1981).

116. *Cohen ex rel Cohen v. Quern*, 608 F. Supp. 1324 (N.D. Ill 1984), *rehearing denied* 617 F.2d 295 (7th Cir. 1984).

117. 42 C.F.R. § 431.625 (1987).

118. Pub. L. No. 100-360, § 301, 102 Stat. 683, 748–50 (1988). The buy-in requirement will be phased in over five years for states that have elected treatment under section 1902(f) of the Social Security Act and that, as of 1 January 1987, used a more restrictive income standard for the aged than the SSI standard. *Id.*

119. 42 C.F.R. § 435.831(c)(1)(i) (1987).

120. *Id.* at §§ 433.139, 433.145 (1987). *See also* 42 U.S.C. § 1396d(p), added by OBRA, § 9403.

121. 42 U.S.C. § 1396a(a)(25), amended by COBRA, § 9503.

122. 42 C.F.R. § 456.1-.657 (1987); 42 U.S.C. § 1396a(a)(30) (1982 & Supp. III 1985).

123. *See e.g.*, *Kessler v. Blum*, 591 F. Supp. 1013 (S.D.N.Y. 1984).

124. 42 C.F.R. § 433.36(g)(3)(iii) (1987); 42 U.S.C. § 1396p(a)(2)(C) (1982 & Supp. III 1985). In the case of a brother or sister, this rule only applies if the sibling lived in your house at least one year before you were admitted to the medical institution. *Id.*

125. 42 C.F.R. § 433.36 (1987).

126. *Id.*; 42 U.S.C. 1396p(a)(1)(B)(i),(ii) (1982 & Supp. III 1985).

127. 42 C.F.R. § 433.36(h) (1987); 42 U.S.C. § 1396p(b) (1982 & Supp. III 1985).

128. *Id.*

129. 42 C.F.R. § 433.36(g)(4) (1987); 42 U.S.C. § 1396p(a)(3) (1982 & Supp. III 1985).

130. 42 C.F.R. § 433.36(g)(1) (1987); 42 U.S.C. § 1396p(a)(1)(A) (1982 & Supp. III 1985).

131. *Coplien v. Dep't. of Health and Social Services*, 119 Wis. 2d 52, 349 N.W.2d 92 (1984); *Smith v. Alabama Medicaid Agency*, 461 So.2d 817 (Ala. Civ. App. 1984); *Hallmark Nursing Center, Inc. v. Menaldino*, 88 A.D.2d 1042, 452 N.Y.S.2d 694 (1982); *Baker v. Sterling*, 39 N.Y.2d 397, 348 N.E.2d 584, 384 N.Y.S.2d 128 (1976).

132. For an excellent discussion of this problem and suggestions on how

to combat cutbacks, see Mullen and Schneider, *Medicaid Cutbacks; a Handbook for Beneficiary Advocates* (Apr. 1976), available from the Nat'l. Clearinghouse for Legal Services, Inc., 407 South Dearborn, Suite 400, Chicago, Illinois, 60605. Recent publications available through the Clearinghouse are National Health Law Program, *An Advocate's Guide to the Medicaid Program* (1985), and Nat'l. Senior Citizens Law Center, *Representing Older Persons; An Advocate's Manual* (1985). Another new publication is *The Best Medicine: Organizing Local Health Care Campaigns* (1985) available from the Villers Foundation, 1334 G Street, N.W., Washington D.C. 20005.

133. 42 C.F.R. § 440.230(b) (1987).

134. *See generally* Nat'l. Health Law Program, *An Advocate's Guide to the Medicaid Program* (1985) at 23.

135. *Fant v. Stumbo*, 552 F. Supp. 617 (W.D. Ky. 1982).

9

Nursing Homes

What is a nursing home?

A place to convalesce after a stay in a hospital. A place to send an aged relative for whom you no longer can care. A place where care is provided lovingly and well or where residents are exploited and abused. The term nursing home encompasses all of these descriptions. Many nursing homes are excellent facilities with competent, compassionate staffs; others are vermin-infested firetraps with abusive staffs and greedy owners, and most are in between these extremes, where many of the most taken-for-granted freedoms of daily life are absent.

More technically, the term is used to describe three kinds of facilities providing some level of medical care to residents, most of whom are elderly. The first of these is the skilled nursing facility (SNF), which is defined as providing skilled nursing care and related services or rehabilitation services to residents who are quite ill but who do not need to be in a hospital. An SNF must have a medical director who is a physician, and a nurse is required to be on duty 24 hours a day.[1] A second type of nursing home is the intermediate care facility (ICF) which is defined as providing "health related care and services to individuals who do not require the degree of care and treatment which a hospital or skilled nursing facility is designed to provide"[2] but who need institutionalized care. ICFs must have a nurse on duty only eight hours a day, seven days a week and are not required to have a medical director.[3]

In late 1987, Congress passed a major nursing home reform law that will alter these requirements. The distinction between skilled and intermediate nursing facilities is to be eliminated by 1 October 1990, by which date all nursing facilities will be required to have a registered nurse on duty eight hours a day, seven days a week and a licensed nurse on duty at all times.[4]

A third type of facility goes by many names—personal-care or board-and-care home or custodial-care or domiciliary-care facility. Although commonly considered nursing homes, these facilities provide only rudimentary medical care. Room, board, and some help in dressing, bathing, and toileting often is provided. Frequently large old private homes have been converted to this use. Unlike the other two types of facilities described above, this type of care is not reimbursed by Medicaid.

In 1985, there were approximately nineteen thousand facilities in the United States providing skilled and/or intermediate care.[5]

Who runs nursing homes?

Approximately 8 percent of the nursing homes in this country are owned and operated by the government. The rest are owned privately—about 22 percent are owned by nonprofit groups such as churches, while about 70 percent of our nursing homes are operated for a profit.[6] The enactment of Medicaid and Medicare in the mid-1960s made vast amounts of government money available to nursing-home operators, and during the late 1960s and early 1970s, nursing homes became big business. Big nursing-home corporations were formed, and nursing-home stocks are traded on the stock exchanges.[7] Recent years have seen the formation of national and regional nursing-home chains, with an increasing percentage of homes operated by these chains.

Public scandals in the 1970s revealed that shady operators made vast fortunes operating nursing homes and that nursing homes often had absentee owners, sometimes doctors or real-estate syndicates. As a result, federal law requires public disclosure of the names of officers, directors, and partners in nursing homes, as well as the names of all persons owning 10 percent or more of a nursing home.[8] In some states, further steps have been taken. For example, New York requires a person applying for authorization to build a new nursing home to reveal his or her partners and investors and requires him or her to establish that all other nursing homes he or she owns are well run.[9] Nursing-home owners and investors in New York likewise are liable to the state and to residents and their families for improprieties resulting from the operation of the nursing home.[10]

To learn who owns a nursing home, contact the nearest office of your state department of health and simply ask for this information. The health department is required to provide this information to the public on request and should readily inform you of the owner(s).

Who lives in nursing homes?

There are approximately 1.5 million elderly Americans in this country's nineteen thousand nursing homes. Most of them are very old (their average age is 82), women outnumber men three to one, and nine out of ten of all residents have no living spouse. Most suffer from several chronic diseases, such as arthritis, heart disease, hypertension, impaired vision, and impaired hearing. Many are quite dependent, frequently needing help with walking, bathing, dressing, eating, and toileting.

The nursing-home population is divided into two groups— short- and long-term residents. Short-term residents usually are admitted to nursing homes from hospitals for skilled nursing care. Recent changes in the way Medicare reimburses hospitals for caring for elderly patients have induced hospitals to release patients to nursing homes sooner than had been the case. As a result, patients admitted to nursing homes are entering them older, sicker, and more dependent than was true a short time ago. Long-term residents generally require personal care, unskilled-nursing care and supervision. The average long-term resident stays in a nursing home over two years. Very often, these residents have no home or apartment to which they can return. Only one nursing-home resident in five will return to their home; some will be transferred to a hospital, but must of them will die in the nursing home.[11]

Who pays for nursing-home care?

More than $33 billion is spent each year to pay for care in nursing homes.[12] Over half of this cost is borne by local, state, and federal governments, with the balance paid by private, paying residents. Private insurance pays for very little long-term care, although this may change in the future as private insurance companies begin to market long-term-care insurance. The largest share of nursing home care is paid by Medicaid, which pays for care by skilled nursing facilities (SNF) and intermediate care facilities (ICF) to eligible residents. In contrast, Medicare pays for only a portion of the cost of care provided by an SNF and only for a maximum of 100 days in a benefit period. Medicare does not pay for ICF care and neither Medicare nor Medicaid pays for care by board-and-care facilities. However, care in these facilities is borne in part by Social Security and Supplemental Security Income (SSI) since many residents of these facilities receive Social Security and SSI; in some states, their SSI payments are increased to cover the high cost of care in these facilities.

Nursing homes also receive government aid for construction and other costs from the Veterans Administration, the Small Business Administration, the Department of Housing and Urban Development, and other agencies of federal, state, and local governments.

How expensive are nursing homes?

Often very expensive. A skilled nursing facility can cost over $4,000 per month. But not all nursing homes are this expensive. Much depends on the size and location of the facility and on whether it is an SNF (the most expensive), an ICF, or a board-and-care home (the least expensive). Before you agree to go to a nursing home, be certain to find out the facility's monthly charge and what the monthly charge covers. Many residents learn too late that the monthly rate does not cover common services like laundry, shampoos, and nonprescription drugs like aspirin. Also investigate alternatives, such as nursing care provided at home from a home health agency, before entering a nursing home.

Federally certified nursing homes are required to tell residents what services are covered in the basic rate, but private paying residents are not always similarly protected except in states such as New York which require nursing homes to execute a contract with each resident spelling out all the charges.[13] Nursing homes, however, rarely give detailed information about costs for services to a prospective resident regardless of the source of their payment. Admission to a nursing home is a critical time. Often in the stress or haste involved, residents or their families do not pause to evaluate the contract or admission agreement they are asked to sign. Recent studies of these agreements suggest that the agreements often contain language that is inappropriate or even illegal. Examples include failures to fully disclose services and rates, attempts to exculpate the facility for harm to the resident, and efforts to require a "responsible party" to cosign the agreement, thereby agreeing to assume financial responsibility for services provided.[14] Some of these clauses may be unenforceable, but it is better to exercise caution by reading the admission agreement carefully before signing.

Medicare and Medicaid residents are protected against financial overreaching in other ways. A nursing home's acceptance of payment from these programs is payment in full, and the nursing home cannot collect extra sums from residents for services covered by the basic rate.[15] Nor can homes ask Medicaid eligible applicants, residents, or their families to make contributions or other gifts to the home as a condition of admission or continued stay in the home. Similarly, a nursing home is not allowed to require that a Medicaid eligible applicant for admission to a nursing home pay the rate charged private paying residents for a period of time as a condition of admission as a Medicaid resident.

These restrictions are designed to assure that Medicaid eligible persons are treated fairly by nursing homes. The reason they are necessary is that in most states nursing homes can charge private paying residents a higher fee than the state will pay for Medicaid residents. Facilities frequently give preference to private paying residents and engage in a variety of practices to reduce the number of Medicaid residents served or to supplement the revenues paid by the state for Medicaid residents. The most blatant of these practices—charging extra for services paid by Medicaid and requiring gifts or donations as a condition of accepting Medicaid residents—are unlawful, but facilities continue these practices, which are regarded by advocates to be of questionable legality. Examples include placing limits on the number of Medicaid patients accepted and providing better facilities or additional services for "private pay" residents. A number of states have moved to outlaw these practices.[16]

What are nursing homes like?

Some nursing homes are excellent facilities with highly trained and motivated staffs in which superb care is available. Others are dingy firetraps. Still others seem nice, but actually provide poor care. The National Citizens Coalition for Nursing Home Reform, an organization dedicated to improving nursing-home care, interviewed current nursing-home residents to determine the characteristics of a good nursing home. The results included such qualities as good food, meaningful activities, trained and responsive staff, and a community presence within the facility, as well as opportunities for choice and as much autonomy as possible for each resident.[17]

In most communities, there are good nursing homes with

trained staff and innovative programs for residents. Regardless of how attractive a nursing home, how attentive the staff, or how progressive the care, residents lose a tremendous amount of autonomy upon entering such a facility. This loss of autonomy is a well-documented effect of any kind of institutionalization and is a factor to keep in mind when choosing a nursing home. It is important to inquire from the staff of the nursing home whether freedom is given to the residents to make as many choices as possible and to observe how much freedom of choice residents are allowed to exercise.

Some nursing homes do not meet the criteria of a good home. Some common problems in nursing homes are excessive use of tranquilizers and physical restraints, bad food, filth, neglect and abuse, theft of money and property, and the lack of respect for privacy and dignity.[18] These problems stem from many sources. Indifferent nursing-home owners, unqualified administrators, inadequate and poorly paid and trained staffs, and a lack of concern by doctors are contributing factors.

Are nursing homes regulated?

Yes. To operate, nursing homes must be licensed by the state in which they are located. To be eligible for reimbursement by Medicare and Medicaid, nursing homes must comply with federal regulations. Thus, all nursing homes are subject to state regulations, and many also are regulated by the federal government. These federal minimum standards are called "conditions of participation" and cover a range of areas such as the construction of the facility, fire safety, physician and nursing services, sanitation, nutrition, physical therapy, recreation, and record-keeping. The Federal regulations exist for the protection of residents' rights. Most states have similar requirements. In addition, the federal government requires the states to regulate nursing-home administrators, and in most states administrators must be licensed.[19]

If adequately enforced these standards should result in good care for nursing home residents. However, the standards and the process by which nursing home compliance with the standards is monitored have been criticized widely in recent years. The principal criticism has been that both the regulations and the inspections to oversee their compliance do not focus enough on the actual care received by residents. In 1983, the federal government commissioned the Institute of Medicine of the National Academy of Sciences to study the need for new federal nursing-home regulations. In 1986, the institute issued its report. Among its recommendations were calls for stronger federal regulations emphasizing the care actually delivered to residents and the quality of life these residents enjoy, a better survey process to ensure compliance with these requirements, improved complaint investigation, and strict penalties for nursing homes violating the rules.[20]

Late in 1987 many of the institute's recommendations were enacted into law as part of the Omnibus Budget Reconciliation Act of 1987 and the Older Americans Act Amendments of 1987.[21] These new laws include the following provisions.

1. Federal nursing home regulations are to be strengthened. The focus of the new regulations is on "quality of life" for residents; periodic assessments of each resident are required and care must be based on the assessments; staffing requirements are increased and nurse's aides (who provide much of the actual care of residents) are required to be trained.
2. Resident rights are strengthened. Protections at the time of admission to and transfer from a nursing home are increased. Also increased are protection against use of restraints and protection of resident funds; access to visitors and to survey results also are strengthened.
3. The survey and certification process is strengthened. States are required to have adequate staff to investigate complaints concerning nursing homes and to monitor deficient homes.
4. Federal and state sanctions for nursing homes failing to comply with federal requirements are strengthened. Prompt action is required where deficiencies immediately jeopardize the health or safety of residents. Additional sanctions available include: civil money penalties; denial of Medicaid payment for new admissions; and authority to temporarily manage deficient facilities and, in emergencies, to close a facility or transfer residents.
5. The long-term-care ombudsman program is strength-

ened. States are required to provide adequate funding and support for the program.

6. Some reforms are effective immediately. Others will be phased in by 1 October 1990.

As a result of these laws, nursing home requirements will be revised considerably in the next several years. For this reason, some sections of this chapter are subject to change. Be certain to consult the long-term care ombudsman in your area for up-to-date information concerning your rights (for a list of ombudsmen see Appendix D).

Board-and-care homes, on the other hand, are not subject to federal regulation; and in many states, the regulations governing these facilities are considerably weaker than the regulations governing SNFs and ICFs.[22]

Are nursing homes inspected?

Yes. Nursing homes usually are inspected annually, typically by the state department of health, to determine the extent of compliance with both federal and state regulations.[23] Ordinarily, an inspection team consists of professionals—such as a sanitation expert and a nurse. If deficiencies are found, the facility is to submit a written "plan of correction" stating how and when the deficiencies will be corrected. If there are no deficiencies, the home's license is issued or renewed, and the home is certified for participation in Medicare and Medicaid. If the deficiencies are major, then enforcement action must be taken to bring the home into compliance.

In 1986, in response to criticism of the failure of these inspections to focus on residents and the care they actually receive, the United States Department of Health and Human Services (DHHS) modified the inspection process to focus more on residents. Called Patient Care and Services (PaCS), the new process requires inspectors to observe nursing home residents and talk with them rather than simply review records as has been done in the past. The DHHS also has initiated a program of "fast track" termination of federal financial participation for facilities found to have deficiencies posing an "immediate and serious threat to health and safety."[24] These initiatives are continued and strengthened by the 1987 reform legislation.

In addition to the annual inspections, states inspect nursing homes in response to complaints. In many states, the department responsible for nursing-home regulation is required by law to respond promptly to complaints by residents, families, and others of nursing home deficiencies. Violations uncovered during complaint investigations can lead to an order of correction or the imposition of sanctions.

Every state also has a long-term care ombudsman program. Created by Congress as part of the Older Americans Act, these programs are required to investigate and resolve complaints made by or on behalf of residents of long-term care facilities.[25] Unlike the health department, however, ombudsmen lack authority to impose sanctions for violations they uncover. Their position is to relay their complaints to the health department and ensure that the department responds appropriately. The programs also monitor laws and issues related to nursing-home residents' rights and serve as advocates for residents rights. The 1987 reform laws strengthen these programs and assure their unimpeded access to nursing home residents.

Are inspection reports available to the public?
Until 1972, the federal government refused to make inspection reports public, claiming they were confidential. That year, the Social Security Act was amended by Congress and summaries of nursing-home inspections now are available at local health and welfare department offices and in the district offices of the Social Security Administration. The summaries and subsequent plans of correction are to be available in these locations no later than ninety days from the date of the most recent inspection.

Further disclosure is needed. Inspection results should be posted in all homes and published in newspapers, just as the results of restaurant inspections are in many communities. A number of states now require widespread disclosure of nursing-home inspection reports.[26] The 1987 reform legislation strengthens federal requirements concerning disclosure of survey results.

Is nursing-home regulation effective?
Efforts to enforce nursing-home standards through inspections and the use of sanctions have been only partially successful. Some of the problems include:

- a survey process that, until recently, focused on the nursing home's ability to provide good care rather than on the care actually provided;
- inspection agencies that are underfinanced and understaffed;
- advance notice given to facilities of the inspection, permitting them to clean up problem areas temporarily;
- the frequent unavailability of sanctions that are appropriate to the particular deficiencies the facility has;
- political pressure exerted by or on behalf nursing homes to thwart enforcement actions;
- the failure of state or federal law to require widespread public disclosure of inspection reports.

Some of these problems and possible solutions are discussed in more detail below.

What can be done if a nursing home doesn't provide good care?

Much nursing-home care continues to be poor in spite of extensive regulations governing quality of care. Important reasons are that enforcement agencies have been meek and have had too few weapons available to punish noncomplying homes. The timidity of these agencies is due in part to the tenacity of the nursing-home lobby. It also stems from the shortage of adequate nursing homes. Decisive action often is not taken against offending nursing homes because if these homes are closed, there is no place for their residents to go. It certainly is true that removing a resident from a nursing home (even a bad one) is a traumatic experience and often results in residents' suffering relapses. In fact, some residents die as a result of the trauma of relocation.[27] Nevertheless, the stalemate must be broken, and effective enforcement must be achieved. Effective enforcement is possible if additional weapons are made available to agencies and if greater public participation is encouraged and maintained.

If a nursing home has serious deficiencies, the state can revoke its license, and the federal government can decertify it and refuse to reimburse it for care provided to residents eligible for Medicaid and Medicare. License revocation is suitable for extreme cases, but is ineffective in most situations. For one thing, it is very slow. In most states a nursing home is entitled to a hearing before its license can be revoked. Nursing homes make good use of these hearings. They are time-consuming, and long delays are common. If the nursing home loses at the hearing, an appeal to the courts inevitably follows. In addition, the sanction is inflexible since it causes the nursing home to close. Enforcement agencies fear this, so nursing homes' licenses rarely are revoked, and horrendous conditions continue. Federal decertification suffers from similar deficiencies. It is too slow, unwieldy, and inflexible. Efforts to decertify a nursing home typically are met with protracted litigation. The new federal initiative to speed decertification in cases where health and safety are at stake is a response to this problem.

Sanctions that are speedier and more flexible must be used. A number of states have developed new enforcement mechanisms aimed at improving nursing home compliance with regulatory requirements. Known as "intermediate sanctions," these mechanisms hold great promise for improving the quality of life for nursing home residents. After a long delay, the federal government began use of this concept in 1986. A brief discussion of intermediate sanctions follows. Among the sanctions are: injunctions, fines, reimbursement control, receivership, criminal sanctions, suspension of new admissions, and the appointment of a monitor to oversee the management of the facility.[28]

Injunctions. State enforcement agencies generally are empowered to seek injunctions against illegal actions by nursing homes. This power can be an effective sanction, because an injunction can be obtained quickly and the nursing home placed under the supervision of a court, which is empowered to penalize any failures to obey the injunction. The injunction seems particularly well suited to violations involving the refusal to correct hazardous conditions or violations of residents' rights, such as efforts to transfer in retaliation for voicing complaints.

Fines. More and more state enforcement agencies have the authority to impose fines or civil penalties for violations of health laws or regulations. Fines are an effective sanction where they are assessed in substantial sums and collected promptly. Compliance efforts are enhanced, since the home has a strong economic incentive to bring itself into compliance.

Appointment of a receiver. As an alternative to decertification or license revocation in situations where a home cannot or will not comply, enforcement agencies in a number of states are authorized to initiate an action for the appointment of a receiver for the facility. The receiver operates or supervises the operation of a noncomplying nursing home and brings the nursing home into compliance when the existing management will not do so. If necessary, the receiver may authorize structural repairs needed to achieve compliance. The advantage of this remedy is that it directly achieves the rehabilitation that license revocation and similar remedies try to induce indirectly without having to move the residents from the facility. Also, relief can be obtained much more quickly since courts usually act promptly in these cases, and owner appeals are unlikely to stay or postpone the receiver's appointment. Problems with receivership include the difficulty of finding a willing and experienced receiver, locating the money needed to achieve compliance, and defining the circumstances under which the original owner can (if ever) resume operation of the facility. Receiverships also are used where a facility is to be closed due to persistent problems not susceptible to correction. In such cases a receiver supervises the closure of the home and the safe and orderly transfer of residents to other facilities.[29]

A related sanction is the use of a public monitor. Available in a few states, a monitor is appointed by the regulatory agency to monitor a home's progress in complying with state and federal regulatory standards. Unlike a receiver who takes over the management of a problem facility, a monitor simply oversees the efforts of the home to carry out the orders of the regulatory agency. The presence of the monitor makes it difficult for a problem home to evade legal requirements.

Suspension of admissions. Another important sanction is the authority to prohibit a nursing home from accepting new residents. Regulatory agencies in a number of states possess this authority. Typically, the sanction is invoked when a facility displays chronic deficiencies in the delivery of care to residents, often due to staffing shortages or deficiencies in the delivery of services by the home's staff. In such situations, the agency can prohibit the home from accepting new residents until the deficiencies are corrected. A variation on this approach is to deny the home reimbursement for Medicaid residents. In 1986, the federal government announced that it would deny Medicare and Medicaid reimbursement for new admissions to homes whose noncompliance with one or more of the basic federal requirements governing nursing homes poses a serious threat to resident health and safety. Once the ban on reimbursement is imposed, it will continue until the home corrects the deficiencies or demonstrates a good faith effort to do so. If neither of these occur, proceedings for decertification of the facility will be commenced.[30]

Reimbursement Controls. Reimbursement controls can be a useful technique to improve the quality of care. Reimbursement is the money paid by the government to a nursing home for the services it provides. Rates can be decreased when deficiencies exist and can be increased when a nursing home provides excellent care. To be effective, reimbursement rate differentials must be sufficiently great to induce a nursing home to make the desired changes, for if the cost of compliance exceeds the changes in reimbursement, the system is ineffective. Many advocates believe that a comprehensive system in which nursing homes are rewarded financially for desirable behavior and penalized financially for improper behavior holds great promise to improve nursing homes.[31]

Criminal sanctions. Most state enforcement agencies and the United States Department of Justice may seek criminal sanctions for misconduct by nursing home operators. Criminal sanctions have not been widely used to force nursing homes to comply with standards involving resident care or fire safety or to penalize facilities or their employees for failure to comply with these requirements. Prosecutors generally are reluctant to spend time with nursing home cases, and judges who do not think these violations are criminal are reluctant to impose jail sentences or large fines. Lengthy trial delays are common, and violations must be proven beyond a reasonable doubt. Moreover, the remedy seeks retribution against the owner rather than rehabilitation of the facility. Despite these barriers, criminal cases have been filed against nursing homes and their employees in cases of extreme abuse or gross neglect.

When financial irregularities are involved, however, criminal sanctions can and should be used. Double-billing, padded payrolls, and conversion of resources to personal use are examples of criminal practices widespread in some segments of the nursing-home industry. Adequate auditing and enforcement make it possible to detect these violations and obtain convictions. The reform legislation enacted late in 1987 provides the

DHHS and the states with many of these sanctions, including the authority to deny Medicaid payment for new admissions, to impose civil money payments, to monitor deficient facilities, to temporarily manage deficient facilities, and, in emergencies, to close facilities and transfer residents. Where a facility's deficiencies immediately threaten resident health or safety and where a facility repeatedly fails to comply with federal requirements, imposition of sanctions and other corrective action are mandated.

Private enforcement devices. Because nursing-home residents are often frail and vulnerable, it is appropriate that the principal burdens of enforcement lie with public agencies. And yet enforcement should not be their exclusive domain; in even the best circumstances, the interests of the public and of agencies charged with protecting the public sometimes diverge. The agencies in charge of enforcing nursing-home regulations often are not model regulators, and the pervasive problems in nursing homes point to the need for alternative enforcement devices.

An illustration of this point is the receivership proposal outlined earlier. The authority to petition for the appointment of a receiver must not be left solely with government agencies. For reasons unrelated to the merits of a particular case, an agency may choose not to seek the appointment of a receiver; thus, residents themselves must be able to exercise this power. Similarly, the power to seek injunctions and other court orders can be a powerful tool in the hands of residents and can augment the efforts of enforcement agencies. Such actions are desirable when resident transfers are proposed and when hazardous conditions continue uncorrected.

Private involvement in public enforcement. The failure of public enforcement agencies to compel compliance with standards for safety and resident care is clear. Why this is so is not so clear, however. Part of the problem is public neglect. The quality of life in nursing homes receives only sporadic public attention. Enforcement agencies are underfunded and understaffed. In addition, the remedies utilized by public agencies often are unsatisfactory, and public enforcement is subject to political and other extralegal pressures that limit effectiveness.

Greater private involvement in the public enforcement process can help rectify these deficiencies. Simple scrutiny by the public is invaluable. Blatant abuses and regulatory favoritism toward the industry are less likely to occur when the enforcement agency's actions are watched by the public. Increased access to regulatory agencies is also required. Inspection results and cost data—already available to some extent—should be distributed more widely, posted in each nursing home, and available in public libraries. When members of the public are rebuffed in efforts to obtain information from agencies, they should file suits under federal and state freedom of information laws to force disclosure.

Concerned members of the public can help enforcement agencies obtain the resources needed to do a good job. If additional sanctions are needed they can lobby the legislature for such authority. If more funding is required to hire and train additional inspectors, they can work to see that the enforcement agency is adequately funded. They also can work with the state nursing home association to obtain adequate Medicaid funding so that homes can afford to provide high quality care to all who need such care. Local, state, and national consumer groups have been extraordinarily successful in obtaining improvements in nursing-home life and in the enforcement mechanisms intended to ensure that homes provide a high quality of life for their residents.[32]

A dramatic illustration of the success of this strategy occurred in Colorado. Unhappy with the quality of care they were receiving, nursing home residents sued the home, the state of Colorado, and the HHS, alleging that the state and federal regulatory agencies had failed to discharge their duty to ensure that Medicaid recipients in nursing homes actually were receiving the high quality care called for by federal nursing home standards. As a result of this suit, the HHS adopted the new PaCS method of inspecting nursing homes which focuses on residents and the care they actually receive. In addition, the residents received damages exceeding $2.5 million from the nursing home.[33] The new PaCS survey system looks to residents of nursing homes for answers about the kind and quality of care they receive in the facilities. The 1987 reform laws continue and strengthen this initiative. The adoption of the new survey process represents a major victory for consumer advocates who have been recommending resident and consumer participation in the inspection process and the regulatory process for many years.[34]

Formal recognition of private involvement in public regulation is needed. Enforcement agencies should be required to
notify nursing-home residents and their families of proposed
actions that may affect them, such as changes in reimbursement
rates, revocation of licenses, or terminations of provider agreements. Residents and other interested persons also should be
able to participate in all proceedings affecting the home. The
form of this participation depends on the nature of the proposed
action and the type of proceeding. Special arrangements may be
needed so nursing-home residents can participate. For example, hearings may have to be held in the nursing home and
special notice procedures devised so that residents and concerned others will have a realistic opportunity to participate.

The Rights of Nursing-home Residents

Does a nursing-home resident have rights?

Absolutely. Although a nursing home can have reasonable
rules that residents must respect, you do not give up your legal
rights when you enter a nursing home. Thus you are free to
vote, marry, enter into contracts, practice your religion, complain, and see your friends just as you could before you entered
the nursing home. Because nursing homes may deny residents
important rights, however, many states and the federal government have issued rules designed to ensure that the rights of
nursing-home residents will be respected.[35] Be aware, however, that these provisions are only partially effective in secur-
ing the rights of nursing-home residents. This is so for several
reasons. The provisions frequently are vague and provide incomplete guidance to residents and staff. In some instances, the
provisions allow rights to be overridden if a doctor so orders.
Also, the provisions are incomplete—some rights important to
residents are not covered. Another problem with the provisions
is their failure to consider the fact that a large number of
nursing-home residents suffer disorientation and memory losses
that make it difficult for them to assert their rights or to
participate fully in decisions affecting their wellbeing. More
generally, enforcement is a problem. Who is to ensure that a
home and its staff respect the rights of residents and what
penalties are available where rights are not respected?[36]

The 1987 reform laws address these problems by strengthening the residents rights protections (reducing, for example, some ambiguities and exceptions noted below) and by enhancing the ability of the states to monitor nursing home compliance with these requirements and to punish noncomplying homes. Also included is a requirement that nurse's aides be trained to respect resident rights.

Do I have a right to personal liberty?

Yes. If you want to leave the nursing home, you are free to do so. Likewise, within the nursing home, the staff cannot lock you in your room, tie you to a bed or chair, or give you a drug to keep you quiet unless a doctor has specified in writing that you be restrained. Unless you have been declared legally incompetent by a court, it is illegal for the staff to prevent you from leaving the nursing home to take a walk, to shop, to visit friends, or simply to go home. They can advise you that you are not strong enough to leave, that you might get hit by a car or otherwise get hurt, and they can try to persuade you to stay. But they should not physically prevent you from leaving. This happened in Texas, when a resident who wanted to leave a nursing home was kept for nearly two months against his will. The resident was barred from using a phone and from having visitors; his clothes were taken away, and he was locked in his room. Several times he got out of the home, and each time he was dragged back. When finally he was able to get away, he filed a lawsuit against the home for false imprisonment and was awarded damages by a jury.[37]

Other ways nursing homes restrain residents is by physically tying them to a bed or chair or by giving them a strong sedative. These practices are permitted only when a doctor has issued a written order authorizing the use of a restraint for a specific, limited period or when a restraint is necessary to prevent a resident from injuring himself or others. The use of restraints except in these circumstances is outlawed by the federal residents' rights provisions for both SNFs and ICFs. In addition, many states have passed laws which further limit the use of restraints by requiring that a restrained resident be checked frequently to ensure that he or she is not injured. Nursing homes are rightly concerned about the safety of confused residents who may wander from the facility. Failure to supervise such residents properly can result in liability to the home if the resident is injured. Homes must respond to this problem in a sensitive manner, however, and cannot utilize restraints except as authorized by state and federal requirements.

Do I have a right of privacy?

Yes. Although moving into a nursing home entails some loss of privacy, you still are entitled to a substantial amount of privacy in a nursing home. You may visit privately with your doctor, your friends and relatives, your minister, your social worker, your lawyer, and others. Likewise you are entitled to send and receive your mail unopened (although the SNF residents' rights regulations permit your doctor to limit this right under certain circumstances), and you are entitled to use a telephone in privacy.[38] In addition, the nursing home cannot reveal any personal, medical, or financial information it has about you without your permission, except where a law expressly authorizes the release of this information (such as to the welfare department for the purpose of informing them that you are no longer ill enough to need nursing home care).[39] Another exception to this rule is that the nursing home can forward your medical records to a hospital to which you are being transferred. You also are entitled to privacy in dressing, bathing, and using the toilet.[40] You are entitled to keep a reasonable number of your personal possessions (books, pictures, chairs, etc.) in the nursing home.[41] Finally, if you are married, you are entitled to private visits with your spouse, and if both of you live in the home, you are entitled to share a room.[42] Thus, the use of bathroom facilities in private and the availability of a place to have private meetings and conversations are basic rights of institutionalized individuals. Denial of these rights can have severe emotional repercussions.

Do I have the right to speak freely?

Yes. Your right to private or public communications cannot be interfered with. The federal residents' rights provisions expressly protect your right to speak out on any issue, including your right to complain about the nursing home.[43] If you are unhappy with the food, the staff, the conditions, anything at all at the nursing home, you are entitled to complain about these conditions to other residents, your friends, the nursing home's owner or administrator, the government, the ombudsman, your congressional representative, the newspapers—in short, to anybody. The rights provisions prohibit a home from retaliating against you for complaining. Nevertheless, many nursing home residents and their families are reluctant to complain for fear of reprisal. Homes should see that this does not occur. The ombudsman, resident councils, and community groups can be helpful in assuring that this right is respected.

Do I have a right to worship?

Yes. Your right to worship is not affected by entering a nursing home. You are free to worship while in a nursing home, and a home cannot interfere with this right. The federal residents' bill of rights does, however, allow your doctor to prohibit your participation in religious activities if he or she believes you would be harmed medically by participating and if he or she notes this opinion in your medical record.[44] Likewise you are free to participate in the activities of social and community groups[45]

Do I have a right to information?

Yes. As a nursing-home resident, there are many things that you need information about—the cost of services, your medical condition, plans to transfer you to another facility, and the existence of your rights, to name just a few. You are entitled to this information. The federal residents' rights provisions clearly require that you be told what services are available in the facility and what the charges are.[46] Some state laws also require that you be given this information.[47]

The federal residents' rights provisions also entitle you to information about your medical condition and give you the right to participate in decisions about your treatment.[48] This right stems from other sources as well. A doctor, hospital, or nursing home must tell you what treatment you are receiving and must inform you of possible adverse consequences of the treatment. This is the doctrine of informed consent. No medical procedure can be performed on you unless you have agreed to the treatment. If the provider fails to tell you these things, he or she can be sued.

As mentioned earlier, you are entitled to see reports of nursing-home inspections, and you are entitled to know who owns the nursing home. This information can be obtained from the state health department.

Nursing-home residents are sometimes transferred to a hospital or to another nursing home. This happens for many reasons. A resident's medical condition may worsen, necessitating transfer to a hospital. Or his or her condition may improve, and if the resident's care is being paid by Medicare or Medicaid, he or she may be forced to go home or move to another facility where less intensive care is provided. Residents are also sometimes transferred from a facility that has lost its license or has been decertified for Medicare and Medicaid. Whatever the reason for the transfer, residents are justifiably upset and are frequently physically or mentally traumatized by being dislocated from the nursing home to which they have become accustomed. For this reason, the federal residents' rights provisions limit the reasons why a resident can be transferred and specify that you are entitled to "reasonable advance notice" of plans to transfer or discharge you from the nursing home.[49] These provisions also require that you be told of the existence and content of the rights provisions and require that you be notified of all the nursing home's rules. [50] OBRA of 1987 strengthens federal protection against transfers and improves residents rights to information.

Do I have a right to adequate treatment?

Yes. Federal regulations specify that an individualized plan of medical treatment be created for you and that it be adhered to.[51] Other regulations require that the nursing home be safe, clean, and adequately staffed, and that you be well fed.[52] It is your absolute right that all of these regulations be observed. You and your family should not hesitate to point out any deficiencies you observe.

Can I decline treatment?

Yes. Unless you have been declared legally incompetent, you cannot be forced to take any drug, accept any therapy, or submit to any treatment that you do not wish administered to you. If you have been declared incompetent, consent must be obtained from another legally authorized individual. The basis for this right is the doctrine of informed consent which requires that a resident's consent be obtained before treatment can proceed. In addition, the federal residents' rights provisions support your right to decline unwanted treatment, although the provisions are not forcefully worded.[53] The SNF regulations explicitly give you only the right to refuse to participate in experimental research, while the ICF regulations say you can decline all treatment. A nursing home or doctor can be sued for treating you after you indicated that you did not want the treatment.

Difficult medical choices often confront nursing-home residents and their families. What diagnostic tests should be used? What medications? Should the resident be transferred to a hospital? If the resident can no longer eat should artificial methods of supplying nutrients be used? If the resident suffers cardiopulmonary arrest, should CPR be employed? These choices are often made more difficult when a resident is not fully incompetent and his or her desires on particular matters unknown. The residents' rights provisions are inadequate to guide such difficult decision-making. A number of states have adopted living will provisions or similar measures to address these concerns, and litigation has been necessary to guide these decisions.

Do I have a right to see my doctor?

Yes. You can be admitted to a nursing home only if a doctor has determined that you need medical care in an institution. Once there, most aspects of your care must be reviewed and approved by a doctor. Federal regulations require that residents in SNFs be seen by a doctor every thirty days during their first ninety days in the facility and at least every sixty days thereafter, and SNFs are required to have a medical director who is a physician.[54] In ICFs, doctors are required to visit their patients every sixty days, but there is no requirement for a medical director.[55]

Although some doctors are very good about seeing their patients in nursing homes, others are not. And even though the federal regulations just mentioned are not exacting, many doctors do not comply even with these lax standards. Residents ignored by their doctors may suffer grave consequences. Their medical problems go undiagnosed and are treated by poorly trained staffs. As a result, it is not unusual for nursing-home residents to suffer severe bed sores, become malnourished and dehydrated, and to lose limbs to gangrene.

You have a right to be seen by a doctor whenever you need one, and it is the nursing home's responsibility to see that a doctor is provided when necessary.[56]

Do I have a right to control my money?

Yes. Unless you have been declared legally incompetent, you are free to continue to manage your finances while you are in a nursing home. If you have been declared incompetent, your guardian has this responsibility. Of course you may delegate management of your finances to a friend, relative, lawyer, or business advisor, but you do not have to do so. You also may give the nursing home authority to manage your finances. If you do, this delegation must be in writing and must conform to laws governing such matters. A nursing home must accept this responsibility, must keep meticulous records of its handling of your finances, and must give you an accounting four times each year.[57] Many states have more exacting requirements.

Nursing-home residents are entitled to a personal allowance for small expenditures. If you are paying for your care privately, a personal allowance should not be a problem. If you are under a guardian, the guardian should give you an allowance for your personal needs. If your care is being paid by Medicare, there is no requirement that you devote your income to the cost of your care. Thus, you are free to spend whatever you like on your personal needs. If your care is being paid by Medicaid, however, the situation is different. Medicaid residents are required to devote the bulk of their income from pensions, Social Security, etc., to pay the nursing home for its services. You are allowed to keep only thirty dollars a month for your personal needs.[58] Most states, however, supplement this federal benefit to increase the amount of the monthly allowance. This "personal needs allowance" is to be used to purchase such monthly personal items as clothing, gifts, snacks, reading materials, cigarettes, and postage and beautician services. Sometimes, however, residents have to use this money to buy medications even though in most instances Medicaid's payment to the facility should cover the cost of these medications.[59] As mentioned earlier, nursing homes do not always clearly indicate what services are and are not covered by the Medicaid payment, and thus residents' personal needs allowance accounts may be billed for items that should already have been paid. Such double billing is a felony and should be reported to your state or local Medicaid fraud and abuse unit.

One other problem in this area arises if you are a Social Security, SSI, or Veterans beneficiary whose check is being sent to a representative payee because the Social Security or Veterans Administration has concluded that you need assistance in handling your benefits. Frequently the representative payee is a relative or friend, but sometimes nursing homes are appointed representative payees for their residents. Although this arrangement is permitted by federal regulations, it should be avoided whenever possible since it presents a conflict of interest for the nursing home which is a creditor of the resident but expected, nevertheless, to manage the resident's funds on behalf of the resident.

What are my rights upon admission to a nursing home?

Admission to a nursing home is usually stressful. Rarely is a person admitted completely voluntarily. Admission may be from a hospital which has announced that it no longer will care for a patient or from home where a family no longer can care for a parent, spouse, or sibling. The prospective resident is often seriously ill and is frequently disoriented. Facilities should be sensitive to these circumstances. Federal residents' rights provisions require that a facility inform prospective residents of three matters—rates, rules, and rights. As mentioned earlier, facilities frequently fail to specify what charges are in their basic rate. Residents also are to be informed of the rules of the facility, and the facility is required to notify residents of their rights under federal law. Where the prospective resident has been adjudicated incompetent or is determined to be incapable of understanding her rights, the provisions specify that this information is to be given to the resident's guardian or family. While it is important for the facility to communicate with a resident's family, it should not exclude the resident from participating in decisions affecting her wellbeing even if the resident suffers some degree of mental impairment. Indeed, the facility should exercise caution in admitting a person in the absence of consent by the resident or her legal guardian. Similarly, a home should admit only those persons it can care for adequately.

OBRA of 1987 tightens the federal requirements concerning admission and also calls for screening of prospective nursing home residents for mental illness or mental retardation to assure that nursing home placement is appropriate. Some states have additional restrictions applicable to the admissions process.[60]

Admissions contracts used by many nursing homes contain

clauses that may be unlawful. Examples include requirements that a responsible party must cosign the contract or that residents must use certain services—such as pharmacy or laundry—as dictated by the facility; waivers of the nursing home's liability for the resident's health, safety, or personal possessions; provisions limiting a resident's right to apply for Medicaid; and the lack of the explicit statement of services covered under the basic Medicaid rate.[61]

A problem often arising when a person seeks admission to a nursing home is whether the person is eligible for Medicaid. Complex eligibility rules restricting the assets and income a Medicaid recipient can have may result in denial of an application for Medicaid. Married applicants face additional difficulties because Medicaid rules may so restrict the income available to the spouse who will not be institutionalized as to make it difficult for him or her to maintain a home. These issues are discussed in the Medicaid chapter.

Also remember that many facilities prefer private pay patients to Medicaid patients and easy-to-care-for patients to those with special needs. A number of steps are being taken to combat these problems.[62] If you encounter difficulty gaining admission to a nursing home, consult the ombudsman or one of the other resources listed later in this chapter.

Can I be required to turn my assets over to the nursing home?
Generally, no. Some nursing homes ask residents to enter into "life-care contracts" with the home, under which the home promises to care for the resident for the remainder of his or her life in exchange for the resident transferring all of his or her assets to the nursing home.

Be careful before signing any contract with a nursing home, particularly one requiring you to turn over your life savings. Check with the state health or welfare department to learn whether life-care contracts are allowed in your state, and have a lawyer review the contract. For example, the contract should have a probationary period during which you can change your mind and have your money and property returned; it should make the nursing home responsible for the cost of your care if you are hospitalized; and it should protect your interests if the nursing home gets into financial difficulties or loses its license.

Do I have a right to go home for visits?

Yes and no. You can leave a nursing home for any reason. Hence you are free to go home to visit friends or relatives on birthdays, holidays, and the like. The problem is that some nursing homes may refuse to readmit you after an overnight visit or after transfer to a hospital for medical care. If there is a waiting list, and often there is, the home may wish to fill your bed as soon as you vacate it.

Medicare and Medicaid have rules that discourage home visits. Under Medicare, nursing homes are paid only for services to residents needing skilled nursing services "on a daily basis."[63] It is the position of HHS that if you are well enough to go home for a visit, you do not need skilled nursing services "on a daily basis." Medicaid has a similar though less stringent rule. Under Medicaid, your bed may be paid for during home visits if your plan of care indicates that these visits are therapeutic.[64] This means that you must arrange in advance with the home and your doctor and, if they agree, you can go home for a visit. Even with such permission, such a home visit may not be possible because your state must have agreed to reimburse nursing homes for such visits. Many states do not include home visits as one of the items reimbursed under Medicaid.

OBRA of 1987 requires nursing homes to develop a "bed hold" policy specifying a Medicaid resident's rights to return to the nursing home following a home visit or hospital transfer. Homes are required to notify residents prior to transfer of this policy and of the state's policy concerning whether Medicaid payment is available for home visits or other temporary absences from a nursing home.

Can I be forced to leave a nursing home against my will?

It depends on the reason you are being asked to leave. The federal residents' rights provisions limit the situations in which a resident can be transferred or discharged from a nursing home against his or her wishes to the following: for medical reasons, for failure to pay the nursing home for its services, or for the resident's "welfare or that of other residents."[65] Discharges for other reasons are forbidden. In particular, a resident cannot be transferred or discharged for complaining about conditions in the home or for otherwise exercising his or her rights.[66] The residents' rights provisions also give residents the right to advance notice before any transfer or discharge.[67] A number of states have supplemented these protections by more specific protections against involuntary transfers.

OBRA of 1987 strengthens these requirements by clarifying and furthering limiting the reasons a resident can be transferred. OBRA also requires that, in most circumstances, notice of the reasons for transfer be supplied thirty days before the transfer is to occur, and requires the states to develop procedures under which residents can appeal proposed transfers.

Several situations involving transfers warrant special attention. One is the utilization-review program. The utilization-review program is a federal requirement that all residents admitted to the nursing home be medically in need of the care provided, that the nursing home be the appropriate level or site of care, and that a periodic review of each resident's need for continued stay in the nursing home be performed.[68] Under utilization review, residents who are found not to need nursing-home care can be forced to leave a nursing home although they would like to stay. Existing residents' rights provisions are not much help to a resident in this situation, and the resident may be forced to rely on other protections discussed later in this chapter.

The other special situation occurs when residents are forced to leave a nursing home that has lost its license or its certification for Medicare and Medicaid. Once again, existing residents' rights provisions are of little help, and residents in this situation must look elsewhere for assistance. The Supreme Court has ruled that nursing-home residents do not have a Constitutional right to notice and a hearing before the government decertifies their facility from participation in the Medicaid program. The Supreme Court decision, however, does not apply to transfers which are requested by facilities or required by circumstances other than decertification. Nursing-home residents whose nursing home is decertified may have a cause of action against the facility for failure to maintain its status as a certified a certified provider.[69] Again, however, many states have provisions designed to assure that residents are protected against abrupt and harmful transfers in this situation.

One other circumstance in which you may have to leave the nursing home against your will is when there is a strike by the nursing home's employees. When this occurs, special arrangements often are made to transfer the residents elsewhere for the duration of the strike. Since transfer often has a detrimental effect on the residents, every effort should be made to avoid this drastic step. Remember that the 1987 reform laws promise additional protections against involuntary transfers, so consult your ombudsman or a lawyer if you are threatened with an involuntary transfer.

Am I entitled to any procedural protections before I am transferred from a nursing home?

Yes. As mentioned earlier, federal regulations require that you be notified of plans to move you from the nursing home. The notice required by the federal rules is supplemented in many states by more stringent state requirements regarding notice. Until OBRA of 1987, federal nursing home regulations did not require a hearing prior to the transfer of a nursing-home resident, but in many states, a nursing-home resident could request a hearing prior to transfer. Effective October 1989, all states will be required to have an appeal process for transfer cases.

Federal Medicare and Medicaid rules offer some help. A common reason for moving residents from a home is a procedure called "utilization review," a cost-control device employed by both Medicare and Medicaid to determine whether a resident continues to need nursing-home care according to each program's criteria. Each nursing home is to have a utilization-review team for this purpose. The team reviews a resident's records and consults with the resident's doctor. If it is determined that the resident has recovered to the point that nursing-home care is no longer needed, the resident and his or her family are notified of this fact and are given a short time in which to make arrangements to transfer the resident elsewhere.[70]

Residents who have been threatened with or notified of a transfer from the nursing home because of an adverse-level-of-care determination can utilize Medicare and Medicaid procedural protections to contest erroneous level-of-care determinations. The Medicare chapter describes the protections available to SNF residents who wish to contest a determination that they no longer require skilled care. The Medicaid chapter outlines the "fair hearing" system available to Medicaid recipients. This system, which provides for notice and a hearing, is available to Medicaid recipients contesting level-of-care determinations.[71]

The level-of-care system has been criticized widely. Reformers have urged that the distinction between skilled and intermediate care be abolished and a single set of standards be adopted for all nursing homes.[72] These reforms were included in OBRA 1987, which abolishes the distinction between skilled and intermediate care, effective 1 October 1990.

How can I assert my rights?

There is no easy answer to this question. The answer depends, in part, on your state and on the nursing-home facility in which you reside. Some possible resources for assistance in asserting your rights are nursing-home resident councils, family councils, nursing-home resident advocacy groups, long-term care ombudsmen, state and local health and welfare departments, and Medicaid fraud and abuse units. Legal remedies may be pursued through legal services programs, your state attorney general, and private lawyers who may sue the nursing home for damages.

Every nursing home is obliged to have a system for the resolution of residents' complaints.[73] In some homes a formal structure has been established; in others the system is informal. Generally, the nursing-home administrator, social worker, or other employee has responsibility for hearing and resolving complaints. If you are uncertain to whom you should complain, speak to the administrator. In some chains, a regional or national office may have responsibility for complaint resolution. Many complaints can be resolved within the home. If you are dissatisfied with the initial resolution of your complaint, do not hesitate to seek further redress within the home or chain. Homes should have clearly established complaint systems. If yours does not, speak to the administrator and urge that a system be established. An idea some homes have adopted is the use of a residents' council to resolve complaints. Similar ideas are the establishment of a family or community council which can help resolve complaints.

You can also complain to the enforcement agency responsible for regulating nursing homes. The agency should send an inspector to investigate your complaint. If a violation is found, the home should be cited for the violation and ordered to correct the violation. Sanctions also may be imposed by the agency.

In some states, health and welfare departments are reluctant to respond to complaints, so be firm with them. Insist that they inform you of the action they intend to take on your complaint and then see that the action promised is carried out.

All states have long-term care ombudsman programs which are responsible for monitoring nursing homes. Although these programs lack the authority to impose sanctions against homes violating resident rights or other nursing home requirements, they can verify your complaint and work with the home to see that your complaint is resolved. They can also relay your complaint to the enforcement agency and insist that it resolve your complaint. Ombudsman programs offer tremendous potential for advancing the rights of nursing-home residents. The 1987 nursing-home reform laws strengthen the ability of state regulatory agencies and long-term care ombudsman programs to respond to complaints.

The department responsible for administering Medicaid (usually the state welfare department) can help with complaints relating to Medicaid. We have mentioned several Medicaid problems experienced frequently by nursing-home residents. If you have one of these problems, seek assistance from the state Medicaid agency.

A number of other groups and agencies involved in regulating or monitoring nursing homes are worth contacting as well. If your home is approved for Medicare, complain to the regional office of the Health Care Financing Administration of the United States Department of Health and Human Services, which has responsibility for seeing that participating nursing homes comply with all Medicare rules. Another agency with some responsibility is the state agency that licenses nursing-home administrators. If your nursing home has a bad administrator, you should inform the licensing agency of this fact. Although these agencies are often ineffectual—in part because they are frequently dominated by nursing-home administrators—it is still important to make them aware of bad administrators among their colleagues. Sometimes the congressional representative, state or local representative, or consumer protection agency in your area will intervene on your behalf.

Thus far we have concentrated on the government agencies

you can turn to for assistance. While you have a right to expect help from these agencies you should not have to rely exclusively on their help. Important private resources available in many areas are consumer groups interested in nursing-home reform. These groups have organized to campaign for nursing-home reform and are very effective in monitoring conditions in nursing homes and in keeping government agencies on their toes. A noteworthy example of such an organization is Citizens for Better Care (CBC), an advocacy organization in Michigan that sends volunteers to nursing homes to hear and resolve complaints and helps individuals select nursing homes. CBC also has sued successfully to obtain access to nursing-home inspection records, has forced the state health and welfare departments to adopt a number of reforms, has convinced the legislature to toughen nursing-home laws, and has published booklets on several important topics concerning nursing homes.

Because of the increasing degree of incapacity of nursing-home residents, it is even more critical that the community—in the form of a community council, a family council, the ombudsman program, or a citizens reform group—establish programs that emphasize a rigorous approach to the enforcement of residents' rights and the overseeing of the quality of life and care in every nursing home. Regular community oversight of a nursing home can have many positive effects. Concerned members of the public, including nursing-home residents and their families, can request voluntary correction, report conditions to enforcement agencies, bring lawsuits, serve on advisory committees, and emphasize the needs and interests of the residents to legislative and governmental bodies.

The nursing-home reform movement has grown dramatically in recent years and now includes individuals, groups, and organizations throughout the country. Important reforms have been achieved by these entities often working in collaboration with senior groups, consumers, and labor organizations, the nursing-home industry, enforcement agencies, legislators, and others interested in the wellbeing of nursing-home residents.[74] The 1987 nursing-home reform legislation was enacted as a result of the efforts of this coalition.

Can I sue a nursing home?

Yes. A nursing home, like a hospital, can be sued by residents who are injured by the home's failure to provide adequate care. Suits can be brought, for example, by a resident who is injured when an employee of the home is careless or abusive or when the resident's requests for assistance are ignored. The nursing home as well as the employee responsible for the injury may be liable in these situations.

In determining whether a nursing home is liable for injuries, a court will consider the resident's age and his or her physical and mental condition. Because of the frailty of many nursing-home residents, most courts have emphasized that nursing homes must be especially careful in treating their residents. The state and federal standards governing nursing homes can be very useful in suits of this kind because a home's failure to comply with these standards can be used to help establish that the home was negligent.

Personal injury and tort actions are becoming more frequent in the nursing-home area.[75] Because most nursing-home residents are quite old, damage awards in nursing-home cases have in the past tended to be smaller than awards in cases involving younger persons. More recently, however, significant damage awards have been obtained in cases involving older persons, often in response to claims of mental and emotional anguish and pain and suffering. Punitive damages can be awarded where it can be established that the home was especially blameworthy, as in the Texas case involving the resident locked up by a nursing-home staff for two months.

Suits also can be filed against a nursing home that fails to provide the services it promised or whose services or facilities do not meet state and federal standards, as well as against a nursing home whose charges exceed those permitted by law. In other areas, such as housing, there have been a number of successful suits of this kind. Nursing-home residents should follow the lead of tenants, filing suits to establish not only that nursing homes must be maintained in compliance with state and federal regulations but also to establish that nursing-home residents may withhold payment when a nursing home does not meet these standards. In addition, nursing-home residents sued by a home for failing to pay for the home's services could use the home's failure to comply with these standards as a defense of nonpayment. Suits also may be filed against health and welfare departments to force them to do their jobs. Approximately twenty states have in some form included the residents' private right to sue explicitly in their nursing-home laws. Residents in other states should press for this important reform.[76]

What should I look for in selecting a nursing home?

The first thing to determine before entering a nursing home is whether you really need a nursing home. Many persons enter nursing homes without thoroughly considering alternatives, such as staying at home and arranging for visiting nurses, housekeepers, etc. or moving to a senior citizens' housing development. It is often difficult to find information about alternatives to nursing-home care, but you should be persistent. Your local, state, or area agency on aging might be helpful. Choose a nursing home only if you need the medical services provided there and are unable to obtain them elsewhere.

As you consider a nursing home, you should learn as much as you can about it from as many sources as possible, including the staff, state or local officials, the long-term care ombudsman, private consumer groups, and the home's residents and their families. You should investigate the physical and sanitary condition of the home, including its fire-safety policies and history. You should find out exactly how much "living space" each resident is entitled to and the kinds of furnishings provided for each resident (without a locked storage area, a private closet, or a bedstand, misplaced or stolen articles may be a problem). You should critically evaluate the quality of life in the home in terms of the nature and number of activities provided for residents and the attitude of the staff toward residents. Location of the nursing home is an important factor — its distance from your family and friends and nearness to civic, cultural, and religious events. Some nursing homes have special rules and do not allow any smoking or drinking of alcoholic beverages by residents. The policy on visitors and visiting hours also should be checked. Consider the cost. What are the charges? Does the home accept Medicare and Medicaid?

No person should enter a nursing home before checking with state and local officials as to whether the facility complies with all applicable laws. You should learn the result of the home's most recent inspection, inquire whether the home has ever been found out of compliance, and the results of any investigation of the home's fiscal policies.

These are just a few of the things you should consider in choosing a nursing home. More detailed suggestions are available in these booklets published by the following organizations: the DHHS, *Nursing Home Care*; Citizens for Better Care, *How to Choose a Nursing Home*; the American Health Care Association, *Thinking About A Nursing Home?*.[77]

Are there alternatives to nursing homes?

Some, but not enough. Programs providing services to older persons—such as meals, transportation, and recreation—are available, as are housing projects for older persons. These programs are beneficial since they enable many older persons to remain in the community.

Most persons receiving long-term care live at home. There is tremendous current interest in exploring how to finance and deliver long-term-care services outside of institutional settings. In recent years, the number of agencies supplying home health services has grown dramatically. At their best, home health services are splendid—high quality care is delivered to a person in his own home at a reasonable cost. Often, however, home health services are chaotic and costly. We are in the early stages of determining what role home health should play in the delivery of long-term care and how we can regulate the quality of such services and deliver them at reasonable cost.[78]

Medicare and Medicaid pay for at least some home health services although as detailed in the Medicare chapter, public reimbursement for home health services is not widely available. Many states are conducting experiments in supplying home health services to Medicaid recipients. Many of these programs include a prescreening mechanism which assesses a person's need for nursing-home care. At best, such programs can help determine what services are needed, thereby avoiding unnecessary institutionalization. At worst, they can result in the denial of needed services.

The expansion of alternatives to nursing-home care is a vital step in the process of improving conditions in nursing homes. Every possible effort should be made to develop these alternatives.

NOTES

1. 42 C.F.R. § 405.1124 (1986).
2. 42 C.F.R. § 440.150(a)(1) (1986).
3. 42 C.F.R. § 442.339(a) (1986).
4. Omnibus Budget Reconciliation Act of 1987, Pub. L. No. 100-203 (1987) [OBRA of 1987].
5. National Center for Health Statistics; *Use of Nursing Homes by the Elderly, Data from the 1985 National Nursing Home Survey.* DDHS Pub. No. (PHS) 87-1250; Inst. of Medicine, *Improving the Quality of Care in Nursing Homes,* (1986) [IoM].
6. IoM, *supra* note 5, at 9.
7. *See generally* B. Vladeck, *Unloving Care: The Nursing Home Tragedy* (1980).
8. 42 C.F.R. § 420.206 (1986).
9. N.Y. Pub. Health Law § 2801-a (McKinney 1985).
10. *Id.*
11. Subcommittee on Health and Long-term Care of the U.S. House of Representatives Select Committee on Aging, "Rights of the Institutionalized Elderly: Lost in Confinement," Briefing Report, 99th Cong., 1st Sess. 1985. [Briefing Report]
12. *Id.*
13. 10 N.Y.C.R.R., 730.2
14. *See, e.g.,* Nemore, "Illegal Terms in Nursing Home Admissions Contracts," 18 *Clearinghouse Rev.* 1165 (1985); Ambrogi & Leonard, "New Study Focuses on Impact of Admission Agreements on Autonomy of Nursing Home Residents," BIFOCAL (ABA Commission on Legal Problems of the Elderly) (Spring 1987) at 1.
15. 42 U.S.C. § 1395cc(a) (1982); 42 U.S.C. § 1396h(d) (1982).
16. *See generally* Edelman, "Discrimination by Nursing Homes Against Medicaid Recipients: Improving Access to Institutional Long-term Care for Poor People," 20 *Clearinghouse Rev.* 330 (1986).
17. *Consumer Statement of Principles for the Nursing Home Regulatory System-State Licensure and Federal Certification Programs* (National Citizens Coalition for Nursing Homes Reform 1983).
18. Briefing Report, *supra* note 11, at ii.
19. *See generally* Brown, "An Appraisal of the Nursing Home Enforcement Process," 17 *Ariz. L. Rev.* 304 (1975).
20. IoM, *supra* note 5, at 1–44.
21. OBRA of 1987, *supra* note 4; Older Americans Act Amendments of 1987, Pub. L. No. 100-175 (1987); N.Y. Times, January 17, 1988 at 1, col. 1.
22. Beyer, Bulkley, Hopkins, "A Model Act Regulating Board and Care

Homes: Guidelines for States," 8 *Mental and Physical Disability L. Rep.* 150 (1984).

23. Butler, "Assuring the Quality of Care and Life in Nursing Homes: the Dilemma of Enforcement," 57 *N.C.L. Rev.* 1317 (1979).

24. PaCS: IoM, *supra* note 5, at 130; "Fast Track Termination," *Quality Care Advocate* (May/June 1986) at 9.

25. 42 U.S.C. § 3027(a)(12) (1982), as amended by Pub. L. No. 100-175, § 129 (1987).

26. *See* Butler, *supra* note 23, at 1378.

27. J. Borup, "The Effects of Varying Degrees of Interinstitutional Environmental Change on Long Term Care Patients," 22 *The Gerontologist* 409 (1982).

28. *See generally* Brown, *supra* note 19; IoM *supra* note 5; Butler, *supra* note 23; ABA Commission on Legal Problems of the Elderly, *Model Recommendations: Intermediate Sanctions for Enforcement of Quality of Care in Nursing Homes* (1981); Jost, "Enforcement of Quality Nursing Home Care in the Legal System," 13 *Law, Medicine and Health Care* 160 (1985); Johnson, "State Regulation of Long-term Care: A Decade of Experience with Intermediate Sanctions," 13 *Law, Medicine and Health Care* 173 (1985).

29. Grad, "Upgrading Health Facilities: Medical Receiverships as an Alternative to License Revocation," 42 *U. Colo. L. Rev.* 419 (1971); Johnson, "Nursing Home Receiverships: Design and Implementation," 24 *St. Louis U.L.J.* 681 (1981).

30. 51 Fed. Reg. 24484 (July 3, 1986); Quality Care Advocate (July/Aug. 1986) at 1.

31. Holahan, "Nursing Home Reimbursement: Implications for Cost Containment, Access and Quality" (Urban Institute 1985).

32. National Citizens' Coalition for Nursing Home Reform, *Advocacy for Quality Nursing Home Care* (1986).

33. *Estate of Smith v. Heckler*, 747 F.2d 583 (10th Cir. 1984); 52 Fed. Reg. 24752 (July 1, 1987); Quality Care Advocate (Jan./Feb. 1987) at 2.

34. *Consumer Statement of Principles, supra* note 17 at 3.

35. 42 C.F.R. § 405.1121(k) (1986); 42 C.F.R. § 442.311 (1986); *see generally* Brown, "Nursing Home Residents' Rights: An Overview and Brief Assessment" in *Legal and Ethical Aspects of Health Care for the Elderly* (1985).

36. Brown, *supra* note 35, at 158.

37. *Big Town Nursing Home, Inc. v. Newman*, 461 S.W.2d 195 (Tex. Civ. App. 1970).

38. 42 C.F.R. § 405.1121(k)(11) (1986); 42 C.F.R. § 442.311(i)(1)(2) (1986).

39. 42 C.F.R. § 405.1121(k)(8) (1986); 42 C.F.R. § 442.311(g)(4) (1986).

40. 42 C.F.R. § 405.1121(k)(9) (1986); 42 C.F.R. § 442.311(g)(2) (1986).
41. 42 C.F.R. § 405.1121(k)(13) (1986); 42 C.F.R. § 442.311(k) (1986).
42. 42 C.F.R. § 405.1121(k)(14) (1986); 42 C.F.R. §§ 442.311(g)(5)(6) (1986).
43. 42 C.F.R. § 405.1121(k)(5) (1986); 42 C.F.R. § 442.311(d)(2) (1986).
44. 42 C.F.R. § 405.1121(k)(12) (1986).
45. 42 C.F.R. § 405.1121(k)(12) (1986); 42 C.F.R. § 442.311(j) (1986).
46. 42 C.F.R. § 405.1121(k)(2) (1986); 42. C.F.R. § 442.311(a)(4) (1986).
47. *E.g.*, 10 N.Y.C.R.R. § 730.2.
48. 42 C.F.R. § 405.1121(k)(3) (1986); 42 C.F.R. § 442.311(b) (1986).
49. 42 C.F.R. § 405.1121(k)(4) (1986); 42 C.F.R. §§ 442.307,311(c) (1986).
50. 42 C.F.R. § 405.1121(k)(1) (1986); 42 C.F.R. § 442.311(a)(1) (1986).
51. 42 C.F.R. § 405.1123(b) (1986); 42 C.F.R. § 442.319(b) (1986).
52. 42 C.F.R. §§ 405.1134, .1124, and .1125 (1986); 42 C.F.R. §§ 442.315, .340 (1986).
53. 42 C.F.R. § 405.1121(k)(3) (1986); 42 C.F.R. § 442.311(b)(1)(iii) (1986).
54. 42 C.F.R. § 405.1123(b) (1986).
55. 42 C.F.R. § 442.346(b) (1986).
56. 42 C.F.R. § 405.1123(b) (1986); 42 C.F.R. § 442.346(a) (1986).
57. 42 C.F.R. § 405.1121(k)(6) (1986); 42 C.F.R. § 442.311(e) (1986).
58. 42 U.S.C. § 1382(e)(1)(B) as amended by P.L. 100-203, § 9119 (Dec. 22, 1987); and by P.L. 100-360 § 411(n)(3) (July 1, 1988), amending P.L. 100-203 § 9119.
59. *See* The Nursing Home Law Letter, Issue No. 90, Mar. 25, 1985; Issue No. 91, Mar. 26, 1985; and Issue No. 93, Apr. 11, 1985, National Senior Citizens Law Center, Washington, D.C.
60. *See generally* Brown, "Contract Rights and Rights Related to Admission, Transfer and Discharge," *American Health Care Ass'n. J.* (May 1985), at 17.
61. *Supra* note 14.
62. *Supra* note 16.
63. 42 C.F.R. § 409.31(b) (1986).
64. 42 C.F.R. § 447.40(a)(1) (1986).
65. 42 C.F.R. § 405.1121(k)(4) (1986); 42 C.F.R. § 442.311(c) (1986).
66. 42 C.F.R. § 405.1121(k)(5) (1986); 42 C.F.R. § 442.311(d)(2) (1986).
67. 42 C.F.R. § 405.1121(k)(4) (1986); 42 C.F.R. § 442.307(b)(1) (1986).
68. 42 C.F.R. § 405.1137 (1986).
69. *O'Bannon v. Town Court Nursing Center, Inc.*, 447 U.S. 773 (1980).
70. 42 C.F.R. § 405.1137(e)(2) (1986); 42 C.F.R. § 442.307(b)(1) (1986).
71. *See* The Nursing Home Law Letter, Issue No. 77, Oct. 1983; Issue No. 78, Nov. 1983; and Issue No. 79, Dec. 1983, Nat'l. Senior Citizens Law Center, Washington, D.C.; *see, e.g., Blum v. Yaretsky*, 457 U.S. 991 (1982).
72. IoM, *supra* note 5, at 71.

73. 42 C.F.R. § 405.1121(k) (1986); 42 C.F.R. § 442.309 (1986).

74. *See generally Advocacy for Quality Nursing Home Care, supra* note 32.

75. *See generally* Nemore, "Protecting Nursing Home Residents," *Trial* (Dec. 1985) at 54; S. Johnson, N. Terry, and M. Wolff, *Nursing Homes and the Law: State Regulations and Private Litigation* (1985) [*Nursing Homes and the Law*].

76. *See, e.g.*, N.Y. Pub. Health Law § 2801-d (McKinney 1985); *See generally Nursing Homes and the Law, supra* note 75.

77. To obtain the booklets, write: U.S. Dep't. of Health and Human Services, 330 Independence Ave., S.W., Washington, D.C. 20201; American Health Care Ass'n., 1200 15th St., N.W., Washington, D.C. 20005; Citizens for Better Care, 1553 Woodward Ave., Suite 525 Detroit, Mich. 48226.

78. *See generally* Chairman of House Select Committee on Aging, 99th Cong., 2d Sess., The Black Box of Home Care Quality (Comm. Print 1986).

PART THREE

The Right to Freedom from Restraints on Life, Liberty, and Property

10

Guardianship and Civil Commitment

In the first edition of this book, this chapter began with the story of Catherine Lake, an older woman who was forgetful, who occasionally wandered from her residence, and who as a result of this behavior—though it posed no danger to herself or to others—was compelled by a court to spend her remaining years in a Washington D.C. mental hospital. At the time, her story was not uncommon. She was one of many elderly people sent against their will to mental hospitals, often large, uncaring, and inhumane facilities. In Ms. Lake's case, her involuntary relocation to a government-run psychiatric hospital, her "civil commitment," was based on hospital psychiatrists' having diagnosed her as suffering from "senile brain disease," an imprecise and questionable determination probably meant to encompass such symptoms as memory loss, depression, and disorientation, the underlying causes for which can include such treatable physical factors as malnutrition, infections, and heart disease.

Today, in most states, it is unlikely that Ms. Lake's story would be repeated. There has been a clear trend away from using large government-run mental hospitals to care for the elderly. Laws that once allowed commitment of older people on the basis of a diagnosis such as "senile brain disease" have been changed and now generally require a court determination that the person to be committed is both mentally ill and poses a danger to self or to others because of the illness. Today's commitment laws may even provide extra safeguards to ensure that older persons are not inappropriately committed, as does Michigan's law which specifies that age alone is not a basis for commitment and which requires special testing of all persons over age 65 made subject to commitment proceedings.[1] Additionally, the legal doctrine of the least restrictive or drastic alternative requires that psychiatric hospitalization be considered only after other residential placements have been found insufficient.

This change, however, does not mean that the elderly are no longer at risk of losing their rights to decide how they will live. Other legal procedures still are used to take away a person's right to control his own life. All states have laws allowing a court to remove either or both the personal or financial decision-making rights of a person found to be "incompetent" or "incapacitated."

We know that people, even those without mental or physical limitations, possess differing abilities and have differing needs. Sometimes physical or mental impairments leave people totally unable to manage their personal or financial affairs, as for example a person in a coma. Sometimes impairments affect only part of a person's ability to care for himself. A person with quadriplegia may be unable to care for himself physically but can direct others in providing his care. Some impairments are temporary, such as the mental confusion that may occur as a side effect of medication, while some impairments seem to be permanent, such as the progressive physical and mental deterioration associated with Alzheimer's Disease. Most impairments pose harm only to their victim, who will suffer the effects of not being able to provide for his needs. Some impairments, however, are alleged to pose a risk of harm to others, such as a patient with schizophrenia whom psychiatrists may believe to be nearly certain to physically assault another. In short, there are a variety of physical and mental conditions which may affect, to varying degrees, for a limited or lasting amount of time, a person's ability to prevent harm to himself or to restrain himself from harming others.

When such conditions exist, and a person no longer can manage to prevent harm to herself or to others, the question is whether, and at what point, the legal system ought to intervene. The means by which legal intervention may be sought, broadly referred to as "protective proceedings," include such processes as guardianship, conservatorship, and civil commitment. These procedures seek to prevent harm from occurring to an impaired person by legally removing, to one extent or other, the impaired person's right to make decisions on her own behalf and appointing a surrogate to make decisions in her place. To appreciate the impact of this, some understanding of what "decision making" entails is needed.

Life presents each of us with a constant succession of choices requiring decisions. Most are minor, such as deciding what to wear in the morning, what newspaper to read, or whether to order fish or fowl in a restaurant. Some are major, such as whether to marry, or whether, near the end of one's life, to move from one's home into a nursing home, or to undergo painful chemotherapy to fight a terminal cancer. All these decisions, for the purpose of understanding protective proceedings, can be placed into two categories: those that affect financial interests and all others. These latter decisions are considered personal decisions. Financial matters that may be acted on can range from buying a candy bar in a vending machine, to giving a gift to a favorite niece, to selling one's home to pay for medical care or a college education. Personal matters that may be acted on range from deciding what book to read or television show to watch to deciding where to live, with whom to associate, or whether to have an organ transplant.

When a person loses part or all of the ability to make decisions, it may become necessary for someone else to have the legal authority to act on his or her behalf. If the impaired person had, at an earlier time, entered into an arrangement (such as a power of attorney or a multiple-party bank account) that would allow another person to act on his behalf, further legal intervention may not be required. If not, however, a protective proceeding may need to be sought. The consequence of such an action is that the impaired person's right to make independent decisions is diminished or eliminated. The right to make decisions is turned over to the guardian or conservator.

Whether losing one's right to make decisions and having to abide by the decisions of another is unfair or unjust depends on the circumstances. It may not be a great loss to a person in a coma, who is unable to participate in any decisionmaking and is unaware of any loss of control, to have his choices made by a guardian. It is a good deal less clear what the impact is of making a mentally ill person who makes "not very good" financial choices subject to a style of life dictated by the financial decisions of a court-appointed conservator, on the presumption that the conservator's decisions will better protect the person's assets. A person who is not mentally ill but who makes the same "not very good" financial decisions could not be subjected involuntarily to such control. Furthermore, the actual outcome of a decision is never certain. All decisions entail a certain amount of risk; well-thought-out plans often fail, and ill-advised schemes often succeed. There is, in addition, the question of values. What is best for an individual may not be the safest and most long-lasting life, but may include the chance to do what that individual believes is best and most important.

Guardians and conservators are often ignorant of, or fail to heed, the concerns and wishes of their wards. Protective proceedings often give little weight to these concerns. These proceedings seem unable to accommodate the differing natures and degrees of impairments and may not recognize that an impairment which affects one area of a person's ability to care for himself may not affect other areas. The result is that the law, in seeking to "help," sometimes takes away rights from those who are merely "different" and not disabled and often fails to respond appropriately to those who need some, but not complete, help.

What is the justification for government intervention into our lives?

A general rule of our legal system is that people are allowed to exercise self-determination; people have both the right and responsibility to make their own decisions about how they will live, on what they will spend their money, and how they will spend their days. For the most part, people are free to think, speak, and do as they please without interference from our government. Yet there are limits. Laws limit our freedom by prohibiting us from injuring others or from harming their property. The legal authority for such laws is the "police power" of the state. This power authorizes the state to proscribe activities which are dangerous to others in order to protect society. A person convicted of violating such laws may, for the protection of society, be deprived of his or her freedom. The loss of liberty suffered by persons "civilly committed," or confined involuntarily in state mental hospitals, is justified in part by the police power, inasmuch as such persons are thought to be dangerous to others. Another limitation on individual freedom is the power of the state to protect individuals incapacitated by disease or other causes who consequently cannot care for themselves, their dependents, or their property. This power is called *parens patriae*, or "parentage of the state." Unlike police power, which is aimed at protecting others, this power focuses on the incapacitated individual and declares that the state has the responsibility of protecting those who cannot protect themselves. Under the *parens patriae* power, the state has the authority to determine when a person cannot care for him- or herself adequately and has the authority to appoint another person, usually called a guardian or conservator, to provide such care.

Because the exercise of police power entails a great loss of liberty (for example, confinement to a prison), procedural protections have long been established to ensure that a person involved in a criminal proceeding is not mistakenly imprisoned or penalized. Examples of these protections are rights to a lawyer, against self-incrimination, to trial by jury, and to cross-examination of witnesses. Unfortunately, not all of these procedural safeguards are provided to persons threatened with such protective proceedings as civil commitment, guardianship, or conservatorship. The reason is that protective proceedings are, for the most part, theoretically founded on the idea that the intervention will benefit the person, in effect "protect" him from himself. Such benevolent proceedings may be felt to pose no real loss of liberty or harm to a person unable to exercise such rights independently. However, in practice, these proceedings are often brought against persons at least partially if not fully able to exercise their rights and for reasons far from benevolent. The resulting genuine deprivations of liberty and property that occur, such as loss of control of one's finances or confinement in an institution such as a psychiatric facility or nursing home, suggest there is no justification for failing to offer procedural and substantive safeguards in protective proceedings. Lawmakers should ensure that the most appropriate and least restrictive processes available are used in seeking intervention in an individual's life.

What are "incompetence" and "incapacity"?

"Incompetence," as a legal term, is a conclusion that a person is unable to care for himself or his property. This determination is made during a court hearing and is used as the basis for the appointment of a guardian or conservator. A term with somewhat similar meaning, "incapacity," is commonly used in more recent protective proceedings statutes,[2] again acting as the trigger for appointment of a guardian or conservator in a court proceeding. While a person may be described by others as being "functionally" incompetent to manage his affairs or diagnosed by medical personnel as being "clinically incompetent" to decide his medical treatment, all adults are presumed under the law to be legally competent, and their status and rights as competent individuals remain until a court hearing is held and a determination on the issue is made.

Most protective proceedings statutes require that two things be proven before a person can be declared incompetent or incapacitated and placed under a guardian or conservator (or both). First, it must be proved the person has a particular physical or mental condition. Second, it must be proved as a result of this condition, the person is unable to manage his personal or financial affairs. A typical example is the Colorado statute, based on the Uniform Probate Code and similar or identical to statutes in a number of states.[3]

> The term "incapacitated person" shall mean any person who is impaired by reason of mental illness, mental deficiency, physical illness or disability, advanced age . . . or other cause to the extent that he or she lacks sufficient understanding or capacity to make or communicate responsible decisions concerning his person.[4]

What is the relationship between incompetence or incapacity, mental illness, and insanity?

Like "incompetence" or "incapacity," "mental illness" and "insanity" as legal terms have no exact medical meaning. Generally speaking, the term "mental illness" is used principally in connection with statutes defining who may be committed to a mental institution involuntarily; the term "insanity" is used principally in conjunction with criminal cases in which a person accused of committing a crime asserts that she should not be convicted because she was "insane" at the time the crime was committed and therefore did not understand what she was doing or that what she did was wrong.

What is a guardian?

Broadly speaking, a guardian is a person appointed by a court to make decisions for an impaired person, usually referred to as a "ward" or a "legally incapacitated person," whom the court has found to be incapable of making reasoned decisions on his or her own. Guardians were once commonly granted both personal and financial powers over a person, but the present trend is for states to regulate "personal" and "financial" decisionmaking under two separate but similar processes. We will follow this trend and discuss "guardian" as a person appointed by a court to make personal decisions for an impaired person and "conservator" as a person appointed by a court to make financial decisions for an impaired person.

The state's authority to appoint a guardian is based on its *parens patriae* power. This power is granted by the state to a particular court—generally called the probate court but known in some states as the county court, chancery court, circuit court, surrogate's court, or superior court. When the court makes a finding that a person brought before it cannot make personal decisions, it has the authority to appoint a guardian to make decisions on his behalf. These decisions are to be made so as to promote the ward's welfare, even against the ward's expressed wishes.

Every state has laws establishing when, how, and why a guardian can be appointed, declaring who can be a guardian, and listing the powers and responsibilities of guardians. State laws vary greatly on these matters. In some states, guardians have total control of their ward's personal decisionmaking. In these states, a guardian who is also appointed as conservator, or a guardian in a state combining both personal and financial decisionmaking in one legal proceeding, has "plenary" or complete control over the ward's life. In other states, guardians' powers may be more limited. Some state laws put restrictions on all guardianships, requiring guardians to seek prior court approval before taking certain actions, such as authorizing sterilization of a ward or placing a ward into an institutional setting.[5] Most states allow the granting of a "limited" or partial guardianship as an alternative to a full guardianship.[6] In these states, a limited guardian's powers may be restricted to certain areas of a ward's personal decisionmaking, such as deciding where a ward should live or consenting to medical care on the ward's behalf. The advantage of such statutes is that they allow the greatest amount of flexibility for restricting only those needs a ward can no longer provide for, while allowing her the use of her remaining abilities. Unfortunately, the statistics indicate that limited guardians are rarely appointed by the courts. Numerous reasons are given, but generally, it is easier for a court to grant a plenary guardianship than to make specific findings about the ward's disability and draw up a guardianship order granting only those powers. A recent conference of judges, however, took issue with this practice, noting that "courts should always consider and utilize limited guardianships as an adjunct of the application of the least restrictive alternative principle, either under existing statutory authority or under the court's inherent power."[7]

In an effort to bring some uniformity to the guardianship process, several model statutes have been proposed. The two most influential model statutes, the Uniform Probate Code (UPC), and the Uniform Guardianship and Protective Proceedings Act (UGPPA), an extension of article 5 of the UPC, provide for the separate regulation of personal and financial decision-making, provide improved due process protections to persons subjected to guardianship proceedings, provide for the imposition of limits upon the powers granted to a guardian, and may help make more uniform the often confusing if not contradictory language of protective proceedings.

What is a conservator?
A conservator is a person appointed by a court to make financial decisions for an impaired person, often referred to as a "ward" or a "protected person," whom the court has found to be incapable of making reasoned decisions independently. A state's authority to appoint a conservator is based on its *parens patriae* power, which is delegated to its probate court. All states provide for the appointment of someone to manage the finances of an impaired person. In a number of states, a conservator is sought in a separate probate proceedings, distinct from a guardianship procedure but under very similar standards and procedures.[8] In the remaining states, the appointment of a guardian automatically ensures that both the financial and the personal decision-making will be undertaken by the guardian. Conservators typically have more specific duties and powers than do guardians.[9] The conservator must be able to show to the court and to the ward how he is managing the ward's affairs by presenting initially an "inventory" of the property he has been able to locate belonging to the ward and thereafter filing annual "accountings" showing the income and expenses of the ward.

Being placed under a conservator does not impair a ward's legal right to make personal decisions, such as voting, marrying, or deciding where to live or whether to receive medical treatment. In this sense, conservatorships are much less restrictive than plenary guardianships. Conservatorship laws as a result may provide somewhat lessened due process rights than do guardianship statutes.[10]

Although a ward retains the right to make personal decisions, a conservator's control over the ward's money may give the conservator a great deal of control over how the ward will live. A ward's only access to spending money is through the conservator. If a ward wants to change her residence, she as a practical matter will be unable to do so unless the conservator agrees to pay the rent or mortgage at the new residence.

Who can be appointed guardian or conservator?

There are few limitations on who can be appointed guardian or conservator. As a general rule, any adult who has the apparent ability and is not clearly antagonistic to the interests of the ward may be appointed. In most states, institutions such as banks, social service agencies, and trust companies may be appointed as well as individuals.

In deciding who should be appointed, the UGPPA, UPC, and a number of states provide a priority list of persons who could be appointed. Usually, the list gives preference to the ward's spouse, child, grandchild, or other next of kin.[11] Many states allow the ward to indicate her own choice, either personally (if the ward is currently able) or by a document (if the ward anticipated the possibility of incapacity and recorded her choice) such as a will, power of attorney, or similar provision.[12] Statutes allowing the ward to choose his guardian or conservator may provide that the ward's determination is to be honored unless unreasonable.[13] In states without priority statutes, there is a strong preference for the appointment of the closest relative or friend.[14]

Often, however, the problem is not in deciding which of several persons vying for the right to be guardian or conservator ought to be appointed, but in finding any individual or institution with appropriate skills willing to serve in this capacity. Financial institutions such as banks or trust companies most often are appointed when there are substantial assets to be managed, and there is need for expertise in financial planning and management. A "public guardian" agency is likely to be appointed when an incapacitated person does not have any relatives or friends willing or able to serve. A public guardian organization may be operated by the court, a social service agency, a for-profit or nonprofit agency, or an independent state agency. Many states currently allow the appointment of a public guardian.[15]

All states grant the judge authority to refuse to appoint a person who has priority or who has volunteered to serve as guardian or conservator if such person is not suitable or qualified. In exercising this discretion, the judge's primary concern is the "best interest" of the ward. A judge may invoke this power if a conflict of interest exists between the proposed guardian or conservator and the ward.[16] An example is the administrator of a nursing home seeking to be appointed either as guardian or conservator for a resident of the facility. Clearly, the administrator would have difficulty protecting the ward's interests, which might dictate leaving the home for a less restrictive or expensive setting, while also being responsible for maintaining a full and profitable nursing home operation.[17] Such potential conflicts of interest may prohibit guardianship or conservatorship by service or health-care providers according to other parts of a state's law, for example a state's public health or licensing statutes.[18]

It seems likely that state agencies serving as public guardians face similar conflicts when they are responsible for delivering care and service to the ward. Additionally, there can be potential conflicts in interest for a close relative, who as guardian or conservator is responsible for providing the ward the best care possible but who—as an heir or beneficiary under the ward's will—stands to receive (as will perhaps other members of her family) the ward's unspent assets upon the ward's death. The other side of the coin, of course, is that a stranger with no conflicting interests is also likely to have no love or knowledge of the ward. Statutory restrictions on a guardian's or conservator's authority and periodic review of his or her acts are intended to reduce or eliminate these concerns.

What are a guardian or conservator's powers and duties?

The powers of guardians and conservators are derived from state statute. In general, the guardian has authority for the care, custody, and control of the ward. Statutes, including the UPC, often describe these powers with broad, all-encompassing language, such as giving the guardian the same power over a ward that a parent has over an unmarried minor child.[19] There may be further statutory definition allowing or requiring the guardian to be responsible for deciding where the ward will live, ensuring the ward has proper clothing, food, housing, and medical care, or seeing that the personal needs of the ward are met. While these powers may seem unrestricted, there usually are some limitations. The authority to consent to truly invasive treatment and/or personal decisions may be reserved for court determination by statute. These might include authority to consent to sterilization, abortion, withdrawal of life-sustaining medical treatment, and removal of a bodily organ, or organ transplant.[20] Most if not all states also prohibit the guardian from placing a ward in a mental institution unless a separate civil commitment proceeding is held, and the ward is found to meet commitment standards.[21]

Most state statutes, including the uniform laws, do not require any kind of periodic review of a guardian's actions regarding personal decisions. Once appointed and unless the ward or a third party takes the affirmative step of seeking court review, a guardian generally has a free hand in determining what is appropriate with respect to the ward's life. A few states—and it is hoped more will follow—require some periodic review of guardianships. Florida, for example, requires that an annual report be filed noting the ward's residence, physical and mental health, and social condition and providing the names of treating physicians and the reasons why the guardianship should be continued.[22]

State statutes are generally more detailed in terms of the powers of a conservator. A conservator is responsible for managing all the ward's property, finances, and business affairs. The conservator receives the ward's income and determines how much of the estate should be spent for food, shelter, and other living expenses. In addition, the conservator has a duty to preserve the ward's estate from loss or damage, invest the ward's assets, and manage the ward's business and property. Conservators are more closely supervised, perhaps because financial matters are more easily reduced to a form that can be measured and understood by the court. The three principal methods of overseeing a conservator's actions are the initial filing of an inventory describing the estate (what the ward owns and its value), the filing of a bond to protect the estate, and the filing of annual or periodic accountings.

Every state has laws authorizing the court to require bonds, and requiring conservators to make regular reports of their performance to the courts or to a state agency.[23] The amount of the bond generally is a percentage of the estate. A conservator who negligently wastes the assets of the ward's estate may be ordered to forfeit all or a portion of his bond. In addition to posting a bond, conservators are required to make periodic accountings of their performance. Failure to make these reports can be grounds for removal.[24]

Guardians and conservators, in all states, are required to take good care of the ward and his or her property. They must not waste the assets of their wards' property. They may be liable for any losses caused by their negligence and may be required to repay any funds that they have misappropriated from the estates.[25] The effectiveness of these controls over guardians and conservators varies from state to state. In a few states, they are supervised closely, but most often a conservator accounts for his performance only at the end of his services or at times when he is sued for specific acts of mismanagement.[26] Too often the ward or some-one who has an interest in the ward is the only real supervisor.

A guardian or conservator who exceeds her authority may be sued by the ward or by a temporary guardian appointed to represent the ward in this lawsuit (called a "guardian *ad litem*"). The result of the suit may be the appointment of a new guardian or conservator or a court order requiring the guardian or conservator to reimburse the ward for any damages caused by his or her actions.

Who pays for a guardian or conservator?

Often, the only source of payment is the ward. Payments to the guardian or conservator may be based either on a certain percentage of the value of the ward's estate or on the basis of what "reasonable" compensation would be for the guardian or conservator's services.[27] The court must approve all requests for payment, although such approval is routinely granted. The larger the ward's estate, the greater are the fees that can be paid, so there is rarely difficulty in finding a conservator or guardian for a ward with substantial assets. Unfortunately, there may be a great problem in finding somebody willing to serve in either capacity for a ward with few assets. Some states have responded to this problem by creating a public guardian who is appointed by the court to serve as guardian or conservator for someone of modest means. Other states have set up a fund from which guardians are paid for acting on behalf of such persons.[28]

How is a guardian or conservator appointed?

Guardian- and conservatorships are initiated with the filing of petitions, as authorized by statute. The format and process for guardian and conservator proceedings basically are the same. If an impaired person can manage neither his personal nor financial affairs, petitions for both guardianship and conservatorship may be filed and a consolidated hearing on both matters held.[29] A petition will allege that the person is incapable of managing her estate or her personal affairs and for that reason is in need of the requested conservator or guardian.[30] Sometimes, the petitions also request the person be declared incompetent. Some states require the person filing a petition to include in it a plan for the rehabilitation of the person over whom a guardianship is requested.[31] In others, petitions must be accompanied by medical certification of the mental condition of the alleged incompetent. Generally, any interested person can file the petition,[32] and in more than half the states, the allegedly incompetent or incapacitated person can file his own petition.[33]

The guardianship or conservatorship petition is filed with the probate court. After the petition is filed, the court will set a date for a hearing and send notice of it to persons who are required to receive it under the state statute. The prospective ward should receive notice, as should certain of her relatives and others who the court determines have sufficient interest in the proceedings. At the hearing, the court will consider all testimony and evidence before it and will determine whether or not a guardian or conservator is required. Often a judge alone will make this determination, but most states also permit (but don't require) jury trials. When a judge alone decides on the need for a guardian or conservator, the hearing is usually informal and may be held in the judge's private chambers.

What must be proven in a guardianship or conservatorship proceeding?

In most states, the court must go through a two-step procedure to determine that a person requires the assistance of a guardian or conservator. First, it must be shown that the person is a member of a class of persons as specified by statue, for whom a guardian or conservator may be appointed. Examples of such classes are the aged, mentally ill, retarded, and alcoholics. Then it must be proven that, as a result of being a member of the specified class, she is unable to care for herself or manage her property. In practice, courts often neglect the second step. A finding that the person is a member of the statutory class may result in the appointment of a guardian or conservator without a separate examination into ability to care for self or property.

To discourage this practice, the model statutes require the analysis applied to be more "functional" than "categorical." They define an "incapacitated person" as one "who is impaired by reason of mental illness, mental deficiency, physical illness or disability, advanced age, chronic use of drugs, chronic intoxication, or other cause (except minority) to the extent of lacking sufficient understanding or capacity to make or communicate responsible decisions."[34] The court is required to balance the medical diagnosis with information about the behavior and limitations of the proposed ward. In Utah, a law based on the UGPPA definition was challenged as being unconstitutionally vague and overbroad.[35] The court held that a determination that "an adult cannot make responsible decisions concerning his person" may only be made when the person's "decision-making process is so impaired that he is unable to care for his personal safety, or unable to attend to and provide for such necessities as food, shelter, clothing and medical care, without which physical injury or illness may occur."[36] This determination implies that irrational or irresponsible decisions alone cannot be the basis for the appointment of a guardian. For similar reasons, other courts have rejected advanced age alone as a sufficient basis for appointing a guardian.[37] Some states have gone further than the uniform laws and have totally eliminated the medical diagnosis as a cause to be proven.[38] The court looks only at the functional limitations and their effect on the individual's ability to make or communicate decisions concerning her person or property.

What type of evidence should be introduced at the hearing?
The issue decided at the hearing is whether or not an individual can properly care for herself or manage her estate. Any evidence that is relevant to this issue should be introduced at the hearing. A person who wishes to challenge guardianship or conservatorship proceedings should arrange to have such witnesses as doctors, friends, business acquaintances, and others to testify at the hearing to his ability to live and make decisions independently. Evidence of a person's business dealings and the successful medical treatment of any illness that might be the basis of the petition also demonstrate legal competence. Evidence

should be prepared to refute the specific facts that are the basis for the guardianship or conservatorship petition.[39] If savings are alleged to have been wasted by improvident investments, one should be prepared to show the investments actually were made with good business judgment. It is important to inform the court of the background of the prospective ward and petitioner's relationship, as well as to explain any reasons for the petitioner's misunderstanding the prospective ward's motives and actions.

Because adequate preparation is so essential, the prospective ward should make all efforts to have an attorney's assistance. An attorney will help collect the evidence and witnesses needed. Assistance at this stage of the proceedings is very important and should be obtained as soon as one learns that a guardianship or conservatorship petition has been filed.

A petitioner seeking the appointment of a guardian or conservator for someone who can no longer manage his or her personal or financial affairs, also needs to provide adequate evidence to allow the court to make an informed decision. A petitioner should be prepared to offer precise, detailed facts to the court to describe how the ward's actions are causing harm, the nature of his or her impairment, the desired outcome of the proceeding, and how this outcome will benefit the ward.

Who has the burden of proof?

Just as defendants in criminal cases are presumed innocent until proven guilty, all persons are presumed to be legally competent and not in need of a guardian or conservator until a court has found them otherwise. Therefore, the person who files the petition for the hearing will be required to prove that a person is incompetent. This proof may consist of a medical certificate of mental capacity,[40] the testimony of witnesses who know the person, documents of recent transactions he or she has made, or any other evidence that supports the allegation of the need for a guardian or conservator.[41]

Courts make determinations on the need for the assistance of a guardian only on the evidence presented to them. A person challenging the procedures has the right to demand that this evidence be reliable and relevant to the issue of guardianship, but this right can be exercised only by active participation in the hearing.

Is a person entitled to notice when a petition for guardianship or conservatorship has been filed?

Yes. All states require that some sort of notice be given of guardianship or conservatorship proceedings. In states where there is no statutory requirement of notice, courts nevertheless have held that it is an essential right that notice be given of the filing of a petition.[42] The purpose of notice is to inform interested persons of the hearing and to give the person under notice an opportunity to prepare his or her defense.

State statutes usually require notice of the date, time, and place of the hearing.[43] Most also require that the notice be given a specified time before the date set for the hearing.[44] Statutes of several states do not require that notice be given if the person who files the petition for the competency determination can show that the person's "best interests" would be served by dispensing with notice.[45] And in some states, notice need not be actually handed to the person whose competence is to be determined.

Are these notice statues adequate?

No. Many present statutes permit too short a period of time between notice of the hearing and the date on which it is held. This hinders preparation of a defense. And statutes that excuse giving notice when a person's "best interests" would thereby be served often result in no one being present to oppose the appointment of a guardian. Because many people are uninformed of their rights, states should require that the notice include all information that might be helpful in preparing a response to the petition for guardianship or conservatorship.[46] Notice should be given of the consequences of being declared incompetent and of the relevant rights—to a jury trial, to be represented by an attorney, to be present at the hearing, to present evidence such as medical documents and witnesses, to cross-examine and subpoena witnesses, and to delay the date of the hearing for good cause. Also, the names of those who will testify at the hearing should be included, and the substance of their testimony should be summarized.

Adequate notice is a fundamental right under the Constitution.[47] Consequently, if a guardianship or conservatorship statute does not provide for adequate notice, it is possible to attack the proceedings as a violation of one's constitutional rights. It may be possible even to reopen a guardianship or conservatorship proceeding that has been completed by alleging that adequate notice was not provided. This happened in New York, when a former mental patient successfully sued to have a court invalidate a guardianship proceeding initiated a decade earlier while she was in a mental hospital.[48]

Does the potential ward have a right to be present at the hearing?

Although the presence of the potential ward at the guardianship or conservatorship hearing is fundamental to a fair procedure and while the potential ward has a right to be present, he or she is rarely present. Only a few states mandate his presence at the hearing, and even in these states the judge may still excuse the person's presence if it is considered to be in the "best interest" of that person. Since some medical experts assert that the stress of a judicial hearing is detrimental to the physical and mental wellbeing of individuals, courts readily accept statements and affidavits from these experts and waive the requirement of the person's presence at the hearing. Unfortunately, the statements and affidavits usually are submitted by the petitioner rather than as a result of an independent judicial investigation. As a result, although the potential ward has the right to be present at the hearing in all states, in practice, he is seldom present. Considering the potential for loss of liberty and property, the ward's presence at the hearing is crucial for the protection of his or her interest. Protective proceeding statutes should assure that the person who is the subject of these proceedings is present to defend him- or herself.

Does the potential ward have a right to a lawyer at a guardianship or conservatorship hearing?

Yes and no. While all states allow representation by a lawyer at a guardianship hearing, most states will not appoint a lawyer for the potential ward if he appears without one or if he cannot afford a lawyer. If the potential ward is wealthy and recognizes the need for a lawyer to represent him, there is no problem. However, if he is poor or does not understand the need for a lawyer, the situation is not good. About half the states either permit or require the judge to appoint a lawyer to represent the potential ward during the proceedings.[50] Others require or allow appointment of a guardian *ad litem*, as discussed below.[51]

The right to counsel may be waived if not affirmatively exercised. The UGPPA requires the appointment of a lawyer to represent the potential ward's interests in all cases in which the ward does not obtain his own lawyer.[52] Sadly, court-appointed lawyers frequently are not much help.[53] Too often they are ineffective in opposing the appointment of a guardian or conservator, sometimes they never even meet their client, and quite often they agree that a guardian or conservator is needed.

A recent conference of judges recommended: (1) that counsel as advocate be appointed in every case; (2) as an advocate, counsel should make a thorough and informed investigation of the situation; and (3) if private funds are not available to pay counsel, then public funds should be used.[54]

There may be a constitutional right to counsel. One court has so held, analogizing guardianship proceedings to involuntary civil commitment.[55] But the issue remains unsettled. In those states where the appointment of a lawyer is discretionary, at least one case has suggested that failure to appoint counsel may be an abuse of discretion.[56] If a court fails to appoint counsel, it should be argued that it has abused its discretion, particularly when the potential ward is unlikely to understand notice concerning the hearing or has failed to appear at a hearing.

What is a guardian *ad litem*?

A guardian *ad litem* is a person appointed during the course of a guardianship or conservatorship proceeding to protect the interests of an allegedly impaired person. Not all states provide for guardians *ad litem*, and the court has great discretion in making such appointments.[57] Guardians *ad litem* are frequently attorneys although they need not be.

The sole function of a guardian *ad litem* is representation at the guardianship or conservatorship hearing or at any other judicial proceeding after a guardian or conservator has been appointed when the guardian or conservator is unwilling or unable to assist. A guardian *ad litem* has no authority over a person or his estate. While the function of a guardian *ad litem* is similar to that of an attorney representing his client, there is a major difference in the theory behind such representation. A guardian *ad litem*'s decisions are to be made in what the guardian *ad litem* believes to be the best interests of the ward, even when contrary to the ward's expressed wishes.[58] An attorney's decisions are made in accordance with the instructions of his client, regardless of what the attorney believes his client's best interests are.[59]

Is there a right to a jury trial?

Yes, although it is seldom exercised. Most states recognize by statute the right to a jury determination of the need for a guardian or conservator.[60] But the potential ward must demand a jury trial; otherwise the right is waived since very few states require jury trials of competence.[61] In practice, jury trials are rarely held in these types of hearings. Usually a judge alone will determine competence. Although there is no guarantee that jury determinations of competence will result in fewer appointments of guardians, notice should be given of a person's right to a jury trial in those states where they are permitted.

What is a temporary or emergency guardian or conservator?

Most states allow the appointment of a temporary or emergency guardian when there is an emergency or life-threatening situation or when a permanent guardian can no longer serve.[62] The normal procedural requirements for appointment of a guardian are relaxed in emergency statutes.[63] There is often no notice provided to the potential ward nor hearing held with counsel.[64] Constitutional due process rights may be abridged by these statutes. Several states have provided some procedural protections—the right to notice, a hearing, and counsel—by statute.[65] And although the statutes refer to "temporary" guardians, in fact, the duration of a temporary guardianship can be quite lengthy.[66] Many statutes also allow a court to temporarily manage a potential ward's property pending appointment of a permanent conservator.[67]

Is there a right to appeal the appointment of a guardian or conservator?

Yes. There is a right to appeal a guardianship or conservatorship, but it is a limited right.

In most states, an appellate court accepts as true all facts that a judge or jury determines to be true at the lower court hearing. The appellate court does not hear new facts or reweigh the evidence given at the hearing. Therefore, the need for adequate representation of counsel at the initial hearing cannot be over-emphasized. An attorney who knows the rules of evidence may be able to exclude much adverse evidence from the hearing and may be able to attack the adequacy and truthfulness of adverse evidence that is introduced.

The appellate court will hear arguments concerning the constitutionality of the state's guardianship or conservatorship statutes; whether certain evidence that was objected to at the hearing was properly excluded or admitted; whether there is some basis in the evidence for the lower court's determinations; and whether certain procedural aspects of the hearing, such as notice, were sufficient to protect one's rights.

How can a guardianship or conservatorship be terminated?

Generally, a guardianship or conservatorship continues until the ward dies. In a few cases it may be terminated when a ward both regains the capacity to care for herself and/or her property and returns to the court to seek an end to the relationship. This process is called "restoration." It is similar to the procedure discussed earlier, by which a guardian or conservator is appointed.[68]

The restoration hearing is initiated by filing a petition in the appropriate court. The petition may state specifically that the condition which was the basis for the initial appointment no longer exists (e.g. drunkenness, sickness, or mental disability), or it may allege generally that the person is now able to care for self, property, or both. It can be filed by the ward in most states and by any interested party in nearly every state.[69]

At the restoration hearing, the guardian or conservator will be required to show further need for her services if she wishes to dispute the ward's competence. The ward, then, must present evidence of his ability to care for himself and his affairs. This evidence might include a medical certificate stating a doctor's opinion that the ward has recovered from the disability that was the basis for guardianship or conservatorship and other documents that demonstrate his ability to care for his own best interests. Friends and business associates should testify at the hearing. Evidence that demonstrates only improper care by a guardian or conservator or evidence that he or she is antagonistic to the ward's best interest will not be enough to restore competence. As with other portions of competence proceedings, there is no right to a court-appointed attorney at a restoration hearing, but an attorney may and should be retained. All states allow restoration. Neither the appointment of a guardian nor of a conservator is necessarily permanent.

Can a ward be institutionalized by his or her guardian?

Yes, under some circumstances. Nearly all states permit a guardian or conservator, as an "interested party," to initiate involuntary civil commitment proceedings to have his ward placed in a state psychiatric hospital.[70] A guardian can also generally arrange for institutionalization in nursing homes, for adult foster care or room and board homes, and for other types of institutional situations without seeking court approval and against the ward's wishes, as part of the guardian's rights with custody of the ward. (Because a conservator's powers extend only to a ward's financial interests, a conservator has no authority to institutionalize a ward.)

What other rights are affected by guardianship and conservatorship statutes?

At one time, the rights affected by guardianship and conservatorship proceedings included a broad spectrum of rights identified with one's citizenship such as the right to contract, vote, marry, hold licenses, make wills, and sue or be sued. The recent trend in protective proceedings makes it more difficult to determine which, if any, of the rights have been affected by these proceedings. For instance, a number of states, as under the UPC and UGPPA, allow for the appointment of limited guardians. Generally, these limitations are fashioned to allow for the greatest amount of individual liberty as possible. However, the appointment often does not address these issues directly, and the effect, therefore, is not always clear.

The right to contract. In one way or another, all states restrict the right of persons under guardianship or conservatorship to make contracts.[71] Generally, most such contracts would be unenforceable. The major exception would be for contracts providing for food, housing, clothing, medical care, and, presumably, legal fees (should one wish to retain counsel to contest a guardian or conservator petition). These and similar expenses, known as "necessities of life"—that is those things reasonably necessary for support, maintenance, and comfort—are usually held to be binding.

The right to vote. In most states, the right to vote is governed by statute and many of these statutes say that persons who are "insane or incompetent" cannot vote.[72] The advent of the limited guardianship as well as changes in the definitions of "incompetent individuals" have severely clouded this issue. Some states, such as New York, have by statute indicated that the appointment of a conservator does not affect a person's civil liberties, including the right to vote.[73] The UPC and UGPPA make it clear that the appointment of a guardian is not an incompetency determination. Thus, a limited guardian appointed under such a statute would raise serious constitutional questions regarding the fundamental right to vote unless the order appointing the guardian specifically limited the ward's authority to do so. Even under those circumstances it could be argued that that portion of the order is unconstitutional.

The right to marry. In many states, a person who has been adjudged incompetent or incapable of making personal decisions cannot marry.[74] The reason for this prohibition is that a person who is incompetent cannot enter into a binding contract, and marriage is regarded by the law as a form of contract. Although few states seem to enforce this prohibition, a person who has been adjudged incompetent probably cannot validly marry without the consent of his guardian and may not be able to marry at all. When a person adjudged incompetent already has married, the marriage can be annulled in many states.

The right to hold licenses. Many states restrict or prohibit the issuance of licenses to practice a profession or to operate a motor vehicle to persons who are insane or incompetent. Many also provide that licenses granted to persons later declared insane or incompetent shall be suspended or revoked.[75] However, some states recognize that the appointment of a guardian should not always result in the loss of such licenses and provide that such an appointment shall not affect the validity of a license already granted.[76]

The right to make wills. Most states distinguish between the requirements for legal competence and those for capacity to make a will. Thus, even a person found to be legally incompetent or in need of a guardian can execute a will in all but a few states. (In these few states, a person found incompetent cannot make a valid will.) In every state, however, evidence of a determination of incompetence is admissible in a later proceeding to challenge the validity of a will; and in most states such evidence will create a presumption of legal incapacity to execute or to revoke a will.[77]

The capacity to sue and be sued. Most states restrict the right of persons found to be incompetent or incapable to sue or be sued. A guardian or conservator may have the authority to initiate and defend suits on the ward's behalf. If the guardian or conservator is unable or unwilling to sue or to defend a suit on behalf of the ward, many states permit courts to appoint a guardian *ad litem* to protect the ward's interests.

Do incompetence and guardianship or conservatorship affect a statute of limitations?

All states have statutes that require a person who wishes to sue another person to begin the suit within a certain time period after the other person has injured him. These are called statutes of limitations. Nearly every state extends its statute of limitations for those persons who have been found legally incompetent.[78]

Planning to Avoid Guardianship or Conservatorship

Earlier in this chapter durable powers of attorney and multiple-party accounts were mentioned as alternatives to guardianship or conservatorship. These planning devices are briefly explored in the following pages. (Readers wishing to create or make use of such devices should first seek professional advice and assistance.) The living will, as discussed in chapter 11, may also be used to obviate the need for a guardian if the decision is the narrow one of withdrawal of an artificial life-support system for a terminally ill person.

How do powers of attorney and durable powers of attorney differ?

A power of attorney is a written document in which one person (the principal) designates another person or organization (the agent or attorney-in-fact) to act in his place. The agent may be granted the general power to do whatever the principal could do, or may be limited to a specific act or acts. In any case, the agent's authority must be specified, and cannot exceed the principal's actual authority. In order to protect the principal, the power of attorney is automatically revoked upon his incapacity, disability, or death. Unfortunately, this feature makes the common law power of attorney useless as a device to plan for possible, future mental incapacity or disability.

By contrast, a durable power of attorney continues in effect even after the principal's disability or incapacity, lasting until revoked or until the principal's death. All states and the District of Columbia authorize by statute the creation of a durable power of attorney. In order to be durable, the written power of attorney must contain language stating it is unaffected by the principal's future incapacity or disability.[79] Generally, any power of attorney is effective upon execution, meaning the agent currently has the power to perform those acts authorized by the principal. Many states also allow a "springing" durable power of attorney which becomes effective only upon the principal's future incapacity or disability. As might be expected, it is difficult to fix the date of effectiveness of a springing durable power since there must be some determination that the principal is legally incapable of acting for himself.

How is a durable power of attorney created?

The universal requirement for making a valid durable power of attorney is the principal must have legal capacity to understand what she is doing in giving up the power to make decisions.[80] The document can generally be created without formalities such as witnesses or a notary certificate, depending upon the acts authorized and the particular state statutes. Transactions involving transfers of real property are the major exception, as they often require notarization and recordation in the jurisdiction where the property is located.[81]

Can a durable power of attorney help avoid conservatorship?

Yes. Durable powers often are used to authorize financial transactions and property management.[82] By arranging property management through an agent, the principal may avoid one of the grounds for appointment of a conservator. Several courts have stated that judicially imposed property management is unnecessary if an incapacitated person has made his or her own arrangements.[83]

Is a durable power also effective in avoiding guardianship?

Yes. Durable powers of attorney can be used to authorize personal decisionmaking, such as arrangements for residential placement, access to records, and probably for health-care decisions. A few state statutes authorize an agent to make health-care decisions through a durable power of attorney.[84] These documents generally require witnesses and notarization.[85] Most commentators believe durable powers of attorney can be used for health-care decisions without specific statutory authorization,[86] and several courts have stated that the existence of a durable power addressing health-care decisions is evidence of the principal's intentions which should be followed.[87] For example, a principal could make her wishes concerning treatment by artificial life-support systems, such as feeding tubes or respirators, known in the power of attorney and could designate an agent to make any relevant necessary decisions.

Is there any way to guarantee a third party's acceptance of the agent's authority?

No. Perhaps the greatest shortcoming of a durable power is third party reluctance to accept the agent's authority. Banks, for instance, often accept only powers of attorney executed on their own forms, and even then reluctantly. Physicians, faced with possible liability, are reluctant to accept an agent's authorization to make life-and-death health-care decisions. Although several states require third-party acceptance of a power of attorney executed in conformity with a model provided by the state law,[88] this remains a problem in most states.

There are several ways to enhance acceptance of the durable power of attorney. First, although most states do not require the power be witnessed and notarized, doing so may make it more acceptable to third parties. Second, the power can be written in a way to encourage acceptance. An inducement clause can be included, holding the third party harmless for acts done by the agent after the power has been revoked. Third, a durable power authorizing health-care decisions can be distributed to physicians in advance to make them aware of the patient's views. In order to protect confidentiality, a principal might want to execute a durable power for health-care decisions in a separate document from a power for financial matters.

What are the agent's duties?

The agent has the duty to act only within the scope of his authority as set forth in the durable power of attorney. This fiduciary responsibility makes the agent liable for actions outside the scope of his authority.[89] The agent must act solely for the principal's benefit. He cannot put his own interests ahead of the principal's. Thus, in managing the principal's finances, the agent cannot commingle the principal's assets with his own or borrow from the principal without specific authority. The agent should keep records and accounts of all transactions, to protect himself against allegations of breach of fiduciary duty.

How is a durable power of attorney revoked?

Several ways. The principal is free to revoke the power so long as he has the capacity to do so. Generally, the revocation should be in writing and should be distributed to the agent and third parties with whom he has transacted business. If the power was recorded, the revocation generally should be recorded as well.

As noted above, the principal's death revokes the power. In most states, if the agent acts after the principal's death but without knowledge of it, the actions are binding on the estate and the principal's heirs or beneficiaries.

What is a multiple-party account?

An account or deposit held in two or more names is a multiple-party account. It may be: a joint account (an account payable to "A or B"); a payable on death (P.O.D.) account (an account held as "A payable on death to B"); or a trust account, which includes a Totten or tentative trust (an account held as "A in trust for B").[90] Some states have statutes modeled after article

6 of the Uniform Probate Code which delineate ownership rights of multiple-party account holders.[91]

How can a multiple-party account help avoid conservatorship?

There are two reasons to create a multiple-party account or deposit. One is to avoid probate. Joint tenants hold whole, undivided interests in the property and the right of survivorship.[92] Upon the death of a cotenant, the survivor continues to hold his undivided interest as before, and that interest survives the cotenant's death. The common understanding of a joint tenancy is a joint tenant takes title to the property upon the death of the cotenant "by operation of law" without the necessity of probate proceedings.

More important for this discussion is the convenience account or deposit, in which one person simply allows another access to the account or deposit. The account owner (that is, the sole depositor) may not wish to transfer title either presently or in the future but—for a variety of reasons—may want to have someone else with access to the account fund. Many older people with physical ailments or who fear mental disability find it convenient to authorize someone else access to an account. By establishing a joint account or deposit for convenience purposes, the property owner has arranged a substituted plan of property management, making court appointment of a surrogate unnecessary.

Are there disadvantages to joint accounts?

Yes. First, the cotenant only has access to the account funds and not to other property. However, a durable power of attorney might be used in conjunction with the joint account or deposit, with the agent designated to sell, store, or otherwise dispose of other personal property.

An even bigger problem may be the risk involved in other parties having access to account or deposit funds. Contribution to an account is unlikely to be even. More commonly, all of the funds initially belonged to one party. The risk of a looted account is magnified by the principal owner's incapacity. But state statutes may determine the parties' ownership rights. The usual rule is the account funds belong to the parties in proportion to the funds contributed.[93]

A significant problem with multiple-party accounts is in establishing the account's purpose—for convenience or to avoid probate. Some state statutes follow the UPC and presume that an account survivor is entitled to the funds.[94] Others follow the opposite rule—an account is presumed to be for convenience purposes if all the funds are contributed by one party.[95] These presumptions can be overcome but often only with great difficulty, time, and expense.[96] Remember, even if probate is avoided, a surviving account holder may be liable for inheritance taxes, depending on state law.

How might a trust help avoid conservatorship?

In several cases, courts have determined that the existence of a trust used to pay for an elder's living and medical expenses made conservatorship unnecessary.[97] In an attempt to avoid conservatorship, several possible trust devices may be useful. An elderly person might establish a revocable living trust (property is transferred to the trustee during the settlor's life, but this trust can be revoked) designating another person as cotrustee. The trust can be written so the cotrustee takes control of all trust funds upon the settlor's incapacity. As with a springing durable power of attorney, there may be difficulty in determining the onset of incapacity, and that issue should be addressed in the trust agreement. With a trustee in place to manage the settlor's property, no conservator should be necessary.

Another possibility is to create a so-called "dry" or unfunded trust in combination with a durable power of attorney. Upon the onset of incapacity the agent under the durable power (preferably someone other than the trustee) funds the trust with the principal's other assets, and the trustee then manages the principal's property.

CIVIL COMMITMENT

What is involuntary civil commitment?

In general terms, it is the legal process of placing someone in a psychiatric hospital against his or her will. The primary purpose of this placement is to diagnose and treat mental disorders, but there is often another purpose—to protect the individual from himself or protect society from the individual. Except in a few states, there must be some kind of court process and a judge's order prior to long-term hospitalization of this nature.[98] Most long-term involuntary commitments are of indefinite duration and are in some instances for life. Psychiatric hospitalization is not, fortunately, the only possible outcome of a civil commitment. Placements to less restrictive kinds of settings such as nursing homes or group homes are appropriate for many individuals. Outpatient commitment is another popular recent development.[99]

How are involuntary civil commitments legally justified?

The most common rationale for committing someone is mental illness and potential danger to self or to others. The legal support for the state's action is its "police power"—to protect society from harm. Some states allow commitment on the grounds the individual is incapable of caring for himself. Several states use the term "gravely disabled" to describe individuals unable to care for their most basic needs of food, shelter, and clothing.[100] These rationales are based on the *parens patriae* theory; the state is presumed to be acting out of benevolent concern for the disabled person's welfare.

A third ground for commitment, albeit somewhat unlikely for elderly persons, is the existence of a developmental disability, such as mental retardation.[101] Many states have separate civil commitment statues for the mentally ill and developmentally disabled persons.

When is involuntary civil commitment justified for an elderly person?

Rarely. Diseases such as Alzheimer's Disease and other forms of dementia are commonly considered mental illnesses,[102] and they often make their victims helpless to care for themselves, if not dangerous to others. In the past, such persons were sometimes involuntarily committed to psychiatric hospitals. However, their conditions seldom warranted such commitments. Many services, such as day-care centers, are available to assist families in caring for these people at home. If home treatment is impossible, foster, nursing-home, or group-home placements can generally be made without invoking civil commitment laws.[103] Families should consider initiation of commitment proceedings a measure of last resort, as most Alzheimer's and other dementia victims do not need psychiatric treatment, nor will they respond to it.

Advanced planning may alleviate the need for civil commitment, particularly for elderly people with nonpsychotic mental disorders. For example, a durable power of attorney authorizing the agent to arrange for nursing-home care, combined with a measure of financial planning, may facilitate placement in a facility previously selected by the person when that person was able to think clearly.

Does an institutionalized person lose all decision-making authority?

Generally, a committed person retains the ability to perform acts such as making contracts or medical treatment decisions, unless and until found specifically incompetent to do so.[104]

Commitment Procedure

Because civil commitments constitute serious intrusions on personal liberty and decisionmaking, procedural protections are required. Exactly what protections remains disputed. One group compares civil commitment to detention for criminal activity and argues the protections should be the same—i.e., proof of dangerousness and mental illness beyond a reasonable doubt should be required. Others argue there is a benevolent aspect to civil commitment;[105] the emphasis is on treatment, and despite the loss of liberty, a more relaxed, nonadversarial procedure is warranted. As a result of these warring views, there is no uniformity in commitment procedures. State statutes and practices vary widely. And the federal and state constitutions are also sources of rights because of the liberty interests involved in involuntary commitment.[106]

What is emergency hospitalization?

Emergency hospitalization is a procedure by which an individual who is thought to present an immediate threat of harm to himself or to others may be detained in an institution for a short period of time (usually a few days). Most states have statutes that authorize emergency detentions.[107] Because the harm to be prevented is immediate, the process frequently is informal, and few procedural safeguards are available.

Emergency detention is often used to observe a person in a hospital setting in hopes of determining whether long-term hospitalization is necessary. Some states have procedures designated as purely observational, in which case no emergency is required to justify a short-term detention.[108]

Because standards justifying emergency hospitalization are vague, and the procedures used are casual, many persons are brought to mental hospitals wrongly. Emergency procedures should be used only in extreme cases, and the procedures should be made more stringent so that abuses will be less common than they now are.

What is nonemergency hospitalization?

A common form of hospitalization is nonemergency or long-term civil commitment. In contrast to emergency commitment, which ordinarily lasts only a few days, long-term commitment is usually for an indefinite period of time, for long periods such as six months or a year. Most states permit long-term commitment not only for persons who are mentally ill and dangerous, but also for persons who are mentally ill and in need of treatment.

Does a person have a right to be notified of a proceeding to hospitalize him or her?

Yes. Every state requires mandatory notice of a commitment proceeding.[109] Many states also require notice to a guardian, spouse, or near relative.[110] The contents of the notification should be clearly stated so as to apprise the individual of what is at stake in the proceedings, the possible consequences, and—of course—the time and place of any hearing.

Is there a right to a lawyer?

Yes. All states except New York[111] give the subject of commitment proceedings the right to select his or her own lawyer.[112] Many states require appointment of a lawyer for an individual unable to secure a lawyer because of poverty or mental or physical condition. In some states the public defender represents at least a portion of persons for whom involuntary commitment is sought. Several courts, although not yet the United States Supreme Court, have stated there is a constitutional right to mandatorily appointed counsel.[113]

Is there a right to be present at the commitment hearing?

Not always. In most states the prospective patient has a right to attend the hearing held to decide whether he needs to be in a mental hospital, but in many he does not.[114] In the latter states the judge can decide that the prospective patient would be upset by attending and can prevent him from being there. Generally the right to attend depends on the prospective patient's demanding to be there. If he does not request to be present, the hearing might be held without him. A few states require the prospective patient to attend. Because attendance at commitment hearings is an important aspect of due process, the presence of the person subjected to a commitment proceeding should be waived only in extreme cases, if at all.

Is there a right to a trial jury?

Sometimes. Fewer than half of the states permit a trial by jury in civil commitment cases, and in most of these states a jury trial will not be held unless it is specifically requested. Of course a prospective patient can argue that a jury trial must be available as a result of the constitution of his state, and this argument may be successful. So far, no court has ordered a trial by jury in a civil commitment case unless it was authorized by statute.

Is there a right to an independent medical examination?

It depends. Both cases and statutes support the right to an independent psychiatric/psychological evaluation in some states.[115] However, questions of who is responsible for paying the examiner often remain. There is no universal right to an independent medical examination.

What must be proved to involuntarily commit someone?

It depends upon the state's statutory requirements and/or caselaw. Most require proof the person is mentally ill and dangerous to himself or others. Proof of a mental illness is provided by expert psychiatric, or possibly, psychological testimony.[116] Most mental health professionals rely upon the Diagnostic and Statistical Manual (DSM-III) for diagnosis of mental disorders. The DSM-III contains a classification system of mental diseases and disorders, and provides signs and symptoms of each (diagnostic criteria). However, a psychiatrist may diagnose mental illness and so testify without the described illness being classified in the DSM-III or meeting exactly the criteria for a particular disorder.[117] Psychiatric diagnosis is far from an exact science.[118] Often, it is the psychiatrist's persuasiveness in presenting his diagnosis, rather than an objective analysis, which establishes the existence of mental illness.

But there must be more than a finding of mental illness to justify an involuntary commitment. Usually the individual must also be determined dangerous to himself or other people. Few mental health professionals claim they can predict future dangerousness with a high degree of accuracy.[119] Consequently, advocates often argue dangerousness must be proved by a recent overtly dangerous act. The courts have divided in response to the argument,[120] and the point remains unsettled. Dangerous acts are usually established by testimony from relatives, friends, and observers. For example, failure to take medications, leaving gas burners blazing, and wandering aimlessly from home are common self-dangerous acts of elderly people. Keep in mind, however, that these actions are often the product of mental disorders which do not require psychiatric hospitalization, and they rarely justify a petition for involuntary commitment. The amount of proof required to establish necessity for involuntary commitment is well settled. The Supreme Court, in *Addington v. Texas*, determined clear and convincing evidence of the existence of—for instance—mental illness is all the federal Constitution requires in civil commitment proceedings. The court rejected the argument that proof beyond a reasonable doubt, the standard to convict, was necessary. States are free to use the more stringent standards if they choose, and several do.[121]

Are there alternatives to psychiatric hospitalization?

Yes. Alternative residential placements such as nursing homes and group homes are increasingly utilized. Each has its own set of problems, but they are usually considered before a psychiatric hospitalization is ordered. Another important alternative to hospitalization is outpatient commitment. Under an outpatient commitment, the individual is allowed to live at home but as a condition, must take medications or participate in counseling. If the individual fails to conform with the treatment ordered, he may then be hospitalized.

These changes have been brought about mainly because of

the doctrine of the least restrictive or drastic alternative, a legal principle recognized in some states statute and by court decision. Under this doctrine, a person cannot be sent to a psychiatric hospital if a less drastic form of treatment—such as by an outpatient commitment or treatment in a nursing home, group home, or foster home—is available.

Adult Protective Services

Thirty-six states and the District of Columbia have special laws and programs that seek to protect impaired adults who are unable to care for themselves and who do not have others to care for them.[122] Usually, these programs are responsible for providing services to all impaired adults, although at least one state restricts services to impaired adults over sixty years of age.[123]

These programs are generally known as adult protective services and are administered by state and local Social Service or Aging departments. These government agencies seek to provide preventive, supportive, and surrogate services to impaired adults living in the community, thereby enabling them to remain independent and free from certain types of physical and financial harm.[124] The situations sought to be protected against are commonly labeled in protective services statutes as "abuse," "neglect," "endangerment" or "exploitation," or some combination thereof. While statutes vary as to the labels used and their content, the following definitions are broadly representative of the harms intended to be prevented or remedied:

1. Abuse. Any harm or threatened harm to an adult's health or welfare caused by another person. This includes nonaccidental physical injury, mental injury, sexual abuse, or maltreatment.
2. Neglect. Any harm to an adult's health or welfare caused by the conduct of a person responsible for the adult's care. This includes failure to provide adequate food, clothing, shelter, or medical care. Self-neglect . . . [may be] included.
3. Exploitation. Any action that involves the misuse of an adult's funds, property, or personal dignity by another person.
4. Endangerment. A life-threatening situation caused by

the inability of the person whose life is threatened to respond.[125]

Impaired adults who face such harmful situations and who will not or cannot voluntarily accept the help of protective services agencies to correct them may have agency help provided involuntarily, by being made the subject of legal intervention. This may occur either under existing protective proceedings laws such as guardianship, conservatorship, or civil commitment, or, in some states, under new and often broad legal authority granted to the administering agency by a particular state's protective services statute. For example, in emergency situations, Florida grants the power to enter into an impaired adult's home against her wishes or to place an impaired adult into an institution, with little or no contemporaneous court overview.[126]

What are protective services?

Adult protective services are typically defined very broadly. Some state laws list general categories of protective services which may be offered to impaired adults, such as "case work, medical care, legal services, fiscal management, and guardianship and placement services."[127] Other states simply define protective services as being any service whose object is to protect an incapacitated person from herself or others.[128] These broad standards allow protective services agencies to provide whatever services are deemed necessary to prevent physical or financial harm to an individual. These may include delivering food to an impaired senior's home, arranging for choreworkers to help clean a senior's home or for visiting nurses to provide medication, or making a home more safe by providing repairs or removing fire hazards. Protective services also may commonly involve taking control of the senior's finances, either voluntarily or through involuntary legal action, and then using the senior's money to pay for property taxes, mortgage payments, health insurance and other necessities.

Who is subject to adult protective services intervention?

Most state statutes limit protective services intervention to persons who both suffer from certain physical or mental conditions, such as "senility" or the "infirmities of aging," and who display certain behavioral disabilities, such as an inability to care for oneself or to protect oneself against abuse, neglect or exploitation.[129] The determination as to whether an impaired person meets these standards is initially made by the workers of the protective services agency, as a precondition to offering services.

How do adult protective service programs operate?

While state programs vary in protective service definition and practice, the following is a general overview of how these programs operate.

A particular state agency is made responsible for providing protective services by statute. In order for the agency to learn of problems suffered by impaired adults in the community, person in certain occupations who are likely to be aware of what occurs in impaired adults' lives may be required to report any suspected cases of abuse, neglect, or exploitation to the agency. Those made subject to mandatory reporting typically include medical practitioners, police, and court, hospital, nursing, and social services personnel.[130] In addition to those who must report, anyone else may voluntarily report suspected problems to the agency.

Once a problem has been reported to the agency, it must begin an investigation to determine if an abusive, neglectful, or exploitive situation involving an impaired adult in fact exists. Most protective services statutes mandate "prompt" investigations, which may be defined as beginning or requiring completion, within 24 to 72 hours. An investigation generally will require a home visit and consultation with persons knowledgeable about the reported problem.[131]

If the agency determines that a statutorily defined situation requiring intervention exists, the agency then becomes responsible for ensuring delivery of whatever protective or remedial services are needed to correct the situation. If these services are not voluntarily accepted by the impaired adult, they may be imposed upon him by court order, either through traditional existing protective proceedings brought at the agency's instigation, such as guardianship, conservatorship, or civil commitment, or through special court procedures authorized under a state's protective services statute. These may include hearings to secure court orders to provide protective services, for placing an impaired adult into an institution for emergency intervention when there is imminent danger to the adult's health or safety, or for allowing entry into an uncooperative adult's house.[132]

Although most statutes require that the services provided be the least restrictive alternative needed to remedy the situation,[133] statistics are unavailable to substantiate whether this happens in practice.[134]

Concerns regarding protective services. Forcing someone to accept protective services may take away his right to decide such matters as how he will live, what he will spend his money on, or where he will stay. Whether this intrusion is justified depends on the person's actual condition and circumstances. An elder who lacks the ability to manage personal or financial affairs and who is incapable of expressing any desires as to how her life should proceed suffers no real loss in having decisions made for her that she can no longer make for herself. An elder with limited abilities who voluntarily accepts protective service assistance suffers no real loss of control, since he has agreed to the provision of help. But an elder who is only partially impaired or merely eccentric, and who is forced to leave her home or to have others provide her services or treatment she may neither want nor be willing to accept is deprived of the right to determine the course of her own life. While the deprivation of rights is certain, actual improvements in the individual's life once services are provided may only be hoped for.

Unless protective services workers are well trained and truly sensitive to the balance between an individual's right to live as he sees fit and the state's need to protect those who are truly incapable of protecting themselves, it is likely that inappropriate intervention will occur. The very general labels used in protective services statutes, such as "abuse," "neglect," or "exploitation," "senility" or "the infirmities of aging," and even "protective services," "case work," or "placement services," allow protective service agencies, their workers, and the courts great leeway to intervene in the lives of people who may simply be peculiar or unconventional. At least one major writer in the field of protective services has expressed the fear that protective services are becoming in many states a mechanism to allow public agencies to assume total dominion over older clients.[135] It is ironic that the outcome of protective services intervention, premised on the idea of maintaining individuals in the community, is in nearly half of all cases placement of the impaired adult into a nursing home.[136]

NOTES

1. MICH. COMP. LAWS ANN. § 330.1402, .1441 (West 1986).
2. *See, e.g.*, ALASKA STAT. § 13.26.005(3) (1985); ARIZ. REV. STAT. ANN § 14-5101 (1975); COLO. REV. STAT. § 15-14-101(1) (1974); D.C. CODE ANN. § 21-2005(11) (Supp. 1987); GA. CODE ANN. § 295-6(a) (Supp. 1987); HAWAII REV. STAT. 560:5–101 (1985); IDAHO CODE § 15-5-101(a) (1979); ME. REV. STAT. ANN. tit. 18A, § 5-101 (1981); MINN. STAT. ANN. § 525.54 (West Supp. 1987); MONT. CODE ANN. § 72-5-101 (1986); NEB. REV. STAT. § 30-2601 (1985); N.H. REV. STAT. ANN. § 464-A:2 XI (Supp. 1986); N.M. STAT. ANN. § 45-5-101 (F) (1978); N.D. CENT. CODE § 30.1-26-01(1) (Supp. 1985); OR. REV. STAT. § 126.003(4) (1985); UTAH CODE ANN. § 75-1-201 (18) (1978).
3. U.P.C. § 5-101 (1974); U.G.P.P.A. § 1-201(7) (1983). The following jurisdictions have enacted either the U.P.C., the U.G.P.P.A. or a close variant. Alaska, Arizona, Colorado, District of Columbia, Hawaii, Idaho, Kansas, Maine, Michigan, Minnesota, Montana, Nebraska, New Hampshire, New Mexico.
4. COLO. REV. STAT. ANN. § 15-14-101(1) (1974).
5. *See, e.g.*, ARK. STAT. ANN. §§ 57-844 to 845 (Supp. 1985); COLO. REV. STAT. § 15-14-312(c) (Supp. 1986); D.C. CODE ANN. § 21-2047 (Supp. 1987); KAN. STAT. ANN. § 59-3018 (1983); MINN. REV. STAT. ANN. § 525.56(4) (Supp. 1987); N.H. REV. STAT. ANN. § 464-A:25 (1983 & Supp. 1986); WASH. REV. CODE ANN. §§ 11.88.090(5), 11.92.040 (1987).
6. S. Brakel, J. Parry, & B. Weiner, *The Mentally Disabled And the Law* 384 (3d ed. 1985).
7. *National Conference of the Judiciary on Guardianship Proceedings for the Elderly, Statement of Recommended Judicial Practices* 4 (American Bar Association Commission on Legal Problems of the Elderly 1986).
8. *See, e.g., The Mentally Disabled and the Law, supra* note 6 (table 7.4).
9. *Compare, e.g.*, U.P.C. § 5-312 (1977) (describing the general powers and duties of guardians) with U.P.C. §§ 5-408, 5-424, 5-425, and 5-426 (1977) (describing permissible court orders and administrative and distributive duties and responsibilites of conservators).
10. *Compare, e.g.*, MICH. COMP. LAWS ANN. § 700.443(2) (West 1986) (which provides a right to present evidence, engage in cross-examina-

tion, and request a jury trial in guardianship hearings) *with* MICH. COMP. LAWS ANN. § 700.467 (West 1986) (which makes no mention of any of the above rights in conservatorship hearings).

11. *See* U.G.P.P.A. §§ 2-205 (guardianship) and 2-309 (conservatorship); COLO. REV. STAT. ANN. §§ 15-14-311 (guardianship), 15-14-410 (conservatorship) (1974).

12. *See, e.g.*, U.G.P.P.A. § 2-206; GA. CODE ANN. § 29-5-6(e)(5) (Supp. 1987); FLA. STAT. ANN. § 744.312(3) (West 1986).

13. MICH. COMP. LAWS ANN. § 700.470(2) (West 1986).

14. The usual practice is to appoint kin as conservators, but if there is an adverse interest, dissent, or other substantial reason, a nonfamily member may be appointed. *Application of Weisman*, 112 App. Div. 2d 871, 493 N.Y.S.2d 151 (App. Div. 1985); *Brown v. Storz*, 710 S.W.2d 402 (Mo. Ct. App. 1986).

15. Public guardianship is becoming increasingly popular. Thirty-four states make statutory provisions for appointment of some form of public guardian, ranging from an office or official designated as public guardian to authorization for an agency or institution as guardian. *Statement of Recommended Judicial Practices, supra* note 7, at 56.

16. *See, e.g.*, *Matter of Guardianship of Brown*, 436 N.E.2d 877 (Ind. Ct. App. 1982).

17. A guardian was removed in a Maine case when there was a possible conflict of interest about the ward's residence. The guardian also was the administrator of the ward's community residential facility. *Estate of Peter C.*, 488 A.2d 468 (Me. 1985).

18. MICH. COMP. LAWS ANN. § 333.21767(1) (West 1986).

19. *See, e.g.*, U.G.P.P.A. § 2-209.

20. *See, e.g.*, statutes *supra* note 5.

21. *The Mentally Disabled and the Law, supra* note 6, at 377.

22. FLA. STAT. ANN. § 744.364 (West 1986).

23. *See generally* 39 Am. Jur. 2d, Guardian and Ward, note 30, at §§ 162-83 (1968 & Supp. 1987).

24. *Id.*

25. *See, e.g.*, *In re Guardianship of Styer*, 24 Ariz. App. 248, 536 P.2d 717 (Ct. App. 1975); *Storms v. Schilling*, 25 Or. App. 209, 207, 548 P.2d 529 (Ct. App. 1976).

26. *The Statement of Recommended Judicial Practices, supra* note 7, at 51-52 details press stories of failures in accounting, as well as a grand jury investigation in Dade County, Florida which found a great majority of 200 randomly selected cases had incomplete reports.

27. *See, e.g.*, U.P.C. § 5-414.

28. *See* D.C. CODE ANN. § 21-2060 (Supp. 1987).

29. *See, e.g.*, U.G.P.P.A. § 1-302(d).

30. The mere allegation that you are aged or senile will not be sufficient to support the petition. *See In re Asa B. Brown*, 45 Mich. 326, 7 N.W. 899 (1881).

31. N.Y. MENTAL HYG. LAW § 77.03 (McKinney 1978).

32. *The Mentally Disabled and the Law*, *supra* note 6, at 379.

33. *Id.* at 380.

34. U.P.C. § 5-103(7), U.G.P.P.A. § 1-201(7).

35. 636 P.2d 1085 (Utah 1981).

36. *Id.* at 1089.

37. *Harvey v. Meador*, 459 So.2d 288 (Miss. 1984); *In re Estate of Wagner*, 367 N.W.2d 736 (Neb. 1985).

38. *See* N.H. REV. STAT. ANN. § 474-A:2 XI (Supp. 1986); D.C. CODE ANN. § 21-2011(11)(16) (Supp. 1987).

39. *See* J. Ziskin, *Coping with Psychiatric and Psychological Testimony* (3d ed. 1981); Horstman, "Protective Services for the Elderly: The Limits of *Parens Patriae*," 40 *Mo. L. Rev.* 215 (1975).

40. Medical evidence relating to competency is required in some states. *See, e.g.*, ARK. STAT. ANN. § 57-615(b) (1971); MASS. ANN. LAWS ch. 201, § 6 (Michie/Law. Coop 1969 & Supp. 1987).

41. *See*, Annot., 9 A.L.R. 3d 774 (1966 & Supp. 1986).

42. *Lessard v. Schmidt*, 349 F. Supp. 1078 (E.D. Wis. 1972) *vacated*, 414 U.S. 473 (1974), *on remand*, 379 F. Supp. 1376 (E.D. Wis. 1974), *vacated and remanded*, 421 U.S. 957 (1975), *on remand*, 413 F. Supp. 1318 (E.D. Wis. 1976) (reinstating prior judgment).

43. *The Mentally Disabled and the Law*, *supra* note 6, (table 7.3).

44. *Id.*

45. *Id.*

46. *Lessard v. Schmidt*, *supra* note 42, the court found that a Wisconsin statute that required notice only of the date, time, and place of the hearing was constitutionally inadequate.

47. Notice must be "reasonably calculated, under all the circumstances, to appraise interested parties of the pendancy of the action and afford them an opportunity to present their objections." *Mullane v. Central Hanover Bank & Trust Co.*, 339 U.S. 306, 314 (1950).

48. *Dale v. Hahn*, 486 F.2d 76 (2d Cir. 1973).

49. *The Mentally Disabled and the Law*, *supra* note 6, at 381, 416-423 (table 7.4).

50. *Id.* at 382.

51. *Id.*

52. U.G.P.P.A. §§ 2-203(b), 2-306(b).

53. Several courts have said that guardians *ad litem* may be neutral fact-

finders or responsible for assisting the court in building a record, rather than advocating for the subject of the proceedings. *Mazza v. Pechacek*, 233 F.2d 666 (D.C. Cir. 1956); *In re Richard N.*, 506 A.2d 221 (Me. 1986)

54. Statement of Recommended Judicial Practices, *supra* note 7, at 3.

55. *In re Guardianship of Deere*, 708 P.2d 1123, 1126 (1985).

56. *Matter of Howes*, 471 A.2d 680 (Me. 1984).

57. *The Mentally Disabled and the Law*, *supra* note 6, at 382 (table 7.4).

58. *See, e.g.*, *In re Jobes*, 210 N.J. Super. Ct. 543, 510 A.2d 133,135 (Super. Ct. 1986).

59. MODEL RULES OF PROFESSIONAL CONDUCT Rule 1.2 (1983); MODEL CODE OF PROFESSIONAL RESPONSIBILITY EC-7-7 (1969).

60. *The Mentally Disabled and the Law*, *supra* note 7, at 382. Court decisions are mixed as to whether there is a right to jury trial. Right to jury trial: *LeJune v. Superior Court*, 218 Cal. 2d 696, 32 Cal. Rptr. 390 (1963). No right to jury trial: *Ward v. Booth*, 197 F.2d 963 (9th Cir. 1952); *Scherz v. Peoples National Bank*, 218 S.W.2d 86 (Ark. 1949).

61. *The Mentally Disabled and the Law*, *supra* note 6, at 382.

62. *The Mentally Disabled and the Law*, *supra* note 6, at 389.

63. *Id.*

64. *See In the Matter of Evatt*, 291 Ark. 153, 722 S.W.2d 851 (1987) for a case in which a temporary guardianship statute was found unconstitutional for lack of a speedy post appointment hearing with counsel and the right to cross-examine witnesses.

65. *See* ALASKA STAT. § 13.26.140 (Supp. 1985); D.C. CODE ANN. § 21-2046 (Supp. 1987); N.H. REV. STAT. ANN. § 464-A:12 (1983).

66. *The Mentally Disabled and the Law*, *supra* note 6, at 389.

67. *See, e.g.*, NEB. REV. STAT. § 30-2637 (1985).

68. *The Mentally Disabled and the Law*, *supra* note 6, at 392–94.

69. *Id.* Only a few states addresss the issue of when a restoration petition may be filed. The U.G.P.P.A authorizes a court to specify a period of up to one year in which a petition for restoration cannot be filed without special leave of the court. U.G.P.P.A. § 2-211.

70. *The Mentally Disabled and the Law* at 101–09 (table 2.3); 377.

71. *See* 2 Williston, *Contracts*, 249-57 (3d ed. 1959).

72. *The Mentally Disabled and the Law*, *supra* note 6, at 445.

73. N.Y. MENTAL HYG. LAW § 77.25 (McKinney 1978 & 1988 Supp.).

74. *The Mentally Disabled and the Law*, *supra* note 6, at 532–38 (table 9.1) The general rule is a guardian cannot consent to or refuse marriage on behalf of the ward. Courts have recognized marriage as a fundamental right and have determined that under some circumstances a guardian may be appointed to approve or disapprove of a

marriage. *In re Guardianship of Mikulanec*, 356 N.W.2d 683 (Minn. 1984).

75. *The Mentally Disabled and the Law*, *supra* note 6, at 441, 479–92. (table 8.2).

76. N.Y. MENTAL HYG. LAW § 77.25 (McKinney 1978 & 1988 Supp.).

77. *See, e.g.*, *Rossi v. Fletcher*, 135 U.S. App. D.C. 333, 418 F.2d 1169 (1969), *cert. denied*, 396 U.S. 1009 (1970); *Tucker v. Jollay*, 43 Tenn. App. 655, 311 S.W.2d 324 (Ct. App. 1957).

78. In some states, a statute of limitations for persons who are legally incompetent may be different depending on whether they have a guardian or not. *E.g.* ALASKA STAT. § 23.30.105 (1984) (relating to workman's compensation cases). *See generally The Mentally Disabled and the Law*, *supra* note 6, at 470.

79. Most state statutes follow the Uniform Probate Code or the Uniform Durable Power of Attorney Act and contain phrases such as "this power of attorney shall not be affected by subsequent disability or incapacity of the principal" or "this power shall become effective upon the disability, or incapacity of the principal." Some allow similar words showing the principal's intent to create a valid durable power of attorney. In three states—Georgia, Louisiana and Oregon—any written power of attorney is durable unless it contains language to the contrary. GA. CODE ANN. § 10-6-36 (1982); LA. CIV. CODE ANN. art. 3027 (B) (West Supp. 1986); OR. REV. STAT. § 126.407 (1985).

80. *See, e.g.*, *Golleher v. Horton*, 148 Ariz. 537, 715 P.2d 1225 (Ct. App. 1965); *Matter of Estate of Taggart*, 95 N.M. 117, 619 P.2d 562 (Ct. App. 1980).

81. *See* F. Collin, Jr., J. Lombard, Jr., A. Moses & H. Spitler, *Drafting the Durable Power of Attorney: A Systems Approach* (1984) for a description of state statutes and practice.

82. Several state statutes list the types of transactions which may be authorized by a durable power of attorney. *See, e.g.* 20 PA. CON. STAT. § 5602 (Supp. 1986); MINN. STAT. ANN. § 523.07 (West Supp. 1987); N.Y. GEN. OBLIG. LAWS § 5-1601 (McKinney 1978 & Supp. 1987).

83. *See, e.g.*, *Matter of Guardianship and Conservatorship of Swandal*, 681 P.2d 701 (Mont. 1984).

84. At least five states authorize general health-care decisions by a durable power of attorney. *See, e.g.*, CAL. CIV CODE §§ 2430-44, (Deering 1986); COLO. REV. STAT. § 14-14-501 (Supp. 1986); ME. REV. STAT. ANN. tit. 18A, § 5-501 (Supp. 1986); 20 PA. CONS STAT. ANN. §§ 5602 (a)(9); 5603(h) (Supp. 1986); R.I. GEN. LAWS § 23.4.10-1 to 2 (Supp. 1986). Two other states allow designation of a

proxy decisionmaker for treatment by artificial life-support system by durable power of attorney. IDAHO CODE § 39-4504 (Supp. 1986); UTAH CODE ANN. § 75-2-1106 (Supp. 1986).

85. Of the states with statutes authorizing health-care decisions only Colorado and Pennsylvania do not require more formalities than for the nonhealth care power.

86. *See* B. Mishkin, *A Matter of Choice* (1987), 28–29 (an information paper prepared for use by the Chairman and Ranking Minority Member of the Special Committee on Aging, United States Senate, distributed by the American Association of Retired Persons in co-operation with the American Bar Association and the American College of Physicians, also available from the Govt. Printing Office); *Drafting the Durable Power of Attorney, supra* note 81, at 24–25.

87. *In re Conroy*, 98 N.J. 321, 486 A. 2d 1209 (1985); *Bartling v. Superior Court*, 163 Cal. App. 3d 186, 209 Cal. Rptr. 220 (Ct. App. 1984).

88. New York and Washington.

89. *See In re Estate of Ward*, 523 A.2d 28 (N.H. 1986).

90. *The Uniform Probate Code Practice Manual* 561 (R. Wellman 2d ed. 1977).

91. *Supra* note 5.

92. Joint tenants have one and the same interests, accruing by one and the same conveyance, commencing at one and the same time, and held by one and the same undivided possession (the four unities). In a joint tenancy, the death of a joint tenant means that the entire tenancy remains with the survivor (the right of survivorship).

93. *See* U.P.C. § 6-103.

94. *See* U.P.C. § 6-104.

95. *See Murray v. Gadsden*, 91 U.S. App. D.C. 38, 197 F.2d 194 (1954); *Owen v. Owen*, 351 N.W.2d 139 (S.D. 1984); *Ebert v. Ritchey*, 458 A.2d 891 (Md. 1983); *Matter of Estate of Lewis*; 97 Idaho 299, 543 P.2d 852 (1975); *Slepkow v. Robinson*, 324 A.2d 321 (R.I. 1974); *O'Hair v. O'Hair*, 109 Ariz. 236, 508 P.2d 66 (1973).

96. If a sole depositor wants to create an account with the right of survivorship, he should use exact words such as "these funds are held by joint tenants with the right of survivorship." *See Chopin v. Interfirst Bank Dallas N.A.* 694 S.W.2d 79 (Tex. Ct. App. 1985).

97. *See Matter of Forward*, 86 App. Div. 2d 850, 447 N.Y.S.2d 286 (App. Div. 1982); *Matter of Waxman*, 96 App. Div. 2d 906, 466 N.Y.S.2d 85 (App. Div. 1983).

98. *The Mentally Disabled and the Law, supra* note 6, at 55–56, 72.

99. *Id.* at 72.

100. *See, e.g.,* CAL. WELF. & INST. CODE § 5008(h) (Deering Supp.

1987). At least nine states use the term gravely disabled in their civil commitment statutes. California has a special conservatorship statute, the Lanterman-Petris-Short Act, under which the conservator may admit his ward to a treatment facility.

101. In this chapter we will discuss involuntary commitments made for reasons of mental illness rather than developmental disability because, to the extent involuntary commitment is applicable to elderly persons, the mental health system is more likely to be used.

102. American Psychiatric Association, *Diagnostic and Statistical Manual* 110–12 (3d ed. 1980) (DSM-III). There is a revised DSM-III, the DSM-IIIR but all citations are to the third edition, unrevised.

103. It has been argued that nursing-home placements are essentially equivalent to involuntary civil commitments, and procedures appropriate to civil commitment should be utilized. *See* Cohen, "Civil Liberties and the Frail Elderly," 15 *Society* 34 (1978).

104. *The Mentally Disabled and the Law*, *supra* note 6, at 405–7 (table 7.2); *See, e.g.*, *In re Boyd*, 403 A.2d 744 (D.C. 1979).

105. Former Chief Justice Warren Burger was strongly identified with this theory. *See, e.g.*, *Addington v. Texas*, 441 U.S. 418 (1979) at 427–29.

106. *See, e.g.*, *Humphrey v. Cady*, 405 U.S. 504 (1972); *Addington*, *supra* at 425.

107. All but three states—Alabama, Arkansas, and Mississippi—allow for emergency detention. *The Mentally Disabled and the Law*, *supra* note 6, at 501.

108. *The Mentally Disabled and the Law*, *supra* note 6, at 54.

109. *Id.* at 65.

110. *Id.*

111. *Id.* at 69. New York has an administrative agency, the Mental Health Information Service, which provides advice and counsel to patients. A statute, N.Y. MENTAL HYG. LAW § 29.09, also provides a right to counsel. In *Project Release v. Prevost*, 722 F.2d 960 (2d Cir. 1983), plaintiff's argued, to no avail, that the existence of the MHIS undermined the statutory entitlement to counsel.

112. *Id.*

113. *See, e.g.*, *Project Release*, *supra* note 111, at 976; *Heryford v. Parker*, 396 F.2d 393, 396 (10th Cir. 1968); *Dixon v. Atty. General*, 325 F. Supp. 966, 974 (M.D. Pa. 1971); *In re Hop*, 29 Cal. 3d 82, 94, 623 P.2d 282, 289, 171 Cal. Rptr. 721, 728 (1981); *In re Fisher*, 39 Ohio St. 2d 71, 72, 313 N.E.2d 851, 858 (1974).

114. *The Mentally Disabled and the Law*, *supra* note 6, at 65.

115. *See, e.g.*, *In re Morrow*, 463 A.2d 689 (D.C. 1983).

116. *See, e.g.*, D.C. CODE ANN. 21-541, 547 (Supp. 1986).

117. The state of Utah does require the diagnosed illness be listed in the *Diagnostic and Statistical Manual*. UTAH CODE ANN. § 64-7-28(1) (1986).

118. *See Addington, supra* note 105, at 429–30.

119. The American Psychiatric Association is on record as opposing involvement in predicting dangerousness. *See The Mentally Disabled and the Law, supra* note 6, at 34, n. 106.

120. Several courts have found a recent overtly dangerous act is required to justify commitment: *Suzuki v. Yuen*, 617 F.2d 173 (9th Cir. 1980); *Stamus v. Leonhardt*, 414 F. Supp. 439 (S.D. Iowa 1976); *Doremus v. Farrell*, 407 F. Supp. 509 (D. Neb. 1975); *Lynch v. Baxley*, 386 F. Supp. 378 (M.D. Ala. 1978); *Lessard v. Schmidt, supra* note 42. Other courts have found no recent overt act is required: *Project Release v. Prevost*, 722 F.2d 960 (2d Cir. 1983); *Colyar v. Third Judicial District Court*, 469 F. Supp. 428 (D. Utah 1979); *United States ex rel. Matthew v. Nelson*, 461 F. Supp. 707 (N.D. Ill. 1978); *In re Snowden*, 423 A.2d 188 (D.C. 1980).

121. *The Mentally Disabled and the Law, supra* note 6, at 68.

122. Salend, Kane, Satz & Pynos, "Elder Abuse Reporting: Limitations of Statutes," 24 *Gerontologist* 61 (1984) [Salend].

123. ILL. ANN. STAT. ch. 23 § 6502(2)(B) (Smith-Hurd 1986).

124. *See generally* M. Kapp & A. Bigot, *Geriatrics and the Law*, 87–111 (1985) [hereafter, Kapp & Bigot].

125. Mich. Dep't. of Social Services, *Adult Protective Services in Michigan*, 3–4, (rev. ed. Sept. 1983).

126. FLA. STAT. ANN. § 410.104 (1)–(4) (West 1986).

127. OHIO REV. CODE ANN. § 5101.60 (N) (Baldwin 1986).

128. ALA. CODE § 38-9-2(9) (1986).

129. Kapp & Bigot, *supra* note 124.

130. Salend, *supra* note 122, at 64.

131. Salend, *supra* note 122, at 62.

132. Regan, "Protecting the Elderly: The New Paternalism," 32 *Hasting L.J.* 1110, at 1113 (1982) [Regan].

133. S.C. CODE ANN. § 43-29-20 (Law. Co-op. 1986); WISC. STAT. ANN. § 55.06(9)(A) (West 1986); *see also*, Note, "Toward Eliminating the Abuse, Neglect, and Exploitation of the Impaired Adults: The District of Columbia Protective Service Act of 1984," 35 *Cath. U.L. Rev.* 1193 (1986) (arguing that the District of Columbia's protective services statute, which is the most recently enacted statute, is effectively providing clients with the least restrictive alternative).

134. Salend, *supra* note 122, at 65.

135. Regan, *supra* note 132, at 1127.

136. Katz, "Elder Abuse," 18 *J. Fam. L.* 695 (1978–80).

11

The Right to Refuse Medical Treatment

Does the right of an individual to decline medical treatment exist, even when such treatment is needed to sustain life? The question has become increasingly important as medical technology has advanced to the point where through the use of intravenous or tubal feeding, respirators, and other medical devices, life can be prolonged beyond the point where disease would normally result in death. To many, the prospect of prolonging life in such a way is an affront to human dignity. Another question arises, then: What can a person do to ensure that unwanted medical measures are not undertaken?

Do I have a right to be told about the treatment a doctor plans to give me?
Yes. Your doctor is required to describe to you the proposed treatment. Information must be given on the probability of the success of the treatment, the alternatives to this kind of treatment, and the risks inherent in accepting or rejecting the treatment.

How detailed must this disclosure be?
Basically a doctor has an obligation to disclose the information you need to enable you to choose among a range of available and potentially beneficial treatments. This disclosure should include a discussion of your current medical status and the likely outcome if no treatment is provided; the interventions that might be helpful to you, including a description of the procedures involved and the likelihood and effect of associated risks and benefits; and, in most cases, a professional opinion as to which is the best choice. In general, the doctor must give you all the information any other doctor would give you in the same situation. In recent years, there has been a trend toward encouraging doctors to provide all the information *you* need to make a proper choice, regardless of whether another person might need less or more information.[1] In any case, you are always free to ask as many questions as you need to understand your situation.

May a doctor give me treatment without first obtaining my consent?

No. A doctor may not provide treatment, administer diagnostic tests, or perform surgery without first fully informing you about the treatment and then obtaining your knowing consent. This is the doctrine of informed consent. If treatment is provided without proper consent or if the doctor has withheld the available information you need in order to properly consent, the doctor may be sued for battery or negligence and may be liable to you for money damages.

May I refuse to consent to medical treatment?

Yes. Every competent adult is entitled to refuse medical treatment, even if that refusal may result in life-threatening conditions or death. Your right to make your own medical decisions—including the right to refuse treatment—is part of your right of self-determination, which has been called your right to be "let alone."[2] A number of state courts have found that the right to refuse medical treatment is also protected by the privacy guarantees of both state and federal constitutions.[3] In limited circumstances your right to refuse treatment could be outweighed by interests the state might have in preserving its citizens' lives. These interests are now very unlikely to outweigh your right to refuse treatment unless the treatment could restore you to a healthy life and refusal of it would result in your death and the subsequent abandonment of your small children to the care of the state.

Are there legal distinctions made between different kinds of medical treatment?

All forms of medical treatment may be rejected. The earlier court cases and discussions of ethical behavior focused on artificial life-sustaining treatment such as respirators, in which the physical "invasiveness" of the treatment was considered in determining whether the patient was entitled to refuse it.[4] Recently it has become clear that whether a treatment is "invasive" depends on whether the patient would want to have it continued. If not, it is considered invasive because it is against the patient's wishes.[5]

Attempts to categorize particular forms of treatment as "ordinary" or "extraordinary" or "heroic" or "usual" have also been discarded.[6] The reason for this is that a particular treatment may be ordinary in one situation and extraordinary in another. For example, a nasogastric tube inserted after an operation which will be removed once the patient recovers from surgery may be "ordinary," while the same tube for a permanently unconscious patient who will never be able to eat on his own or recover to cognitive life may be "extraordinary." The patient or substitute decisionmaker is entitled to reject any unwanted treatment.

There has been debate in recent years as to whether artificially or technologically supplied nutrition and hydration ("tube feeding") is medical treatment that can be forgone. The courts of a number of states have now considered this issue and have held that artificial feeding is equivalent to other forms of high technology medical treatment and can be withheld or withdrawn.[7] The symbolism of feeding cannot be denied, but it is widely (although not unanimously) accepted that there is a clear distinction between the nurturing aspects of normal feeding and the provision of sustenance by technology.[8] In hospices, for instance, artificial feeding is rarely recommended precisely because its provision can impede the family's and friends' ability to touch and hold the patient. The distinction has been stated by the New Jersey Supreme Court as follows:

> Certainly, feeding has an emotional significance. As infants we could breathe without assistance, but we were dependent on others for our lifeline of nourishment. Even more, feeding is an expression of nurturing and caring, certainly for infants and children, and in many cases for adults as well. Once one enters the realm of complex, high-technology medical care, it is hard to shed the "emotional symbolism" of food. However, artificial feedings such as nasogastric tubes, gastrostomies, and intravenous infusions are significantly different from bottle-feeding or spoon-feeding—they are medical procedures with inherent risks and possible side effects, instituted by skilled healthcare providers to compensate for impaired physical functioning. Analytically, artificial feeding by means of a nasogastric tube or intravenous infusion can be seen as equivalent to artificial breathing by means of a respirator. Both prolong life

through mechanical means when the body is no longer able to perform a vital bodily function on its own.[9]

In some states the right to refuse medical treatment (including artificial feeding) has been found to be constitutionally protected, which means that it cannot be restricted by legislation.[10]

How will my competence to make medical decisions be determined?

You are assumed to be competent unless you are proven to be otherwise. If you can understand your medical condition and the effects of treatment and nontreatment, you are legally competent to make your own medical decisions. What is at issue is a common-sense evaluation of whether a person has, or lacks, "decision-making capacity" about this particular decision.[11] Refusing treatment that a physician recommends, forgetfulness in other areas of life, and even diagnosed mental illness, do not alone justify a conclusion of incompetence to make medical decisions. A person who has been adjudicated incompetent may still be able to make medical decisions. Similarly, some people not adjudicated incompetent may be unable to make such decisions. The only question to be asked is whether the patient has the ability to understand the particular medical situation and to make a choice in light of that understanding.[12]

What rights will I have to authorize or reject medical care when I am unconscious or otherwise unable to make medical decisions?

You keep the rights you had when you were competent when you become unable to make current medical decisions. The question becomes how should the people around you—your family, friends, and medical providers—determine what you would have wanted in your present condition. In general, they are required to make the decision you would have made, regardless of whether they agree with you or whether most people would make the same decision. This is known as "substituted judgment." As one court has stated, the standard is "a subjective one consistent with the notion that the right we are seeking to effectuate is a very personal right to control one's own life. The question is not what a reasonable or average person would have chosen to do under the circumstances but what the particular patient would have done if able to choose for himself."[13]

There are two kinds of substituted judgment. The first occurs when the patient's specific wishes are known and can be reported by family or representatives.[14] The second involves decisions which can be made by a family member or representative, based upon the patient's general known attitudes even though no specific discussions about the treatment at issue have taken place.[15] Decisions made on behalf of people who have never been able to make their own medical decisions (e.g., some of the mentally retarded) must be based on the second approach.[16]

The subjective standard is different from a "best interests" standard. The latter is based upon what most people would want in similar circumstances. Decisions made in the best interests of the patient are acceptable only if it is impossible to ascertain the patient's actual or inferred wishes.[17] When determining a patient's best interests the "benefits" and "burdens" of the proposed treatment are weighed against each other.[18]

In practice, adherence to the patient's known or inferred choice usually will also be in the patient's best interest. In recognition of this, some courts have intermingled the two tests.[19]

How can I best protect my rights to have the kind of medical treatment I want if I become unable to make decisions?

There are a variety of ways you can protect your rights to have your choice about medical treatment carried out when you are permanently unconscious or otherwise permanently unable to make decisions. It is important to note that there is a vast difference between planning for treatment at the end of your life, when there is no hope of recovery, and planning for treatment in situations in which you are temporarily incapacitated, but with medical assistance, will be able to recover and make future decisions. In these latter situations, it will be assumed (unless you explicitly state otherwise in advance) that you *do* want treatment, and you will receive all the treatment available to restore you. This is the "emergency exception" to the doctrine of informed consent.

Your right to accept or refuse treatment when you are unable to make decisions and have no prospects for recovery can be protected by executing an "advance directive" (often known as a "living will") and by appointing another person as your proxy decisionmaker. Living wills can be useful both in states with "natural death" statutes and in states which have not yet enacted such legislation.

Thirty-eight states and the District of Columbia have enacted natural death or living will laws.[20] Although no two of these statutes are identical, all provide for execution of a document in advance which can be used to state that you do not want certain kinds of life-sustaining treatment if you are in a "terminal condition" (usually defined in the statute.) All the statutes provide immunity, civil and criminal, for physicians who act in accordance with your directive. The statutes all require that you be given care needed for your comfort. All also permit easy revocation of your advance directive. Each statute requires the advance directive to be signed and witnessed, and in most states, the people who may witness are restricted to those who will not inherit from you or otherwise "benefit" from your death. Most of the statutes permit you to add personal instructions to your advance directive. In most, physicians who are unwilling to comply with your wishes are required to transfer you or help with your transfer to another physician. All the statutes state that refusal of life support under the statute does not constitute suicide and that insurance is not affected by execution of an advance directive.

Some natural death statutes also provide procedures for decisionmaking for people who have not executed advance directives (the decision is usually assigned to family members in a stated order of priority) and for oral directives by patients before they become incompetent. The suggested forms vary from state to state, but one recommended form to which personal instructions can be added is as follows:[21]

> If I should have an incurable or irreversible condition that will cause my death within a relatively short time, and I am no longer able to make decisions regarding my medical treatment, I direct my attending physician, pursuant to the [Natural Death Act in the state], to withhold or withdraw treatment that only prolongs the process of dying and is not necessary to my comfort or to alleviate pain.

Signed this _____ day of _____, _____

Signature _____

Address _____
The declarant voluntarily signed this writing in my presence.

Witness _____
Address _____
Witness _____
Address _____

Even without legislation, living wills offer important protection because they constitute evidence of your wishes which guide your substitute decisionmakers. Here is one widely available form for use in such states.[22]

LIVING WILL DECLARATION

To My Family Doctors, and All Those Concerned with My Care

I, _____, being of sound mind, make this statement as a directive to be followed if I become unable to participate in decisions regarding my medical care.

If I should be in an incurable or irreversible mental or physical condition with no reasonable expectation of recovery, I direct my attending physician to withhold or withdraw treatment that merely prolongs my dying. I further direct that treatment be limited to measures to keep me comfortable and to relieve pain.

These directions express my right to refuse treatment. Therefore I expect my family, doctor, and everyone concerned with my care to regard themselves as legally and morally bound to act in accord with my wishes, and in so doing to be free of any legal liability for having followed my direction.

I especially do not want: _____
Other instructions/comments: _____

Proxy designation Clause: Should I become unable to communicate my instructions as stated above, I designate the following person to act in my behalf:

Name _____
Address _____

If the person I have named is unable to act in my behalf, I authorize the following person to do so:

Name _____

Address_____

Signed: _____ Date: _____

Witness: (Name & Address)   Witness: (Name & Address)

Keep the signed original with your personal papers at home. Give signed copies to your doctors, family, and to your proxy. Make sure that if you change doctors, your new doctor also gets a copy. Initial and date it periodically to show that it stills represents your wishes.

Several natural death statutes expressly recognize the appointment of a proxy to make decisions on the patient's behalf.[23] Sometimes the statute makes reference, in this context, to the state's durable power of attorney statute.

All fifty states and the District of Columbia now have durable power of attorney statutes.[24] Some of these specifically provide that an agent appointed under the statute is empowered to make medical decisions on the principal's behalf;[25] others have been interpreted to permit medical decisionmaking.[26] Several have special forms for appointment of such an agent. The majority of durable power of attorney statutes do not specifically mention the power to make medical decisions on the principal's behalf, but many people think that they should be read to include this power.

The advantage of appointing an agent is that it singles out one particular friend or family member to make decisions for you and tells your doctor that this is the person you have chosen and have entrusted with your wishes. It is also a valuable adjunct in making choices and interpreting ambiguities in your living will should the need arise. A personal advocate can also give weight to your living will.

Written living wills and proxy appointments are not, however, the only way of having your wishes carried out. The natural death acts usually define the group of patients to whom they apply (the definitions of "terminal condition" or permanent unconsciousness vary from state to state) and the procedures which may be withheld under the act (which also vary from state to state). You do, however, keep your rights to refuse treatment even if you are not in a condition covered by the statute or have not appointed an agent or proxy. Numerous courts have now held that treatment may be refused on an incompetent patient's behalf when (1) there is no statute;[27] (2) there is a statute, but the patient is not covered by it because, for instance, the patient is not "terminally ill" or has not executed a directive;[28] (3) the treatment at issue (for instance artificially supplied nutrition and hydration) is not a treatment that is included in the statute's definition of those that may be withheld or withdrawn.[29] In these situations the courts in each case have looked for evidence of what the patient would have wanted, whether in written form, reports of conversations with family and friends, or in general attitudes toward medical care and religious beliefs. There is a growing acceptance that close family members or appointed representatives are the best people to make these decisions on behalf of the incompetent patient. Prior court approval is not usually necessary.[30]

What kind of instructions should I put in my living will and what should I discuss with my agent, proxy, family, and friends?

It is important that your instructions for treatment at the end of life be as personal and specific as possible. You may wish to specify the kinds of treatment you do and do not wish to have. Many people state their preferences, for instance, about artificial feeding, cardiac resuscitation, respirator support, antibiotics, dialysis, surgery, chemotherapy, insulin, and radiation. Many people ask for relief from pain, and some specify that if possible they wish to die at home. Some people state that they do not want life sustaining medical treatment if, with reasonable medical certainty, there is no chance that they will regain cognitive abilities.

As part of a proxy appointment, you might wish to authorize your agent in writing to make decisions to give or withhold consent to specific medical or surgical measures with reference to your condition, prognosis, and known wishes regarding terminal care; to authorize appropriate end-of-life care, including pain-relieving procedures; to grant releases to medical personnel; to employ and discharge medical personnel; to have access to and to disclose medical records and other personal information; to resort to court, if necessary, to obtain court authorization regarding withholding or withdrawal of medical treatment; and to expend (or withhold) funds necessary to carry out medical treatment.

What will happen if my doctor does not follow my advance directive?

In nearly all the states with living will legislation, doctors who do not wish to comply with a person's directive are required to transfer or effect the transfer of the patient to another doctor. As a general matter, a living will or oral directions to an agent or family member or friend are evidence of your refusal of consent; and as a matter of legal theory, the provision of even life-sustaining treatment in contravention of a patient's known wishes is an actionable battery for which damages against medical care providers could be sought.[31]

NOTES

1. *See* President's Commission for the Study of Ethical Problems in Medicine and Biomedical and Behavioral Research, *Making Health Care Decisions*, p. 23 (1982).

2. *Olmstead v. United States*, 277 U.S. 438 (1928).

3. *See, e.g., Bartling v. Superior Court*, 163 Cal. App. 3d 186, 209 Cal. Rptr. 220 (Ct. App. 1984); *Bouvia v. Superior Court* (Glenchur), 179 Cal. App. 3d 1127, 225 Cal. Rptr. 297 (Ct. App. 1986), *review denied* (Cal. June 5, 1986); *Brophy v. New England Sinai Hospital, Inc.*, 398 Mass. 417, 497 N.E.2d 626 (1986); *Corbett v. D'Alessandro*, 487 So. 2d 368 (Fla. Dist. Ct. App.), *review denied*, 492 So. 2d 1331 (Fla. 1986); *Foody v. Manchester Memorial Hospital*, 40 Conn. Supp. 127, 482 A.2d 713 (Super. Ct. 1984); *In re L.H.R.*, 253 Ga. 439, 321 S.E.2d 716 (1984); *Leach v. Akron General Medical Center*, 68 Ohio Misc. 1, 426 N.E.2d 809 (Com. Pl. 1980); *In re Quinlan*, 70 N.J. 10, 355 A.2d 647, *cert. denied sub nom. Garger v. New Jersey*, 429 U.S. 922 (1976), *overruled in part on other grounds, In re Conroy* N.J. 321, 486 A.2d 1209 (1985); *Rasmussen v. Fleming*, 154 Ariz. 207, 741 P.2d 674 (1987); *In re Torres*, 357 N.W.2d 332 (Minn. 1984); *Tune v. Walter Reed Army Medical Hospital*, 602 F. Supp. 1452 (D.D.C. 1985).

4. *See, e.g., In re Quinlan*, 70 N.J. 10, 355 A.2d 647, *cert. denied sub nom. Gerger v. New Jersey*, 429 U.S. 922 (1976), *overruled in part on other grounds, In re Conroy* N.J. 321, 486 A.2d 1209 (1985).

5. *Brophy v. New England Sinai Hospital, Inc.*, 398 Mass. 417, 497 N.E.2d 626 (1986). *See also Superintendent of Belchertown State School v. Saikewicz*, 373 Mass. 728, 370 N.E.2d 417 (1977); *In re Requena*, 213 N.J. Super. 475, 517 A.2d 886 (Super. Ct. Ch. Div.),

aff'd, 213 N.J. Super. 443, 517 A.2d 869 (Super. Ct. App. Div. 1986). (*per curiam*).

6. *See, e.g., Barber v. Superior Court*, 147 Cal. App. 3d 1006, 195 Cal. Rptr. 484 (Ct. App. 1983); *In re Conroy*, 98 N.J. 321, 486 A.2d 1209 (1985).

7. *See, e.g., Barber v. Superior Court*, 147 Cal. App. 3d 1006, 195 Cal. Rptr. 484 (Ct. App. 1983); *In re Bayer*, No. 4131 (N.D. Burleigh County Ct. Feb. 5, 11, 1987) (Riskedahl, J.); *Bouvia v. Superior Court (Glenchur)*, 179 Cal. App. 3d 1127, 225 Cal. Rptr. 297 (Ct. App. 1986), *review denied* (Cal. June 5, 1986); *Brophy v. New England Sinai Hospital, Inc.*, 398 Mass. 417, 197 N.E.2d 626 (1986); *Cantor v. Weiss*, No. 626 163 (Cal. Super. Ct. Los Angeles County Dec. 30, 1986) (Newman, J.); *In re Conroy*, 98 N.J. 321, 486 A.2d 1209 (1985). *Corbett v. D'Alessandro*, 487 So. 2d 368 (Fla. Dist. Ct. App.), *review denied*, 492 So. 2d 1331 (Fla. 1986); *Delio v. Westchester County Medical Center*, 129 A.D.2d 1, 516 N.Y.S.2d 677 (App. Div. 2d Dep't 1987); *In re Jane Doe*, No. 2560 (Pa. Ct. Com. Pl. Aug. 19, 1987) (Lehrer, J.); Legal Intelligencer, Sept. 2, 1987, at 1, col. 2; *Gary v. California* (Hirth), No. 576 123 (Cal. Super Ct. San Diego County March 23, *modified in part*, April 15, 1987) (Milkes, J.); *In re Gardner*, 534 A.2d 947 (Me. 1987); *In re Guardianship of Grant*, 109 Wash. 2d 545, 747 P.2d 445 (1987); *Hazelton [sic] v. Powhatan Nursing Home, Inc.*, No. CH 98287 (Va. Cir. Ct. Fairfax County Aug. 29, 1986), *order signed* (Sept. 2, 1986), (Fortkort, J.), *appeal denied*, Record No. 860814 (Va. Sept. 2, 1986); *In re Jobes*, 108 N.J. 394, 529 A.2d 133 (1987); *In re Peter*, 108 N.J. 365, 529 A.2d 419 (1987); *In re Requena*, 213 N.J. Super. 475, 517 A.2d 886 (Super. Ct. Ch. Div.) *aff'd*, 213 N.J. Super. 443, 517 A.2d 869 (Super. Ct. App. Div. 1986) (per curiam); *In re Rodas*, No. 86PR139 (Colo. Dist. Ct. Mesa County Jan. 22, 1987) (Buss, J.); *Wilcox v. Hawaii*, Civ. No. 860116 (Hawaii Cir. Ct. 5th Cir. June 16, 1986) (Hirano, J.).

8. *See, e.g.* Opinion of the American Medical Association, Council on Ethical and Judicial Affairs, Mar. 15, 1986.

9. *In re Conroy*, 98 N.J. 321, 372, 486 A.2d 1209, 1236 (1985).

10. *See, e.g., Corbett v. D'Alessandro*, 487 So. 2d 368 (Fla. Dist. Ct. App.), *review denied*, 492 So. 2d 1331 (Fla. 1986).

11. President's Commission for the Study of Ethical Problems in Medicine and Biomedical Behavioral Research, *Deciding to Forego Life-Sustaining Treatment* (1983) p. 121 ff.

12. Courts' discussions of this issue are found in *e.g. Lane v. Candura*, 6 Mass. App. 377, 576 N.E.2d 435 (1978); *In re Estate of Brooks*, 32 Ill. 2d 361, 205 N.E.2d 435 (1965); *In re Yetter*, 62 Pa. D & C2d 619

(1973); *State Dept. of Human Services v. Northern*, 563 S.W.2d 197 (Tenn. Ct. App. 1978).

13. *In re Conroy*, 98 N.J. 321, 486 A.2d 1209 (1985).

14. *See, e.g., In re Peter*, 108 N.J. 365, 529 A.2d 419 (1987).

15. *See, e.g., In re Jobes*, 108 N.J. 394, 529 A.2d 434 (1987).

16. *See, e.g., Superintendent of Belchertown State School v. Saikewics*, 373 Mass. 728, 370 N.E.2d 417 (1977).

17. *See, e.g., Rasmussen v. Fleming*, 154 Ariz. 207, 741 P.2d 674 (1987).

18. *Barber v. Superior Court*, 147 Cal. App. 3d 1006, 195 Cal. Rptr. 484 (Ct. App. 1983).

19. *See, e.g., In re Torres*, 357 N.W.2d 332 (Minn. 1984); *Foody v. Manchester Memorial Hospital*, 40 Conn. Supp. 127, 482 A.2d 713 (Super. Ct. 1984).

20. Alabama Natural Death Act, Ala. Code §§ 22-8A-1 to -10 (1984); Alaska Rights of Terminally Ill Act, ALASKA STAT §§ 18.12.010–.100 (Supp. 1986); Arizona Medical Treatment Decision Act, ARIZ. REV. STAT. ANN. §§ 36–3201 to –3210 (1986); Arkansas Rights of the Terminally Ill or Permanently Unconscious Act, 1987 Ark. Acts 713; California Natural Death Act, CAL. HEALTH & SAFETY CODE §§ 7185–7195 (Supp. 1987); Colorado Medical Treatment Decision Act, COLO. REV. STAT. §§ 15-18-101 to -113 (Supp. 1986); Connecticut Removal of Life Support Systems Act, CONN. GEN. STAT. §§ 19a-570 to -575 (1987); Delaware Death with Dignity Act, DEL. CODE ANN. tit. 16, §§ 2501-2509 (1983); District of Columbia Natural Death Act of 1981, D.C. CODE ANN. §§ 6-2421 to -2430 (Supp. 1986); Florida Life-Prolonging Procedure Act, FLA. STAT. ANN. §§ 765.01 to -.15 (1986); Georgia Living Wills Act, GA. CODE ANN. §§ 31-32-1 to -12 (1985 & Supp. 1986), amended 1987 Ga. Laws 488; Hawaii Medical Treatment Decisions Act, HAWAII REV. STAT. §§ 327D-1 to -27 (Supp. 1986); Idaho Natural Death Act, IDAHO CODE §§ 39-4501 to -4508 (1985 & Supp. 1986); Illinois Living Will Act, ILL. ANN. STAT. ch. 110 ½ §§ 701-710 (Smith-Hurd Supp. 1986); Indiana Living Wills and Life-Prolonging Procedures Act, IND. CODE ANN. §§ 16-8-11-1 to -17 (Burns Supp. 1986); Iowa Life-Sustaining Procedures Act, IOWA CODE ANN. §§ 144A.1 to -.11 (West Supp. 1986), amended H.F. 360, 1987 Session, 72nd Iowa General Assembly; Kansas Natural Death Act, KAN. STAT. ANN. §§ 65-28,101 to -28,109 (1985); Louisiana Life-Sustaining Procedures Act, LA. REV. STAT. ANN. §§ 40:1299.58.1 to -.10 (West Supp. 1987); Maine Living Wills Act, ME. REV. STAT. ANN. tit. 22, §§ 2921-2931 (Supp. 1986); Maryland Life-Sustaining Procedures Act, MD. HEALTH-GENERAL CODE ANN. §§ 5-601 to -614 (Supp. 1986); Mississippi

Withdrawal of Life-Saving Mechanisms Act, Miss. Code Ann. §§ 41-41-101 to -121 (Supp. 1986); Missouri Life Support Declarations Act, Mo. Ann. Stat. §§ 459.010 to -.055 (Vernon Supp. 1987); Montana Living Will Act, Mont. Code Ann. §§ 50-9-101 to -104, -111, -201 to -206 (1985); Nevada Withholding or Withdrawal of Life-Sustaining Procedures Act, Nev. Rev. Stat. §§ 449.540 to -.690 (1986); New Hampshire Terminal Care Document Act, N.H. Rev. Stat. Ann. §§ 137-H:1 to -H:16 (Supp. 1986); New Mexico Right to Die Act, N.M. Stat. Ann. §§ 24-7-1 to -11 (1986); North Carolina Right to Natural Death Act, N.C. Gen. Stat. Ann. §§ 90-320 to -322 (1985); Oklahoma Natural Death Act, Okla. Stat. Ann. tit. 63, §§ 3101-3111 (West Supp. 1987); Oregon Rights with Respect to Terminal Illness Act, Or. Rev. Stat. §§ 97.050 to -.090 (1985); South Carolina Death with Dignity Act, S.C. Code Ann. §§ 44-77-10 to -160 (Law. Co-op Supp. 1986); Tennessee Right to Natural Death Act, Tenn. Code Ann. §§ 32-11-101 to -110 (Supp. 1986); Texas Natural Death Act, Tex. Rev. Civ. Stat. Ann. art. 4590h (Vernon Supp. 1987); Utah Personal Choice and Living Will Act, Utah Code Ann. §§ 75-2-1101 to -1118 (Supp. 1986); Vermont Terminal Care Document Act, Vt. Stat. Ann. tit. 18, §§ 5251-5262 and tit. 13, § 1801 (Supp. 1985); Virginia Natural Death Act, Va. Code §§ 54-325.8:1 to -:13 (Supp. 1986); Washington Natural Death Act, Wash. Rev. Code Ann. §§ 70.122.010 to -.905 (Supp. 1987); West Virginia Natural Death Act, W. Va. Code §§ 16-30-1 to -10 (1985); Wisconsin Natural Death Act, Wisc. Stat. Ann. §§ 154.01 to -.15 (West Supp. 1986); Wyoming Act, Wyo. Stat. §§ 33-26-144 to -152 (Supp. 1986). *See also* Uniform Rights of Terminally Ill Act, §§ 1-18, 9A U.L.A. 456 (Supp. 1986).

21. This form is taken from the Uniform Rights of the Terminally Ill Act, §§ 1-18, 9A U.L.A. 456 (Supp. 1986) adopted by the National Conference of Commissioners on Uniform State Laws (and endorsed by the American Bar Association). The commissioners proposed this act as a model for enactment in all the states to provide uniformity.

22. This form is distributed by the Society for the Right to Die. The appropriate form for use in each state, with guidelines for its execution is available, free of charge, from the Society for the Right to Die, 250 West 57th Street, New York, NY 10107.

23. *See, e.g.*, Arizona Medical Treatment Decision Act (1985); Ariz. Rev. Stat. Ann. §§ 36-3201 to -3210 (1986); Florida Life-Prolonging Procedure Act (1984); Fla. Stat. Ann. §§ 765.01 to -.15 (1986). *See* Checklist Chart of Living Will Laws, Society for the Right to Die (1987).

24. Ala. Code § 26-1-2 (Supp. 1985); Alaska Stat. §§ 13.26.325, 13.26.330

(1985); ARIZ. REV. STAT. ANN. §§ 14-5501, 14-5502 (1975); ARK. STAT. ANN. §§ 58-501 to 58-511 (Repl. 1971, Supp. 1985), §§ 58-701 to 58-704 (Supp. 1985); CAL. CIV CODE §§ 2400-07, 2430-44, 2500-08, 2510-13 (West Supp. 1986); COLO. REV. STAT. §§ 15-14-501 to 15-14-502 (Supp. 1985); CONN. GEN. STAT. ANN. §§ 1-42 to 1-56 (West 1969) § 45-690 (West Supp. 1986); D.C. CODE ANN. §§ 21-2001 to -2081 (Supp. 1987); DEL. CODE ANN. tit. 12, §§ 4901 to 4905 (Supp. 1984); FLA. STAT. ANN. §§ 709.08 (West 1969, West. Supp. 1986); GA. CODE ANN. §§ 10-6-5 to 10-6-36 (1982); HAWAII REV. STAT. §§ 560:5-501,5-502 (Supp. 1985); IDAHO CODE §§ 15-5-501 to 15-5-505 (Supp. 1985); H.B. No. 498 (amendment to §§ 39-4502 to 39-4506) (1986); ILL. ANN. STAT. ch. 110 ½ § 11a-23 (Smith-Hurd Supp. 1986); IND. CODE ANN. § 30-2-11-1 to 30-2-11-7 (Burns Supp. 1986); IOWA CODE ANN. §§ 663.705, 633.707 (West Supp. 1985); KAN. STAT. ANN. §§ 58-610 to 58-617 (1983); KY. REV. STAT. ANN. § 386.093 (Michie 1984); LA. CIV. CODE ANN. art. 3027 (West Supp. 1986); ME. REV. STAT. ANN. tit. 18-A, §§ 5-502 (1981); MD. EST. & TRUST CODE ANN. §§ 13-601 to 13-603 (1974); MASS. GEN. LAWS ANN ch. 201B, §§ 1 to 7 (West Supp. 1986); MICH. COMP. LAWS ANN. § 700.495 (West 1980); MINN. STAT. ANN. §§ 523.01 to 523.25 (West Supp. 1986); MISS. CODE ANN. §§ 87-3-13 (Supp. 1985); MO. ANN. STAT. § 486.550 to 486.595 (Vernon Supp. 1986); MONT. CODE ANN. §§ 72-5-501, 72-5-502 (1985); NEB. REV. STAT. §§ 30-2664 to 30-2672 (Supp. 1985); NEV. REV. STAT. §§ 111.460, 111.470 (1986); N.H. REV. STAT. ANN. § 506:6 (Supp. 1985); N.J. STAT. ANN. §§ 46:2B-8, 2B-9 (West Supp. 1985); N.M. STAT. ANN. §§ 45-5-501, 45-6-502 (1978); N.Y. GEN. OBLIG. LAWS §§ 5-15-1 to 5-1601, (McKinney 1978, Supp. 1986); N.C. GEN. STAT. §§ 32A-1 to 32A-14 (1984, Supp. 1985); N.D. CENT. CODE §§ 30.1-30-01 to 30.1-30-05 (Supp. 1985); OHIO REV. CODE ANN. §§ 1337.09, 1337.091 (Page Supp. 1985); OKLA. STAT. ANN. tit. 58, §§ 1051 to 1062 (West Supp. 1985); OR. REV. STAT. §§ 126.407, 126.413 (Repl. 1985); PA. STAT. ANN. tit. 20, §§ 5601 to 5607 (Purdon Supp. 1986); R.I. GEN. LAWS § 34-22-6.1 (1984), §§ 23-4.9-1 to 23-4.9-2 (1986) (Ch. 190 of Public Laws, 1986); S.C. CODE ANN. §§ 32-13-10 (Law. Co-op Supp. 1985); S.D. CODIFIED LAWS ANN. §§ 59-7-2.1 to 59-7-2.4 (Repl. 1978); TENN. CODE ANN. §§ 34-6-101 to 34-6-107 (Repl. 1984); TEX. PROB. CODE ANN. § 36A (Vernon 1980); UTAH CODE ANN. §§ 75-5-501, 75-5-502 (Repl. 1978); VT. STAT. ANN. tit. 14, §§ 3051, 3052 (1985); VA. CODE §§ 11-9.1, 11-9.2, 11-9.3 (Repl. 1985); WASH. REV. CODE ANN. §§ 11.94.010 to 11.94.060 (Supp. 1986); W. VA. CODE § 27-11-6 (1985); WISC. STAT. ANN. § 243.07 (West Supp. 1985); WYO. STAT. §§ 3-5-101 to 3-5-103 (Supp. 1985).

25. For complete information *see* Society for the Right to Die,

"Appointing a Proxy for Health Care Decisions," available from the Society for the Right to Die, 250 West 57th Street, New York, NY 10107.

26. *See, e.g., In re Peter*, 108 N.J. 365, 529 A.2d 419 (1987).

27. *See, e.g., In re Quinlan*, 70 N.J. 10, 355 A.2d 647, *cert. denied sub nom Garger v. New Jersey*, 429 U.S. 922 (1976), *overruled in part on other grounds, In re Conroy* 98 N.J. 321, 486 A.2d 1209 (1985); *Brophy v. New England Sinai Hospital, Inc.*, 398 Mass. 417, 497 N.E.2d 626 (1986); *Delio v. Westchester County Medical Center*, 129 A.D.2d 1, 516 N.Y.S.2d 677 (App. Div. 2d. Dep't 1987).

28. *See, e.g., In re Rodas*, No. 86PR139 (Colo. Dist. Ct. Mesa County Jan. 22, 1987) (Buss, J.); *In re Colyer*, 99 Wash. 2d 114, 660 P.2d 738 (1983), *overruled in part on other grounds, In re Guardianship of Hamlin*, 102 Wash. 2d 810, 689 P.2d 1372 (1984); *In re L.H.R.*, 253 Ga. 439, 321 S.E.2d 716 (1984); *Rasmussen v. Fleming*, 154 Ariz. 207, 741 P.2d 674 (1987).

29. *Corbett v. D'Alessandro*, 487 So. 2d 368 (Fla. Dist. Ct. App.) *review denied*, 492 So. 2d 1331 (Fla. 1986).

30. *See, e.g., In re Jobes*, 108 N.J. 394, 529 A.2d 434 (1987).

31. *Leach v. Shapiro*, 13 Ohio App. 3d 393, 469 N.E.2d 1047 (Ct. App. 1984).

Appendix A
National Legal Organizations for the Elderly

The following is a brief list of national legal programs specializing in the legal problems of the elderly. These organizations assist attorneys throughout the country on legal problems affecting older persons.

American Bar Association Commission on
Legal Problems of the Elderly
1800 M St., N.W., Suite 200
Washington, D.C. 20036
(202) 331-2297

Center for Social Gerontology
117 No. 1st Street, Suite 204
Ann Arbor, MI 48104
(313) 665-1126

Legal Counsel for the Elderly (LCE)
1909 K St., N.W.
Washington, D.C. 20049
(202) 662–4933

Legal Services for the Elderly (LSE)
132 W. 43rd St., 3rd Floor
New York, NY 10036
(212) 595-1340

National Health Law Program
2639 S. La Cienega Blvd.
Los Angeles, CA 90034
(213) 204-6010, or
2025 M St., N.W.
Washington, D.C. 20036
(202) 887-5310

National Senior Citizens Law Center (NSCLC)
1052 W. 6th St., 7th Floor
Los Angeles, CA 90017
(213) 482-3550, or
2025 M St., N.W., Suite 400
Washington, D.C. 20036
(202) 887-5280

Appendix B
National Organizations for the Elderly

The following is a brief list of national organizations actively interested in the rights of the elderly.

American Association of Retired Persons (AARP)
1909 K St., N.W.
Washington, D.C. 20049
(202) 872-4700

American Society of Aging
833 Market St., Suite 516
San Francisco, CA 94103
(415) 543-2617

The Gerontological Society
1411 K St., N.W., Suite 300
Washington, D.C. 20005
(202) 393-1411

Gray Panthers
311 S. Juniper St., Suite 601
Philadelphia, PA 19107
(215) 545-6555

National Association of Area Agencies on Aging
600 Maryland Ave., S.W.
West Wing, Suite 208
Washington, D.C. 20024
(202) 484-7520

National Association of Retired Federal Employees
1533 New Hampshire Avenue, N.W.
Washington, D.C. 20036
(202) 234-0832

National Association of State Units on Aging
600 Maryland Avenue, S.W., Suite 208
Washington, D.C. 20024
(202) 484-7182

National Caucus and Center on Black Aged
1424 K St., N.W.
Suite 500
Washington, D.C. 20005
(202) 637-8400

National Center on Rural Aging (NCRA)
c/o National Council on the Aging
600 Maryland Ave., S.W., West Wing 100
Washington, D.C. 20024
(202) 479-1200

National Citizens Coalition on Nursing Home Reform
1424 16th St., N.W., Suite L2
Washington, D.C. 20036
(202) 797-0657

National Council of Senior Citizens
925 15th St., N.W.
Washington, D.C. 20005
(202) 347-8800

National Council on the Aging
600 Maryland Avenue, S.W.
West Wing, Suite 100
Washington, D.C. 20024
(202) 479-1200

National Indian Council on Aging
P.O. Box 2088
Albuquerque, NM 87103
(505) 242-9505

National Pacific/Asian Resource Center on Aging
2033 6th Ave., Suite 410
Seattle, WA 98121
(206) 448-0313

Older Women's League
1325 G. St., N.W., Lower Level B
Washington, D.C. 20005
(202) 783-6686

Pension Rights Center
918 16th St., N.W., Suite 704
Washington, D.C. 20006
9202) 296-3776

Society for the Right to Die
250 W. 57 St.
New York, NY 10107
(212) 246-6973

Villers Foundation
1334 G St., N.W.
Washington, D.C. 20005
(202) 628-3030

Appendix C
Congressional Committees

Two committees in Congress focus all of their attention on the problems of the elderly. Neither has authority to initiate legislation, but both study the problems of the elderly, monitor implementation of legislation affecting the elderly, recommend legislative changes, and issue reports on a wide variety of topics affecting the elderly.

House Select Committee on Aging
712 House Office Building Annex #1
Washington, D.C. 20515-6361
(202) 226-3375

Senate Special Committee on Aging
Dirksen Senate Office Bldg., Rm. SD-G41
Washington, D.C. 20510-6400
(202) 224-5364

Appendix D

State Offices of Aging, Legal Services Developers, and Long-term Care Ombudsmen

Every state has an office responsible for developing programs and policies benefitting older persons. Usually called the Office of Aging (sometimes a different name is used), these offices provide funding for a wide variety of programs for older persons, such as nutrition programs, senior centers, and legal services programs. While the state office may operate some of these programs itself, in most instances it forwards funds to local governments and private organizations to enable them to run these programs. If you have questions about what programs are available in your area, you can contact the state office.

Every state is required to have a legal services developer whose job is to work with law schools, bar associations, private lawyers, and public legal services programs to increase the number of lawyers serving older persons. If you need a lawyer and are uncertain where to find one, contact the legal services developer for your state. Most legal services developers have an office at the State Office of Aging. In those states in which the developer is located elsewhere, the state office can provide you with an address and phone number for the developer.

Every state is required to have a long-term care ombudsman program. The purpose of these programs is to improve the quality of life for nursing-home residents by receiving and resolving complaints, monitoring the state health department's regulation of nursing homes, studying the need for additional laws to protect nursing-home residents, etc. If you need help with a nursing-home problem and are not sure where to turn, contact the long-term care ombudsman. Most ombudsmen have an office at the State Office of Aging. In those states in which the ombudsman is located elsewhere, the state office can provide you with an address and phone number for the ombudsman. A list of state offices of aging follows.

ALABAMA

Commission on Aging
State Capitol
Montgomery, Ala. 36130
(205) 261-5743

ALASKA

Older Alaskans Commission
Pouch C, Mail Stop 0209
Juneau, Alaska 99811
(907) 465-3250

ARIZONA

Aging and Adult Administration; (P.O. Box 6123)
1400 West Washington St.
Phoenix, Ariz. 85005
(602) 255-4446

ARKANSAS

Arkansas State Office on Aging
Donaghey Building, suite 1428, 7th & Main Sts.
Little Rock, Ark. 72201
(501) 371-2441

CALIFORNIA

Department of Aging
1020 19th St.
Sacramento, Calif. 95814
(916) 322-5290

COLORADO

Aging and Adult Services Division
Department of Social Services, room 503, 1575 Sherman St.
Denver, Colo. 80220
(303) 866-2586

CONNECTICUT

Department on Aging
175 Main Street
Hartford, Conn. 06106
(203) 566-7725

DELAWARE

Division of Aging
Department of Health and Social Services
1901 North Dupont Highway
New Castle, Del. 19720
(302) 421-6791

DISTRICT OF COLUMBIA

Executive Director, Office on Aging, Office of the Mayor
1424 K St., NW.
Washington, D.C. 20005
(202) 724-5622

FLORIDA

Program Office of Aging and Adult Services
Department of Health and Rehabilitation Services
1323 Winewood Blvd.
Tallahassee, Fla. 32301
(904) 488-8922

GEORGIA

Office of Aging
878 Peachtree Street, N.E., Room 632
Atlanta, Ga. 30309
(404) 894-5333

HAWAII

Executive Office on Aging, Office of the Governor, State of Hawaii
1149 Bethel Street, room 307
Honolulu, Hawaii 96813
(808) 548-2593

IDAHO

Idaho Office on Aging
Room 114-Statehouse
Boise, Idaho 83720
(208) 334-3833

ILLINOIS

Department on Aging
421 East Capitol Ave.
Springfield, Ill. 62706
(217) 785-3356

INDIANA

Indiana Department on Aging & Community Services
Suite 1350, 115 N. Pa. St.
Indianapolis, Ind. 46204
(317) 232-7006

IOWA

Commission on Aging
914 Grand Avenue, Suite 236, Jewett Bldg.
Des Moines, Iowa 50319
(515) 281-5187

KANSAS

Department of Aging
610 West 10th St.
Topeka, Kans. 66612
(913) 296-4986

KENTUCKY

Division for Aging Services, Department of Human Resources
DHR Bldg., 6th floor, 275 East Main St.
Frankfort, Ky. 40601
(502) 564-6930

LOUISIANA

Office of Elderly Affairs
4528 Bennington Ave., P.O. Box 80374
Baton Rouge, La. 70898-0374
(504) 925-1700

MAINE

Bureau of Maine's Elderly, Department of Human Services
State House, Station No. 11
Augusta, Maine 04333
(207) 289-2561

MARYLAND

Office on Aging, State Office Bldg.
301 West Preston St.
Baltimore, Md. 21201
(301) 383-5064

MASSACHUSETTS

Secretary, Department of Elder Affairs
38 Chauncy St.
Boston, Mass. 02111
(617) 727-7751

MICHIGAN

Office of Services to the Aging
P.O. Box 30026
Lansing, Mich. 48909
(517) 373-8230

MINNESOTA

Minnesota Board on Aging
Metro Square Bldg., room 204
7th and Robert Sts.
St. Paul Minn. 55101
(612) 296-2544

MISSISSIPPI

Mississippi Council on Aging
Executive Building, suite 301
Jackson, Miss. 39201
(601) 354-6590

MISSOURI

Division on Aging, Department of Social Services
Broadway State, P.O. Box 570
Jefferson City, Mo. 65101
(314) 751-3082

MONTANA

Community Services Division
P.O. Box 4210
Helena, Mont. 59604
(406) 444-3865

NEBRASKA

Department on Aging
P.O. Box 95044, 301 Centennial Mall South
Lincoln, Nebr. 68509
(402) 471-2306

NEVADA

Division for Aging Services, Department of Human Resources
505 East King St., Kinkead Bldg., room 101
Carson City, Nev. 89710
(702) 885-4210

NEW HAMPSHIRE

Council on Aging
14 Depot St.
Concord, N.H. 03301
(603) 271-2751

NEW JERSEY

Division on Aging
Department of Community Affairs
363 West State St., CN 807
Trenton N.J. 08625-0807
(609) 292-4833

NEW MEXICO

State Agency on Aging
224 East Palace Ave., 4th floor
La Villa Rivera Building
Santa Fe, N. Mex. 87501
(505) 827-7640

NEW YORK

Office for the Aging, New York State Executive Department
Empire State Plaza, Agency Building No. 2
Albany, N.Y. 12223
(518) 474-5731

NORTH CAROLINA

Division of Aging
708 Hillsboro St., suite 200
Raleigh, N.C. 27603
(919) 733-3983

NORTH DAKOTA

Aging Services, Department of Human Services
State Capitol Bldg.
Bismarck, N. Dak. 58505
(701) 224-2577

OHIO

Ohio Department of Aging
50 West Broad St., 9th Floor
Columbus, Ohio 43215
(614) 466-5500

OKLAHOMA

Special Unit on Aging, Department of Human Services
P.O. Box 25352
Oklahoma City, Okla. 73125
(405) 521-2281

OREGON

Oregon Senior Services Division
313 Public Service Bldg.
Salem, Oreg. 97310
(503) 378-4728

PENNSYLVANIA

Department of Aging
231 State St., Room 307, Finance Bldg.
Harrisburg, Pa. 17120
(717) 783-1550

RHODE ISLAND

Department of Elderly Affairs
79 Washington St.
Providence, R.I. 02903
(401) 277-2858

SOUTH CAROLINA

Commission on Aging
915 Main St.
Columbia, S.C. 29201
(803) 758-2576

SOUTH DAKOTA

Office of Adult Services and Aging, Department of Social Services
Richard F. Kneip Bldg., 700 North Illinois St.
Pierre, S. Dak. 57501-2291
(605) 773-3656

TENNESSEE

Commission on Aging
703 Tennessee Bldg., 535 Church St.
Nashville, Tenn. 37219
(615) 741-2056

TEXAS

Texas Department on Aging
210 Barton Springs Rd., 5th floor, P.O. Box 12786, Capital Station
Austin, Tex. 78704
(512) 475-2717

UTAH

Division of Aging and Adult Services, Department of Social Services
150 West North Temple, Box 2500
Salt Lake City, Utah 84110-2500
(801) 533-6422

VERMONT

Office on Aging
103 South Main St.
Waterbury, Vt. 05676
(802) 241-2400

VIRGINIA

Office on Aging
101 N. 14th St., 18th floor, James Monroe Bldg.
Richmond, Va. 23219
(804) 225-2271

WASHINGTON

Bureau of Aging and Adult Services
Department of Social and Health Services, OB-43G
Olympia, Wash. 98504
(206) 753-2502

WEST VIRGINIA

Commission on Aging
State Capitol
Charleston, W. Va. 25305
(304) 348-3317

WISCONSIN

Bureau on Aging
1 West Wilson St., room 685
Madison, Wis. 53702
(608) 272-8606

WYOMING

State of Wyoming, Wyoming Commission on Aging
Hathaway Bldg., #139
Cheyenne, Wyo. 82002
(307) 777-7986

AMERICAN SAMOA

Territorial Aging Program, Government of American Samoa
Office of the Governor
Pago Pago, American Samoa 96799
Samoa 3-1254 or 3-4116

GUAM

Office of Aging, Social Service
Department of Public Health, Government of Guam
P.O. Box 2618
Agana, Guam 96910
749-9901 extension 423

PUERTO RICO

Gericulture Commission, Department of Social Services
P.O. Box 11398
Santurce, P.R. 00910
(809) 722-2429

TRUST TERRITORY OF THE PACIFIC ISLANDS

Office on Aging
Trust Territory of the Pacific Islands
Saipan, CM 96950
Telephone Nos. 9335 or 9328

VIRGIN ISLANDS

Commission on Aging
6F Havensight Mall
Charlotte Amalie
St. Thomas, Virgin Islands 00801
(809) 774-5884

Appendix E
Computing Your Social Security Benefits

The following is a reprint of a Social Security Administration pamphlet entitled *Estimating Your Social Security Retirement Check*.

You are probably wondering how much your Social Security checks will be. You can get an approximate answer from the information in this leaflet.

The information given here is limited to retirement checks for workers who reach 62 after 1982. Specific estimates can be made by people who reach 62 in 1984 through 1987. People who reach 62 after 1987 can also make an approximate estimate of their benefit. But the estimate will not be as accurate because of future changes in the cost of living and wages. Social Security also pays disability and survivors benefits, but for information about these benefits, call any Social Security office.

Under the method of figuring benefits described in this leaflet, actual earnings for past years will be adjusted or indexed to take account of changes in average wages since the year the earnings were received. These adjusted earnings are averaged together and the benefit rate figured from this average. The indexing method of figuring benefits is intended to insure that benefits will reflect changes in wage levels over a person's working lifetime and will have a relatively constant relationship to preretirement earnings.

The method described in this leaflet up through Step 7 on page 8 can be used by all workers who reach 62 after 1979. The formula used in Step 8 to figure the benefit rate applies only to workers who reach 62 in 1984–87. People who reach 62 after 1987 cannot figure a specific estimate based on the figures provided in this leaflet. An approximate estimate can be made by using Step 8 for workers who reach 62 in 1987.

The formula in Step 8 of this leaflet cannot be used to estimate benefits by people who reach 62 after 1985 and who also become eligible after 1985 for a pension based on work not covered by Social Security. For information on the formula to be used, contact any Social Security office and ask for the leaflet, *How your Social Security check is affected by a pension—from work not covered by Social Security*.

All benefit rates estimated by following the steps in this pamphlet are effective beginning December 1986 (checks payable in January 1987 or later).

Source: SSA Publication No. 05-10070. U.S. Department of Health and Human Services, Social Security Administration. February 1987.

WORKSHEET

You Reach 62 In

Year	A	B	C 1984	C 1985	C 1986	C 1987	D
1951	3,600		5.2	5.4	5.8	6.0	
1952	3,600		4.9	5.1	5.4	5.7	
1953	3,600		4.6	4.9	5.1	5.4	
1954	3,600		4.6	4.8	5.1	5.3	
1955	4,200		4.4	4.6	4.9	5.1	
1956	4,200		4.1	4.3	4.6	4.8	
1957	4,200		4.0	4.2	4.4	4.6	
1958	4,200		4.0	4.1	4.4	4.6	
1959	4,800		3.8	4.0	4.2	4.4	
1960	4,800		3.6	3.8	4.0	4.2	
1961	4,800		3.6	3.7	3.9	4.1	
1962	4,800		3.4	3.6	3.8	3.9	
1963	4,800		3.3	3.5	3.7	3.8	
1964	4,800		3.2	3.3	3.5	3.7	
1965	4,800		3.1	3.3	3.5	3.6	
1966	6,600		2.9	3.1	3.3	3.4	
1967	6,600		2.8	2.9	3.1	3.2	
1968	7,800		2.6	2.7	2.9	3.0	
1969	7,800		2.5	2.6	2.7	2.9	
1970	7,800		2.3	2.5	2.6	2.7	
1971	7,800		2.2	2.3	2.5	2.6	
1972	9,000		2.0	2.1	2.3	2.4	
1973	10,800		1.9	2.0	2.1	2.2	
1974	13,200		1.8	1.9	2.0	2.1	
1975	14,100		1.7	1.8	1.9	1.9	
1976	15,300		1.6	1.7	1.7	1.8	
1977	16,500		1.5	1.6	1.6	1.7	
1978	17,700		1.4	1.4	1.5	1.6	
1979	22,900		1.3	1.3	1.4	1.5	

WORKSHEET continued

You Reach 62 In

Year	A	B	C 1984	C 1985	C 1986	C 1987	D
1980	25,900		1.2	1.2	1.3	1.3	
1981	29,700		1.1	1.1	1.2	1.2	
1982	32,400		1.0	1.0	1.1	1.2	
1983	35,700		1.0	1.0	1.1	1.1	
1984	37,800		1.0	1.0	1.0	1.0	
1985	39,600		1.0	1.0	1.0	1.0	
1986	42,000		1.0	1.0	1.0	1.0	
1987	43,800		1.0	1.0	1.0	1.0	
1988	43,800*		1.0	1.0	1.0	1.0	
TOTAL					$		

*The maximum amount of annual earnings that counts for Social Security rises automatically as earnings levels increase. Because of this, the base in 1988 and later may be higher than $43,800.

Here's how to estimate the amount

Follow the directions below and you'll find out the approximate amount of the monthly checks you'll get from Social Security after you retire.

Step 1. The amount of your check is based on your earnings over a period of years. Based on the year you were born, pick the number of years you need to count from the following chart:

Retirement benefits

Year you were born	Years needed
1922	28
1923	29
1924	30
1925	31
1926	32
1929 or later	35*

*Maximum number of years that count

Step 2. Fill in the worksheet for the year you reach 62. Column A shows maximum earnings covered by Social Security. In Column B, list your earnings beginning with 1951. Write 0 for a year of no earnings. If you entered more than the maximum in any year, list only the maximum for each year. Estimate your earnings for future years, including any years you plan to work past 65. Stop with the year before you retire or plan to retire.

Step 3. Multiply the amount in Column B (not to exceed the maximum) for each year by the factor in Column C for the year you reach 62. Write the result in Column D.

Step 4. Cross off your list, in Column D, the years of your lowest earnings until the number of years left is the same as your answer to Step 1. (You may have to leave some years of 0 earnings on your list.)

Step 5. Add up the earnings for the years left on your list. Write this figure in the space marked TOTAL at the bottom of the worksheet and here.

$ _____

Step 6. Divide this total by the number you wrote for Step 1. The result is your average indexed *yearly* earnings covered by Social Security. Write the figure here.

$ _____

Step 7. Divided your average indexed yearly earnings by 12. The result is your *average indexed montly earnings*. Round the result to the next lower dollar. Write your figure here.

$ _____

Step 8 (for workers who reach 62 in 1984). Multiply the first $267 of your average indexed monthly earnings by 90 percent. Write the result here.

$ _____

Multiply the next $1,345 of your average indexed monthly earnings by 32 percent. Write the result here.

$ _____

Multiply any remaining amount by 15 percent. Write the result here.

$ _____

Add the figures. Round the total to the next lower dime. Write your answer here. Total: $ _____ This is the estimate of your basic benefit.

You are eligible for "cost-of-living" increases starting with the year you reach 62. To figure your benefit rate as of December 1986, multiply your total by 1.081.

Round to the next lower dollar. This is the estimate of your age 65 benefit (excluding any "cost-of-living" increases after 1986).

$ _____

Step 8 (for workers who reach 62 in 1985). Multiply the first $280 of your average indexed monthly earnings by 90 percent. Write the result here.

$ _____

Multiply the next $1,411 of your average indexed monthly earnings by 32 percent. Write the result here.

$ _____

Multiply any remaining amount by 15 percent. Write the result here.

$ _____

Add the figures. Round the total to the next lower dime. Write your answer here. Total: $ _____ This is the estimate of your basic benefit.

You are eligible for "cost-of-living" increases starting with the year you reach 62. To figure your benefit rate as of December 1986, multiply your total by 1.044.

Round to the next lower dollar. This is the estimate of your age 65 benefit (excluding any "cost-of-living" increases after 1986).

$ _____

Step 8 (for workers who reached 62 in 1986). Multiply the first $297 of your average indexed monthly earnings by 90 percent. Write the result here.

$ _____

Multiply the next $1,493 of your average indexed monthly

earnings by 32 percent. Write the result here.

$ _____

Multiply any remaining amount by 15 percent. Write the result here.

$ _____

Add the figures. Round the total to the next lower dime. Write the answer here. Total $ _____ This is the estimate of your basic benefit.

You are eligible for "cost-of-living" increases starting with the year you reach 62. To figure your benefit rate as of December 1986, multiply your total by 1.013.

Round to the next lower dollar. This is the estimate of your age 65 benefit (excluding any "cost-of-living" increases after 1986).

$ _____

Step 8 (for workers who reached 62 in 1987). Multiply the first $310 of your average indexed monthly earnings by 90 percent. Write the result here.

$ _____

Multiply the next $1,556 of your indexed monthly earnings by 32 percent. Write the result here.

$ _____

Multiply any remaining amount by 15 percent. Write the result here.

$ _____

Add the figures. Round the total to the next lower dime. Write your answer here. Total: $ _____ This is the estimate of your basic benefit.

You are eligible for "cost-of-living" increases starting with the year you reach 62.

Round to the next lower dollar. This is an estimate of your age 65 benefit (excluding any "cost-of-living" increases).

$ _____

If you choose benefits before 65

If you choose to receive retirement benefits before 65, your basic benefit is permanently reduced. The amount of the reduction depends on the number of months you receive benefits before 65. For example, the reduction is 20 percent if benefits start at 62; 13⅓ percent at 63; and 6⅔ percent at 64.

Wives' and husbands' benefits

The benefit for your wife or husband at 65 is one-half of your 65 benefit, rounded to the next lower dollar. If your wife or husband starts to get benefits before 65, the benefit is permanently reduced. The amount of reduction depends on the number of months he or she receives benefits before 65. For example, the reduction is 25 percent if benefits start at 62; 16⅔ percent at 63; and 8⅓ percent at 64.

The "notch" effect

The method of figuring benefits explained in this leaflet was enacted as part of the 1977 Social Security Amendments. This legislation made significant changes in the way benefits are figured in order to correct a flaw in the prior-law benefit formula that overadjusted for inflation and threatened the solvency of the Social Security trust funds.

Benefit levels under the new system are slightly lower than those prevailing under the old law. Thus, some workers born in 1916 and earlier—with benefits figured under the method in effect before the 1977 amendments—can receive higher monthly benefits than workers born in 1917 and later who have similar earnings histories and who retire at the same age with benefits figured under the new indexing method. This effect is sometimes referred to as the "notch."

To ease the transition from the old to the new formula, special computation provisions apply to workers born between 1917 and 1921. Their benefits are figured two ways—under the new indexing method and under a modified version of the method in effect before the 1977 amendments. Workers in these age groups are paid a benefit rate based on the higher of the two calculations. Workers born after 1921 have their benefits figured only under the indexing method.

For more information

The information contained in this leaflet is complex. If you need assistance in estimating your benefit, contact your local Social Security office.

Appendix F
Computing Your Supplemental Security Income Benefits

A new method of determining SSI eligibility and computing benefits has been adopted. Called "retrospective monthly accounting" or RMA, it works as follows.

First are five definitions. (1) The month for which eligibility is being determined is called the "computation" or "current" month. This is normally the same month in which an application is filed or benefits are payable. (2) The month from which income is taken to compute the benefit is called the "budget" month. The budget month may be the computation month or the month before the computation month or the second month before the computation month. (3) FBR is the federal benefit rate, a standardized rate under law, of $354 (effective 1 January 1988) for an individual and $532 (1 January 1988) for a couple. (4) The payment limit is $30 for an individual in an institution which receives Medicaid and $60 for a couple in a similar institution. (5) "Countable income" is the amount of earned and unearned income which remains after all allowable exclusions have been deducted from gross income.

Calculations for eligibility are based upon countable income received in the computation month and other factors such as resources and size of household but never the $30 or $60 limits. Calculations for the amount of payment are based upon the FBR for the computation month minus countable income received in the budget month. In some states and the District of Columbia there is either an optional or mandatory state supplementation. Countable income is deducted first from the FBR, and any excess is then deducted from the state supplementary payment level. Usually, the budget month is two months before the computation month. For the first two months of eligibility this is not so. The process is as follows:

When an applicant first applies (or is reinstated) for SSI payments, his or her countable income for the computation month is determined and a review of other previously named factors conducted to determine his or her eligibility. Once he or she is found eligible, the payment amount for that entry month only is calculated, based upon the appropriate FBR minus countable income for that same month.

For the second month after his or her entry into the SSI system, eligibility is based upon income and other factors in the computation month as always, but the payment amount is computed on the appropriate FBR or limit for the computation month minus countable income for the previous month.

Thereafter, for all succeeding months while he or she is continuously eligible, computations for eligibility each month are based upon countable income and other factors for the computation month, but calculations for the payment amount are based upon the FBR or limit for the computation month minus the countable income for the budget month, which is two months prior to the computation month. An example of which months the computations are based on follows.

Example showing the months on which computations are based for an individual who first becomes eligible in January.

For the months below:	Computations for eligibility are based on income (and other factors) received in the month of:	Computations for payment amount are based on FBR minus income received in the month of:
January (first eligible)	January	January
February	February	January
March	March	January
April	April	February
May	May	March
June	June	April
July	July	May
August	August	June
September	September	July, etc.

Source: Disability Practice Manual, p. 7 (Legal Counsel for the Elderly, AARP, Washington, D.C. 1985).

List of Contributors

Robert N. Brown is a Professor of Law at the University of Detroit School of Law and Director of its Health Law Center. He has been involved actively with older persons' rights since 1971 when he was Associate Director of Legal Research and Services for the Elderly in Washington, D.C. A former Chairman of the Aging and the Law section of the Association of American Law Schools and a member of the Senior Justice Committee of the State Bar of Michigan, Brown has lectured and written extensively on issues affecting the elderly. He serves currently as a Commissioner of the American Bar Association Commission on Legal Problems of the Elderly. Brown was the editor and principal author of the first edition of this book and served in the same capacity for this edition.

Legal Counsel For The Elderly (LCE) is both a free legal services program for elderly residents of the District of Columbia and a national support center specializing in expanding and improving the delivery of legal services to persons age 60 and older. LCE's national activities include: providing statewide training events for lawyers and other advocates, recruiting volunteers for local advocacy projects and providing technical assistance, operating statewide legal hotlines in several states, operating volunteer advocacy and financial management programs in communities nationwide, operating a national home study paralegal course, and producing and distributing legal publications and audio-visual materials. Wayne Moore is its director.

Wiliam A. Dombi is the Director of the Center for Health Care Law based in Washington, D.C. In his current position and as former Director of Legal Assistance to Medicare Patients, Dombi has represented thousands of Medicare beneficiaries through class-action litigation and administrative appeals and has lectured extensively on Medicare advocacy and the development of Medicare advocacy projects.

M. Anne Hart received a Master of Science in Gerontology and a Master of Public Administration from the Andrus Gerontology Center at the University of Southern California. She has worked as a nursing assistant in a nursing home and as a nursing-home inspector and is now the Long-term Care Ombudsman for the District of Columbia.

Robert L. Liebross, an attorney with the Pension Rights Center in Washington, D.C., provides legal assistance to working and retired people on pension matters. He has a master's degree in labor relations law from Georgetown University Law Center and has worked previously in the field of Occupational Safety and Health Law.

Virginia R. Long is a graduate of the University of Southern California and George Washington University's Institute of Law and Aging. Since 1981 she has been a paralegal with Legal Counsel for the Elderly. A public benefits specialist, she has been a contributor to the Elderly Law Manual and other LCE publications.

Da Costa R. Mason, a graduate of Syracuse University and Catholic University School of Law, is the Senior Legal Program Coordinator at LCE. He has over eight years of experience in the area of protective services and was a drafter of the District of Columbia Guardianship, Protective Proceedings and Durable Power of Attorney Act of 1986.

Jan Allen May is a graduate of Brown University and Antioch School of Law. He is the Managing Attorney at LCE in Washington, D.C. where he has handled Social Security cases for ten years. He has written extensively on Social Security law and conducted training programs on Social Security law throughout the country for attorneys and paralegals.

J. Kenneth L. Morse is an attorney working with the Equal Employment Opportunity Commission's Office of General Counsel. Mr. Morse has been involved in litigating age discrimination in employment cases at the trial and appellate levels for the past eight years. In addition to his work with the Commission, Mr. Morse also has written and lectured extensively on age discrimination in employment for organizations such as the National Senior Citizens Law Center, legal services programs, state and national bar associations, and age advocacy groups.

Fenella Rouse, a graduate of Columbia University School of Law, is Director of Legal Services for the Society for the Right to Die, a national nonprofit patients' rights organization based in New York City. The society serves as a central information service on all aspects of the right to refuse treatment. It distributes "living wills," counsels and advises people about their rights, and seeks to clarify the law by working for natural death legislation and by participating as amicus curiae in court cases involving the right to refuse treatment. Ms. Rouse has written extensively on the patient's right to self-determination and has lectured on the topic throughout the country.

Michael R. Schuster is a graduate of the College of St. Thomas in St. Paul, Minnesota and of the University of Notre Dame Law School. He is the Director of Litigation at LCE. He has been involved in Social Security and Supplemental Security Income litigation and administrative hearings for over ten years and wrote the Disability Practice Manual (published by LCE) as well as other Social Security and Supplemental Security Income publications.

Thomas V. Trainer is a graduate of Grand Valley State Colleges and the University of Detroit School of Law. He is the Education and Advocacy Coordinator for the Walter P. Reuther Senior Centers of Metropolitan Detroit and is also the Medicare Recovery Project manager for the Michigan Office of Services to the Aging. He serves on the State Bar of Michigan Senior Justice Committee and recently chaired the Legal, Insurance, and Finance Committee of the Michigan Task Force on Alzheimer's Disease and Related Conditions.

Bruce B. Vignery is a graduate of the University of Colorado and the Catholic University School of Law. He has worked in the Civil Rights Division of the United States Department of Justice and in the Neighborhood Legal Services program in Washington, D.C. and is currently with the National Protective Services Support Center of LCE. He is one of the principal drafters of the new District of Columbia guardianship statute.